NEW ENGLAND'S
BEST TRIPS

31 AMAZING ROAD TRIPS

This edition written and researched by

Gregor Clark
Carolyn Bain, Mara Vorhees, Benedict Walker

SYMBOLS IN THIS BOOK

 Top Tips

 History & Culture

 Essential Photo

 Link Your Trips

 Family

 Walking Tour

Tips from Locals

 Food & Drink

 Eating

Trip Detour

 Outdoors

 Sleeping

📞 Telephone Number

⊘ Opening Hours

🅿 Parking

⊖ Nonsmoking

❄ Air-Conditioning

@ Internet Access

🛜 Wi-Fi Access

🥗 Vegetarian Selection

🏊 Swimming Pool

👪 Family-Friendly

🐾 Pet-Friendly

MAP LEGEND

Routes

Trip Route
Trip Detour
Linked Trip
Walk Route
Tollway
Freeway
Primary
Secondary
Tertiary
Lane
Unsealed Road
Plaza/Mall
Steps
Tunnel
Pedestrian Overpass
Walk Track/Path

Boundaries

--- International
--- State/Province
--- Cliff

Hydrography

River/Creek
Intermittent River
Swamp/Mangrove
Canal
Water
Dry/Salt/ Intermittent Lake
Glacier

Route Markers

97 US National Hwy
5 US Interstate Hwy
44 State Hwy

Trips

1 Trip Numbers
9 Trip Stop
🏃 Walking tour
↩ Trip Detour

Population

✪ Capital (National)
◉ Capital (State/Province)
● City/Large Town
● Town/Village

Areas

Beach
Cemetery (Christian)
Cemetery (Other)
Park
Forest
Reservation
Urban Area
Sportsground

Transport

✈ Airport
Ⓑ BART station
Ⓣ Boston T station
Cable Car/ Funicular
Ⓜ Metro/Muni station
Ⓟ Parking
Ⓢ Subway station
Train/Railway
Tram
Ⓤ Underground station

Note: Not all symbols displayed above appear on the maps in this book

---

PLAN YOUR TRIP

ON THE ROAD

CONTENTS

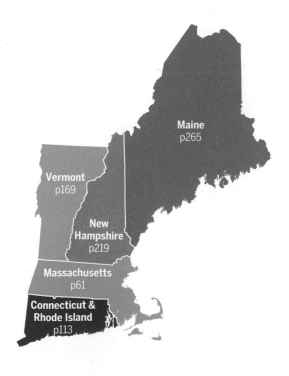

Maine
p265

Vermont
p169

New
Hampshire
p219

Massachusetts
p61

Connecticut &
Rhode Island
p113

Contents cont.

ROAD TRIP ESSENTIALS

Vermont Hardwood forest in the Green Mountains

WELCOME TO
NEW ENGLAND

Steeped in Colonial history, graced with gorgeous mountains and coastlines, and packed with culinary and cultural attractions, New England is an irresistible road trip destination.

The trips in this book embrace the thrill of the open road, taking in both well-known travel hot spots and off-the-beaten-track treasures. Come cruise the fabled coastlines of Maine and Cape Cod, the White Mountains' spectacular granite summits and the fiery fall foliage of the Berkshires and Green Mountains.

From historic sites such as Plimoth Plantation and Nantucket to big cities and contemporary art museums, these trips wind past pumpkin patches and cranberry bogs, red barns and white-steepled churches, covered bridges and lighthouses. Along the way, sample cuisine from the best clam shacks, lobster joints and farm-to-table eateries, while staying at cozy B&Bs, vintage hotels and classic roadside motels. And if you've only got time for one trip, make it one of our Classic Trips, which take you to the very best of New England.

NEW ENGLAND HIGHLIGHTS

Classic Trip 26
Acadia National Park
Swoop up Cadillac Mountain, then roll past cliffs on Mt Desert Island. **3 DAYS**

Classic Trip 25
Maritime Maine
Lighthouses, lobster shacks, maritime museums and early sunrises. **5 DAYS**

Classic Trip 2
Fall Foliage Tour
The ultimate fall foliage trip, featuring dappled trails and awesome views. **5–7 DAYS**

NEW BRUNSWICK

St Leonard
Perth-Andover
Woodstock
Fredericton
St Stephen
Passamaquoddy Bay
Lubec

Presque Isle
Bridgewater
Ashland
Knoles Corner
Clair
Dickey

CANADA
USA

Allagash Wilderness Waterway

Baxter State Park
Mt Katahdin (5267ft)
Millinocket

Howland
Milo
Bangor

West Grand Lake

Bar Harbor
Acadia National Park

Penobscot Bay
Camden
Rockland
Belfast

MAINE

Moosehead Lake
Rockwood
Kennebec River
Appalachian Trail

Pittsfield
Waterville
Augusta

Bingham
Jackman

St Lawrence River

Quebec City

Luc St-François

QUEBEC

Sherbrooke

Oquossoc
Mooselookmeguntic Lake

Rumford

Mt Washington (6288ft)
North Conway
White Mountain National Forest
Lincoln

Berlin
Littleton

Brunswick
Sebago Lake

VERMONT

Morrisville
Stowe
Montpelier

Long Trail

St Albans
Lake Champlain
Burlington
Middlebury

Saranac Lake
Lake Placid
Adirondack Park

NEW YORK

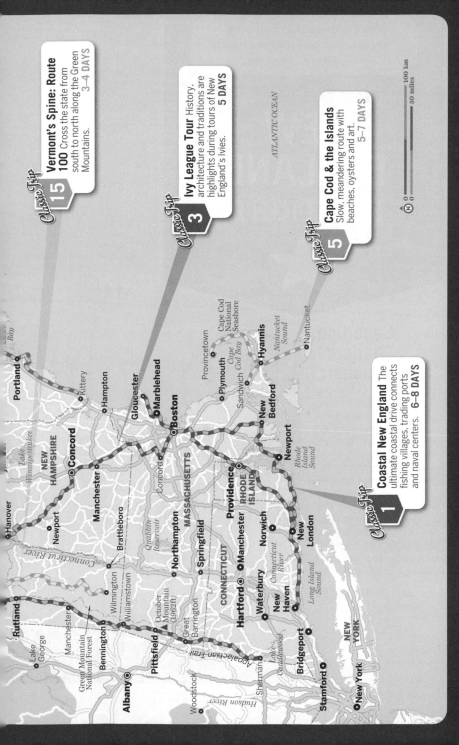

> New England's best sights and experiences, and the road trips that will take you there.

NEW ENGLAND
HIGHLIGHTS

Cape Cod National Seashore

The outer edge of Cape Cod is a collage of sand dunes, salt marshes and seaside forest, home to prolific bird and marine life. Since the 1960s, this wild world is all preserved under the auspices of the Cape Cod National Seashore. Drive along the shoreline on **Trip 5: Cape Cod & the Islands**, stopping to climb historic lighthouses, swim at wind-whipped beaches and stroll along scenic boardwalks.

Trips 4 5

Cape Cod National Seashore Beach on Cape Cod

Fall Foliage Sugar maples in Peacham

Fall Foliage

New England is radiant in autumn, when entire mountainsides burst into a mosaic of red, gold, orange and crimson leaves, juxtaposed against verdant meadows and granite crags. On **Trip 2: Fall Foliage Tour** or **Trip 15: Vermont's Spine: Route 100**, drive through vivid streamers of seasonal foliage – stopping to sample fresh-pressed cider – before the earth goes to sleep under a thick blanket of snow.

Trips 2 7 8 14 15 16 17 19 20

Acadia National Park

The Precipice. The Beehive. Thunder Hole. Is this a James Bond movie or Acadia National Park? The dilemma on **Trip 26: Acadia National Park**: stop to explore or keep on driving? Park Loop Rd, with its gentle curves and crafted viewpoints, was designed with drivers in mind. It tugs you forward. But the adventures pull you sideways. So drive it twice – first without stopping, then to explore.

Trip 26

Appalachian Trail

The AT traverses 14 states and more than 2100 miles. Five of those states and 730 of those miles are in New England. **Trip 7: Berkshire Back Roads** offers access to the lush slopes of western Massachusetts; **Trip 20: White Mountains Loop** hits New Hampshire's majestic granite peaks; and **Trip 28: Great North Woods** traverses – yes – the Great North Woods of Maine.

Trips 2 3 7 8 14 20 28 31

Lighthouses West Quoddy Light, Lubec

BEST BEACHES

Herring Cove Miles of secret Cape Cod dunes for strolling and sunbathing. **Trip** 5

Hammonasset Beach Long pine-backed beach set amid salt marshes and meadows. **Trip** 12

Ellacoya State Beach Family fun on the shores of New Hampshire's favorite lake. **Trip** 22

Sand Beach Ponder the Milky Way over the Atlantic at an evening ranger talk. **Trip** 26

Weston's Beach Kayak, canoe or tube to this sandy bend along Maine's Saco River. **Trip** 29

Lighthouses

More than 60 lighthouses pepper Maine's coast, with dozens more in Massachusetts, Rhode Island and Connecticut. Their historic importance is evident on **Trip 25: Maritime Maine**, which curves past fishing villages, ports and maritime museums. But their vital connection to local lives doesn't truly grab you until you visit on a fog-thick morning, with foghorns wailing and waves smashing against the rocks.

Trips 1 5 10 25 26

White Mountains Presidential Range in the White Mountain National Forest

White Mountains

Gamblers have Vegas. Gourmands have San Francisco. And hikers have the White Mountains, a region of soaring peaks and lush valleys that covers one quarter of New Hampshire. More than 700,000 acres are protected in the White Mountain National Forest. As you'll see on **Trip 20: White Mountains Loop**, this wilderness is made accessible by the Appalachian Mountain Club, which manages the hut-to-hut hiking network.

Trips 20 24

BEST HIKES

- - - - - - - - - - - - - - - - - - - -

Housatonic River Walk Follow the foliage-clad banks of this idyllic river. **Trip** 7

- - - - - - - - - - - - - - - - - - - -

Mt Greylock Climb Massachusetts' tallest mountain for glorious views of five states. **Trip** 8

- - - - - - - - - - - - - - - - - - - -

Camel's Hump Enjoy sweeping vistas from an iconic Vermont peak. **Trip** 17

- - - - - - - - - - - - - - - - - - - -

Mt Monadnock Tread in Thoreau's footsteps up America's most-climbed mountain. **Trip** 23

- - - - - - - - - - - - - - - - - - - -

Jordan Cliffs Scale cliff-side ladders in Maine's Acadia National Park. **Trip** 26

Ivy League Universities Harvard University, Cambridge

Vermont Farms Pumpkin harvest

Ivy League Universities

New England is home to four of the eight Ivy League universities. Steeped in tradition, these institutions are known for academic excellence and rich histories. Study up on **Trip 3: Ivy League Tour**, starting on the bucolic green of Dartmouth College, with subsequent stops at the more urban campuses of Harvard, Brown and Yale.

Trip 3

Colonial History

New England's rural hinterland presents a rich tableau of the country's Colonial past. On **Trip 11: Quiet Corner** or **Trip 14: Litchfield Hills Loop**, trace the footsteps of Revolutionary heroes, human rights activists, religious thinkers and reformists, and discover the region's deep historical roots.

Trips 1 4 11 14

Vermont Farms

From apple and blueberry picking to artisanal-cheese sampling to pumpkin festivals, Vermont farms welcome visitors and encourage you to learn how they produce the fare that lands on your plate. Experience the state's agricultural bounty to the max on **Trip 16: Cider Season Sampler**, when the harvest hits full swing and leaves erupt in red, yellow and copper.

Trips 16 17 18 21

Mansions of Newport

Newport's natural beauty has long attracted wealthy holidaymakers. As early as the 18th century, Manhattan's 'society' families flocked here for relaxing escapes, purchasing generous parcels of land and erecting sumptuous summer mansions. On **Trip 9: Rhode Island: East Bay**, take our walking tour down ritzy Bellevue Ave and admire Italianate palazzos, French chateaux and English manors, cloned from steeple to cellar.

Trips `1` `9`

Maritime New England

The southeastern corner of Connecticut is unlike any other in New England. The heritage of its seafaring days lives on in the country's largest maritime museum, Mystic Seaport, and the US naval base in Groton, visited on **Trip 1: Coastal New England**. Come for seafaring tales, as well as cruises in tall ships, wooden-boat regattas and restaurants serving seafood.

Trips `1` `5` `6` `9` `10` `25` `26`

(left) **Mansions of Newport** Breakers mansion

(below) **Ben & Jerry's Ice-Cream Factory** Iconic ice-cream

Ben & Jerry's Ice-Cream Factory

After winding your way through the scenic curves and rural villages on **Trip 15: Vermont's Spine: Route 100**, there's only one thing left to do – eat ice cream at Chunky Monkey HQ, aka the Ben & Jerry's Factory. Take a tour and learn how two schoolmates turned a $5 ice-cream-making correspondence course into Vermont's most delicious export.

Trip 15

BEST DRIVING ROADS

Mohawk Trail This scenic byway follows a former Native American footpath. **Trip** 8

CT 169 Explore Connecticut's farms and 200-year-old villages. **Trip** 11

VT 100 Meander through the scenic heart of Vermont's Green Mountains. **Trip** 15

Hwy 2, Champlain Islands Island-hop across Lake Champlain. **Trip** 18

Kancamagus Hwy Cruise past majestic vistas of granite peaks. **Trip** 20

19

IF YOU LIKE...

Maine Lobster bake on the shore

Seafood

As a rule, when in New England, one should eat as much lobster as possible. But there's more to life than the celebrity crustacean. There are also crabs, clams, oysters, scallops and fresh flaky fish.

5 Cape Cod & the Islands Feast on clams, oysters and seafood galore at some of the region's best restaurants.

6 Around Cape Ann Pull up a picnic table for fried clams and steamed lobsters at a waterfront clam shack.

10 Rhode Island: Coastal Culture Celebrate summer with clam cakes on a sunny bayside terrace or fresh-caught fish by the ferry dock.

25 Maritime Maine Lobster rolls, fried haddock and clam chowder – look for the shacks and no-frills eateries along the coast.

Outdoor Activities

Rolling hills and rocky peaks; rushing rivers and glass-like lakes; windswept beaches and sandy dunes: this is what draws millions of outdoor adventurers to New England.

2 Fall Foliage Tour Go zip-lining in Bretton Woods or cruise Lake Champlain on a 43ft schooner.

20 White Mountains Loop Embrace the views on a hut-to-hut hike amid New England's highest peaks.

26 Acadia National Park Hike, bike, kayak and stargaze on Mt Desert Island, a multisport mecca.

28 Great North Woods Canoe and fish on magnificent Moosehead Lake, or climb Mt Katahdin, Maine's highest peak.

Beer & Wine

Despite the region's Puritan roots, modern-day New England is jam-packed with microbreweries and wineries where you can wet your whistle. Just don't drink and drive!

12 Connecticut Wine Trail Tour Connecticut's Atlantic-facing vineyards for award-winning Cabernet Franc.

16 Cider Season Sampler Sample organic brews, crisp hard ciders, and an unconventional wine made with Vermont maple syrup.

18 Lake Champlain Byway Pull yourself away from the lake to visit Vermont's most creative microbrewery.

27 Old Canada Road The Liberal Cup and the Kennebec River Brewery are mug-lifting members of the Maine Beer Trail.

Provincetown Humpback whale-watching

Art & Architecture

New England's art and architecture span the centuries, from historic homes to contemporary museums and galleries.

3 Ivy League Tour Discover Orozco murals, a magnificent Shaker dwelling and the brick and stone beauty of America's oldest college campuses.

8 Mohawk Trail Take in Deerfield's collection of period homes and Mass MoCA's ever-changing exhibits.

17 Northeast Kingdom to Camel's Hump Visit villages lost in time, tour a historic round church and explore a barn full of larger-than-life puppets.

30 Mainely Art With galleries and art walks galore, you can take home the local scenery in Belfast, Camden and Rockport.

History

From Plymouth Rock to Revolutionary War sites to Mark Twain's Victorian mansion, New England's multilayered history is palpable at every turn.

4 Pilgrim Trail Chart the arrival and settlement of the New World's earliest incomers from Europe.

9 Rhode Island: East Bay Tour Pilgrims' houses and ancient burial grounds, and the grand mansions of pirates and privateers.

19 Southern Vermont Loop Learn about Bennington's role in the American Revolution, the Lincoln family home and Norman Rockwell's place in Vermont.

25 Maritime Maine Maine's coastal heritage, from shipbuilding to seafaring to fishing, is traced at museums along the coast.

Wildlife

The northern states are home to moose, bears, deer and other land mammals; dolphins, whales and seals frolic in the coastal waters; and the region's forests, lakes and marshes are full of migrating and resident birdlife.

5 Cape Cod & the Islands Onshore sanctuaries shelter abundant birdlife, while Stellwagen Bank attracts magnificent marine mammals.

13 Lower River Valley Spot bald and golden eagles migrating down from Canada for the winter.

22 Lake Winnipesaukee Bobcats, mountain lions and loons inhabit the quieter nooks of Lake Winn.

24 Woodland Heritage Trail With a 95% success rate, odds are good you'll see a moose on the Gorham Moose Tour.

NEED ^{TO} KNOW

CURRENCY
US Dollars ($)

LANGUAGE
English

VISAS
The United States' Visa Waiver Program allows pre-approved citizens of many countries to visit for 90 days or less without a visa. See https://travel.state.gov for details.

FUEL
Gas stations are ubiquitous. Prices averaged $2.30 per US gallon at the time of research.

RENTAL CARS
Rental cars are readily available region-wide. Companies include:

Avis (www.avis.com)

Enterprise (www.enterprise.com)

Hertz (www.hertz.com)

National (www.nationalcar.com)

IMPORTANT NUMBERS
Emergency (911)

AAA roadside assistance (1-800-222-4357)

Climate

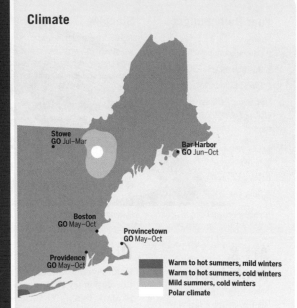

Warm to hot summers, mild winters
Warm to hot summers, cold winters
Mild summers, cold winters
Polar climate

When to Go

High Season (May–Oct)
» Accommodation prices increase by 50% to 100%; book in advance.

» Temperate spring weather and blooming fruit trees. July and August are hot and humid, except in mountain areas.

» Cooler in September and October.

Shoulder (Mar & Apr)
» Weather remains wintry throughout March; April sees some sunshine and spring buds.

» Less demand for accommodations; negotiate lower prices (also applies to beach areas in May and early June).

Low Season (Nov–Feb)
» Significantly lower prices for accommodations.

» Some sights in seasonal destinations close.

» With snow comes ski season (December to March), meaning higher prices in ski resorts.

Your Daily Budget

Budget: Less than $100
» Camping or dorm bed: $30–60
» Bus tickets: $10–20
» Street food mains: $8–12
» National Park Service (NPS) walking tours and free-admission days at museums: free

Midrange: $100–250
» Double room in a midrange hotel: $100–250
» Daily car rental: from $50
» Admission to museums and parks: $10–20

Top End: More than $250
» Double room in high-end hotel: from $250
» Eat at the region's finest restaurants: mains from $25
» Tickets to concerts, events and tours: $30–100

Eating

Restaurants Serving everything from clam chowder to gourmet international cuisine.

Cafes, diners & bakeries Ideal for coffee and casual meals.

Seafood shacks Specializing in lobster rolls, fried clams and summery seafood treats.

Bars, taverns & pubs Drinking establishments featuring 'pub grub' or full-fledged dinners.

Vegetarians Well-served in cities and college towns.

Price indicators represent the cost of a main course:

$	less than $15
$$	$15–25
$$$	more than $25

Sleeping

B&Bs Intimate, family-run guesthouses varying widely in price; often in charming historic homes or attractive country settings.

Camping From rustic National Forest tent sites to upscale private campgrounds with electricity/water hookups and recreational facilities.

Hotels Run-of-the-mill chains to stylish urban boutique hotels.

Motels America's iconic no-frills, low-cost roadside lodgings.

Price indicators represent the high-season rate for a double room with bathroom:

$	less than $100
$$	$100–250
$$$	more than $250

Arriving in New England

Boston Logan International Airport
Rental cars Catch a free shuttle bus to the Rental Car Center. The Sumner or Ted Williams tunnel toll into downtown Boston costs $3.50.

Silver Line bus Travels downtown ($1.70 to $2).

Subway Free shuttle goes to blue-line Airport station; subway fares are $2.25 to $2.75.

Taxis To downtown Boston $25 to $40, 20 minutes.

Manchester International Airport
Rental cars Take the free shuttle bus to rental car offices.

Shared vans Rides (from $39) to southern New Hampshire and northern Massachusetts.

TF Green Airport (Warwick, RI)
Rental cars Take the free shuttle bus to rental car offices.

Trains Run to downtown Providence ($6.25, 20 minutes) and Boston ($12, 90 minutes).

Cell Phones

Most US cell-phone systems are incompatible with the GSM 900/1800 standard used throughout Europe and Asia. Check with your cellular service provider before departure.

Internet Access

Many hotels, restaurants, cafes, libraries and public spaces offer free or low-cost wireless access.

Money

ATMs are widely available, and credit cards are accepted at most hotels and restaurants.

Useful Websites

Lonely Planet (www.lonelyplanet.com/usa/new-england) Destination information, hotel bookings and traveler forum.

Visit New England (www.visitnewengland.com) Listings for events, sights, restaurants and hotels in all six states.

New England Guide (www.boston.com/travel/newengland) Travel tips and itineraries from the *Boston Globe*.

Appalachian Mountain Club (www.outdoors.org) Hiking, biking, camping, climbing and paddling.

For more, see New England Driving Guide (p331).

CITY GUIDE

BOSTON

Narrow streets and stately architecture recall a history of revolution and transformation. Today, Boston is still forward-thinking and barrier-breaking. Follow the Freedom Trail to learn about the past; stroll along the Rose Kennedy Greenway to appreciate the present; and visit the galleries, clubs and student haunts to envision the future.

Boston The harbor at night

Getting Around

Park your car and explore the city on foot, with Boston's fabulous **Hubway** (www.thehubway.com; 24/72hr membership $6/12, per 30/60/90min free/$2/4; ⏲24hr) bike-share program, or aboard the USA's oldest subway system, the **MBTA** (📞617-222-5215; www.mbta.com; per ride $1.70-2.75), known locally as 'the T'.

Parking

Parking is scarce and meter readers are ruthless. Relatively affordable lots are located under the Boston Common and in the Seaport District.

Where to Eat

Boston's most famous eating area is the North End, packed with *salumeria* (delis), *pasticceria* (pastry shops) and ristoranti. The Seaport District is the place to go for seafood, while the giant Quincy Market food court offers something for everyone.

Where to Stay

Boston is small enough that almost all neighborhoods offer easy access to great sights, dining and entertainment. Beacon Hill and Back Bay are particularly charming. Although the West End is desolate, its hotels offer excellent value for their convenience to downtown Boston.

Useful Websites

Lonely Planet (www.lonelyplanet.com/boston)

Boston.com (www.boston.com) The *Boston Globe*'s online presence.

Universal Hub (www.universalhub.com) Bostonians talking to each other.

Sons of Sam Horn (www.sonsofsamhorn.com) Discussion of all things Red Sox.

Trips Through Boston: 1 4

For more, check out our city and country guides. www.lonelyplanet.com

TOP EXPERIENCES

➡ Boston Common & Public Garden

Picnic on the 50-acre lawn of America's oldest public park, or cruise the lake in a pedal-powered Swan Boat at the adjacent Public Garden.

➡ Freedom Trail

Sample Boston's Revolutionary sights along the well-marked red-brick road from Boston Common to Bunker Hill. (www.thefreedomtrail.org)

➡ Baseball at Fenway Park

Join the 'Fenway faithful' in rooting for the Red Sox at America's oldest major league baseball stadium. (www.redsox.com)

➡ Museum of Fine Arts

Ogle the encyclopedic collection at Boston's premier arts museum, including an entire gallery devoted to American painter John Singer Sargent. (www.mfa.org)

➡ Harvard University

Absorb four centuries of academic prestige on a campus tour of America's oldest college, which has graduated eight American presidents and dozens of Nobel laureates. (www.harvard.edu)

➡ Beacon Hill

Wander the lantern-lit cobblestone streets and flower-bedecked brick town houses of Boston's loveliest neighborhood.

➡ North End

Crunch cannoli in the bakeries of Boston's quintessential Italian neighborhood, or prowl among the 17th-century tombstones in the Old North Church cemetery.

➡ Seaport District

Snag a waterside table, tie on a bib, crack open a lobster claw and down a microbrew or two in this trendy restaurant district with glorious city and harbor views.

NEW ENGLAND
BY REGION

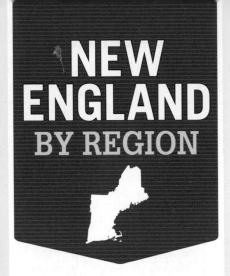

New England's six states are a road-tripper's dream, whether you're lobster shack-hopping along Maine's Atlantic shoreline or climbing through a canopy of multicolored autumn maples on a Vermont back road. Here's your guide to what each state has to offer.

Vermont (p169)

Framed by blazing fall leaves, blankets of snow or the exuberant greens of spring and summer, Vermont's blend of bucolic farmland, mountains and small villages is road-trip heaven. The delightful lakeside city of Burlington is just icing on the cake.

Sip cider and follow fiery foliage on Trip 16

Connecticut & Rhode Island (p113)

Flying largely below the tourist radar, New England's tiniest two states are best known for Newport's opulent mansions and the Ivy League campuses of Brown and Yale. Dig deeper to find historic Yankee settlements, maritime museums, the Litchfield Hills' idyllic greenery and an impressively long coastline.

Marvel at Newport's mansions on Trip 9

Maine (p265)

Sequestered in the nation's northeastern corner, Maine is a world unto itself. Choose between the bustling summer scene along its supremely scenic coastline – or decamp to the Great North Woods for fishing, boating and a feeling of wild isolation unparalleled east of the Mississippi.

Ogle lighthouses and linger over lobster on Trip 25

New Hampshire (p219)

Wherever you go in New Hampshire, nature is always close at hand. Zigzag through the White Mountains' breathtaking granite notches, loll about on the family-friendly shores of Lake Winnepesaukee, or take a cultural break in the artsy villages around Mt Monadnock and the history-packed seaside streets of Portsmouth.

Embrace lakeside living on Trip 22

Massachusetts (p61)

Cradle of the American Revolution, Massachusetts is New England's most populous and culturally vibrant state. Here museums, galleries and historic sites vie for attention with an amazing diversity of landscapes, from Cape Cod's windswept dunes to the Berkshires' pastoral mountain scenery.

Prowl Cape Cod's antique shops and sandy beaches on Trip 5

NEW ENGLAND

Classic Trips

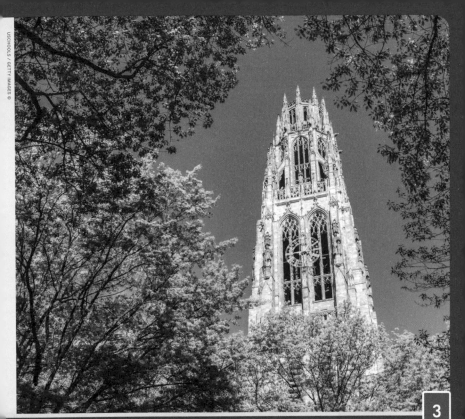

3

What Is a Classic Trip?

All the trips in this book show you the best of New England, but we've chosen seven as our all-time favorites. These are our Classic Trips – the ones that lead you to New England's iconic sights, top activities and unique experiences. Turn the page to see our multi-state Classic Trips, and look out for more Classic Trips on the following pages:

Above: Harkness Tower, Yale University, New Haven
Left: Cape Cod beach

29

Classic Trip

Coastal New England

1

This drive follows the southern New England coast. A week of whale-watching, maritime museums and sailboats will leave you feeling pleasantly waterlogged.

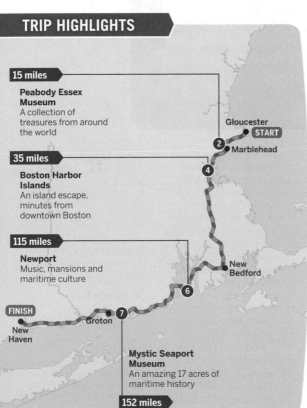

TRIP HIGHLIGHTS

15 miles

Peabody Essex Museum
A collection of treasures from around the world

35 miles

Boston Harbor Islands
An island escape, minutes from downtown Boston

115 miles

Newport
Music, mansions and maritime culture

152 miles

Mystic Seaport Museum
An amazing 17 acres of maritime history

 Gloucester **START**
Marblehead
New Bedford
FINISH
New Haven
Groton
New Bedford

6–8 DAYS
240 MILES / 386KM

GREAT FOR...

BEST TIME TO GO
Sites are open and weather is fine from May to September.

ESSENTIAL PHOTO
Pose for a snap alongside The Gloucester Fisherman.

BEST TWO DAYS
The first 35 miles (stops one to four) showcase coastal New England, past and present.

Salem The tall ship *Friendship* at Derby Wharf

Classic Trip

1 Coastal New England

From a pirate's perspective, there was no better base in Colonial America than Newport, given the easy access to trade routes and friendly local merchants. Until 1723, that is, when the new governor ceremoniously hanged 26 sea bandits at Gravelly Point. This classic trip highlights the region's intrinsic connection to the sea, from upstart pirates to upper-crust merchants, from Gloucester fisherfolk to New Bedford whalers, from clipper ships to submarines.

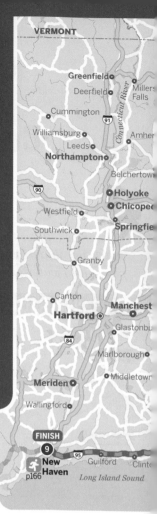

① Gloucester

Founded in 1623 by English fisherfolk, Gloucester is among New England's oldest towns. This port on Cape Ann has made its living from fishing for almost 400 years, and has inspired works including Rudyard Kipling's *Captains Courageous* and Sebastian Junger's *The Perfect Storm*. Visit the **Marine Heritage Center** (www. maritimegloucester.org; 23 Harbor Loop; adult/child $6/4; ⊙10am-5pm Jun-Oct; 🚻) to see the working waterfront in action. There is plenty of hands-on educational fun, including an outdoor aquarium and an excellent exhibit dedicated to Stellwagen Bank, the nearby National Marine Sanctuary. **Capt Bill & Sons Whale Watch** (☎978-283-6995; www.captainbillandsons.com; 24 Harbor Loop; adult/child $48/32; 🚻) boats also depart from here.

Don't leave Gloucester before you pay your respects at the **Gloucester Fishermen's Memorial**, where Leonard Craske's famous statue *The Gloucester Fisherman* stands.

✕ 🛏 p39, p89

The Drive ❯❯ Head out of town on Western Ave (MA 127), cruising past *The Gloucester Fisherman* and Stage Fort Park. This road follows the coastline south through swanky seaside towns, including Manchester-by-the-Sea and Beverly Farms, with

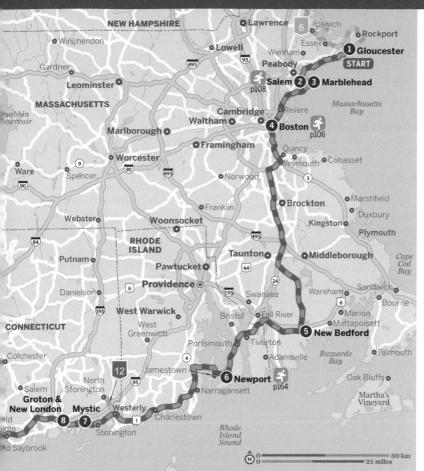

glimpses of the bay. After about 14 miles, cross Essex Bridge and continue south into Salem. For a quicker trip, take MA 128 south to MA 114.

TRIP HIGHLIGHT

2 Salem

Salem's glory dates to the 18th century, when it was a center for clipper-ship trade with the Far East,

LINK YOUR TRIP

6 Around Cape Ann

Head north from Gloucester for more quaint coastal culture.

12 Connecticut Wine Trail

Continue south along the coast for a tasty tour through New England wine country.

thanks to the enterprising efforts of merchant

Elias Hasket Derby. His namesake, Derby Wharf,

Classic Trip

is now the center of the **Salem Maritime National Historic Site** (www.nps.gov/ sama; 193 Derby St; ⊗9am-5pm), which includes the 1871 lighthouse, the tall ship *Friendship* and the state custom house.

Many Salem vessels followed Derby's ship *Grand Turk* around the Cape of Good Hope, and soon the owners founded the East India Marine Society to provide warehousing services for their ships' logs and charts. The new company's charter required the establishment of 'a museum in which to house the natural and artificial

curiosities' brought back by members' ships. The collection was the basis for what is now the world-class **Peabody Essex Museum** (www. pem.org; 161 Essex St; adult/ child $20/free; ⊗10am-5pm Tue-Sun; 🚻). Still today, the museum contains an amazing collection of Asian art, among other treasures.

A stroll around town (p108) reveals some impressive architecture – grand houses that were once sea captains' homes.

✕ 🛏 p39, p71

The Drive » Take Lafayette St (MA 114) south out of Salem center, driving past the campus of Salem State College. After crossing an inlet, the road bends east and becomes Pleasant St as it enters Marblehead center.

---

3 **Marblehead**

First settled in 1629, Marblehead is a maritime village with winding streets, brightly painted Colonial houses, and 1000 sailing yachts bobbing at moorings in the harbor. This is the Boston area's premier yachting port and one of New England's most prestigious addresses. Clustered around the harbor, Marblehead center is dotted with historic houses, art galleries and waterside parks.

The Drive » Drive south on MA 129, exiting Marblehead and continuing through the seaside town of Swampscott. At the traffic circle, take the first exit onto MA 1A, which continues south through Lynn and Revere. Take the VFW Pkwy (MA 1A) to

---

REVERE BEACH

Cruising through Revere, MA 1A parallels the wide, sandy stretch of Revere Beach, which proudly proclaims itself America's first public beach, established in 1896. Scenic but soulless, the condo-fronted beach belies the history of this place, which was a raucous boardwalk and amusement park for most of the 20th century. Famous for roller coasters, dance halls and the Wonderland dog track, Revere Beach attracted hundreds of thousands of sunbathers and fun-seekers during summer months.

The area deteriorated in the 1970s due to crime and pollution. In 1978 a historic blizzard wiped out many of the remaining buildings and businesses, and the 'Coney Island of New England' was relegated to the annals of history.

Revere Beach benefitted from a clean-up effort in the 1980s; nowadays, the beach itself is lovely to look at and a safe place to swim. Unfortunately, dominated by high-end condominium complexes, the area retains nothing of its former charm. Only one vestige of 'old' Revere Beach remains: the world-famous **Kelly's Roast Beef** (www.kellysroastbeef.com; 410 Revere Beach Blvd; sandwiches $8-12, mains $12-25; ⊗5am-2:30am), which has been around since 1951, and still serves up the best roast-beef sandwiches and clam chowder in town. There's no indoor seating, so pull up some sand and enjoy the view. Beware of the seagulls: they're crazy for roast beef.

the Revere Beach Pkwy (MA 16) to the Northeast Expwy (US 1), which goes over Tobin Bridge and into Boston.

TRIP HIGHLIGHT

❹ Boston

Boston's seaside location has influenced every aspect of its history, but it's only in recent years that the waterfront has become an attractive and accessible destination for visitors. Now you can stroll along the **Rose Kennedy Greenway** (www.rosekennedygreenway. org; ⚑; Ⓣ Aquarium, Haymarket), with the sea on one side and the city on the other. The focal point of the waterfront is the excellent **New England Aquarium** (www.neaq. org; Central Wharf; adult/ child $27/19; ⊙9am-5pm Mon-Fri, to 6pm Sat & Sun, 1hr later Jul & Aug; Ⓟ ⚑; Ⓣ Aquarium), home to seals, penguins, turtles and oodles of fish. Parking is $18.

From Long Wharf, you can catch a ferry out to the **Boston Harbor Islands** (www.bostonharbor islands.org; ⊙9am-dusk mid-Apr–mid-Oct; 🚢 from Long Wharf) for berry picking, beachcombing and sunbathing. Harbor cruises and trolley tours also depart from these docks. If you prefer to keep your feet on dry land, take a walk (p106) to explore Boston's flower-filled parks and shop-lined streets.

> ## PARKING IN BOSTON
>
> Parking in downtown Boston is prohibitively expensive. For more affordable rates, cross the Fort Point Channel and park in the Seaport District. Park in lots on Northern Ave (near the Institute of Contemporary Art) for a flat rate of $12; the Necco Street Garage (further south, off A St) is only $6.

✕ ➩ p39, p71

The Drive » Drive south out of Boston on I-93. You'll recognize the urban 'hood of Dorchester by pretty Savin Hill Cove and the landmark Rainbow Swash painted on the gas tank. At exit 4, take MA 24 south towards Brockton, then MA 140 south towards New Bedford. Take I-195 east for 2 miles, exiting onto MA 18 for New Bedford.

---

❺ New Bedford

During its heyday as a whaling port (1765–1860), New Bedford commanded some 400 whaling ships – a vast fleet that brought in hundreds of thousands of barrels of whale oil for lighting lamps. Novelist Herman Melville worked on one of these ships for four years, and thus set his celebrated novel *Moby-Dick* in New Bedford.

The excellent, hands-on **New Bedford Whaling Museum** (www.whaling museum.org; 18 Johnny Cake Hill; adult/child/student/senior $16/6/9/14; ⊙9am-5pm Apr-Dec, 9am-4pm Tue-Sat, 11am-4pm Sun Jan-Mar) commemorates this history. A 66ft skeleton of a blue whale welcomes you at the entrance. Inside, you can tramp the decks of the *Lagoda,* a fully rigged, half-size replica of an actual whaling bark.

The Drive » Take I-195 west for about 10 miles. In Fall River, head south on MA 24, which becomes RI 24 as you cross into Rhode Island. Cross the bridge, with views of Mt Hope Bay to the north and Sakonnet River to the south, then merge onto RI 114, heading south into Newport.

TRIP HIGHLIGHT

❻ Newport

Blessed with a deep-water harbor, Newport has been a shipbuilding base since 1646. Bowen's and Bannister's Wharf, once working wharves, now typify Newport's transformation from a working city-by-the-sea to a resort town. Take a narrated cruise with **Classic Cruises of Newport** (☏401-847-0298; www.cruisenewport.com; Bannister's Wharf; adult/child from $25/20; ⊙mid-May–mid-Oct) on *Rum Runner II,* a Prohibition-era bootlegging vessel, or *Madeleine,* a 72ft schooner.

Classic Trip

WHY THIS IS A CLASSIC TRIP
MARA VORHEES, WRITER

Nothing evokes New England's salty air like driving along the old coastal roads. MA 127 winds through some of the state's prettiest seaside towns, giving glimpses of gracious mansions perched at the ocean's edge. Even better, I love cruising along MA 1A with the windows down, feeling the ocean breeze, hearing the seagulls' cries and recalling the glory days of Revere Beach.

Top: Peabody Essex Museum, Salem
Left: Promenade at Revere Beach
Right: New Bedford Whaling Museum, New Bedford

WALTER BIBIKOW / GETTY IMAGES ©

Although its pirate days are over, Newport's harbor remains one of the most active yachting centers in the country. Visit the **Museum of Yachting** (MoY; ☎401-848-5777; www.iyrs.edu; 449 Thames St; ◷ noon-5pm Tue-Sat May-Oct) for a quick history lesson in the America's Cup Gallery and to watch students at work in the restoration school. Looming beside the museum is **Fort Adams** (www.fortadams. org; tours adult/child $10/5; ◷10am-4pm May-Oct), one of the largest seacoast fortifications in the US. In August it's the venue for the **Newport Jazz Festival** (www.newport jazzfest.org; Fort Adams State Park; tickets $40-85, 3 days $155; ◷Jul & Aug) and the **Newport Folk Festival** (www.newportfolk.org; Fort Adams State Park; 1-/3-day pass $49/120, parking $18; ◷late Jul).

✕ ⌷ p39, p123

The Drive ❯❯ Head west out of Newport on RI 138, swooping over Newport Bridge onto Conanicut Island and then over Jamestown Bridge to pick up US 1 for the drive into Mystic. The views of the bay from both bridges are a highlight.

- - - - - - - - - - - - - -

TRIP HIGHLIGHT

❼ Mystic

Many of Mystic's clipper ships launched from George Greenman & Co Shipyard, now the site

Classic Trip

of the **Mystic Seaport Museum** (☎860-572-0711; www.mysticseaport.org; 75 Greenmanville Ave; adult/child $26/17; ☻9am-5pm Apr-Oct, 10am-4pm Thu-Sun Nov-Mar; P ♿). Today the museum covers 17 acres and includes more than 60 historic buildings, four tall ships and almost 500 smaller vessels. Interpreters staffing all the buildings are glad to discuss their crafts and trades. Most illuminating are the demonstrations on such topics as ship rescue, oystering and whaleboat launching. The museum's exhibits also include a replica of the 77ft slave ship *Amistad.*

If the call of the sea beckons, set sail on the **Argia** (☎860-536-0416; www.argiamystic.com; 15 Holmes St; adult/child $49/39), a replica of a 19th-century schooner, which cruises down the Mystic River to Fishers' Island Sound.

🛏 p39

The Drive » The 7-mile drive from Mystic to Groton along US 1 south is through built-up suburbs and light industrial areas. To hop across the Thames River to New London, head north along North St to pick up I-95 south.

❽ Groton & New London

Groton is home to the US Naval Submarine Base, the first and the largest in the country. It is off-limits to the public, but you can visit the **Historic Ship Nautilus & Submarine Force Museum** (☎800-343-0079; www.ussnautilus.org; 1 Crystal Lake Rd; ☻9am-4pm Wed-Mon; P), which is home to *Nautilus,* the world's first nuclear-powered submarine and the first sub to transit the North Pole.

Across the river, New London has a similarly illustrious seafaring history, although these days it's built a reputation for itself as a budding creative center. Each summer it hosts Sailfest (www.sailfest.org), a three-day festival with free entertainment, topped off by the second-largest fireworks display in the Northeast. There's also a **Summer Concert Series**, organized by **Hygienic Art** (☎860-443-8001; www.hygienic.org; 79 Bank St; price varies for some exhibitions; ☻11am-3pm Tue-Thu, to 6pm Fri & Sat, from noon Sun).

✖ p39

The Drive » It's a 52-mile drive from Groton or New London to New Haven along I-95 south. The initial stages of the drive plow through the suburbs, but after that the interstate runs through old coastal towns such as Old Lyme, Old Saybrook and Guilford.

❾ New Haven

Although most famous for its Ivy League university, Yale, New Haven also played an important role in the burgeoning anti-slavery movement when, in 1839, the trial of mutineering Mendi tribesmen was held in New Haven's District Court.

Following their illegal capture by Spanish slave traders, the tribesmen, led by Joseph Cinqué, seized the schooner *Amistad* and sailed to New Haven seeking refuge. Pending the successful outcome of the trial, the men were held in a jailhouse on the green, where a 14ft-high bronze memorial now stands. It was the first civil-rights case held in the country.

For a unique take on the New Haven shoreline, take the 3-mile round-trip on the **Shore Line Trolley** (☎203-467-6927; www.shorelinetrolley.org; 17 River St, East Haven; adult/child $10/6; ☻10:30am-4:30pm daily Jun-Aug, Sat & Sun May, Sep & Oct; ♿), the oldest operating suburban trolley in the country, which takes you from East Haven to Short Beach in Branford. A wealth of art and architecture is packed into the streets of downtown New Haven (p166).

✖ 🛏 p39, p59, p147

Eating & Sleeping

Gloucester ❶

✗ Two Sisters Coffee Shop   Diner $

(www.facebook.com/TwoSistersCoffeeShop; 27 Washington St; mains $5-8; ⊙6:30am-1pm; 🖋) This local place is where the fisherfolk go for breakfast when they come in from their catch. They're early risers, so you may have to wait for a table. Corned-beef hash, eggs in a hole and pancakes all get rave reviews. Service is a little salty.

Salem ❷

🛏 Stephen Daniels House   B&B $$

(📞978-744-5709; www.thedanielshouse.com; 1 Daniels St; r $125-150; P🖋) This must be Salem's oldest lodging, with parts dating from 1667. Two walk-in fireplaces grace the common area, and the rooms are filled with period antiques.

Boston ❹

✗ Barking Crab   Seafood $$

(www.barkingcrab.com; 88 Sleeper St; sandwiches from $9, mains $17-27; ⊙11:30am-10pm; 🚇SL1, SL2; Ⓣ South Station, Aquarium) Big buckets of crabs (bairdi, king, snow, Dungeness etc), steamers dripping in lemon and butter, paper plates piled high with all things fried, pitchers of ice-cold beer...Devour your feast at communal picnic tables overlooking the water. Service is slack, noise levels are high, but the atmosphere is jovial.

🛏 Harborside Inn   Boutique Hotel $$$

(📞617-723-7500; www.harborsideinnboston.com; 185 State St; r from $269; P❄@🖋; Ⓣ Aquarium) Steps from Faneuil Hall and the waterfront, this boutique hotel inhabits a respectfully renovated 19th-century mercantile warehouse. The 116 rooms are on the small side, but comfortable and appropriately nautically themed. Note that Atrium Rooms face the atrium (ahem) and Cabin Rooms have no windows at all. Add $20 for a city view (worth it).

Newport ❻

✗ White Horse Tavern   Tavern $$$

(📞401-849-3600; www.whitehorsenewport.com; 26 Marlborough St; meals $28-58; ⊙11:30am-9pm) If you'd like to eat at a tavern opened by a 17th-century pirate that once served as an annual meeting place for the colonial Rhode Island General Assembly, try this historic beauty. Menus for dinner (at which men should wear a jacket) might include baked escargot, truffle-crusted Atlantic halibut or beef Wellington.

Mystic ❼

🛏 Whaler's Inn   Inn $$

(📞860-536-1506; www.whalersinnmystic.com; 20 E Main St; d from $170; P@🖋) In downtown Mystic, beside its historic drawbridge, this hotel combines an 1865 Victorian house with a reconstructed luxury hotel and a modern motel. Rates include continental breakfast, a small gym and complimentary bicycles.

New London ❽

✗ Captain Scott's Lobster Dock   Seafood $$

(📞860-439-1741; www.captscotts.com; 80 Hamilton St; mains $7-21; ⊙11am-9pm May-Oct; 🖋) Captain Scott's is *the* place for seafood in the summer. The setting's just a series of picnic tables by the water, but you can feast on succulent (hot or cold) lobster rolls, followed by steamers, fried whole-belly clams, scallops or lobsters.

New Haven ❾

✗ Miya's Sushi   Sushi $$$

(📞203-777-9760; www.miyassushi.com; 68 Howe St; mains $8-35; ⊙4-10pm; 🖋) Two-time winner of the Taste of the Nation Award, Chef Bun Lai's immaculately presented, sustainable sushi and sashimi concoctions sport fantastic names. Even more fantastic are the freshness and flavours of the raw ingredients.

Classic Trip

Fall Foliage Tour

2

Touring New England in search of autumn's changing colors has become so popular that it has sprouted its own subculture of 'leaf-peepers.' Immerse yourself in the fall harvest spirit.

TRIP HIGHLIGHTS

212 miles

Lake Champlain
Cruise the lake on a 43ft schooner for the best views

7

St Johnsbury

8

North Conway
FINISH

327 miles

Bretton Woods
Zip-line 1000ft through a golden leaf canopy

● Manchester

47 miles

Berkshires
Pack a picnic in the Berkshires' gourmet shops

4

2

Sherman ●
START

10 miles

Kent
Autumn foliage framing the Housatonic River

5–7 DAYS
375 MILES / 603KM

GREAT FOR...

BEST TIME TO GO
Mid-September to late October are best for the harvest and autumn leaves.

☒ ESSENTIAL PHOTO
Kent Falls set against a backdrop of autumnal colors.

☑ BEST FOR OUTDOORS
Zip-lining through the tree canopy in Bretton Woods.

umpkin pie

Classic Trip

2 Fall Foliage Tour

The brilliance of fall in New England is legendary. Scarlet and sugar maples, ash, birch, beech, dogwood, tulip tree, oak and sassafras all contribute to the carnival of autumn color. But this trip is about much more than just flora and fauna: the harvest spirit makes for family outings to pick-your-own farms, leisurely walks along dappled trails and tables groaning beneath delicious seasonal produce.

① Lake Candlewood

With a surface area of 8.4 sq miles, Candlewood is the largest lake in Connecticut. On the western shore, the **Squantz Pond State Park** (☎203-312-5013; www.ct.gov/deep/squantzpond; 178 Shortwoods Rd, New Fairfield; residents $9-13, nonresidents $15-22; ☺8am-sunset; P🐾) is popular with leaf-peepers, who come to amble the pretty shoreline. In Brookfield and Sherman, quiet vineyards with acres of gnarled grapevines line the hillsides. Visitors can tour the intimate **White Silo Farm** (☎860-355-0271; www.whitesilowinery.com; 32 CT 37; tastings $7; ☺11am-6pm Fri-Sun Apr-Dec; 🐾), where the focus is on specialty

wines made from farm-grown fruit.

For the ultimate bird's-eye view of the foliage, consider a late-afternoon hot-air balloon ride with **GONE Ballooning** (☎203-262-6625; www.flygoneballooning.com; 88 Sylvan Crest Dr, Southbury; adult/under 12yr $250/125; 🐾) in nearby Southbury.

✕ p49

The Drive » From Danbury, at the southern tip of the lake, you have a choice of heading 28 miles north via US 7, taking in Brookfield and New Milford (or trailing the scenic eastern shoreline along Candlewood Lake Rd S); or heading 26 miles north along CT 37 and CT 39 via New Fairfield, Squantz Pond and Sherman, before reconnecting with US 7 to Kent.

TRIP HIGHLIGHT

❷ Kent

Kent has previously been voted *the* spot in all of New England (yes, even beating Vermont) for fall foliage viewing. Situated prettily in the Litchfield Hills on the banks of the Housatonic River, it is surrounded by dense woodlands. For a sweeping view of them, hike up Cobble Mountain in **Macedonia State Park** (☏860-927-3238; www.ct.gov/deep/macedoniabrook; 159 Macedonia Brook Rd; residents/nonresidents $14/24; ⏱mid-Apr–Sep; P🚲), a wooded oasis 2 miles north of town. The steep climb to the rocky ridge affords panoramic views of the foliage against a backdrop of the Taconic and Catskill mountain ranges.

🔗 LINK YOUR TRIP

8 **Mohawk Trail**
Pick up the Mohawk Trail at Williamstown for more spectacular mountain vistas and rural New England charm.

15 **Vermont's Spine: Route 100**
Branch off US 7 at Manchester and take Vermont's dazzlingly scenic VT 100 north along the eastern slopes of the Green Mountains.

Classic Trip

The 2175-mile Georgia-to-Maine Appalachian National Scenic Trail (www.appalachiantrail.com) also runs through Kent and up to Salisbury on the Massachusetts border. Unlike much of the trail, the Kent section offers a mostly flat 5-mile river walk alongside the Housatonic, the longest river walk along the entire length of the trail. The trailhead is accessed on River Rd, off CT 341.

 p163

The Drive » The 15-mile drive from Kent to Housatonic Meadows State Park along US 7 is one of the most scenic drives in Connecticut. The single-lane road dips and weaves between thick stands of forest, past Kent Falls State Park with its tumbling waterfall (visible from the road), and through West Cornwall's

picturesque covered bridge, which spans the Housatonic River.

❸ Housatonic Meadows State Park

During the spring thaw, the churning waters of the Housatonic challenge kayakers and canoeists. By summer the scenic waterway transforms into a lazy, flat river, perfect for fly-fishing. In **Housatonic Meadows State Park** (☎860-927-3238; www.ct.gov/deep/housatonicmeadows; 90 CT 7 North, Sharon; ⊙8am-sunset), campers vie for a spot on the banks of the river while hikers take to the hills on the Appalachian Trail. **Housatonic River Outfitters** (☎860-672-1010; www.dryflies.com; 24 Kent Rd, Cornwall Bridge) runs guided fishing trips with gourmet picnics.

Popular with artists and photographers, one of the most photographed fall scenes is the **Cornwall**

Bridge (West Cornwall), an antique, covered bridge that stretches across the broad river, framed by vibrantly colored foliage.

On Labor Day weekend, in the nearby town of Goshen, you can visit the Goshen Fair (www.goshenfair.org) – one of Connecticut's best old-fashioned fairs, with ox-pulling and wood-cutting contests.

The Drive » Continue north along US 7 toward the Massachusetts border and Great Barrington, 27 miles away. After a few miles you leave the forested slopes of the park behind and enter expansive rolling countryside dotted with large, red-and-white barns. Look out for hand-painted signs advertising farm produce and consider stopping overnight in Falls Village, which has an excellent B&B (p49).

TRIP HIGHLIGHT

❹ Berkshires

Blanketing the western-most part of Massachusetts, the rounded mountains of the Berkshires turn crimson and gold as early as mid-September. The effective capital of the Berkshires is **Great Barrington**, a formerly industrial town whose streets are now lined with art galleries and upscale restaurants. It's the perfect place to pack your picnic or rest your legs before or after a hike in nearby **Beartown State Forest** (www.mass.gov/dcr; 69 Blue Hill Rd, Monterey; parking

LOCAL KNOWLEDGE: KENT FALLS

Kent is a great place to base yourself in the fall, with lots of accessible spots for viewing the leaves and good amenities in the pretty town center. The best hiking trail in season is the section that connects with the Appalachian Trail at Caleb's Peak, affording fantastic views. If you're less able to hike, the easiest way to get a beautiful vista is to head 5 miles south out of town on US 7 to **Kent Falls State Park**, which is unmissable on your right. The falls' wonderfully lazy cascade is right before you and there are lots of easy trails into the forest.

$8-10). Crisscrossing some 12,000 acres, **hiking trails** yield spectacular views of wooded hillsides and pretty Benedict Pond.

Further north, **October Mountain State Forest** (www.mass.gov/dcr; 317 Woodland Rd) is the state's largest tract of green space (16,127 acres), also interwoven with hiking trails. The name – attributed to Herman Melville – gives a good indication of when this park is at its loveliest, with its multicolored tapestry of hemlocks, birches and oaks.

p49, p97

The Drive ›› Drive north on US 7, the spine of the Berkshires, cruising 11 miles through Great Barrington and Stockbridge. In Lee, the highway merges with scenic US 20, from where you can access October Mountain. Continue 16 miles north through Lenox and Pittsfield to Lanesborough. Turn right on N Main St and follow the signs to the Mt Greylock State Reservation entrance.

---

⑤ Mt Greylock State Reservation

At 3491ft, Massachusetts' highest peak is perhaps not very high, but a climb up the 92ft **War Veterans Memorial Tower** rewards you with a panorama stretching up to 100 verdant miles, across the Taconic, Housatonic and Catskill ranges, and over five states. Even if the weather seems drab from the foot, driving up to

LOCAL KNOWLEDGE: NORTHERN BERKSHIRE FALL FOLIAGE PARADE

If your timing is right, you can stop in North Adams for the **Northern Berkshire Fall Foliage Parade** (www.fallfoliageparade.com; ⊗Oct), held in late September or early October. Held for over 60 years, the event follows a changing theme, but it always features music, food and fun – and, of course, foliage.

the summit may well lift you above the gray blanket, and the view with a layer of cloud floating between tree line and sky is simply magical.

Mt Greylock State Reservation (☎413-499-4262; www.mass.gov/dcr; 30 Rockwell Rd, Lanesborough; ⊗9am-5pm Jun-Aug, to 4.30pm Sep-May) has some 45 miles of **hiking trails**, including a portion of the Appalachian Trail. Frequent trail pull-offs on the road up – including some that lead to waterfalls – make it easy to get at least a little hike in before reaching the top of Mt Greylock.

p49

The Drive ›› Return to US 7 and continue north through the quintessential college town of Williamstown. Cross the Vermont border and continue north through the historic village of Bennington. Just north of Bennington, turn left on VT 7A and continue north to Manchester (51 miles total).

---

⑥ Manchester

Stylish Manchester is known for its magnificent New England architecture. For fall foliage views, head south of the center and take the **Mt Equinox Skyline Drive** (☎802-362-1114; www.equinoxmountain.com; VT 7A, btwn Manchester & Arlington; car & driver $15, each additional passenger $5, under 10yr free; ⊗9am-4pm late May-Oct) to the summit of 3828ft Mt Equinox, the highest mountain accessible by car in the Taconic Range. Wind up the 5.2 miles – with gasp-inducing scenery at every hairpin turn – seemingly to the top of the world, where the 360-degree panorama unfolds, offering views of the Adirondacks, the lush Battenkill Valley and Montreal's Mt Royal.

If early snow makes Mt Equinox inaccessible, visit 412-acre **Hildene** (☎802-362-1788; www.hildene.org; 1005 Hildene Rd/VT 7A; adult/child $20/5, guided tours $7.50/2; ⊗9:30am-4:30pm), a Georgian Revival mansion that was once home to the Lincoln family. It's filled with presidential memorabilia and sits nestled at the edge of

Classic Trip

WHY THIS IS A CLASSIC TRIP
BENEDICT WALKER, WRITER

There's something truly magical about Mother Nature's autumnal palette. If she's on time and you're in sync, this classic leaf-peeping itinerary will show you the full spectrum of yellows, golds, oranges, crimsons and reds. The route takes enough time and heads far enough north to offer real variety. Throw in a lake cruise and a zip line above the forest canopy and we've got you covered!

Top: Covered bridge, West Cornwall
Left: Mt Equinox Skyline Drive
Right: Sailboat, Lake Champlain

LARRY GERBRANDT / GETTY IMAGES ©

the Green Mountains, with access to 8 miles of wooded **walking trails**.

✕ ⊨ p49, p213

The Drive » Take VT 7 north, following the western slopes of the Green Mountains through Rutland and Middlebury to reach Burlington (100 miles) on the shores of Lake Champlain.

- - - - - - - - - - - - - -

TRIP HIGHLIGHT

❼ Lake Champlain

With a surface area of 490 sq miles straddling New York, Vermont and Quebec, Lake Champlain is the largest freshwater lake in the US after the Great Lakes.

On its eastern side, **Burlington** is a gorgeous base for enjoying the lake. Explore it on foot (p216), then scoot down to the wooden promenade, take a swing on the four-person rocking benches and consider a bike ride along the 7.5-mile lakeside bike path.

For the best offshore foliage views, we love the *Friend Ship* sailboat at **Whistling Man Schooner Company** (☏802-598-6504; www.whistlingman. com; Burlington Community Boathouse, 1 College St, at Lake Champlain; 2hr cruises adult/child $50/35; ⏱3 trips daily late May–early Oct), a 43ft sloop that accommodates just 17 passengers. Next door, **ECHO Lake Aquarium & Science Center** (☏802-864-1848; www.echovermont. org; 1 College St; adult/child

$13.50/10.50; 🕙10am-5pm; 🚹) explores the history and ecosystem of the lake, including a famous snapshot of 'Champ,' Lake Champlain's mythical sea creature.

🍴 p49

The Drive » Take I-89 southeast to Montpelier, savoring gorgeous views of Vermont's iconic Mt Mansfield and Camel's Hump, then continue northeast on US 2 to St Johnsbury, where you can pick up I-93 southeast across the New Hampshire line to Littleton. Take the eastbound US 302 exit and continue towards Crawford Notch State Park and Bretton Woods. The drive is 115 miles.

TRIP HIGHLIGHT

8 Bretton Woods

Unbuckle your seat belts and step away from the car. You're not just peeping at leaves today, you're swooping past them on zip lines that drop 1000ft at 30mph. The four-season **Bretton Woods Canopy Tour** (📞603-278-4947; www.brettonwoods.com; US 302; per person $89-110; 🕙tours 10am & 1:30pm year-round, plus additional times during peak periods) includes a hike through the woods, a stroll over sky bridges and a swoosh down 10 cables to tree platforms.

If this leaves you craving even higher views, cross US 302 and drive 6 miles on Base Rd to the coal-burning, steam-powered **Mt Washington Cog Railway** (📞603-278-5404; www.thecog.com; 3168 Bass Station Rd; adult $68-73, child $39; 🕙daily Jun-Oct, Sat & Sun late Apr, May & Nov) at the western base of Mt Washington, the highest peak in New England. This historic railway has been hauling sightseers to the mountain's 6288ft summit since 1869.

🛏 p229

The Drive » Cross through Crawford Notch and continue 20 miles southeast on US 302, a gorgeous route through the White Mountains that parallels the Saco River and the Conway Scenic Railroad. At the junction of NH 16 and US 302, continue 5 miles on US 302 into North Conway.

---

9 North Conway

Many of the best restaurants, pubs and inns in North Conway come with expansive views of the nearby mountains, making it an ideal place to wrap up a fall foliage road trip. If you're traveling with kids or you skipped the cog railway ride up Mt Washington, consider an excursion on the antique steam Valley Train with the **Conway Scenic Railroad** (📞800-232-5251, 603-356-5251; www.conwayscenic.com; 38 Norcross Circle; Notch Train coach/1st class/dome car $62/76/90, Valley Train coach/1st class/dome/dining car from $17/21/25.50/36.50; 🕙mid-Jun–Oct; 🚹); it's a short but sweet round-trip ride through the Mt Washington Valley from North Conway to Conway, 11 miles south, with the Moat Mountains and the Saco River as your scenic backdrop. First-class seats are usually in a restored Pullman observation car.

🍴🛏 p49, p229

DETOUR: KANCAMAGUS SCENIC BYWAY

Start: 9 North Conway

Just south of North Conway, the 34.5-mile Kancamagus Scenic Byway, otherwise known as NH 112, passes through the White Mountains from Conway to Lincoln, NH. You'll drive alongside the Saco River and enjoy sweeping views of the Presidential Range from Kancamagus Pass. Inviting trailheads and pull-offs line the road. From Lincoln at the highway's western end, a short drive north on I-93 leads to Franconia Notch State Park, where the foliage in September and October is simply spectacular.

Eating & Sleeping

Lake Candlewood ❶

✕ American Pie   Bakery $$

(☎860-350-0662; www.americanpiecompany.
com; 29 Sherman Rd/CT 37, Sherman; mains
$10-22; ⏰7am-9pm Tue-Sun, to 3pm Mon) A local
favorite serving up 20 varieties of homemade
pie, including pumpkin and blueberry crumb,
alongside burgers, steaks and salads.

Housatonic Meadows State Park ❸

🛏 Falls Village Inn   Inn $$$

(☎860-824-0033; www.thefallsvillageinn.com; 33
Railroad St, Falls Village; d/ste $209/299; P🛜)
The heart and soul of one of the smallest villages
in Connecticut, this inn originally served the
Housatonic Railroad. Now the six rooms are styled
by interior decorator Bunny Williams, and the Tap
Room is a hangout for Lime Rock's racers.

Berkshires (Great Barrington) ❹

✕ Castle
Street Café   Modern American $$$

(☎413-528-5244; www.castlestreetcafe.com; 10
Castle St; mains $22-32; ⏰5-9:30pm Wed-Mon;
🛜) Castle Street Café's menu reads like a who's
who of local farms: Pineland Farm grass-fed
natural beef, Rawson Brook chevre and Equinox
Farm mesclun greens. Chef-owner Michael Ballon's
preparations range from innovative vegetarian fare
to classics such as rack of lamb. The setting is as
engaging as the food, with both a jazzy bar with a
pub menu and an art-filled dining room.

Mt Greylock State Reservation ❺

🛏 Bascom Lodge   Lodge $

(☎413-743-1591; www.bascomlodge.net; 1
Summit Rd; dm/d/q $40/125/150, mains $8-12;
⏰restaurant 8am-4:30pm Sat & Sun May & daily
Jun-Oct, dinner by reservation; P) High atop
Mt Greylock, this truly rustic hostelry was built
as a federal work project in the 1930s. Rooms
have shared bathrooms, comfortable beds and
wonderful views. The meals – fresh, hot and

individually prepared – are excellent and filling,
providing perfect sustenance for hikers.

Manchester ❻

🛏 Equinox   Resort $$$

(☎800-362-4747, reservations 877-854-7625;
www.equinoxresort.com; 3567 Main St/VT 7A; r
$299-489, ste $419-719; @🛜🐾) Manchester's
most famous resort encompasses many worlds:
cottages with wood-burning fireplaces, luxury
town houses with full kitchens, the main house's
elegant suites, and the Federal-style 1811 House's
antique-filled rooms, canopied beds and oriental
rugs. High-end extras abound: an 18-hole golf
course, two tennis courts, a state-of-the-art
fitness center, a full-service spa and endless
activities, including falconry, archery and
snowmobiling.

Lake Champlain ❼

✕ American Flatbread   Pizza $$

(☎802-861-2999; www.americanflatbread.com/
restaurants/burlington-vt; 115 St Paul St; flatbreads
$14-23; ⏰restaurant 11:30am-3pm & 5-11:30pm
Mon-Fri, 11:30am-11:30pm Sat & Sun) Central
downtown location, bustling atmosphere, great
beers on tap from the in-house Zero Gravity
microbrewery, and superb flatbread (thin-crust
pizza) with locally sourced ingredients are reason
enough to make this one of your first lunch or
dinner stops in Burlington. Throw in an outdoor
terrace in the back alleyway in warm weather, and
you've got one of Vermont's finest eateries.

North Conway ❾

🛏 Red Elephant Inn   Inn $$

(☎800-642-0749, 603-356-3548; www.
redelephantinn.com; 28 Locust Lane; r $120-239;
🛜) Set on a quiet street behind the Red Jacket
Mountain View Inn, this lovely Victorian is a hidden
gem. The eight rooms are individually decorated
in colorful, eclectic themes with telling names
including the Hippie Room, Country Quilts and
Neiman Marcus.

Classic Trip

Ivy League Tour

3

This trip celebrates history and education as it rolls between New England's Ivies, where campus tours sneak behind the gates for an up-close look at the USA's greatest universities.

TRIP HIGHLIGHTS

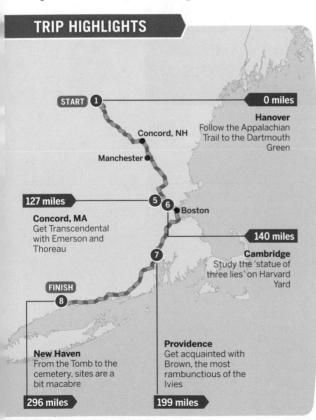

START ① 0 miles

Hanover
Follow the Appalachian Trail to the Dartmouth Green

Concord, NH

Manchester

127 miles

⑤ ⑥ Boston

Concord, MA
Get Transcendental with Emerson and Thoreau

140 miles

Cambridge
Study the 'statue of three lies' on Harvard Yard

⑦

FINISH
⑧

New Haven
From the Tomb to the cemetery, sites are a bit macabre

296 miles

Providence
Get acquainted with Brown, the most rambunctious of the Ivies

199 miles

5 DAYS
296 MILES / 476KM

GREAT FOR...

BEST TIME TO GO
Catch student-filled campuses from September to November.

 ESSENTIAL PHOTO
Stand beside the statue of John Harvard, the man who didn't found Harvard.

 BEST HISTORY
Learn about the USA's oldest university during a Harvard tour.

3 Ivy League Tour

What's most surprising about a tour of the Ivy League? The distinct personalities of the different campuses, which are symbiotically fused with their surrounding landscapes. Compare fresh-faced Dartmouth, with its breezy embrace of New Hampshire's outdoors, to enclaved Yale, its Gothic buildings fortressed against the urban wilds of New Haven. But the schools all share one trait – vibrant, diverse and engaged students who dispel any notions that they're out-of-touch elites.

❶ Hanover, New Hampshire

When the first big snowfall hits **Dartmouth College** (📞603-646-1110; www.dartmouth.edu), an email blasts across campus, calling everyone to the central **Green** for a midnight snowball fight. The Green is also the site of elaborate ice sculptures during Dartmouth's **Winter Carnival** (www.dartmouth.edu/~sao/events/carnival; ◷Feb), a weeklong celebration that's been held annually for more than 100 years.

North of the Green is **Baker Berry Library** (📞603-646-2560; http://dartmouth.edu/education/libraries; 25 N Main St; ◷8am-2am Mon-Fri, 10am-2am Sat & Sun), which holds an impressive mural called the *Epic of American Civilization*. Painted by Jose Clemente Orozco, it traces the course of civilization in the Americas from the Aztec era to modern times. At 4pm, stop by the adjacent **Sanborn House Library** (Dartmouth College), where tea is served during the academic year for 10¢.

This tradition honors a 19th-century English professor who invited students for chats and afternoon tea. For a free student-led **walking tour** (☎603-646-2875; http://dartmouth.edu/visit; 6016 Mc-Nutt Hall) of the campus, stop by the admissions office on the 2nd floor of McNutt Hall on the west side of the Green. Call or check online to confirm departure times.

The collection at Dartmouth's **Hood Museum of Art** (☎603-646-2808; http://hoodmuseum.dartmouth.edu; 6 E Wheelock St; ⊙10am-5pm Tue & Thu-Sat, to 9pm Wed, noon-5pm Sun) includes nearly 70,000 items. The collection is particularly strong in American pieces, including Native American art. One highlight is a set of Assyrian reliefs dating to the 9th century BC.

From the museum, turn left onto E Wheelock St and walk toward

LINK YOUR TRIP

12 Connecticut Wine Trail

Jump from grades to grapes in New Haven by heading north along US 1.

21 Connecticut River Byway

From Hanover, drive south on NE 10 for riverside history.

53

the Hanover Inn. You'll soon cross the **Appalachian Trail**, which runs through downtown. From here, it's 431 miles to Mt Katahdin in Maine.

 p59

The Drive ⟩⟩ From Hanover, follow NH 120 east to I-89 south. Take exit 117 to NH 4 east, following it to NH 4A. Turn right and follow NH 4A 3.5 miles to the museum.

- - - - - - - - - - - -

❷ Enfield Shaker Museum

The Enfield Shaker site sits in stark contrast to today's college campuses. In fact, the two couldn't be more different – except for the required communal housing with a bunch of non-relatives. But a trip here is illuminating. Set in a valley overlooking Mascoma Lake, the Enfield Shaker site dates to the late 18th century. At its peak, some 300 members lived in Enfield. Farmers and craftspeople, they built impressive wood and brick buildings and took in converts, orphans and children of the poor – essential for the Shaker future since sex was not allowed in the pacifist, rule-abiding community. By the early 1900s the

community had gone into decline and the last family left in 1917.

The **museum** (☎603-632-4346; www.shakermuseum.org; 447 NH 4A, Enfield; adult/youth/child $12/8/3; ☉10am-4pm Mon-Sat, noon-4pm Sun Apr-late Dec) centers on the Great Stone Dwelling, the largest Shaker dwelling house ever built. You can also explore the gardens and grounds. The guide might even let you ring the rooftop bell. Spend the night on the 3rd and 4th floor of the building. **Accommodations** (☎603-632-4346; www.shakermuseum.org/staywithus.htm; 447 NH 4A, Enfield; s/d/tr $110/135/160; ☎) feature traditional Shaker furniture, but not phones or TVs, although there is wi-fi.

The Drive ⟩⟩ Return to I-89 south. After 54 miles, take I-93 north 3 miles to exit 15E for I-393 east. From there, take exit 1 and follow the signs.

- - - - - - - - - - - -

❸ Concord, New Hampshire

New Hampshire's capital is a trim and tidy city with a wide Main St dominated by the striking **State House** (☎603-271-2154; www.gencourt.state.nh.us; 107 N Main St; ☉8am-4pm Mon-Fri), a granite-hewed 19th-century edifice topped with a glittering dome.

Nearby, the New Hampshire schoolteacher Christa McAuliffe,

chosen to be America's first teacher-astronaut, is honored at the **McAuliffe-Shepard Discovery Center** (☎603-271-7827; www.starhop.com; 2 Institute Dr; adult/child 3-12yr $10/7; ☉10:30am-4pm daily mid-Jun–early Sep, Fri-Sun rest of year). She died in the *Challenger* explosion on January 28, 1986. The museum also honors New Hampshire native Alan B Shepard, a member of NASA's elite Mercury corps who became America's first astronaut in 1961. Intriguing exhibits chronicle their lives and spotlight aviation, and earth and space sciences. There's also a planetarium.

 p59

The Drive ⟩⟩ Return to I-93 south, passing through Manchester before entering Massachusetts. Follow I-495 south toward Lowell.

- - - - - - - - - - - -

❹ Lowell, Massachusetts

In the early 19th century, textile mills in Lowell churned out cloth by the mile, driven by the abundant waterpower of Pawtucket Falls. Today, the historic buildings in the city center – connected by the trolley and canal boats – comprise the Lowell National Historic Park, which gives a fascinating peek at the workings of a 19th-century industrial town. Stop first at the **Market Mills**

Visitors Center (www.
nps.gov/lowe; 246 Market St,
Market Mills; ☺9am-5pm) to
pick up a map and check
out the general exhibits.
Five blocks northeast
along the river, the **Boott
Cotton Mills Museum**
(www.nps.gov/lowe; 115 John
St; adult/child/student $6/3/4;
☺9:30am-5pm; ⓘ) has ex-
hibits that chronicle the
rise and fall of the industrial revolution in Lowell,
including technological
changes, labor move-
ments and immigration.
The highlight is a work-
ing weave room, with 88
power looms. A special
exhibit on **Mill Girls &
Immigrants** (40 French St;
☺11am-5pm Jun-Sep, 1:30-
5pm Oct-Nov) examines the
lives of working people,
while seasonal exhibits
are sometimes on display
in other historic build-
ings around town.

The Drive » Take the Lowell
Connector to US 3 heading
south. In Billerica, exit to
Concord Rd. Continue south on
Concord Rd (MA 62) through
Bedford. This road becomes
Monument St and terminates
at Monument Sq in Concord
center. Walden Pond is about
3 miles south of Monument Sq,
along Walden St (MA 126) south
of MA 2.

❺ Concord, Massachusetts

Tall, white church
steeples rise above
ancient oaks in Colonial
Concord, giving the town
a stateliness that belies
the American Revolution

drama that occurred cen-
turies ago. It is easy to
see how so many writers
found their inspiration
here in the 1800s.

Ralph Waldo Emerson
was the paterfamilias of
literary Concord and the
founder of the Transcen-
dentalist movement (and,
incidentally, a graduate
of Harvard College). His
home of nearly 50 years,
the **Ralph Waldo Emer-
son Memorial House** (28
Cambridge Turnpike; adult/
child $9/7; ☺10am-4:30pm
Thu-Sat, 1-4:30pm Sun mid-
Apr–Oct), often hosted
his renowned circle of
friends.

One of them was Henry
David Thoreau (another
Harvard grad), who put
Transcendentalist beliefs
into practice when he
spent two years in a
rustic cabin on the shores
of **Walden Pond** (www.
mass.gov/dcr/parks/walden;
915 Walden St; parking $8-10;
☺dawn-dusk). The glacial
pond is now a state park,
surrounded by acres of
forest. A footpath circles
the pond, leading to the
site of Thoreau's cabin on
the northeast side.

The Drive » Take MA 2 east
to its terminus in Cambridge.
Go left on the Alewife Brook
Pkwy (MA 16), then right on

Massachusetts Ave and into
Harvard Sq. Parking spaces
are in short supply, but you
can usually find one on the
street around the Cambridge
Common.

❻ Cambridge, Massachusetts

Founded in 1636 to edu-
cate men for the minis-
try, Harvard is America's
oldest **college** (www.
harvard.edu; Massachusetts
Ave; tours free; Ⓣ Harvard).
The geographic heart of
the university – where
red-brick buildings and
leaf-covered paths exude
academia – is **Harvard
Yard**. For maximum
visual impact, enter
the yard through the
wrought-iron Johnston
Gate, which is flanked by
the two oldest buildings
on campus, **Harvard Hall**
and **Massachusetts Hall**.

The focal point of the
yard is the **John Harvard
statue**, by Daniel Chester
French. Inscribed 'John
Harvard, Founder of Har-
vard College, 1638,' it is
commonly known as the
'statue of three lies': John
Harvard was *not* the
college's founder but its
first benefactor; Harvard
was actually founded

ALL ABOUT HAAAHHHVAAAHHHD

Want to know more? Get the inside scoop from savvy
students on the unofficial **Hahvahd Tour** (Trademark
Tours; www.harvardtour.com; adult/child $10/7; Ⓣ Harvard).

Classic Trip

WHY THIS IS A CLASSIC TRIP
MARA VORHEES, WRITER

One of my favorite ways to spend an afternoon is absorbing the energy of Harvard Sq – befriending the buskers, browsing the shelves at Harvard Bookstore and drinking coffee (and reviewing my purchases) at Cafe Pamplona. Typical of the Ivies, Harvard exudes tradition, elitism and academia, but it also fosters innovation and creativity. You'll feel it as you wander the leafy campuses and see the students in action.

Top: Connecticut River near Dartmouth College
Left: Harvard University, Cambridge
Right: Lowell House, Harvard University, Cambridge

JOHN COLETTI / GETTY IMAGES ©

in 1636; and the man depicted isn't even Mr Harvard himself! This symbol hardly lives up to the university's motto, *Veritas* (truth).

Most Harvard hopefuls rub the statue's shiny foot for good luck; little do they know that campus pranksters regularly use the foot like dogs use a fire hydrant.

So, what's the best thing about Harvard University? The architecture? The history? Arguably, it's the location. Overflowing with coffeehouses and pubs, bookstores and record stores, street musicians and sidewalk artists, panhandlers and professors, **Harvard Square** exudes energy, creativity and nonconformity – and it's all packed into a handful of streets between the university and the river. Spend an afternoon browsing bookstores, riffling through records and trying on vintage clothing; then camp out in a local cafe.

✕ ⊨ p59

The Drive » Hop on Memorial Dr and drive east along the Charles River. At Western Ave, cross the river and follow the signs to I-90 heading east ($1.25 toll). Cruise through the tunnel (product of the notorious Big Dig) and merge with I-93 south. Follow I-93 south to I-95 south. Take I-95 south to Providence.

Classic Trip

TRIP HIGHLIGHT

❼ Providence, Rhode Island

College Hill rises east of the Providence River, and atop it sits Brown University (www.brown. edu), the rambunctious younger child of an uptight New England household. Big brothers Harvard and Yale carefully manicure their public image, while the little black sheep of the family prides itself on staunch liberalism. Founded in 1764, Brown was the first American college to accept students regardless of religious affiliation, and the first to appoint an African American woman, Ruth Simmons, as president, in 2001. Of its small 700-strong faculty, five Brown professors and two alumni have been honored as Nobel laureates.

The campus, consisting of 235 buildings, is divided into the Main Green and Lincoln Field. Enter through the wrought-iron **Van Wickle Gates** on College St. The oldest building on the campus is **University Hall**, a 1770 brick edifice, which was used as a barracks during the Revolutionary War. Free tours of the campus begin from the **Brown University Admissions Office** (📞401-863-2378; Corliss Brackett House, 45 Prospect St).

✗ 🛏 p59, p123, p131

The Drive ❯❯ Take Memorial Blvd out of Providence and merge with I-95 south. The generally pleasant tree-lined interstate will take you around the periphery of Groton, Old Lyme, Guilford and Madison, where you may want to stop for a coffee or snack. Exit at junction 47 for downtown New Haven.

TRIP HIGHLIGHT

❽ New Haven, Connecticut

Gorgeous, Gothic Yale University is America's third-oldest university. Head to the **Yale University Visitor Center** (📞203-432-2300; http://visitorcenter. yale.edu; 149 Elm St; ⏰9am-4:30pm Mon-Fri, 11am-4pm Sat & Sun) to pick up a free map or take a free one-hour **tour**.

The tour does a good job of fusing historical and academic facts and passes by several standout monuments, including Yale's tallest building, **Harkness Tower**. Guides refrain, however, from mentioning the tombs scattered around the campus. No, these aren't filled with corpses; they're secret hangouts for senior students. The most notorious **Tomb** (64 High St) is the HQ for the Skull & Bones Club, founded in 1832. Its list of members reads like a who's who of high-powered politicos and financiers over the last two centuries.

New Haven's spacious **green** has been the spiritual center of the city since its Puritan fathers designed it in 1638 as the prospective site for Christ's second coming. Since then it has held the municipal burial grounds – graves were later moved to Grove St Cemetery – several statehouses and an array of churches, three of which still stand.

✗ 🛏 p39, p59, p147

Eating & Sleeping

Hanover ❶

✗ Lou's   Diner $

(☎603-643-3321; www.lousrestaurant.
net; 30 S Main St; mains $10-15; ⏱6am-3pm
Mon-Fri, 7am-3pm Sat & Sun) A Dartmouth
institution since 1947, this is Hanover's oldest
establishment, always packed with students
meeting for a coffee or perusing their books.
From the retro tables or the Formica-topped
counter, order typical diner food such as
eggs, sandwiches and burgers. Breakfast is
served all day, and the bakery items are highly
recommended.

Concord, NH ❸

✗ Granite   Modern American $$

(☎603-227-9005; www.graniterestaurant.com;
96 Pleasant St; lunch mains $10-18, dinner mains
$16-34; ⏱7-10am, 11:30am-2:30pm & 5-9pm
Mon-Thu, to 10pm Fri & Sat, 10:30am-2:30pm
& 5-8pm Sun) In a grand turreted Victorian
building, Granite serves fine New American
cuisine all day long, from breakfasts of smoked
turkey and sweet potato hash, to crab cake BLTs
with lemon-basil aioli at lunchtime, to braised
rabbit stroganoff for dinner.

Cambridge ❻

✗ Café Pamplona   Cafe

(http://cafepamplona.weebly.com; 12 Bow St;
⏱11am-midnight; 🛜; Ⓣ Harvard) Located
in a cozy cellar on a backstreet, this no-frills
European cafe is the choice among old-time
Cantabrigians. In addition to tea and coffee,
Pamplona has light snacks, such as gazpacho,
sandwiches and biscotti. The tiny outdoor
terrace is a delight in summer.

🛏 Irving House
at Harvard   Guesthouse $$

(☎617-547-4600; www.irvinghouse.com; 24
Irving St; r from $225, without bath from $135;

Ⓟ❄@🛜; Ⓣ Harvard) Call it a big inn or a
homey hotel, this property welcomes the world-
weariest of travelers. The 44 rooms range in
size, but every bed is covered with a quilt, and big
windows let in plenty of light. There is a bistro-
style atmosphere in the brick-lined basement,
where you can browse its books, plan your travels
or munch on free continental breakfast.

Providence ❼

✗ Louis Family Restaurant   Diner $

(☎401-861-5225; www.louisrestaurant.org; 286
Brook St; mains from $6; ⏱5am-3pm; ♿) Wake
up early to watch bleary-eyed students and
carpenters eat strawberry-banana pancakes
and drink drip coffee at their favorite greasy
spoon long before the rest of College Hill shows
signs of life.

New Haven ❽

✗ Frank Pepe   Pizza $

(☎203-865-5762; www.pepespizzeria.com;
157 Wooster St; pizza from $12; ⏱11am-10pm;
🖍♿) Pepe's lays claim to baking the 'best
pizza in America,' a title it's won three times
running. We'll let you be the judge, but can
confirm this joint cranks out tasty pies fired
in a coal oven, just as it has since 1925; only
now it has a bunch of other locations across
Connecticut, making consistency harder to
master. Cash only. The white-clam pizza is the
pie the people praise.

🛏 Farnam Guest House   B&B $$

(☎203-562-7121; www.farnamguesthouse.
com; 616 Prospect St; r from $159; Ⓟ❄🛜)
The Farnams have a long association with Yale
as alums, donors and professors, and you can
stay in their grand Georgian Colonial mansion
in the best neighborhood in town. Expect
old-world ambience, with Chippendale sofas,
wingback chairs, Victorian antiques and plush
oriental carpets. There's a Steinway grand
piano in the parlor!

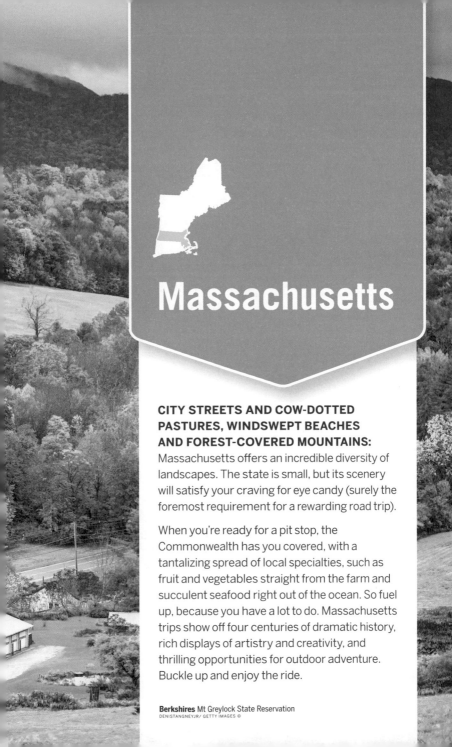

Massachusetts

CITY STREETS AND COW-DOTTED PASTURES, WINDSWEPT BEACHES AND FOREST-COVERED MOUNTAINS: Massachusetts offers an incredible diversity of landscapes. The state is small, but its scenery will satisfy your craving for eye candy (surely the foremost requirement for a rewarding road trip).

When you're ready for a pit stop, the Commonwealth has you covered, with a tantalizing spread of local specialties, such as fruit and vegetables straight from the farm and succulent seafood right out of the ocean. So fuel up, because you have a lot to do. Massachusetts trips show off four centuries of dramatic history, rich displays of artistry and creativity, and thrilling opportunities for outdoor adventure. Buckle up and enjoy the ride.

Berkshires Mt Greylock State Reservation
DENISTANGNEYJR/ GETTY IMAGES ©

Massachusetts

Stellwagen Bank

This National Marine Sanctuary is a rich feeding ground for humpback whales. See them on Trips **1** **5**

Gould's Sugar House

Fluffy pancakes and homemade ice cream show off delicious maple syrup, made at this family farm. Taste the goodness on Trip **8**

Rocky Neck Art Colony

Artists have converted Gloucester's colorful fishing shacks into galleries and studio space, open for your visit on Trips **1** **6**

Nauset Light

The iconic red-and-white beacon has been shining the light since 1877. Climb to the top on Trip **5**

Commercial Street

'Eclectic' doesn't begin to describe Provincetown's main drag, with art galleries, pet parades and gay cabaret. See the show on Trips **4** **5**

Cape Cod National Seashore Truro Lighthouse

Pilgrim Trail

4

Follow in the footsteps of the country's earliest European settlers, visiting the sites that commemorate their struggles and celebrate their successes in making their home in the New World.

TRIP HIGHLIGHTS

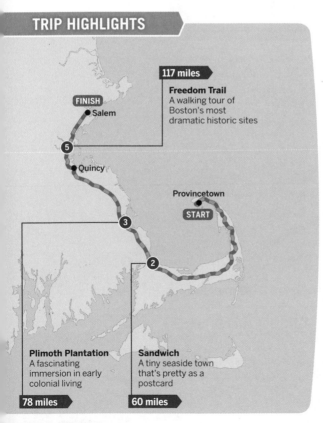

117 miles

Freedom Trail
A walking tour of Boston's most dramatic historic sites

FINISH
Salem

5

Quincy

Provincetown

START

3

2

Plimoth Plantation
A fascinating immersion in early colonial living

78 miles

Sandwich
A tiny seaside town that's pretty as a postcard

60 miles

4–5 DAYS
147 MILES / 235KM

GREAT FOR...

BEST TIME TO GO
Most sites are open from April to November.

ESSENTIAL PHOTO
The Dexter Grist Mill in Sandwich is photogenic.

BEST FOR FAMILIES
Plymouth is packed with interesting and educational fun.

4 Pilgrim Trail

Your car is a time machine, transporting you back 400 years. The region's living museums allow you to experience firsthand what life was like for the colonists as they settled in the New World. Explore the sites and structures – churches and trading posts, homesteads and grist mills – that are still standing from those early days.

❶ Provincetown

Most people don't know that months before the 'official' landing on Plymouth Rock, the Pilgrims arrived at the tip of Cape Cod. Despite the protected harbor and good fishing, they were unable to find a reliable source of freshwater, so they headed off to Plymouth. But not before signing the Mayflower Compact, which is considered the first governing document of the Plymouth Colony. The **Pilgrim Monument** (☏508-487-1310; www.

DETOUR: BOURNE

Start: ❷ Sandwich

Bourne is not as picturesque as nearby Sandwich, but it is historically significant, thanks to its strategic location at the northeastern corner of Buzzards Bay, halfway between the Manomet and Scusset Rivers. Here, in 1627, the Pilgrims founded the Aptucxet Trading Post, which allowed easy access to the Dutch settlements to the south. The trading center would eventually lead to the construction of the Cape Cod Canal, which was built so traders could avoid the cape's hazardous eastern shore.

Nowadays, the **Aptucxet Trading Post Museum** (www.bournehistoricalsociety.org; 6 Aptucxet Rd; ☺10am-5pm Tue-Sat Jun-Aug) is an eclectic little museum, built on what are believed to be the oldest remains of a Pilgrim building ever found. Although the simple, unpainted clapboard structure standing today is a replica built on the original foundation, it's still possible to imagine Pilgrims, Wampanoag and Dutch coming here to barter goods, seeds, tools and food.

To reach the Aptucxet Trading Post, take MA 6A out of Sandwich and continue on Sandwich Rd for 7 miles along the Cape Cod Canal. Once in Bourne, turn right on Perry Rd and take the first left on Aptucxet Rd.

pilgrim-monument.org; 1 High Pole Hill Rd; adult/child $12/4; ☺9am-5pm Apr, May & Sep-Nov, to 7pm Jun-Aug) commemorates the signing of the compact, as do a few exhibits at the on-site **Provincetown Museum**. Climb 252ft (116 steps)

LINK YOUR TRIP

1 Coastal New England

See more of maritime Massachusetts, Rhode Island and Connecticut.

25 Maritime Maine

For a round of lighthouse photos and lobster feasts, take I-95 to Kittery.

to the top of the tall tower for magnificent views of Provincetown Harbor and the National Seashore.

In addition to its historic interest, Provincetown is a cauldron of contemporary creativity, which you can see for yourself on a walk (p110) along artsy Commercial St.

✕ 🛏 p71, 81

The Drive » Head out of Provincetown on US 6, passing picturesque East Harbor and windblown beach shacks. You'll also pass Pilgrim Heights, where the settlers found freshwater, and First Encounter Beach, site of the first violent clash with the native population. From Orleans, continue west on US 6 or take slower, more scenic MA 6A, which shows off the cape's historic villages.

TRIP HIGHLIGHT

❷ Sandwich

With the waterwheel at the old mill, the white clapboard houses, and the swans on the pond, the center of Sandwich is as pretty as a Cape Cod town can be. The restored 17th-century **Dexter Grist Mill** (☎508-888-4361; Water St; adult/child $4/3; ☺11am-4.30pm Mon-Sat, 1-4pm Sun mid-Jun–mid-Oct) on the edge of Shawme Pond has centuries-old gears that still grind cornmeal. Nearby, **Hoxie House** (☎508-888-4361; 18 Water St; adult/child $4/3; ☺11am-4:30pm Mon-Sat, 1-4:30pm Sun mid-Jun–mid-Oct) is one of the oldest houses on Cape Cod. The 1640 salt box–style structure has been faithfully restored, complete with antiques and brick hearth, giving a good sense of early-settler home life.

The Drive » Hop on US 6 heading west over the Sagamore Bridge. Stay on MA 3 or branch off to MA 3A, which hugs the coast for the 14 miles north to Plymouth.

- - - - - - - - - - -

TRIP HIGHLIGHT

❸ Plymouth

Plymouth is 'America's Home Town,' where the Pilgrims first settled in the winter of 1620. An innocuous, weathered ball of granite – the famous **Plymouth Rock** – marks the spot where they (might have) stepped ashore in this foreign land, while **Mayflower II** (www.plimoth.org; State Pier, Water St; adult/child $12.50/8.50; ☺9am-5pm Apr-Nov; 🚻) is a replica of the small ship in which they made the fateful voyage. Many museums and historic sites in the surrounding streets recall the Pilgrims' struggles, sacrifices and triumphs.

The best is **Plimoth Plantation** (www.plimoth.org; 137 Warren Ave; adult/child $28/16; ☺9am-5pm Apr-Nov; 🚻), a historically accurate recreation of the Pilgrims' settlement. Everything in the 1627 English Village – costumes, implements, vocabulary, artistry, recipes and crops – has been painstakingly researched and remade. Costumed interpreters, acting in character, explain the details of daily life and answer your questions as you watch them work and play. The on-site **Wampanoag Homesite** replicates the life of a Native American community in the same area during that time. Unlike the English Village, the homesite is staffed by indigenous people speaking from a modern perspective.

✕ 🛏 p71

The Drive » Take MA 3 north for about 25 miles. In Quincy, take the Burgin Pkwy 2 miles north into the center.

Provincetown Race Point Beach

④ Quincy

Quincy was first settled in 1625 by a handful of raucous colonists who could not stand the strict and stoic ways in Plymouth. History has it that this group went so far as to drink beer, dance around a maypole and engage in other festive Old English customs, which enraged the Pilgrims down the road. Nathaniel Hawthorne immortalized this history in his fictional account *The Maypole of Merrimount*. Eventually, Myles Standish arrived from Plymouth to restore order to the wayward colony.

What earns this town the nickname 'The City of Presidents' is that it is the birthplace of John Adams and John Quincy Adams. The collection of houses where the Adams family lived now composes the **Adams National Historic Park** (www.nps.gov/adam; 1250 Hancock St; adult/child $10/ free; ⊙9am-5pm mid-Apr– mid-Nov; ⊤Quincy Center). Besides the homes, you can also see where the presidents and their wives are interred in the crypt of the **United First Parish Church** (www.ufpc.org; 1306 Hancock St; donation adult/child/senior & student $5/free/3; ☺11am-4pm Mon-Fri, noon-4pm Sat & Sun mid-Apr–mid-Nov; TQuincy Center).

The Drive » Take Newport Ave north out of town and merge onto I-93 heading north. Continue on the Central Artery straight through (and under) Boston, experiencing firsthand the benefits of the infamous Big Dig. Take exit 26 onto Storrow Dr for downtown Boston.

TRIP HIGHLIGHT

❺ Boston

Ten years after the Pilgrims settled in Plymouth, they were followed by a group of Puritans – also fleeing the repressive Church of England – who founded the Massachusetts Bay Colony about 40 miles up the coast. The Puritans' first seat of government was on the north shore of the Charles River, where excavations have uncovered the foundations of Governor John Winthrop's home, known as the **Great House** (City Sq; ☺dawn-dusk; 🛥Inner Harbor Ferry from Long Wharf, TNorth Station). Winthrop is buried alongside other early settlers in the **King's Chapel Burying Ground** (www.kings-chapel.org; 58 Tremont St; donation $2, Bells & Bones tour $10;

☺10am-5pm Mon-Sat, 1:30-5pm Sun; TState).

Not too many physical structures remain from these earliest days of Boston's settlement. The city's oldest dwelling (1680) is **Paul Revere House** (www.paulreverehouse.org; 19 North Sq; adult/child $3.50/1; ☺9:30am-5:15pm mid-Apr–Oct, to 4:15pm Nov–mid-Apr, closed Mon Jan-Mar; 🚻; THaymarket), where the celebrated patriot lived. The oldest church (1723) is **Old North Church** (www.oldnorth.com; 193 Salem St; requested donation $3, tour adult/child $6/4; ☺9am-5pm Mar-Dec, to 6pm Jun-Oct, 10am-4pm Nov-Feb; THaymarket, North Station), where two lanterns were hung on the eve of the American Revolution. To see these and other sites from Boston's revolutionary history, follow the **Freedom Trail** (TPark), which connects the most prominent historic landmarks. For a contemporary perspective, stroll (p106) around the city's green spaces and shopping places.

✖ 🛏 p39, p71

The Drive » As you exit Boston to the north, take US 93 to US 95/MA 128. At the fork, stay on MA 128. Take exit 25A to MA 114, and follow the signs to Salem center. Alternatively, for a scenic seaside route, take MA 1A all the way up the coast through Swampscott and Marblehead.

- - - - - - - - - -

❻ Salem

Founded by English fisherfolk in 1626, Salem was part of the Massachusetts Bay Colony. **Salem Pioneer Village** (www.pioneervillagesalem.com; Forest River Park; $6; ☺tours 12:30pm, 1:30pm & 2:30pm Sat & Sun) is an outdoor, interactive museum that gives visitors an idea of what daily life was like for settlers.

Salem is most famous – or infamous – as the site of the witch trials in 1692, when 19 people were hanged as a result of witch-hunt hysteria. Don't miss the **Witch Trials Memorial** (Charter St), a simple but dramatic monument that honors the innocent victims. To understand more about how this hysteria snowballed, visit the **Witch House** (Jonathan Corwin House; www.witchhouse.info; 310 Essex St; adult/child $8.25/4.25, tour $2; ☺10am-5pm Mar-Nov). This was the home of Jonathan Corwin, a local magistrate who investigated witchcraft claims.

The town has dozens of other related sites, as well as a month-long Halloween extravaganza in October. But there's a lot more to Salem than bed knobs and broomsticks. Take a walk (p108) and discover the town's many historical charms.

✖ 🛏 p39, p71

Eating & Sleeping

Provincetown ❶

✗ Mews Restaurant & Cafe — Modern American $$$

(☎508-487-1500; www.mews.com; 429 Commercial St; mains bistro $13-21, restaurant $22-35; ⏰5:30-10pm) A fantastic water view, the hottest martini bar in town and scrumptious food add up to Provincetown's finest dining scene. There are two sections. Opt to dine gourmet on lobster risotto and filet mignon downstairs, where you're right on the sand, or go casual with a juicy Angus burger from the bistro menu upstairs. Reservations recommended.

Plymouth ❸

✗ Blue Blinds Bakery — Bakery $

(www.blueblindsbakery.com; 7 North St; ⏰6am-9pm Mon-Thu, 7am-3pm Fri & Sun; 🍴👶) Blue Blinds is a cozy house – it feels like a home, really – with plants in the windows and a fire in the fireplace and folks sipping coffee on the shady front porch. The baked goods are out of this world, including fresh-baked organic breads, muffins and pastries. Breakfast is served all day, but the sandwiches and homemade soups are also divine.

🛏 Pilgrim Sands — Hotel $$

(☎800-729-7263; www.pilgrimsands.com; 150 Warren Ave; d without ocean view $139-189, with ocean view $219-229; P❄@🏊) This mini resort is a good option for families as it's right on a private beach and directly opposite Plimoth Plantation. The exterior is not much to look at, but most of the rooms are recently refurbished and quite smart, while service is top notch.

Boston ❺

🍷 Warren Tavern — Pub

(www.warrentavern.com; 2 Pleasant St; ⏰11am-1am Mon-Fri, 10am-1am Sat & Sun; Community College) One of the oldest pubs in Boston, the Warren Tavern has been pouring pints for its customers since George Washington and Paul Revere drank here. It is named for General Joseph Warren, a fallen hero of the Battle of Bunker Hill (shortly after which – in 1780 – this pub was opened). Also recommended as a lunch stop.

🛏 Ames Hotel — Boutique Hotel $$$

(☎617-979-8100; www.ameshotel.com; 1 Court St; r from $369; P❄🛜; Ⓣ State) It's easy to miss this understated hotel, tucked behind the granite facade of the historic Ames Building (Boston's first skyscraper). Starting in the lobby and extending to the guest rooms, the style is elegant but eclectic, artfully blending modern minimalism and old-fashioned ornamental details. The upper floors yield wonderful views over the city.

Salem ❻

✗ Red's Sandwich Shop — Diner $

(www.redssandwichshop.com; 15 Central St; mains $5-8; ⏰5am-3pm Mon-Sat, 6am-1pm Sun) This Salem institution has been serving eggs and sandwiches to faithful customers for more than 50 years. The food is hearty and basic, but the real attraction is Red's old-school decor, complete with counter service and friendly faces. It's housed in the old London Coffee House building (around since 1698).

🛏 Stephen Daniels House — B&B $$

(☎978-744-5709; www.thedanielshouse. com; 1 Daniels St; r $125-150; P🛜) This must be Salem's oldest lodging, with parts dating from 1667. Two walk-in fireplaces grace the common area, and the rooms are filled with period antiques. It's appropriate in this spooky town that such an old house be haunted: rumor has it that a ghost cat roams the ancient halls, and it's even been known to jump into bed with guests.

Classic Trip

Cape Cod & the Islands

5

A drive down the cape offers a beach for every mood. Besides sun, surf and sand, there are lighthouses to climb, oysters to eat, art and antiques to buy, and trails to hike.

TRIP HIGHLIGHTS

128 miles
Provincetown
A breeding ground for artistic, intellectual and alternative culture

FINISH **8**

Wellfleet **6**

105 miles
Cape Cod National Seashore
Hiking, biking, swimming and sunbathing amid miles of pristine dunes and beaches

START
Sandwich
Yarmouth Port
5
Hyannis

96 miles
Brewster Tidal Flats
A spectacular seascape for a sunset

3

Nantucket
Cobblestone streets lined with blooming trees and 19th-century mansions

46 miles

5–7 DAYS
128 MILES / 206KM

GREAT FOR...

BEST TIME TO GO

Enjoy fine weather but avoid the crowds in May, June or September.

ESSENTIAL PHOTO

Brewster's otherworldly tidal flats are particularly photogenic at sunset.

BEST FOR FOOD & DRINK

Slurp oysters and devour classic pastries in Wellfleet.

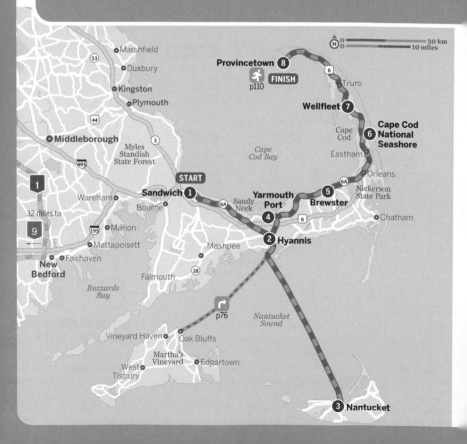

Classic Trip

5 Cape Cod & the Islands

As the sun sets and the sky darkens, you slide your car into place alongside dozens of others facing the massive screen. Roll down the window, feel the salty breeze and recline your seat. After an exhilarating day at the beach, it's time to sit back and enjoy a double feature at the drive-in. Sounds like something out of a 1950s fantasy? It's summer on Cape Cod.

0   20 km
0   10 miles

Marshfield
53
Duxbury

Provincetown 8
p110 **FINISH**
6
Truro

Kingston
Plymouth
Wellfleet 7

44
Cape Cod
Middleborough
Myles
Standish
State Forest
3
6 National
Seashore
Cape
Cod
Eastham

495
Cape
Cod Bay
Orleans
6A
Nickerson
State Park

1
START
Sandwich 1
Yarmouth
Port
5
Brewster

32 miles to
Wareham
Bourne
6A
Sandy
Neck
4
6
Chatham

9
195 Marion
Mattapoisett
Mashpee
2 **Hyannis**

New
Bedford
Fairhaven
Falmouth
28
Buzzards
Bay
p76
Nantucket
Sound

Vineyard Haven
Oak Bluffs
Martha's
Vineyard Edgartown
West
Tisbury

3 **Nantucket**

❶ Sandwich

Cape Cod's oldest town (founded in 1637) makes a perfect first impression as you cross over the canal from the mainland. In the village center, white-steepled churches, period homes and a working grist mill surround a picturesque swan pond.

Fun for kids and adults alike, the nearby 100-acre **Heritage Museums & Gardens** (☎508-888-3300; www.heritagemuseumsand gardens.org; 67 Grove St; adult/child $18/8; ⏰9am-5pm mid-Apr–mid-Oct; 👪) sports a vintage-automobile collection, an authentic 1908 carousel and unusual folk-art collections. Too tame? A new part of the complex houses zip

LINK YOUR TRIP

1 **Coastal New England**

From Hyannis, take I-195 to New Bedford to intersect with this trip through maritime New England.

9 **Rhode Island: East Bay**

A longer trip on I-195 will zip you to Providence to take in the pleasures of picturesque Rhode Island.

CAPE COD POTATO CHIP FACTORY

On your way into Hyannis, stop at the **Cape Cod Potato Chip Factory** (☎888-881-2447; www.capecodchips.com; 100 Breed's Hill Rd; ⏰9am-5pm Mon-Fri) for a free self-guided tour and a free sample. From MA 132 (just west of the airport), take Independence Dr a half-mile north to the factory.

---

lines, rope bridges and aerial trails.

Before leaving town, take a stroll across the **Sandwich boardwalk** (parking is $15 in summer), which extends 1350 scenic feet across an expansive marsh to **Town Neck Beach**. From MA 6A, head north onto Jarves St, left at Factory St and right onto Boardwalk Rd.

The Drive » Heading east on MA 6A, also known as Old King's Hwy, wind your way past cranberry bogs, wetlands and Shaker-shingle cottages. In Barnstable, take a right on MA 132 and head to the more commercial southern side of the cape. For a faster but less scenic version of this trip, take the Mid-Cape Hwy (US 6) instead of 6A.

---

❷ Hyannis

Most people traveling through Hyannis are here to catch a ferry to Nantucket or Martha's Vineyard (just like you). Fortunately, the village port has a few sights to keep you entertained while you wait for your boat – or even longer.

Take a walk through the **HyArts District**

(☎508-862-4678; www.hyartsdistrict.com; 250 South St; ⏰ shanties daily mid-Jun–mid-Oct, Fri-Sun mid-May–mid-Jun), which includes the Guyer Barn community art space and neighboring studios, the colorful artist shanties near the ferry docks, and the art-strewn Walkway to the Sea.

Politics aficionados will know that Hyannis has been the summer home of the Kennedy clan for generations. Back in the day, JFK spent his summers here – times that are beautifully documented with photographs and video at the **John F Kennedy Hyannis Museum** (☎508-790-3077; www.jfkhyannismuseum.org; 397 Main St; adult/child $10/5; ⏰9am-5pm Mon-Sat, noon-5pm Sun Jun-Oct, 10am-4pm Mon-Sat, noon-4pm Sun mid-Apr–May & Nov). There's also a JFK Memorial at the family-friendly **Veterans Beach** (Ocean St; 👪), about a half-mile south of the Hy-Line Cruise dock.

🛏 p81

The Drive » Leave your car in Hyannis and take a one-hour

catamaran trip or a cheaper two-hour ferry trip to Nantucket. Don't miss the picturesque Brant Point Lighthouse as the ferry pulls into Nantucket harbor.

TRIP HIGHLIGHT

❸ Nantucket

Nantucket is New England at its most rose-covered, cobblestoned, picture-postcard perfect. The island's main population center, Nantucket Town was once home port to the world's largest whaling fleet. Now a National Historic Landmark, the town boasts leafy streets lined with gracious period homes and public buildings. For the finest stroll, walk up cobbled **Main Street**, just past the Pacific National Bank (c 1818), where the grandest whaling-era mansions are lined up in a row.

While strolling the streets, pay a visit to the excellent **Nantucket Whaling Museum** (📞508-228-1894; www.nha.org; 13 Broad St; adult/child $20/5; ◷11am-4pm Apr & May, 10am-5pm Jun-Oct, hours vary Sat & Sun Nov, Dec & mid-Feb–Mar), which occupies a former spermaceti (whale oil) candle factory. The evocative exhibits relive Nantucket's 19th-century

DETOUR: MARTHA'S VINEYARD

Start: ❷ Hyannis (p75) or ❸ Nantucket

Your island destination is Oak Bluffs, the Vineyard's mecca for summer fun. Originally a retreat for a revivalist church group, it's now a retreat for beach-bound, ice-cream-eating party people.

In the mid-19th century, the members of the Methodist Camp Meeting Association (CMA) enjoyed a day at the beach as much as a good gospel service. They first camped out in tents, then built some 300 wooden cottages, each adorned with whimsical filigree trim. From bustling Circuit Ave, slip down the alley to discover the **Campgrounds**, a world of gingerbread houses adorned with Candyland colors. For a peek inside one, visit the **Cottage Museum** (📞508-693-0525; www.mvcma. org; 2 Trinity Park; adult/child $2/50¢; ◷10am-4pm Mon-Sat, 1-4pm Sun late May–early Sep), which contains exhibits on CMA history. The brightly painted cottages surround emerald-green **Trinity Park** and its open-air **Tabernacle** (1879), where the lucky descendants of the campers still gather for community singalongs and concerts.

Further north on Circuit Ave, you can take a nostalgic ride on the **Flying Horses Carousel** (www.mvpreservation.org; 15 Lake Ave; $3; ◷10am-10pm late May–mid-Sep, shorter hours rest of year; 👪), a National Historic Landmark that has been captivating kids of all ages since 1876. It's the country's oldest continuously operating merry-go-round, where the antique horses have manes of real horse hair.

Beginning just south of the Steamship Authority's ferry terminal, a narrow strip of sandy **beach** runs unbroken for several miles. There is also a scenic **bike trail** (with plenty of places to rent) connecting Oak Bluffs with other parts of the Vineyard.

From Hyannis, **Hy-Line Cruises** (📞508-778-2600; www.hylinecruises.com; Ocean St Dock) operates a high-speed passenger ferry (adult/child round-trip $59/39, one hour) to Oak Bluffs several times daily from May to October. It also has a ferry link between Nantucket and Oak Bluffs from June to September.

heyday as the whaling center of the world.

Close to town, there's a pair of family-friendly beaches where you can cool off. For wilder, less-frequented strands, you'll need to pedal a bike or hop on a bus to **Surfside** or **Nobadeer Beach**, 3 to 4 miles south of town.

 p81

The Drive ⟫ Ferry back to Hyannis Port to pick up your car. From South St, turn north on Lewis Bay Rd/Camp St, and then turn right on Yarmouth Rd. Continue north for 3 miles, then turn right on MA 6A and continue into Yarmouth Port.

---

❹ Yarmouth Port

Nearly 50 historic sea captains' homes are lined up along MA 6A in Yarmouth Port, in a stretch known as **Captains' Mile**. Most of them are private homes; however, the Historical Society of Old Yarmouth maintains the 1840 **Captain Bangs Hallett House** (☎508-362-3021; www.hsoy.org; 11 Strawberry Lane, Yarmouth Port; tour adult/child $3/free; ⊙1-4pm Fri-Sun mid-Jun–mid-Oct). For more historic sites in Yarmouth Port, pick up the free self-guided Captains' Mile walking-tour booklet.

Alternatively, stroll or walk 1 mile up Center St to **Grey's Beach**, also known as Bass Hole. A terrific quarter-mile-long boardwalk extends over

a tidal marsh and creek, offering a unique vantage point for viewing all sorts of sea life.

The Drive ⟫ Continue east on MA 6A through the classy village of Dennis and on to Brewster. This section of road (between Barnstable and Brewster) is lined with old homes that have been converted into antique shops. Take the time to stop and browse, and come home with treasures ranging from nautical kitsch to art-deco cool.

TRIP HIGHLIGHT

❺ Brewster

Brewster's best-known landmark is the **Brewster Store** (☎508-896-3744; www.brewsterstore.com; 1935 MA 6A, at MA 124; ⊙6am-10pm Jun-Sep, shorter hours Oct-May), an old-fashioned country store that has been in operation since 1866. Penny candy is still sold alongside the local newspaper. Upstairs, you'll discover a stash of museum-quality memorabilia as old as the building.

When the tide goes out on Cape Cod Bay, the bayside beach becomes a giant sandbar, offering opportunities to commune with crabs, clams and gulls, and to take in brilliant sunsets. Best access to the tidal flats is via the **Point of Rocks** or **Ellis Landing Beaches** (parking is $15 in summer). Pick up a parking sticker and check the tide charts at the town hall.

✗ ⌂ p81

The Drive ⟫ Head east on MA 6A out of Brewster, then hop on US 6, lined with roadside motels and clam shacks. It's a quick trip through Orleans and Eastham to your next destination.

TRIP HIGHLIGHT

❻ Cape Cod National Seashore

Extending some 40 miles around the curve of the Outer Cape, the Cape Cod National Seashore is a treasure trove of unspoiled beaches, dunes, salt marshes, nature trails and forests. Start your explorations at the **Salt Pond Visitor Center** (☎508-255-3421; www.nps.gov/caco; 50 Nauset Rd, cnr US 6; ⊙9am-5pm), which offers a wonderful view of the namesake salt pond. Numerous walking and cycling trails begin right at the visitor center; this is also the place to purchase a parking permit if you intend to spend time at any of the National Seashore beaches.

After this brief introduction, take Nauset Rd and Doane Rd to the picturesque **Coast Guard Beach** for swimming and bodysurfing. Afterwards, drive along the aptly named Ocean View Dr to **Nauset Light** (☎508-240-2612; www.nausetlight.org; Ocean View Dr; ⊙tours Sun May-Oct, plus Tue & Wed Jul & Aug), which has been shining on the cape since 1877 (and gracing the

Classic Trip

WHY THIS IS A CLASSIC TRIP
CAROLYN BAIN, WRITER

As a non-American, for me the name 'Cape Cod' has deep resonance – it speaks of the Kennedys' Camelot, wholesome family vacations, seafood and salt spray. This trip takes those stereotypes and turns them into something real, with tangible character in the form of deep-rooted whaling history, P-town counterculture, and lobster and oyster feasts. Plus, sometimes it's hard not to think you've landed in a real-life Ralph Lauren ad.

Top: Fishermen off the coast of Chatham
Left: Shells, Wellfleet
Right: Nantucket, Massachusetts

packets of Cape Cod potato chips for more than 30 years).

The Drive » Take Nauset Rd back to the Mid-Cape Hwy and continue north to Main St in Wellfleet. For a scenic detour, turn right off the highway onto Le Count Hollow Rd, then left on Ocean View Dr. From here, Long Pond Rd will cross the highway and deposit you on Main St in Wellfleet center.

⑦ Wellfleet

Wellfleet is one of Cape Cod's unsung gems, offering some unspoiled beaches, a charming historic center and plenty of opportunities to slurp glorious oysters.

By day, browse the **galleries** that are sprinkled around town. (The Wellfleet Art Galleries Association map has descriptive listings.) Or spy on the birdlife at Mass Audubon's 1100-acre **Wellfleet Bay Wildlife Sanctuary** (☏508-349-2615; www.massaudubon.org; 291 US 6, South Wellfleet; adult/child $5/3; ☻trails 8am-dusk, nature center 8:30am-5pm; 👪), where trails cross tidal creeks, salt marshes and sandy beaches.

By night, park your car at the 1950s-era **Wellfleet Drive-In** (☏508-349-7176; www.wellfleetcinemas.com; 51 US 6, South Wellfleet; adult/child $10/7.50; ☻late May–mid-Sep; 👪), where everything except the feature flick is true to the era.

Classic Trip

Grab a bite to eat at the old-fashioned snack bar, hook the mono speaker over the car window and settle in for a double feature.

For a more raucous night, head to Cahoon Hallow Beach, where the cape's coolest summer-time hangout is housed in the former lifeguard station, now known as the **Beachcomber** (☎508-349-6055; www. thebeachcomber.com; 1120 Cahoon Hollow Rd; ☺5pm-1am late May–early Sep).

 p81

The Drive » US 6 continues north through Truro, passing Truro Vineyards and Pilgrim Heights. On the right, the picturesque East Harbor is backed by pristine parabolic dunes; on the left, wind-blown beach shacks front Provincetown Harbor. Alternatively, take the slower-going Shore Rd (MA 6A), which branches off in North Truro and eventually becomes Commercial St in Provincetown.

LGBTQ PROVINCETOWN

While other cities have their gay districts, in Provincetown the entire town is the gay district.

A-House (Atlantic House; ☎508-487-3169; www.ahouse. com; 4 Masonic Pl; ☺bar noon-1am, club 10pm-1am) P-town's gay scene got its start here and it's still the leading bar in town.

Boatslip Beach Club (☎508-487-1669; www. boatslipresort.com; 161 Commercial St) Hosts wildly popular tea dances each afternoon.

Pied Bar (☎508-487-1527; www.piedbar.net; 193 Commercial St; ☺noon-1am May-Oct) A popular waterfront lounge that attracts lesbians and gay men. Particularly hot at sunset.

TRIP HIGHLIGHT

⑧ Provincetown

Provincetown is far out. We're not just talking geographically (though it does occupy the outermost point on Cape Cod); we're also talking about the flamboyant street scenes, brilliant art galleries and unbridled nightlife. Once an outpost for fringe writers and artists, Provincetown has morphed into the hottest gay and lesbian destination in the Northeast. Even if you're only in town for a day, you'll want to spend part of it admiring the art and watching the local life as you stroll (p110) along Commercial Street.

Provincetown is also the perfect launching point for whale-watching, since it's the closest port to Stellwagen Bank National Marine Sanctuary, the summer feeding ground for humpback whales. **Dolphin Fleet Whale Watch** (☎800-826-9300; www.whalewatch.com; MacMillan Pier; adult/child $47/31; ☺mid-Apr-Oct;) offers up to nine tours daily, each lasting three to four hours.

✕ ⊨ p71, p81

Eating & Sleeping

Hyannis ❷

🛏 Anchor-In   Hotel $$$

(📞508-775-0357; www.anchorin.com; 1 South
St; r $94-374; ✳ @ 🛜 🏊) This family-run
boutique hotel puts the chains to shame. The
harborfront location offers a fine sense of place,
and the heated outdoor pool is a perfect perch
from which to watch fishing boats unload their
catch. The rooms are bright and smart, with
water-view balconies. If you're planning a day
trip to Nantucket, the ferry is just a stroll away.
Winter rates are a bargain.

Nantucket ❸

✗ Black-Eyed
Susan's   Modern American $$$

(📞508-325-0308; www.black-eyedsusans.
com; 10 India St; breakfast $8-12, dinner $26-30;
⏱7am-1pm daily, 6-10pm Mon-Sat Apr-Oct; 🖋)
It's hard to find anyone who doesn't adore this
petite, long-running, quietly gourmet place.
At breakfast, try the sourdough French toast
topped with cinnamon pecans and orange
butter; at dinner, sit at the bar to watch chefs
perform magic in a *tiny* space. The fish of
the day often takes top honors (with strong
competition). BYOB.

Brewster ❺

✗ Brewster Fish House   Seafood $$$

(📞508-896-7867; www.brewsterfishhouse.
com; 2208 MA 6A; lunch $12-19, dinner $21-37;
⏱11:30am-3pm & 5-9:30pm) It's not an eye-
catcher from the outside, but it's heaven inside
for seafood lovers. Start with the lobster bisque,
naturally sweet and with chunks of fresh lobster.
From there it's safe to cast your net in any
direction; dishes are fresh and creative. Just a
dozen tables, and no reservations, so try lunch
or early dinner to avoid long waits.

🛏 Nickerson State Park   Campground $

(📞877-422-6762, 518-884-4959; www.
reserveamerica.com; 3488 MA 6A; campsite $27,

yurt $50-60; ⏱mid-Apr–Oct; 🚲) Head here
for Cape Cod's best camping, with more than
400 wooded campsites and a handful of yurts
set in pond- and trail-filled grounds. It often fills
up, so reserve your spot early. You can make
reservations up to six months in advance.

Wellfleet ❼

✗ PB Boulangerie & Bistro   Bakery $

(📞508-349-1600; www.pbboulangeriebistro.
com; 15 Lecount Hollow Rd, South Wellfleet;
pastries $3-5, sandwiches $10-12; ⏱bakery
7am-7pm, bistro 5-10pm Wed-Sun & 10am-
2:30pm Sun) A Michelin-starred French baker
setting up shop in tiny Wellfleet? You might
think he'd gone crazy, if not for the line out the
door. You can't miss PB: it's painted pink and set
back from US 6. Scan the cabinets full of fruit
tarts, chocolate-almond croissants and filled
baguettes and you'll think you've died and gone
to Paris.

✗ Bookstore & Restaurant   Seafood $$

(📞508-349-3154; www.wellfleetoyster.com; 50
Kendrick Ave; mains $9-29; ⏱11:30am-9pm)
This friendly place serves oysters and littleneck
clams harvested at low tide in the waters right
across the street – can't get fresher than that.
Sit out on the deck and enjoy the view. It's been
going strong since 1964 and the menu covers a
broad spectrum, from fish sandwiches to chicken
Parmesan, seafood linguini and prime rib.

Provincetown ❽

🛏 Carpe Diem   Boutique Hotel $$$

(📞508-487-4242; www.carpediemguesthouse.
com; 12-14 Johnson St; r $139-549; 🅿 ✳ 🛜)
Sophisticated yet relaxed, this boutique inn
blends a soothing mix of smiling Buddhas,
orchid sprays and artistic decor. Each guest
room is inspired by a different gay literary
genius; the room themed on poet Raj Rao, for
example, has sumptuous embroidered fabrics
and hand-carved Indian furniture. The on-site
spa includes a Finnish sauna, hot tub and
massage therapy.

Around Cape Ann

6

There's more to Cape Ann than widows' walks and sailing lore. This drive offers salt marshes and windswept beaches, oases of art and antiques, and more clam shacks than you can shake a shucker at.

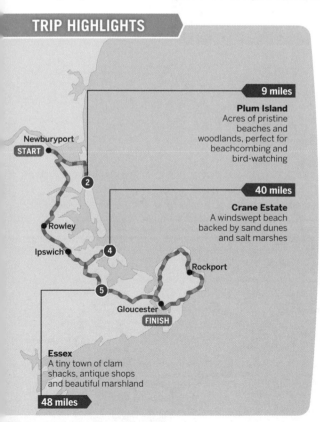

9 miles

Plum Island
Acres of pristine beaches and woodlands, perfect for beachcombing and bird-watching

40 miles

Crane Estate
A windswept beach backed by sand dunes and salt marshes

Essex
A tiny town of clam shacks, antique shops and beautiful marshland

48 miles

2–3 DAYS
54 MILES / 86KM

GREAT FOR...

BEST TIME TO GO
The water is warmest from July to September.

ESSENTIAL PHOTO
The red fishing shack at Rockport Harbor is called Motif No 1 for its artistic appeal.

BEST FOR OUTDOORS
Parker River Wildlife Refuge offers excellent hiking, swimming, kayaking and canoeing.

Plum Island Birdlife in Parker River Wildlife Refuge

6 Around Cape Ann

Somebody – a New Englander, no doubt – once said that 'the humble clam...reaches its quintessence when coated and fried.' The big-bellied bivalve – lightly battered and deeply fried – supposedly originated in Essex, Massachusetts, so Cape Ann is an ideal place to sample the New England specialty. This North Shore route takes you from clam shack to clam shack, with breaks in between eating for beachcombing, bird-watching and gallery hopping.

❶ Newburyport

Situated at the mouth of the Merrimack River, the town of Newburyport prospered as a shipping port and silversmith center during the late 18th century. Not too much has changed in the last 200 years, as Newburyport's brick buildings and graceful churches still show off the Federal style that was popular back then.

Today the center of town is a model of historic preservation and gentrification. Admire the public art as you take a stroll

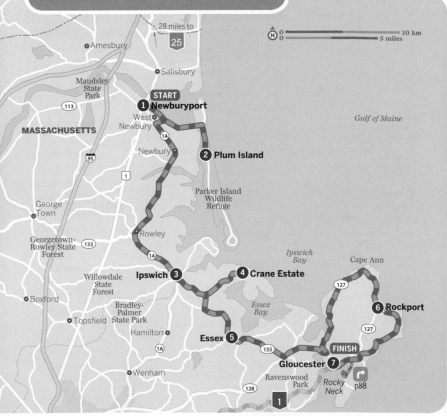

along the **Matthews Memorial Boardwalk**, which runs along the Merrimack and ends at the granite **Custom House Maritime Museum** (www.customhouse maritimemuseum.org; 25 Water St; adult/senior & child $7/5; ◷10am-4pm Tue-Sat, noon-4pm Sun May-Dec, 10am-4pm Sat & Sun only Jan-Apr). From here, you can browse in the boutiques along State St or admire the art galleries on Water St.

The Drive » Go east on Water St, which follows the coastline out of town. It becomes the Plum Island Turnpike before passing the eponymous airport and the Parker River Visitor Center. Cross the river onto Plum Island and turn right on Sunset Dr to reach the wildlife refuge.

TRIP HIGHLIGHT

❷ Plum Island

A barrier island off the coast of Massachusetts,

LINK YOUR TRIP

1 Coastal New England

Continue south from Gloucester and follow the coastline all the way through Connecticut.

25 Maritime Maine

From Newburyport, drive 26 miles north on I-95 to Kittery to experience the coastal culture of Maine.

Plum Island has 9 miles of wide, sandy beaches surrounded by acres of wildlife sanctuary. These are among the most pristine beaches on the North Shore, especially if you head to the furthest points on the island. **Sandy Point** (www.mass.gov/dcr; ◷dawn-8pm;), on the southern tip, is a state park that's popular for swimming, sunning and tide pooling.

Parker River Wildlife Refuge (www.fws.gov/refuge/parker_river; car/bike & pedestrian $5/2; ◷dawn-dusk) is the 4662-acre sanctuary that occupies the southern three-quarters of Plum Island. More than 800 species of bird, plant and animal reside in its many ecological habitats, including beaches, sand dunes, salt pans, salt marshes, freshwater impoundments and maritime forests. Several miles of foot trails allow access to the inland area, with observation towers and platforms punctuating the trails at prime bird-watching spots. Stop at the **visitor center** (www.fws.gov/refuge/parker_river; 6 Plum Island Turnpike; ◷11am-4pm) for information and exhibits about the refuge.

🛏 p89

The Drive » Depart the island on the Plum Island Turnpike. After 2 miles, turn left on Ocean Ave, then left on High Rd (MA 1A). Continue south through picturesque farmland, stopping

at farm stands along the way. Go through the tiny town of Newbury and picturesque Rowley, with the famous Sunday-morning Todd Farm Flea Market. Continue south into Ipswich.

- - - - - - - - - - - -

❸ Ipswich

Ipswich is one of those New England towns that are pretty today because they were poor in the past. It had no harbor and no source of waterpower for factories, so commercial and industrial development went elsewhere. As a result, Ipswich's 17th-century houses were not torn down to build grander residences. Nowadays, there are 58 existent First Period homes, including the 1677 **Whipple House** (www.ipswichmuseum.org; 1 South Village Green; adult/child $10/5; ◷10am-4pm Thu-Sat Apr & May, plus Wed & Sun Jun-Oct), which is open to the public. For more historic homes, pick up a map from the **Ipswich Museum** (www.ipswich museum.org; 54 S Main St; 1/3 houses $10/15; ◷10am-4pm Thu-Sat Apr & May, plus Wed & Sun Jun-Oct).

🍴 p89

The Drive » Head out of town on S Main St (MA 133) and turn left on Argilla Rd. Drive for about 4 miles through beautiful woods and marshland. The entrance to the Great House is on the left, while the beach is straight ahead.

❹ Crane Estate

One of the longest, widest, sandiest beaches in the region is **Crane Beach** (www.thetrustees. org; Argilla Rd, Ipswich; pedestrian & cyclist $2, car weekday/weekend $25/30; ☺8am-dusk; 👫), which has 4 miles of fine-sand barrier beach on Ipswich Bay. The beach is set in the midst of the Crane Wildlife Refuge, so the entire surrounding area is wildly beautiful. Five miles of trails traverse the dunes.

Above the beach, on Castle Hill, sits the 1920s **estate** (www.thetrustees. org; Argilla Rd, Ipswich; house tours $15-20, grounds car/bike $10/2; ☺ house 10am-4pm Tue-Sun Jun-Oct, Sat & Sun Apr & May, grounds 8am-dusk year-round; P 👫) of Chicago plumbing-fixture magnate Richard T Crane. The 59-room Stuart-style Great House is sometimes open for tours. The lovely landscaped grounds, which are open daily, contain several miles of walking trails.

🛏 p89

Newburyport Harbor at dusk

The Drive » Depart by way of Argilla Rd, but turn left on Northgate Rd, which will take you back to MA 133. Turn left and continue 2.6 miles east into Essex.

- - - - - - - - - - - -

TRIP HIGHLIGHT

5 Essex

The meandering Essex River shares its name with this tiny town, home to some 3500 souls. The town's proud maritime history is on display at the **Essex Shipbuilding Museum** (www.essexshipbuildingmuseum. org; 66 Main St; guided tour adult/child $10/5, self-guided tour $7; ◷10am-5pm Wed-Sun Jun-Oct, Sat & Sun Nov-May;). Most of the collection of photos, tools and ship models came from local basements and attics, allowing Essex to truly preserve its history. The collection is housed in the town's 1835 school house (check out the **Old Burying Ground** behind it). The historical society also operates a museum shipyard, a section of waterfront property where shipbuilding activities have taken place for hundreds of years.

Despite centuries of maritime history,

nowadays the town is more famous for its ample antique shops and succulent clams. With plenty of picnic tables overlooking the namesake estuary, there is no better lunch stop.

 p89, p155

The Drive ≫ Continue east on MA 133, then merge onto MA 128 heading north. At the traffic circle, take the third exit to Washington St (MA 127), which circles Cape Ann. Heading up the cape's western side, the winding road follows the Annisquam River, with a long bridge over the inlet at Goose Cove. Rounding the tip of the cape, you'll pass through tiny Lanesville and Pigeon Cove before arriving in Rockport.

---

❻ Rockport

Rockport is named for its 19th-century role as a shipping center for gran-

ite cut from local quarries. The stone is still ubiquitous: monuments, building foundations, pavements and piers remain as a testament to Rockport's past.

That's about all that's left of this industrial history, however. A century ago, Winslow Homer, Childe Hassam, Fitz Henry Lane and other acclaimed artists arrived, inspired by the hearty fisherfolk who wrested a hard-won but satisfying living from the sea. Today Rockport's main revenue source is the tourists who come to look at the artists. (The artists have long since given up looking for hearty fisherfolk because their descendants are all running B&Bs.)

The town hub is Dock Sq, recognizable by the

oft-painted red fishing shack, decorated with colorful buoys. From here, **Bearskin Neck**, lined with galleries, lobster shacks and souvenir shops, juts into the harbor.

 p89

The Drive ≫ Leave Rockport on South St (MA 127A), heading south past Delmater Sanctuary. Now Thatcher St, the road passes the lovely Good Harbor Beach, which is a fine spot for a cool-off. Merge onto Main St as you enter Gloucester center.

---

❼ Gloucester

Gritty Gloucester offers a remarkable contrast to the rest of Cape Ann. The working waterfront is dominated by marinas and shipyards, with a backdrop of fish-processing plants. This hardworking town has its own unexpected charm, which is particularly visible in the brick buildings along Main St. Nearby, the tiny **Cape Ann Museum** (www.capeannmuseum. org; 27 Pleasant St; adult/ children $10/free; ⊘10am-5pm Tue-Sat, 1-4pm Sun) is a gem – particularly for its impressive collection of paintings by Gloucester native Fitz Henry Lane. Exhibits also showcase the region's granite-quarrying industry and – of course – its maritime history.

 p39, p89

DETOUR: ROCKY NECK ART COLONY

Start: ❻ Rockport

The narrow peninsula of Rocky Neck, jutting into Gloucester Harbor, offers inspiring views of the ocean and the harbor. Between WWI and WWII, artists began renting the local fisherfolk's seaside shacks, which they used as studios. Today these same shanties, considerably gentrified, constitute the Rocky Neck Art Colony (www.rockyneckartcolony.org), home to dozens of studios and galleries. In addition to the cooperative **Gallery 53 on Rocky Neck** (53 Rocky Neck Ave; ⊘10am-6pm Sun-Thu, to 8pm Fri & Sat Jun–mid-Oct), about a dozen galleries and studios are open to visitors. There's also a couple of restaurants.

From MA 127A (at the junction with MA 128), turn left onto E Main St and right onto Rocky Neck Ave.

Eating & Sleeping

Plum Island ❷

🛏 Blue   Inn $$$

(📞855-255-2583; www.blueinn.com; 20
Fordham Way, Plum Island; d from $460;
🅿 ❄ 📶 🐾) In a drop-dead-gorgeous location
on a beautiful beach, this sophisticated inn is
quite a surprise on unassuming Plum Island.
Rooms feature high ceilings, contemporary
decor, fresh white linen and streaming sunlight.
Private decks, shared hot tubs and in-room
fireplaces are a few of the perks – all steps from
the surf. Breakfast is delivered to your room.

Ipswich ❸

🍽 Clam Box   Seafood $$

(www.clamboxipswich.com; 246 High St/MA 133,
Essex; mains $15-32; ⏱11am-8pm) You can't
miss this classic clam shack, just north of Ipswich
center. Built in 1938, it actually looks like a clam
box, spruced up with striped awnings. Folks line
up out the door for crispy fried clams and onion
rings – some claim they're the best in the land.

Crane Estate ❹

🛏 Inn at Castle Hill   Inn $$$

(📞978-412-2555; http://innatcastlehill.
thetrustees.org; 280 Argilla Rd, Ipswich; r
woodland view $235-285, ocean view $395-515;
🅿 ❄ 📶) On the beautiful grounds of the Crane
Estate, this inn is an example of understated
luxury, its 10 rooms each uniquely decorated
with subtle elegance. Turndown service, plush
robes and afternoon tea are some of the perks.
Instead of televisions (of which there are
none), guests enjoy a wraparound veranda and
its magnificent views of sand dunes and salt
marshes.

Essex ❺

🍽 JT Farnham's   Seafood $$

(88 Eastern Ave, Essex; mains $15-25; ⏱11am-
8pm; 👶) When the Food Network came to

Essex to weigh in on the fried-clam debate
for the show *Food Feud*, the winner was JT
Farnham's, thanks to the crispiness of his clams.
Pull up a picnic table and enjoy the amazing
estuary view.

🍽 Woodman's   Seafood $$$

(www.woodmans.com; 121 Main St/MA 133,
Essex; sandwiches $8-20, mains $15-32;
⏱11am-8pm Sun-Thu, to 9pm Fri & Sat) This
roadhouse is the most famous spot in the area
to come for clams, any way you like them.
The specialty is Chubby's original fried clams
and crispy onion rings, but this place serves
everything from boiled lobsters to homemade
clam cakes to a seasonal raw bar.

Rockport ❻

🍽 Roy Moore
Lobster Company   Seafood $$

(39 Bearskin Neck; lobster $15; ⏱9am-6pm)
This takeout kitchen has the cheapest lobster-
in-the-rough on the Neck. Your beast comes on
a tray with melted butter, a fork and a wet wipe
for cleanup. Find a seat at a picnic table on the
back patio and dig in. Don't forget to bring your
own beer or wine.

Gloucester ❼

🛏 Rocky Neck
Accommodations   Apartment $$

(📞978-381-9848; www.rockyneckaccomm
odations.com; 43 Rocky Neck Ave; r $155-165, ste
$265-285; 🅿 📶) You don't have to be an artist
to live the bohemian life in Gloucester. The colony
association offers light-filled efficiencies – all
equipped with kitchenettes – at the Rocky Neck
Artist Colony. The rooms are sweet and simple,
most with beautiful views of Smith Cove. Weekly
rates also available.

Berkshire Back Roads

7

These country roads offer a mix of cultural riches, sweet farmland and mountain scenery. In summer, enjoy music and dance in the open air; in autumn, indulge in apples straight from the orchard.

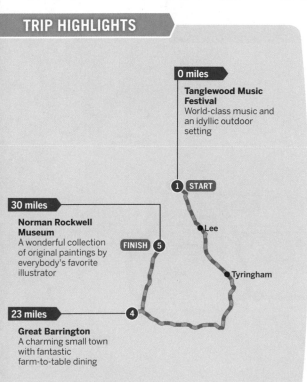

0 miles

Tanglewood Music Festival
World-class music and an idyllic outdoor setting

1 START

30 miles

Norman Rockwell Museum
A wonderful collection of original paintings by everybody's favorite illustrator

FINISH 5

Lee

Tyringham

23 miles

4

Great Barrington
A charming small town with fantastic farm-to-table dining

2–3 DAYS
30 MILES / 48KM

GREAT FOR...

BEST TIME TO GO

Cultural events are in full swing from mid-June to September; fall foliage is best in October.

 ESSENTIAL PHOTO

Compare your photo of Main St, Stockbridge, to the Rockwell painting.

 BEST FOR FOODIES

Great Barrington practically invented the locavore movement.

7 Berkshire Back Roads

Pack a picnic of farm-fresh fruit and local cheese, spread your blanket on the lush green lawns, and settle in for an evening of world-class music under the stars. Or world-class dance. Or Shakespeare. Or experimental theater. Indeed, for every day you spend hiking the hills and photographing the scenery, you can spend an evening taking in a cultural masterwork.

TRIP HIGHLIGHT

1 Lenox

Prized for its bucolic peace, this gracious town was a summer retreat for wealthy families with surnames such as Carnegie, Vanderbilt and Westinghouse. Lenox is the cultural heart of the Berkshires, and its illustrious past remains tangibly present today.

In the 19th century, writers such as Nathaniel Hawthorne and Edith Wharton set up shop here. Wharton's fabulous

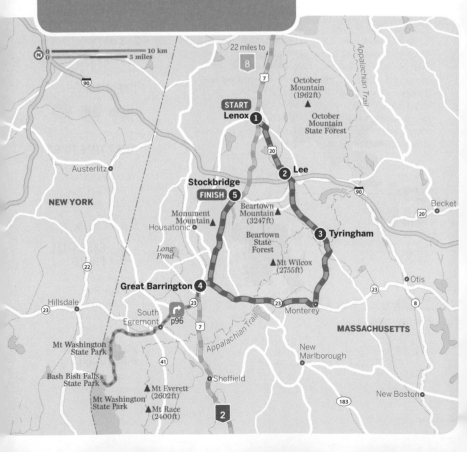

SUMMER FESTIVALS

Aston Magna (www.astonmagna.org; ☉Jun & Jul) Listen to Bach, Brahms and Buxtehude and other early classical music in Great Barrington during June and July.

Shakespeare & Company (☑413-637-1199; www.shakespeare.org; 70 Kemble St; ☉late Jun–early Sep) Shakespearean plays are performed outdoors in a bucolic context in Lenox in July and August.

Berkshire Theatre Festival (☑413-997-9444; www.berkshiretheatre.org; 83 E Main St; ☉Jun-Oct) Stop by for experimental summer theater in an old playhouse in Stockbridge from late July through October.

Jacob's Pillow (☑413-243-9919; www.jacobspillow.org; 358 George Carter Rd, Becket; ☉mid-Jun–Aug) The best dance troupes of most cities can't top the stupefying and groundbreaking dance of Jacob's Pillow, which runs from mid-June through August near Lee.

Tanglewood Music Festival (☑888-266-1200; www.tanglewood.org; 297 West St/MA 183, Lenox; lawn tickets $15-22, kids free; ☉late Jun–early Sep) For many, the Berkshires' most famous festival and its outstanding orchestral music are reason enough to return to Lenox each summer.

mansion, **The Mount** (www.edithwharton.org; 2 Plunkett St; adult/child $18/free; ☉10am-5pm May-Oct), shows off a magnificent interior and formal gardens, demonstrating the principles that she describes in her book *The Decoration of Houses*.

LINK YOUR TRIP

2 **Fall Foliage Tour**
Expand your leaf-peeping to the other New England states.

8 **Mohawk Trail**
For more beautiful Berkshire scenery and artistic offerings, drive north on US 7 to Williamstown.

About a mile west of Lenox center, **Tanglewood** is the summer home of the esteemed Boston Symphony Orchestra. From June to September, these beautifully manicured grounds host concerts of pop and rock, chamber music, folk, jazz and blues, in addition to the symphony. Traditionally, the July 4 extravaganza features Massachusetts native James Taylor.

✗ ⛏ p97

The Drive » Head out of Lenox on Walker St (MA 183), passing the historic Ventfort Hall, an impressive Jacobean Revival mansion that was a Morgan family home. One mile southeast of the center, turn right onto US 20 and drive 3 miles south, passing pretty Laurel Lake. Cross the bridge over the Housatonic River as you enter Lee.

- - - - - - - - - - - - - -

❷ Lee
Welcome to the Berkshires' towniest town, at once cute and gritty. The main street runs through the center, curving to cross some railroad tracks. On it you'll find a hardware store, a bar and a few places to eat, including a proper diner featured in a famous Norman Rockwell painting. The biggest draw to Lee is **Jacob's Pillow**, the prestigious summertime dance festival that takes place in neighboring Becket. Free **Inside/Out performances** are held on the outdoor Simon Stage, which has an amazing backdrop of the Berkshire hills.

✗ p97

The Drive » Continue east on US 20, crossing under the turnpike. Turn right on MA 102, then make an immediate left on Tyringham Rd. Hugging the Housatonic River, this scenic road passes some pretty homesteads and woodsy hillsides before entering Tyringham as Main St.

---

❸ Tyringham

Once the home of a Shaker community (1792–1874), this tiny village enjoys a gorgeous setting in the midst of the Tyringham Valley. To get some perspective on the pastoral splendor, take a 2-mile hike over the knobs of **Tyringham Cobble** (www.thetrustees.org; Jerusalem Rd; ⊘ dawn-dusk), which offers wildflower-strewn hillsides and spectacular views.

You don't have to get out of your car to see the village's most famous attraction: the **Tyringham Gingerbread House** (Santarella; www.santarella.us; 75 Main St), an architectural fantasy designed by sculptor Henry Hudson Kitson. This fairy-tale thatched-roofed cottage is readily visible from the road, though the

Stockbridge Norman Rockwell Museum

interior is not open to the public.

The Drive >> Depart Tyringham on Main St. Turn right on Monterey Rd, passing the inviting Monterey Town Beach. Look for the old-fashioned General Store in Monterey, then head west on MA 23. Pass Beartown State Forest and Butternut Mountain as you enter Great Barrington. Continue on State Rd, cross the bridge over the Housatonic River and turn left onto Main St.

TRIP HIGHLIGHT

❹ Great Barrington

Woolworths, diners and hardware stores have given way to galleries, boutiques and 'locavore' restaurants on Main St, Great Barrington, once named the 'best small town in America' by the Smithsonian Institution. The picturesque Housatonic River flows through the center of town, with the parallel **River Walk** (www.gbriver walk.org) offering a perfect perch from which to admire it. Access the walking path from Main St (behind Rite-Aid) or from Bridge St.

After a few hours' rest in small-town America, you might hanker for a hike in the hills. Head

95

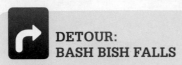

DETOUR:
BASH BISH FALLS

Start: ❹ Great Barrington (p95)

In the southwesternmost corner of the state, near the New York state line, is **Bash Bish Falls** (www.mass.gov/dcr; Falls Rd, Mt Washington; ☼ sunrise-sunset), the largest waterfall in Massachusetts. The water feeding the falls runs down a series of gorges before the torrent is sliced in two by a massive boulder perched directly above a pool. There it drops as a photogenic double waterfall. These 60ft-high falls are a popular spot for landscape painters to set up their easels.

To get here from Great Barrington, take MA 23 west to South Egremont. Turn right onto MA 41 south and then take the immediate right onto Mt Washington Rd (which becomes East St) and continue for 7.5 miles. Turn right onto Cross Rd, then right onto West St and continue 1 mile. Turn left onto Falls Rd and follow that for 1.5 miles.

There are two trailheads. The first is for a short, steep trail that descends 300ft over the course of a quarter-mile. For a more leisurely, level hike, continue another mile over the New York state line. This 0.75-mile trail takes about 20 minutes in each direction.

---

to **Monument Mountain** (www.thetrustees.org; US 7; parking $5; ☼ sunrise-sunset), 5 miles north. In 1850, Nathaniel Hawthorne climbed this mountain with Oliver Wendell Holmes and Herman Melville, thus sealing a lifelong friendship. You can follow their footsteps on one of two hiking trails to the 1642ft summit of Squaw Peak. From the top you'll get fabulous views all the way to Mt Greylock in the northwestern corner of the state and to the Catskills in New York.

✕ 🛏 p49, p97

The Drive ≫ Head north out of town on Main St and turn right on State St to cross the Housatonic River. Drive north on US 7, passing the pretty Fountain Pond on the right and Monument Mountain on the left. Turn left on MA 102, which is Main St, Stockbridge.

TRIP HIGHLIGHT

❺ Stockbridge

Main St, Stockbridge, is so postcard-perfect it looks like something out of a Norman Rockwell painting. In fact, it was depicted in the painting *Stockbridge Main Street at Christmas*. Stockbridge people and places inspired many of Rockwell's illustrations, as the artist lived here for 25 years. The **Norman Rockwell Museum** (www.nrm.org; 9 Glendale Rd/MA 183; adult/child $18/6; ☼ 10am-4pm May-Oct, to 5pm Nov-Apr) displays the world's largest collection of Rockwell's original art, including the beloved *Four Freedoms* and a complete collection of *Saturday Evening Post* covers.

Norman Rockwell is the main draw, but Stockbridge was also home to Daniel Chester French in an earlier era. Sculptor of *Abraham Lincoln* at the Lincoln Memorial and *The Minuteman* in Concord, French spent his summers at **Chesterwood** (www.chesterwood. org; 4 Williamsville Rd; adult/child/student $18/free/13; ☼ 10am-5pm late May–mid-Oct), a 122-acre estate. His house and studio are substantially as they were when he lived here, with nearly 500 pieces of sculpture, finished and unfinished, in the studio.

✕ p97

Eating & Sleeping

Lenox ❶

✘ Nudel — American $$$
(☎413-551-7183; www.nudelrestaurant.com;
37 Church St; mains $22-26; ⏱5:30-9:30pm
Tue-Sun) Nudel is a driving force in the area's
sustainable-food movement, with just about
everything on the menu seasonally inspired and
locally sourced. The back-to-basics approach
rings through in inventive dishes, which change
daily but never disappoint. Incredible flavors.
Nudel has a loyal following, so reservations are
recommended in high season.

🛏 Stonover Farm B&B — B&B $$$
(☎413-637-9100; www.stonoverfarm.com; 169
Under Mountain Rd; ste $385-485; ✳ @ 🛜) If
you're looking for a break from musty Victorians
with floral wallpaper, you'll love this contemporary
inn wrapped in a century-old farmhouse. The
three suites in the main house groan with casual
luxury. Oversized Jacuzzis, marble bathrooms,
wine and cheese in the evening – this is
pampering fitting its Tanglewood neighborhood
setting. There are also two private stand-alone
cottages. Breakfast – fresh, homemade,
decadent – is served in the creamery overlooking
the pond or outside in the courtyard.

Lee ❷

✘ Joe's Diner — Diner $
(☎413-243-9756; 85 Center St; mains $4-9;
⏱5:30am-8:30pm Mon-Sat, 7am-2pm Sun)
There's no better slice of blue-collar Americana in
the Berkshires than Joe's Diner, at the north end
of Main St. Norman Rockwell's famous painting of
a policeman sitting at a counter talking to a young
boy, *The Runaway* (1958), was inspired by this
diner. Joe's has barely changed a wink – not the
bar stools and not the old-fashioned diner fare.

Great Barrington ❹

✘ Allium — Modern American $$
(☎413-528-2118; www.alliumberkshires.
com; 42 Railroad St; small plates $9-16, mains

$16-28; ⏱5-9:30pm) Allium subscribes to the
slow-food movement, with a seasonal menu
that relies on fresh organic produce, cheeses
and meats. Go for cocktails and small plates in
the lounge area, with windows facing the street,
or a more formal meal in the dining room, with
a view into the kitchen. This stylish restaurant
combines rustic and modern design elements
to great effect.

✘ Berkshire Co-op Market Cafe — Cafe $
(www.berkshire.coop; 42 Bridge St; meals
$6-10; ⏱8am-8pm; 🍴) You don't need to
spend a bundle to eat green, wholesome and
local. This cafe inside the Berkshire Co-op
Market, just off Main St, has a crunchy farm-
fresh salad bar, generous made-to-order
sandwiches (both meat and veggie) and
fair-trade coffees.

🛏 Wainwright Inn — B&B $$$
(☎413-528-2062; www.wainwrightinn.
com; 518 S Main St; r $169-219; ✳ 🛜) Great
Barrington's finest place to lay your head,
this c 1766 inn exudes historical appeal from
its wraparound porches and spacious parlors
to the period room decor. Most of the eight
guest rooms come with working fireplaces.
Breakfast is a decadent experience. The inn
is a short walk from the center of town on a
busy road.

Stockbridge ❺

✘ Once Upon a Table — American $$$
(☎413-298-3870; www.onceuponatablebistro.
com; 36 Main St; mains lunch $10-14, dinner
$20-30; ⏱11am-8:30pm Mon-Sat, to 3pm
Sun) This bright spot in the Mews shopping
arcade serves upscale fare in a sunny dining
room. It's the best place in town for lunch,
with choices like daily-changing omelets and
sophisticated sandwiches. The dinner menu
features reliably delicious treats such as
pecan-crusted rainbow trout and fine dessert
pastries.

Mohawk Trail

8

New England's oldest scenic highway offers invigorating art and architecture, stimulating action and adventure, and spectacular mountain scenery – everything you need for a weekend getaway.

TRIP HIGHLIGHTS

43 miles

MASS MoCA
An industrial relic turned into an incredible venue for installation art

24 miles

Deerfield Valley Canopy Tours
A thrilling ride through the treetops

FINISH
Williamstown

⑤ ④

③

Shelburne Falls

Deerfield

START

Western Summit
Jaw-dropping views and heart-pounding hikes along the Hoosac Ridge

38 miles

2–3 DAYS
46 MILES / 74KM

GREAT FOR...

BEST TIME TO GO
Enjoy clear views and open access to sites from June to October.

ESSENTIAL PHOTO
Snap a photo of the vast three-state vista from the Western Summit.

BEST FOR SCENERY
The 19 miles from stops three to five offer hair-raising turns and jaw-dropping views.

8 | Mohawk Trail

The road winds ever upward. Suddenly, around a bend, there's a clearing in the forest and the landscape sprawls out in a colorful tapestry, yielding views across the valley and into neighboring states. Welcome to the Western Summit of the Mohawk Trail, a 63-mile stretch of scenic byway, showing off raging rivers, idyllic farms and forest-covered mountains. Drivers, beware: it's practically impossible to keep your eyes on the road.

❶ Deerfield

Start your tour in **Historic Deerfield Village** (www.historic-deerfield. org; Old Main St; adult/child $14/5; ⏰9:30am-4:30pm Apr-Dec; ♿), an enchanting farming settlement that has escaped the ravages of time. Old Main St now presents a noble prospect: a dozen houses dating from the 1700s and 1800s, well preserved and open to the public. The homes have been restored and furnished according to actual historical records, reflecting

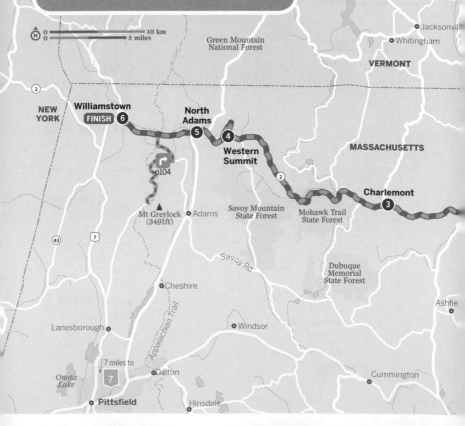

different periods in the village's history.

One block east of Old Main St, **Memorial Hall Museum** (www.americancenturies.mass.edu; cnr Memorial St, US 5 & MA 10; adult/child $6/3; ☺11am-4:30pm Sat & Sun May, Tue-Sun Jun-Oct) contains lots of original artifacts from local homes, including the storied Indian House Door. This farming family's front door was hacked through by attackers during the infamous 1704 raid, when Native Americans massacred

or captured most of the village residents.

🛏 p105

The Drive » From Historic Deerfield Village, drive north on MA 10 (US 5) for 3 miles and turn left to head west on MA 2A. At the traffic circle, take the second exit onto the Mohawk Trail (MA 2). For souvenirs, look for the Native American–owned Mohawk Trading Post as you enter Shelburne. Turn left on Bridge St to continue into Shelburne Falls.

----

❷ Shelburne Falls

The main drag in this artisan community is only three blocks long — a tiny but charming stretch of turn-of-the-20th-century buildings, housing art galleries and coffee shops alongside a barber shop, a general store and an old-fashioned pharmacy. Forming the background are the forested mountains, the Deerfield River and a pair of picturesque bridges across it — one made of iron, the other covered in flowers.

One paid gardener and a host of volunteers have been maintaining the **Bridge of Flowers** (www.bridgeofflowersmass.org; ☺Apr-Oct) since 1929. From April to October, more than 500 varieties of flowering plant, shrub and vine flaunt their colors on the 400ft-long span.

Two blocks south, the swirling of water around rocks in the Deerfield River has created an

LINK YOUR TRIP

7 **Berkshire Back Roads**

From Williamstown, drive south on US 7 to hook up with this loop around the Massachusetts mountains.

21 **Connecticut River Byway**

Drive north from Deerfield to explore the mighty New England waterway.

impressive collection of **glacial potholes** (Deerfield Ave) – near-perfect circular craters in the river bed. There are more than 50 potholes on display, including the world's largest, which has a 39ft diameter.

✕ p105

The Drive ⟫ At the end of Bridge St, cross the metal bridge and turn right on State St, which runs parallel to the Deerfield River. Turn left on MA 2, saluting the Big Indian as you leave Shelburne Falls. The Mohawk Trail continues to follow the raging river, with Charlemont spread out along this road for several miles.

TRIP HIGHLIGHT

❸ Charlemont

Tucked between the Deerfield River and the Hoosac hills, tiny Charlemont is worth a stop if you're craving an adrenaline rush. This is the home of **Zoar Outdoor** (☏800-532-7483; www.zoaroutdoor.com; 7 Main St/MA 2, Charlemont; kayak from $33, rafting $61-89; ⏱9am-5pm; ♿), offering canoeing, kayaking and whitewater rafting on the river rapids for all skill levels, including trips for children as young as seven. Come in spring for high-water adventure or in autumn for fall-foliage brilliance.

If you prefer to keep your feet dry, **Deerfield Valley Canopy Tours** (☏800-532-7483; www.deer fieldzipline.com; 7 Main St/

MA 2, Charlemont; zip $79-92; ⏱10am-5pm) lets you unleash your inner Tarzan on a treetop glide above the river valley. All in all, the three-hour outing includes three rappels, two sky bridges and 11 zips that get progressively longer. The hardest part is stepping off the first platform – the rest is pure exhilaration!

The Drive ⟫ Leaving Charlemont, you'll pass the *Hail to the Sunrise* statue, honoring the Five Indian Nations of the Mohawk Trail. The next stretch is the highlight of the route, as it cuts across the eponymous state forest. Continue climbing through the town of Florida, punctuated by three lookouts: the unmarked Eastern Summit, the Whitcomb Summit (the highest along the trail) and the Western Summit.

TRIP HIGHLIGHT

❹ Western Summit

Also known as Perry's Peak, the Western Summit (2100ft) shows off amazing views of the surrounding Hoosac Range. On a clear day, you can see into Vermont and even New York. The summit is topped with a ticky-tacky tourist shop, so you can buy some fudge.

You'll also find the trailhead for the **Hoosac Range** just east of the gift shop. This scenic 6-mile round-trip hike follows the ridgeline south to Spruce Hill summit, located in Savoy Mountain State

PHIL HABER PHOTOGRAPHY / GETTY IMAGES ©

Forest. Allow at least four hours for the hike; if you're pressed for time, the 1.5-mile loop to Sunset Rock is a shorter alternative.

The Drive ⟫ Back in the car, you'll find that the Mohawk Trail descends quickly, with an exhilarating spin around the Hairpin Turn to make your heart beat a little faster. Entering North Adams, the road follows

Shelburne Falls Bridge of Flowers

the Hoosac River past vestiges of the industrial era.

TRIP HIGHLIGHT

5 North Adams

North Adams' beautiful and bleak 19th-century downtown seems out of sync with the rest of the Berkshires. And nestled into this industrial-era assemblage is a contemporary-art museum of staggering proportions.

MASS MoCA (Massachusetts Museum of Contemporary Art; www.massmoca.org; 87 Marshall St; adult/child $18/8; 10am-6pm Jul & Aug, 11am-5pm Wed-Mon Sep-Jun;) sprawls over 13 acres of downtown North Adams. After the Sprague Electric Company packed up in 1985, more than $31 million was spent to modernize the property into the country's biggest art gallery, which now encompasses 222,000 sq ft and more than 25 buildings, including art-construction areas, performance centers and 19 galleries. One gallery is the size of a football field, giving installation

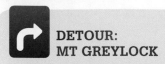

DETOUR: MT GREYLOCK

Start ❺ North Adams (p103)

Just west of downtown North Adams, look for the turn-off to Notch Rd, which will take you about 5 miles south to **Mt Greylock State Reservation** (☎413-499-4262; www.mass.gov/dcr; 30 Rockwell Rd, Lanesborough; ⏰9am-5pm Jun-Aug, to 4:30pm Sep-May). In summer (mid-May to mid-October) you can drive up; otherwise, park your car at the entrance and hike 5 miles to the summit, where you will be rewarded with a 360-degree vista, taking in five states and hundreds of miles.

At 3491ft, Mt Greylock is the state's highest peak. In the 19th century, Greylock was a favorite destination for New England's nature-loving writers, including Nathaniel Hawthorne and Henry David Thoreau. Herman Melville even dedicated a novel to 'Greylock's Most Excellent Majesty.' Nowadays, it is ceremoniously topped with the 92ft-high War Memorial Tower, which you can climb (making the mountain effectively 3583ft). From May to October, you can also eat and sleep at the magnificently sited Bascom Lodge.

artists the opportunity to take things into a whole new dimension.

In addition to ever-changing, description-defying installations, there is a fascinating Sol LeWitt retrospective, on display until 2033. Little ones can always create and speculate in Kidspace, while the on-site theater space hosts music festivals, dance parties, poetry recitals and every kind of performance art imaginable.

✕ 🛏 p105

The Drive » Exiting North Adams, the Mohawk Trail crosses the Hoosac River several times before becoming Main St, Williamstown.

❻ Williamstown

Tiny Williamstown is nestled in the heart of the Purple Valley, so named because the surrounding mountains often seem shrouded in a lavender veil at dusk. It is the quintessential college town, dominated by the marble-and-brick buildings of elite Williams College.

In addition to welcoming green spaces and academic architecture, Williamstown is home to a pair of exceptional art museums. The **Clark Art Institute** (www.clarkart.edu; 225 South St; adult/child $20/free; ⏰10am-5pm Tue-Sun) is a gem, with wonderful collections of paintings by French Impressionists and their American contemporaries, all set amid 140 gorgeous acres of expansive lawns.

Down the road, the **Williams College Museum of Art** (www.wcma.org; 15 Lawrence Hall Dr; ⏰10am-5pm, to 8pm Thu, closed Wed Sep-May) has an impressive collection of its own. The American Collection includes substantial works by notables such as Edward Hopper, Winslow Homer and Grant Wood, to name only a few. The photography collection is also noteworthy, with images by Man Ray and Alfred Stieglitz.

✕ 🛏 p105

Eating & Sleeping

Deerfield ❶

🛏 Deerfield Inn · Inn $$

(📞413-774-5587; www.deerfieldinn.com; 81 Old
Main St; tw from $150, d $160-200; ✳🔌📶)
This establishment, smack in the heart of
the historic district, has 24 rooms furnished
with antiques and housed in a gracious Greek
revival farmhouse. The included hot, hearty
breakfast – as well as other meals – are served
in the attached restaurant, which sources many
ingredients from the surrounding farmland.

Shelburne Falls ❷

🍴 Gould's Sugar House · Breakfast $$

(www.goulds-sugarhouse.com; 270 Mohawk
Trail; mains $8-12; ⏱8:30am-2pm Mar, Apr &
Sep-Nov) The standard order at this family-run
farm is fluffy pancake perfection, drizzled with
maple heaven. Other unexpected highlights
include the sugar pickles (yes, you read that
right), maple ice cream and corn fritters. While
you wait (and you will wait), you can watch the
syrup being made. Located right on the Mohawk
Hwy, east of the Shelburne Falls turn-off.

North Adams ❺

🍴 Public Eat & Drink · Pub Food $$

(www.publiceatanddrink.com; 34 Holden
St; mains $10-22; ⏱11:30am-10pm; 🍴)
With exposed-brick walls and big windows
overlooking the street, this cozy pub is the
most popular dinner spot in North Adams.
Come for an excellent selection of craft beers
and gourmet pub fare, such as brie burgers,
flatbread pizzas and bistro steak. Some decent
vegetarian options as well.

🛏 Porches · Boutique Hotel $$

(📞413-664-0400; www.porches.com; 231 River
St; d/ste from $239/279; ✳🔌📶🏊) Across

the street from MASS MoCA, the artsy rooms
here combine well-considered color palettes,
ample lighting and French doors into a pleasant
sleeping experience. It seems pricey for North
Adams, but they got all the details right (and
they are the only game in town).

Williamstown ❻

🍴 Mezze Bistro & Bar · Fusion $$

(📞413-458-0123; www.mezzerestaurant.com;
777 Cold Spring Rd/US 7; mains $14-28; ⏱5-
9pm) You don't know exactly what you're going
to get at this contemporary chic restaurant – as
the menu changes frequently – but you know
it's going to be good. Situated on 3 spectacular
acres, Mezze's farm-to-table approach begins
with an edible garden right on-site. Much of the
rest of the seasonal menu, from small-batch
microbrews to organic meats, is locally sourced
as well.

🛏 Guest House at Field Farm · Inn $$$

(📞413-458-3135; www.thetrustees.org/
field-farm; 554 Sloan Rd; r $195-295; @📶🏊)
About 6 miles south of Williamstown, this
one-of-a-kind inn offers an artful blend of mid-
20th-century modernity and timeless mountain
scenery. The six rooms are spacious and fitted
with handcrafted furnishings that reflect the
modernist style of the house. The sculpture-
laden grounds feature miles of lightly trodden
walking trails and a pair of Adirondack chairs set
perfectly for unobstructed star gazing.

🛏 Maple Terrace Motel · Motel $$

(📞413-458-9677; www.mapleterrace.com; 555
Main St; d $99-139; 📶🏊) The Maple Terrace is
a simple yet cozy 15-room place on the eastern
outskirts of town. The Swedish innkeepers
have snazzed up the grounds with gardens that
make you want to linger. There's nothing fancy
going on here, but the place is comfortable and
service is warmly attentive.

STRETCH YOUR LEGS
BOSTON

Start/Finish Boston Common

Distance 2.5 miles

Duration Three hours

Everybody knows about its world-class museums and historical sites, but Boston also offers a network of verdant parks, welcoming waterways and delightful shopping streets, making it a wonderful walking city.

Take this walk on Trips

Boston Common

Welcome to the country's oldest **public park** (btwn Tremont, Charles, Beacon & Park Sts; ◷6am-midnight; [P] [♿]; [T]Park St), with a convenient underground parking facility below – what foresight! A **bronze plaque** is emblazoned with the words of the treaty between Governor Winthrop and William Blaxton, who sold this land for £30 in 1634. The **Massachusetts State House** (www.sec.state.ma.us; cnr Beacon & Bowdoin Sts; ◷9am-5pm, tours 10am-3:30pm Mon-Fri; [T]Park St) commands a prominent position in the park's northeastern corner.

The Walk ≫ Follow the busy Bostonians crisscrossing the common. Exit the park from the western side, cross Charles St and enter the tranquil Public Garden.

Public Garden

The **Public Garden** (www.friendsofthepublic garden.org; Arlington St; ◷6am-midnight; [♿]; [T]Arlington) is a 24-acre botanical oasis of Victorian flower beds, verdant grass and weeping willows shading a tranquil lagoon. At any time of year, it is an island of loveliness, awash in seasonal blooms, gold-toned leaves or untrammeled snow. Taking a ride on the **Swan Boats** (www. swanboats.com; Public Garden; adult/child $3.50/2; ◷10am-5pm Jun-Aug, to 4pm mid-Apr–May, noon-4pm Sep; [T]Arlington) in the lagoon has been a Boston tradition since 1877. And don't miss the famous statue **Make Way for Ducklings**, based on the beloved children's book by Robert McCloskey.

The Walk ≫ Cross the bridge and exit the garden through the southwestern gate to Arlington St. Stroll west on swanky Newbury St, perfect for window-shopping and gallery hopping. Take a left on Clarendon St and continue to Boylston St.

Copley Square

Boston's most exquisite architecture is clustered around this stately Back Bay plaza. The centerpiece is the Romanesque **Trinity Church** (www.trinitychurch boston.org; 206 Clarendon St; adult/child $7/free; ◷10am-5pm Tue-Sat, 1-5pm Sun; [T]Copley), famed for its stained-glass

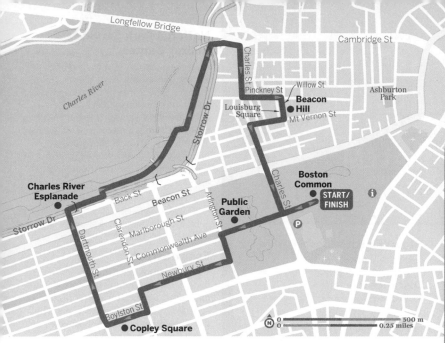

windows. It's particularly lovely as reflected in the facade of the modern **John Hancock Tower**. This assemblage faces off against the elegant neo-Renaissance **Boston Public Library** (www.bpl.org; 700 Boylston St; ⊕9am-9pm Mon-Thu, to 5pm Fri & Sat year-round, also 1-5pm Sun Oct-May; ⊤Copley), packed with sculpture, murals and other treasures.

The Walk » Head north on Dartmouth St, crossing the stately, dual-carriageway Commonwealth Ave, the grandest of Back Bay's grand avenues. Continue three more blocks to Back St, from where a pedestrian walkway crosses Storrow Dr to the esplanade.

Charles River Esplanade

The southern bank of the **Charles River Basin** (www.esplanadeassociation.org; ⛹; ⊤Charles/MGH, Kenmore) is an enticing urban escape, with grassy knolls and cooling waterways, all designed by Frederick Law Olmsted. The park is dotted with public art, including an oversized bust of **Arthur Fiedler**, the longtime conductor of the Boston Pops. The **Hatch Memorial Shell** hosts free outdoor concerts and movies, including the famed July 4 concert by the Boston Pops.

The Walk » Walk east along the esplanade, enjoying the breezes and views of the Charles River. It's about a half-mile to the Longfellow Bridge, where you can climb the ramp and find yourself at the top of Charles St.

Beacon Hill

With an intriguing history and iconic architecture, Beacon Hill is Boston's most prestigious address. Charles Street is an enchanting spot for browsing boutiques and haggling over antiques. To explore further, wander down the residential streets lit with gas lanterns, admire the brick town houses decked with purple windowpanes and blooming flower boxes, and discover streets such as stately **Louisburg Square** that capture the neighborhood's grandeur.

The Walk » Take your time strolling south along charming Charles St. For a glimpse of Louisburg Sq, walk two blocks east on Pinckney St. Then continue south to Boston Common.

107

STRETCH YOUR LEGS
SALEM

Start/Finish National Park Service Visitor Center

Distance 2.5 miles

Duration Two hours

A lot of history is packed into this gritty city of witches and sailors — even more than you read in the textbooks. This walk highlights the architectural gems and little-known stories that are often overlooked.

Take this walk on Trips

National Park Service Visitor Center

Start your explorations at the **NPS Visitor Center** (www.nps.gov/sama; 2 New Liberty St; ☺9am-5pm Wed-Sun), which offers information on Salem. For a good overview, catch a free screening of *Where Past Is Present,* a short film about Salem history. You can also pick up a map and description of several self-guided walking tours and other area attractions.

The Walk ›› From the visitor center, walk south on New Liberty St for half a block. The excellent Peabody Essex Museum sits at the corner of Essex St. Turn right and continue down Essex St.

Essex Street

The main drag in Salem is Essex St, a pedestrian mall that is lined with shops and cafes, a few historic buildings and several witch-themed attractions. The most prominent building is the **old Town Hall**, the red-brick beauty that was the seat of government in the 19th century. At the corner of Washington St stands a statue of Samantha Stephens, the spell-casting, nose-twitching beauty from the classic TV show *Bewitched.*

The Walk ›› Cross Washington St and continue west on Essex St. At Summer St, turn left and walk one block south to Chestnut St.

Chestnut Street

Lovers of old houses will revel in the grand antique homes on Chestnut St, which is among the most architecturally lovely streets in the country. One of these stately homes is the **Phillips House** (www.phillipsmuseum.org; 34 Chestnut St; adult/child/senior & student $8/4/7; ☺11am-4pm Tue-Sun Jun-Oct, Sat & Sun Nov-May), which displays the family furnishings of Salem sea captains, including a collection of antique carriages and cars.

The Walk ›› Retrace your steps on Chestnut St. Cross Summer St and continue walking on

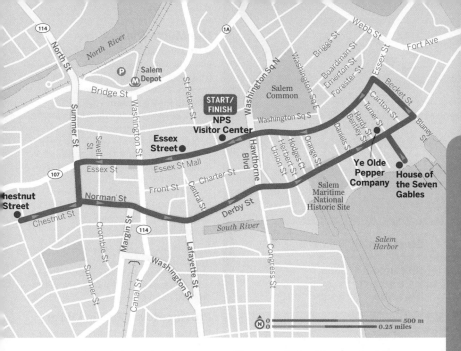

Norman St. Cross Washington St and continue walking on Derby St, passing through the heart of the Salem Maritime National Historic Site.

Ye Olde Pepper Companie

In 1806, Englishwoman Mrs Spencer survived a shipwreck en route to the New World. She arrived in Salem with nary a penny to her name, but, with a small loan, she bought a barrel of sugar and created 'Salem Gibraltar,' a candy that sated the sweet teeth of sea captains and merchants. Two centuries later, **Ye Olde Pepper Companie** (www. peppercandy.net; 122 Derby St; ☺10am-6pm) still uses her recipes for old-fashioned delights such as Black Jacks (flavored with blackstrap molasses) and Gibraltars (lemon and peppermint treats).

The Walk » From Derby St, turn right on Turner St and stroll to the end of this lovely residential lane.

House of the Seven Gables

'Half-way down a by-street of one of our New England towns, stands a rusty wooden house, with seven acutely-peaked gables, facing towards various points of the compass, and a huge clustered chimney in the midst.' So wrote Nathaniel Hawthorne in his 1851 novel about the **House of the Seven Gables** (www.7gables.org; 54 Turner St; adult/child/teen $13/8/10; ☺10am-7pm Jul-Oct, to 5pm Nov-Jun). The admission fee allows entrance to the site's four historic buildings, as well as the luxuriant gardens on the waterfront.

The Walk » Continue east on Derby St. Peek inside the whimsical world of metal sculpture on the corner of Blaney St before walking up Becket St. Turn left on Essex St and walk a half-mile back to the NPS Visitor Center.

STRETCH YOUR LEGS
PROVINCETOWN

Start/Finish MacMillan Pier

Distance 1.3 miles

Duration Two hours

Ever since Charles Hawthorne opened the Cape Cod School of Art back in 1899, this little town at the tip of the cape has attracted artists, writers and other creative types exploring 'alternative' lifestyles.

Take this walk on Trips

MacMillan Pier

Start your walking tour at the central pier, where fishing boats dock alongside passenger ferries and whale-watching cruisers. Perched out on the dock, the **Whydah Pirate Museum** (☎508-487-8899; www.whydah.com; MacMillan Pier; adult/child $10/8; ⊙10am-5pm May-Oct) is an unexpected curiosity. Captained by 'Black Sam' Bellamy, the *Whydah* sank in 1717 and to this day remains the only authenticated pirate ship ever salvaged. A local expedition recovered more than 100,000 items of booty – coins, jewelry, weapons – some of which are on display.

The Walk » From MacMillan Pier, stroll east on Commercial St. Take a quick detour to see an incredible, fantastical sculpture garden behind the wrought-iron fence on Center St. Then cross the street and enter the library.

Provincetown Public Library

Erected in 1860 as a church, this handsome belfry-topped building later became a museum, complete with a half-size replica of Provincetown's famed race-winning schooner *Rose Dorothea*. When the museum went bust, the town converted the multifunctional building to the **Provincetown Public Library** (☎508-487-7094; www.provincetownlibrary.org; 356 Commercial St; ⊙10am-5pm Mon & Fri, to 8pm Tue-Thu, 1-5pm Sat & Sun; ♿). One catch: the boat was too big to remove, so it still occupies the upper deck, with bookshelves built around it.

The Walk » Continue east on Commercial St. Grab a coffee at the ever-popular Wired Puppy, then turn left and walk up Pearl St. Cross Bradford St and continue to your next destination.

Fine Arts Work Center

The **Fine Arts Work Center** (☎508-487-9960; www.fawc.org; 24 Pearl St) is one reason that this far-flung corner of Massachusetts continues to attract daring and creative minds. The progressive foundation supports emerging artists and writers, offering fellowships and facilities so they can immerse themselves in their creative endeavors.

The on-site **Hudson D Walker Gallery** (📞508-487-9960; www.fawc.org; 24 Pearl St; 🕑9am-5pm Mon-Fri) often hosts exhibits of work by past and present fellows, while readings, talks and presentations take place in the **Stanley Kunitz Common Room**.

The Walk » Return to Bradford St and turn left. Stroll for a few blocks along this backbone of Provincetown, which sees much less action than Commercial St. Bang a right on Bangs St and return to the main drag.

Provincetown Art Association & Museum

Founded in 1914, the **Provincetown Art Association & Museum** (PAAM; 📞508-487-1750; www.paam.org; 460 Commercial St; adult/child $10/free; 🕑11am-8pm Mon-Thu, to 10pm Fri, to 6pm Sat, to 5pm Sun Jul & Aug, shorter hours rest of year, closed Mon-Wed Oct-May) celebrates the town's thriving art community, displaying the works of hundreds of artists who have found their inspiration on the Lower Cape. Among the impressionist, modernist and contemporary works are pieces by Charles Hawthorne, who led the early Provincetown art movement, and Edward Hopper, who had a home and gallery in the Truro dunes.

The Walk » Walk west on Commercial St, passing through the eclectic East End.

East End

As you walk back along Commercial St toward MacMillan Pier, you are traversing the **Provincetown East End Gallery District**. Between Bangs and Standish Sts, P-town's main drag is lined with galleries showcasing local and national (and some international) artists. Browse at your leisure, but don't miss the **Albert Merola Gallery** (📞508-487-4424; www.albertmerolagallery.com; 424 Commercial St; 🕑hours vary), which showcases works by both contemporary and notable past Provincetown artists. Pick up the free *Provincetown Art Guide* for a map and complete list of galleries.

The Walk » Continue walking west on Commercial St to return to MacMillan Pier.

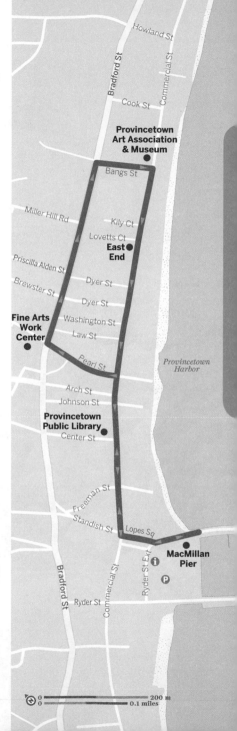

Connecticut & Rhode Island

WITH LAKES, ORCHARDS, VINEYARDS AND COASTAL CLIFF WALKS, Connecticut and Rhode Island pack a big punch – even though they're two of the smallest states in the Union. Connecticut's pristine scenery has been luring artists, celebrities and moneyed Manhattanites since the 1900s and it's easy to see what drew them here: a historic rural landscape, genteel pre-Colonial towns, clam shacks and oyster harvests.

Just down the road, tiny Rhode Island sports a jagged coastline trimmed with some of the best beaches in the northeast, while the cities of Providence and Newport brim with museums, galleries and gorgeous old cobbled neighborhoods. No wonder the Vanderbilts and their friends decamped here for summer balls and swimming. You'd be wise to follow suit.

Watch Hill Watch Hill lighthouse
ENZO FIGUERES / GETTY IMAGES ©

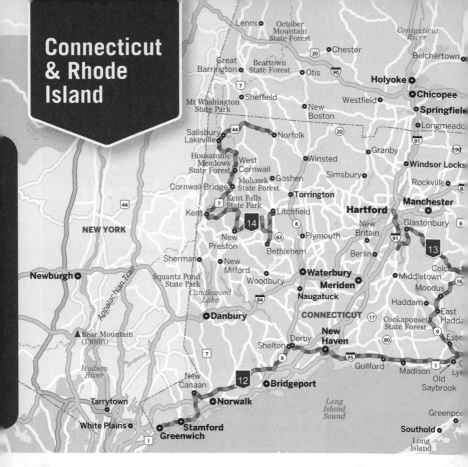

Connecticut & Rhode Island

9 **Rhode Island: East Bay 3–4 Days**
A historic drive exploring the founding days of America. (p117)

10 **Rhode Island: Coastal Culture 4 Days**
A meandering tour combining big-city culture with islands and beaches. (p125)

11 **Quiet Corner 3 Days**
Drive along a National Scenic Byway amid gorgeous pastoral scenery. (p133)

12 **Connecticut Wine Trail 5 Days**
Visit rural and coastal vineyards with a dose of modern architecture in between. (p141)

13 **Lower River Valley 4 Days**
Tour the Connecticut River, visiting castles and cruising for eagles. (p149)

14 **Litchfield Hills Loop 5 Days**
A gourmet trip around the rolling hills and lakes of Connecticut's 'Hamptons.' (p157)

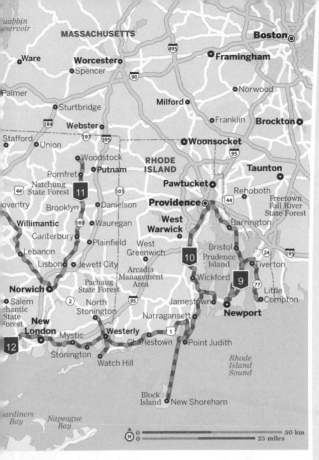

DON'T MISS

Polo in Rhode Island

Enjoy polo in Portsmouth at the Glen Farm country estate on Trip 9

Golden Lamb Buttery

Mingle over drinks, head off for a hayride and then settle down for a gourmet dinner. Reserve ahead on Trip 11

Jonathan Edwards Winery

Those in the know pick up lunch along the way to this 48-acre estate overlooking the Atlantic. Perfect for afternoon picnics on Trip 12

Philip Johnson Glass House

Tour Connecticut's newest National Trust Historic Site and one of the world's most famous modern houses on Trip 12

Bantam Cinema

Watch stylish independent and foreign films in a converted red barn next to Lake Bantam on Trip 14

Westerly Misquamicut State Beach

115

Rhode Island: East Bay

9

East Bay is Rhode Island's historical heart. Tour the shoreline, and follow the trail from America's humble Colonial roots in Little Compton to the industrial boomtowns of Newport and Providence.

TRIP HIGHLIGHTS

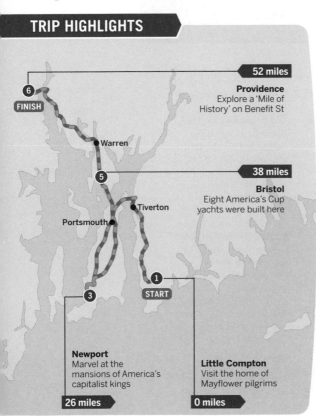

52 miles

Providence
Explore a 'Mile of History' on Benefit St

● Warren

38 miles

Bristol
Eight America's Cup yachts were built here

● Tiverton

Portsmouth ●

START

Newport
Marvel at the mansions of America's capitalist kings

26 miles

Little Compton
Visit the home of Mayflower pilgrims

0 miles

3–4 DAYS
52 MILES / 83KM

GREAT FOR...

BEST TIME TO GO
May to October for good weather and farm food.

 ESSENTIAL PHOTO
Capture the mansions and sheer cliffs along Cliff Walk.

 BEST FOR HISTORY
Find modern America's beginnings in Little Compton.

Rhode Island Newport coastline

9 Rhode Island: East Bay

Rhode Island's jagged East Bay tells the American story in microcosm. Start in Little Compton with the grave of Elizabeth Pabodie (1623–1717), the first European settler born in New England. Then meander through historic Tiverton and Bristol, where slave dealers and merchants grew rich. Prosperous as they were, their modest homes barely hold a candle to the mansions, museums and libraries of Newport's capitalist kings and Providence's intelligentsia.

TRIP HIGHLIGHT

1 Little Compton

No doubt tiring of the big-city bustle of 17th-century Portsmouth, early settler Samuel Wilbor crossed the Sakonnet River to Little Compton. His plain family home, **Wilbor House** (☎401-635-4035; www.littlecompton.org; 548 West Main Rd; adult/child $6/3; ☺1-5pm Thu-Mon Apr-Oct, 9am-3pm Tue-Fri Nov-Mar), built in 1690, still stands on a manicured lawn behind a traditional five-bar gate and tells the story of eight generations of Wilbors who lived here.

The rest of Little Compton, from the hand-hewn clapboard houses to the white-steepled **United Congregational Church**, overlooking the **Old Commons Burial Ground**, is one of the oldest and most quaint villages in all of New England. Elizabeth Pabodie, daughter of Mayflower pilgrims Priscilla and John Alden and the first settler born in New England, is buried here.

Lovely, ocean-facing **Goosewing Beach** (☺dawn-dusk) is the only good public beach. Parking costs $10 at **South Shore Beach**, from where you can walk across a small tidal inlet.

🛏 p123

The Drive » Head north along RI 77 at a leisurely pace,

enjoying the peaceful country scenery of rambling stone walls and clapboard farmhouses. As you approach Tiverton, look out to your left and you'll occasionally get glimpses out to the water, which are particularly pretty in the late afternoon.

- - - - - - - - - - - -

❷ Tiverton

En route to Tiverton's historic Four Corners, stop in at **Sakonnet Vineyards** (☎401-635-8486; www.sakonnetwine.com; 162 West Main Rd; ⏲11am-5pm) for free daily wine tastings and guided tours. This will set you up nicely for the gourmet treats that await in Tiverton: **Gray's Ice Cream** (☎401-624-4500; www.graysicecream.com; 16 East Rd; scoops from $3; ⏲7am-7pm), where over 40 flavors are made on-site daily; artisanal cheeses from the **Milk & Honey Bazaar** (☎401-624-1974; www.milkandhoneyri.com;

❙ LINK YOUR TRIP

4 **Pilgrim Trail**
Continue the historical journey in Plymouth with the Massachusetts Pilgrim Trail.

10 **Rhode Island: Coastal Culture**
Explore Rhode Island's coastal culture, heading west along I-95 from Providence.

3838 Main Rd; 10am-5pm
Wed-Sat, noon-5pm Sun); and
the gourmet deli bar at
Provender Fine Foods
(401-624-8084; www.
provenderfinefoods.com; 3883
Main Rd; items $4-18), **where**
you can munch on giant
cookies or forage for
picnic fare.

Tiverton is an artists'
colony so it also offers
some of the best shopping
in the state, including
handwoven Shaker-
style rugs from **Amy C
Lund** (401-816-0000;
www.aclhandweaver.com;
3964 Main Rd; 10am-5pm
Wed-Sat, noon-5pm Sun) and
museum-quality art from
Gallery 4 (401-816-0999;
www.gallery4tiverton.com;
3848 Main Rd; 11am-4:30pm
Wed-Sat, noon-4:30pm Sun).

The Drive » Head north up
Main St, leaving Tiverton and
its green fields behind you, and
merge onto the westbound RI
138/RI 24 south, which leads
you directly into Newport.

TRIP HIGHLIGHT

❸ Newport

Established by reli-
gious moderates fleeing
persecution from Mas-
sachusetts Puritans, the
'new port' flourished
to become the fourth-
richest city in the newly
independent colony.
Downtown, the Colonial-
era architecture is beau-
tifully preserved along
with notable landmarks,
such as Washington Sq's
Colony House, where
Rhode Island's declara-
tion of independence was
read in May 1776.

Just off the square, the
gaslights of the **White
Horse Tavern** (401-849-
3600; www.whitehorsenew
port.com; 26 Marlborough St;
meals $28-58; 11:30am-
9pm), America's oldest
tavern, still burn, and
on Touro St, America's
first synagogue, **Touro**

Synagogue (401-847-
4794; www.tourosynagogue.
org; 85 Touro St; adult/child
$12/free; noon-1.30pm Sun-
Fri May-Jun, 10am-4pm Sun-Fri
Jul & Aug, to 1:30pm Sun-Fri
Sep & Oct, noon-1.30pm Sun
Nov-Apr), still stands. Tour
the past on a guided walk
with **Newport History
Tours** (401-841-8770;
www.newporthistorytours.org;
Brick Market Museum & Shop,
127 Thames St; tours adult/
child $12/5; tour times
vary;).

Fascinating as New-
port's early history is,
it struggles to compete
with the town's latter-day
success, when wealthy
industrialists made
Newport their summer
vacation spot and built
country 'cottages' down
lantern-lined Bellevue
Ave, modeled on Ital-
ianate palazzos, French
chateaux and Elizabe-
than manor houses, and
decorated them with
priceless furnishings and
artworks. Tour the most
outstanding with the
**Preservation Society of
Newport County** (401-
847-1000; www.newport
mansions.org; 424 Bellevue
Ave; 5-site ticket adult/child
$33/11).

✕ 🛏 p39, p123

The Drive » Leave Newport
by way of 10-mile Ocean Dr,
which starts just south of Fort
Adams and curls around the
southern shore, past the grand
mansions, and up Bellevue
Ave before intersecting with
Memorial Blvd. Turn right
here for a straight shot into
Middletown.

DETOUR: PRUDENCE ISLAND

Start: ❺ Bristol (p121)

Idyllic **Prudence Island** (401-683-0430; www.
prudencebayislandstransport.com; 6am-6pm Mon-Fri, to
4pm Sat & Sun) sits in the middle of Narragansett Bay,
an easy 25-minute ferry ride from Bristol. Originally
used for farming and later as a summer vacation
spot for families from Providence and New York, who
travelled here on the Fall River Line Steamer, the
island now has only 88 inhabitants. There are some
fine Victorian and Beaux Arts houses near Stone
Wharf, a lighthouse and a small store, but otherwise
it's wild and unspoiled. Perfect for mountain biking,
barbecues, fishing and paddling.

YIMING CHEN / GETTY IMAGES ©

Providence City skyline

④ Middletown

Flo's (📞401-847-8141; www.flosclamshacks.com; 4 Wave Ave, Middletown; mains $8-18; 🕐 closed Jan & Feb) jaunty red-and-white clam shack would be enough reason to visit Middletown, which now merges seamlessly with Newport. But the best fried clams in town taste better after a day on **Sachuest Beach** (Second Beach; 📞401-846-6273), the largest and most beautiful beach on Aquidneck Island. Curving around Sachuest Bay, it is backed by the 450-acre **Norman Bird Sanctuary** (📞401-846-2577; www.norman birdsanctuary.org; 583 Third Beach Rd; adult/child $6/3; 🕐9am-5pm), which teems with migrating birds.

The Drive ≫ Leave Aquidneck Island via East Main Rd, which takes you north through the suburbs of Middletown and Portsmouth. After 6.5 miles, pick up the RI 114 and cross the bay via the scenic Mt Hope suspension bridge. From here it's a short 3-mile drive into Bristol.

TRIP HIGHLIGHT

⑤ Bristol

One-fifth of all slaves transported to America were brought in Bristol ships and by the 18th century the town was one of the country's major commercial ports. The world-class **Herreshoff Marine Museum** (📞401-253-5000; www.herres hoff.org; 1 Burnside St; adult/ child $10/free; 🕐10am-5pm May-Oct; ♿) showcases some of America's finest yachts, including eight that were built for the America's Cup.

Local resident Augustus Van Wickle bought a 72ft Herreshoff yacht for his wife Bessie in 1895, but having nowhere suitable to moor it, he then had to build **Blithewold Mansion** (📞401-253-2707; www.blithewold.org; 101 Ferry

LOCAL KNOWLEDGE: POLO IN PORTSMOUTH

Drab though the urban environs of Portsmouth may seem, in-the-know locals rate Portsmouth as a family-friendly destination. Not least because the polo matches hosted at Glen Farm make for a great family day out. Home to the **Newport Polo Club** (☎401-846-0200; www.nptpolo.com; 250 Linden Lane; lawn seats adult/child $12/free; ⏰gates open 1pm), the 700-acre 'farm' was assembled by New York businessman Henry Taylor, who sought to create a gentleman's country seat in the grand English tradition. In summer, the farm is host to the club's polo matches (check the website for dates), which are a perfect way to enjoy the property and get an authentic taste of Newport high life.

Rd; adult/child $11/3; ⏰10am-4pm Tue-Sun mid-Apr–Oct; P). The arts-and-crafts mansion sits in a peerless position on Narragansett Bay and is particularly lovely in spring, when the daffodils line the shore. Other local magnates included slave trader General George DeWolf who built **Linden Place** (☎401-253-0390; www.lindenplace.org; 500 Hope St; adult/child $8/6; ⏰10am-4pm Thu-Sat May-Oct; P), famous as a location for the 1974 film *The Great Gatsby*.

Bristol's **Colt State Park** (www.riparks.com; RI 114; ⏰8:30am-4:30pm; P) is Rhode Island's most scenic park, with its entire western border fronting Narragansett

Bay, fringed by 4 miles of cycling trails and shaded picnic tables.

🛏 p123

The Drive » From Bristol it's a straight drive north along RI 114, through the suburbs of Warren and Barrington, to Providence. After 17 miles, merge onto the I-195 W, which takes you the remaining 18 miles into the center of town.

- - - - - - - - - - -

TRIP HIGHLIGHT

❻ Providence

Providence, the first town of religious liberal Roger Williams' new Rhode Island and Providence Plantation colony, was established so that 'no man should be molested for his conscience sake.' **Benefit Street's 'Mile of**

History' gives a quick lesson in the city's architectural legacy with more than 100 Colonial, Federal and Revival houses. Amid them you'll find William Strickland's 1838 **Providence Athenaeum** (☎401-421-6970; www.providenceathenaeum.org; 251 Benefit St; ⏰9am-7pm Mon-Thu, to 5pm Fri & Sat, 1-5pm Sun), inside which plaster busts of Greek gods and philosophers preside over a collection that dates to 1753.

Atop the hill sits Brown University (www.brown.edu), with its Gothic and Beaux Arts buildings arranged around the College Green. Nearby is **John Brown House** (☎401-273-7507; www.rihs.org; 52 Power St; adult/child $10/6; ⏰tours 1:30pm & 3pm Tue-Fri, 10:30am, noon, 1:30pm & 3pm Sat Apr-Dec), which President John Quincy Adams thought to be 'the most magnificent and elegant mansion...on this continent.'

End the tour with a nod toward the bronze statue of *Independent Man,* which graces the pearly white dome of the **Rhode Island State House** (☎401-222-2357; www.rilin.state.ri.us; 82 Smith St; ⏰tours by appointment).

🍴🛏 p59, p123, p131

Eating & Sleeping

Little Compton ❶

🛏 Stone House Inn   Historic Inn $$$

(📞401-635-2222; 122 Sakonnet Point Rd; d from $295; P🛜) When this unashamedly upmarket inn opened its doors in 2016, Little Compton's notoriously private elite feared it meant the out-of-towners were coming. With only 13 rooms (lavish as they may be), it's hardly cause for an invasion. If you have cash and the inclination, this is your chance to take a peek at how the other half live.

Newport ❸

✖ Fluke Wine Bar   Seafood $$$

(📞401-849-7778; http://flukewinebar.com; 41 Bowen's Wharf; mains $40-60; ⏲5-11pm Wed-Sat Nov-Apr, daily summer) Fluke's Scandinavian-inspired dining room, with its blond wood and picture windows, offers an accomplished seafood menu featuring roasted monkfish, seasonal striped sea bass and plump scallops. Upstairs, the bar serves a rock-and-roll cocktail list.

✖ The Mooring   Seafood $$$

(📞401-846-2260; www.mooringrestaurant.com; Sayer's Wharf; sandwiches $12-16, mains $19-38; ⏲11:30am-10pm) A harborfront setting and a menu brimming with fresh seafood make this an unbeatable combination for seaside dining. Tip: if it's packed, take the side entrance to the bar, grab a stool and order the meaty clam chowder and a 'bag of doughnuts' (tangy lobster fritters).

🛏 Marshall Slocum Guest House   B&B $$$

(📞401-841-5120; www.marshallslocuminn.com; 29 Kay St; d $89-295; 🛜) This clapboard colonial house, a former parsonage, is situated in a quiet residential street between Historic Hill and downtown Newport. The period feel is wonderfully preserved in gorgeous rooms featuring canopy beds, cool linen bed sheets, wide wooden floorboards and shuttered windows. Book well in advance.

Bristol ❺

🛏 Governor Bradford Inn   Inn $$

(📞401-254-1745; www.mounthopefarm.org/the-inn; 250 Metacom Ave; r from $135; P❄) Administered by the Mount Hope Trust, the Governor Bradford offers four individually styled rooms in a 300-year-old Georgian farmhouse. Once owned by the Haffenreffer family, of beer-brewing fortune, the house sits on 200 acres of pristine farmland.

Providence ❻

✖ Haven Brothers Diner   Diner $

(📞401-603-8124; www.havenbrothersmobile.com; cnr Dorrance & Fulton Sts; meals $5-12; ⏲5pm-3am) Parked next to City Hall, this diner sits on the back of a truck that has rolled into the same spot every evening for decades. Climb up a rickety ladder to get basic diner fare alongside everyone from prominent politicians to college kids pulling an all-nighter to drunks. The murder burger ($4.50) comes highly recommended.

✖ Local 121   Modern American $$

(📞401-274-2121; www.local121.com; 121 Washington St; mains $14-36; ⏲5pm-midnight Mon-Fri, from 10am Sat & Sun) Locavore mania comes to Providence with this opulent, old-school restaurant with contemporary aspirations. Housed in the old Dreyfus hotel (built in the 1890s), a building owned by the arts organization AS220, Local 121 has an easy, unpretentious grandeur – and some damn fine food. The menu is seasonal, but recent options include a perfect (local) scallop po'boy and (local) duck ham pizza.

🛏 Providence Biltmore   Historic Hotel $$

(📞401-421-0700; www.providencebiltmore.com; 11 Dorrance St; r from $169; P🛜) The granddaddy of Providence's hotels, the Biltmore dates to the 1920s. The lobby, both intimate and regal, nicely combines dark wood, twisting staircases and chandeliers, while well-appointed rooms stretch many stories above the old city. Ask for one of the 292 rooms that are on a high floor.

Rhode Island: Coastal Culture

10

After traveling this route along the state's jagged coastline and visiting the islands floating in Narragansett Bay, you will understand why Rhode Island earned the honorable title of Ocean State.

TRIP HIGHLIGHTS

START **1** — **0 miles**

Providence
Explore Rhode Island
School of Design

Wickford

3 — **30 miles**

Narragansett

Charlestown

Westerly

Galilee

Jamestown
Sundowners and the
best sunsets in Rhode
Island

7

FINISH

5

Watch Hill
Millionaire homes and
a yacht-studded bay

111 miles

Block Island
Best for bird-watching
and beach hopping

60 miles

**4 DAYS
111 MILES / 178KM**

GREAT FOR...

BEST TIME TO GO
June to September for
sun, sand and surfing.

 **ESSENTIAL
PHOTO**

The Southeast Light
atop red clay cliffs.

 **BEST FOR
OUTDOORS**

Block Island's 25
miles of trails weave
through wildflowers
and nesting birds.

10 Rhode Island: Coastal Culture

Rhode Island might only take 45 minutes to drive across, but it packs 400 miles of coastline into its tiny boundaries. Much of this takes the form of white sandy beaches, arguably the finest places for ocean swimming in the northeast. Then there are islands to explore, sea cliffs to walk along and isolated lighthouses to frame that perfect sunset shot.

TRIP HIGHLIGHT

① Providence

Rhode Island's capital presents visitors with some fine urban strolling, from Brown University's campus on 18th-century **College Hill** to the city's **Riverwalk** and the historic downtown along Weybosset St. Along the way, visit the **Rhode Island School of Design** (RISD; ☎401-454-6300; www.risd. edu; 20 N Main St), the top art institution in the US and home to the **RISD Museum of Art** (☎401-454-6500; www.risdmuseum.

org; 224 Benefit St; adult/youth $12/3; ⏰10am-5pm Tue-Sun, to 9pm Thu; ♿), with its collection of Roman and Etruscan artifacts, medieval and Renaissance works, and 19th-century French paintings. RISD maintains several fine galleries. **Sol Koffler** (☎401-277-4809; 169 Weybosset St; ⏰noon-5pm Wed-Sat) serves as the main exhibition space for graduate students, while **risd|works** (☎401-277-4949; www.risdworks.com; 10 Westminster St; ⏰10am-5pm Tue-Sun; ♿) offers some of their work for sale.

If you're in town on the third Thursday of the month, you can catch **Gallery Night** (www.gallerynight. info), when 23 galleries and museums open their doors for free viewings.

✖ 🛏 p59, p123, p131

LINK YOUR TRIP

9 **Rhode Island: East Bay**

Head east down RI 114 for a trip back in time to the earliest days of the colony.

12 **Connecticut Wine Trail**

From Westerly, drive west to Stonington on US 1 for a gourmet tour of Connecticut's vineyards and farms.

LOCAL KNOWLEDGE: ALLIE'S

Poll a couple of Rhode Islanders for the state's best souvenir, and one of them will probably say a treat from **Allie's Donuts** (☎401-295-8036; 3661 Quaker Lane/RI 2; ⏰5am-3pm Mon-Fri, 6am-1pm Sat & Sun). Allie has been turning out hot-to-trot homemade doughnuts from her roadside shack on RI 2 for more than 40 years and Rhode Islanders travel from across the state to take them away by the dozen ($7.20). Light as air, they are filled and topped with delectable condiments such as flaked coconut, chocolate and lemon cream, and cherry jelly.

The Drive » Leave Providence via Memorial Blvd and pick up the I-95 S. Meander through the suburbs for 1.5 miles and veer left onto RI 4 S toward North Kingstown. Exit at 7A–7B onto RI 403 east toward Quonset and after a couple of miles turn onto US 1 for Wickford.

----

② Wickford

Bypassed by the era of steamboats and train travel, Wickford's Main St and Pleasant St languished sleepily through the industrial revolution and are still lined with 18th-century Colonial and Federal homes, which lead down to the harbor where fishermen cast their lines off the pier. Rent kayaks from the **Kayak Centre** (www.kayakcentre.com; 9 Phillips St, Waterside Wickford; rental per 2hr $28; ⏰10am-5pm Wed-Mon) for a paddle around the bay.

Then visit the **Old Narragansett Church** (☎401-294-4357; www.stpaulswickford.org; 60 Church Lane; ⏰11am-4pm Thu-Sun Jul & Aug or by appointment). It dates from 1707 and retains its box pews and upstairs gallery where plantation slaves were allowed to worship. Local artist Gilbert Scott (1755–1828), who painted the portrait of George Washington that graces the one-dollar bill, was baptized here in the silver baptismal font.

The Drive » It is a short 4-mile drive along RI 1A S from Wickford to Conanicut Island. Once you're through the Wickford suburbs, take the RI 138 ramp over the Jamestown Bridge, which affords expansive views of the bay. Once on the island, turn right down North Rd to Jamestown past the old smock windmill.

----

③ Jamestown

More rural than its prosperous neighbor, Newport, Jamestown's first inhabitants were Quaker farmers, shepherds and pirates. Captain Kidd spent considerable time here and is said to have buried his treasure hereabouts.

These days, the real treasure in Jamestown is the peace and quiet. The waterfront is undeveloped and you can walk along **Conanicus Avenue** and take a bench overlooking the harbor. The **Jamestown Newport Ferry** (☏401-423-9900; www.jamestownnewportferry. com; Conanicut Marina; return adult/child $24/10; ☺May-Oct) sails to Newport with stops at Fort Adams and Rose Island. It is the best deal going for a harbor tour.

At the southernmost tip of Conanicut Island is **Beavertail State Park**, where you can enjoy one of the best vistas – and sunsets – in the Ocean State. Many vacationers bring lawn chairs, barbecues and picnics, and spend all day enjoying the walking trails and cliff-top views. At the point, picturesque **Beavertail Lighthouse** (☏401-423-3270; www. beavertaillight.org; Beavertail State Park; donations welcome; ☺10am-4:30pm Jun-Sep), one of the oldest along the Atlantic coast, still signals ships into Narragansett Bay.

✗ p131

The Drive ›› Leaving Conanicut Island, head south along the scenic

JIM PHOTOGRAPHY / SHUTTERSTOCK ©

route RI 1A, along which you'll enjoy woodsy roads around Saunderstown and glimpses of the bay as you skirt the shoreline south of Narragansett Pier.

- - - - - - - - - - -

❹ **Narragansett**

Scarborough State Beach (970 Ocean Rd), just south of Narragansett Pier, is one of the state's biggest

beaches and is considered by many the best.

A few miles further south is **Galilee**, the departure point for the **Block Island Express** (☏860-444-4624; www. goblockisland.com) to Block Island. Sometimes called Point Judith in ferry schedules, Galilee is a workaday fishing town. Arrive in time and eat

Jamestown Newport Bridge

at dockside **Champlin's Seafood** (📞401-783-3152; 256 Great Rd; dishes $3-15; 🕐11am-9pm summer, shorter hours rest of year), where they haul the fish right out of the bay onto your plate.

Further south still, the **Roger W Wheeler State Beach** (100 Sand Hill Cove Rd) is a good spot for families with small children. Not only does

it have a playground and other facilities, it also has a very gradual drop-off and little surf. All-day parking in Galilee costs $10 in any of the several lots.

🛏 p131

The Drive ≫ Car-and-passenger ferries run from Galilee State Pier, Point Judith, to Old Harbor, Block Island.

- - - - - - - - - -
TRIP HIGHLIGHT

❺ Block Island

From the deck of the ferry you'll see a cluster of mansard roofs and gingerbread houses rising picturesquely from **Old Harbor**, Block Island's main centre of activity.

Beyond here, the island's attractions are

FANTASTIC UMBRELLA FACTORY

A collection of 19th-century farm buildings and unkempt gardens, the **Fantastic Umbrella Factory** (☎401-364-6616; www.fantasticumbrellafactory.com; 4820 Old Post Rd, Charlestown; ☺10am-6pm), a former commune, got its start as one of Rhode Island's strangest stores in 1968. You can find almost anything in a series of shacks filled with gift items, flowers, toys, handmade jewelry and authentic hippie hemp clothing. Exotic birds and farm animals walk all over the place, much to the delight of children.

simple. Stretching for several miles to the north of Old Harbor is the 3-mile **State Beach**, long enough to find a quiet spot even on a busy day. Otherwise, bike or hike around the island's rolling farmland, pausing to admire the island's lighthouses: **Southeast Light**, set dramatically atop 200ft red clay cliffs, and **North Light** (☺museum 10am-5pm Jun-Labor Day), which stands at the end of a long sandy lane lined with beach roses. In spring and fall, when migratory species fly south along the Atlantic Flyway, bird-watching opportunities abound.

Hire bikes from **Island Moped and Bike Rentals** (☎401-741-2329; www.bimopeds.com; 41 Water St, Old Harbor; bikes/mopeds per day from $20/45; ☺9am-8pm).

✕ ⊨ p131

The Drive » Take the ferry back to Galilee and follow the signs to the main interstate RI 1.

This 20-mile stretch of highway to Westerly is pleasant enough, lined with thick woods and plenty of opportunities to detour to various beaches.

- - - - - - - - - - - - -

❻ Westerly

Westerly sits on Rhode Island's western border, sharing the banks of the Pawcatuck River with Connecticut. In the 19th century it was a town of some wealth, thanks to its high-grade granite quarries. That heyday is long gone, although local **Misquamicut State Beach** still draws the weekending crowds who favor its scenic situation on Winnapaug Pond.

Nearby is the old-fashioned amusement resort of **Atlantic Beach Park** (☎401-322-0504; www.atlanticbeachpark.com; 321-338 Atlantic Ave, Misquamicut), which offers miniature golf, wave rides, batting cages and the like.

✕ ⊨ p131

The Drive » It's a short and scenic 2-mile drive south down RI 1A from the centre of Westerly to the heady heights of mansion-clad Watch Hill. Along the way, enjoy views over Little Narragansett Bay across landscaped lawns and gardens.

- - - - - - - - - - - -

TRIP HIGHLIGHT

❼ Watch Hill

The wealthy summer colony of Watch Hill, with its huge Queen Anne summerhouses, occupies a spit of land at the southwesternmost point of Rhode Island.

Visitors here spend their time at **East Beach**, which stretches for several miles from Watch Hill lighthouse all the way to Misquamicut. (The public access to the beach is located on Bluff Ave near Larkin Rd.) For children, an ice-cream cone and a twirl on the **Flying Horses Carousel** (Bay St; rides $1; ☺11am-9pm Mon-Fri, 10am-9pm Sat & Sun) provide immediate gratification. The antique carousel dates from 1883 and its horses, suspended on chains, really do appear to 'fly' when the carousel spins.

For a leisurely beach walk, the half-mile stroll to **Napatree Point** is unbeatable with the Atlantic on one side and yacht-studded Little Narragansett Bay on the other.

Eating & Sleeping

Providence ❶

✖ Loie Fullers — Modern American $$

(☎401-273-4375; www.loiefullers.com; 1455 Westminster St; mains $15-21; ◎5-11pm Mon-Sat, 10am-2pm & 5-11pm Sun) This wonderfully original, atmospheric little bistro on the outskirts of the Federal Hill neighborhood is an oasis of fun and deliciousness on an otherwise drab trunk road. Inside, candles, ornate polished woods, frescos and art-nouveau elements transport you to another time, another place. On the French-inspired Modern American menu, comfort is king. Somebody had to let the cat outta the bag...

◻ Christopher Dodge House — B&B $$

(☎401-351-6111; www.providence-hotel. com; 11 W Park St; r $129-189; P) This 1858 Federal-style house is furnished with early American reproduction furniture and marble fireplaces. Austere on the outside, it has elegant proportions, large, shuttered windows and wooden floors.

Jamestown ❸

✖ Village Hearth Artisan Bakery — Bakery $

(☎401-423-9282; www.villagehearthbakerycafe. com; 2 Watson Ave; items $4-12; ◎7am-4pm Fri & Sat, 7am-2pm & 4.30-7pm Sun) This low-slung yellow shack is situated a block north of the Jamestown village centre. It houses a community bakery and, on Sundays only, a pizzeria. It's a good pit stop for picnic fare, selling excellent country loaves and pastries. The bakery accepts cash only.

Narragansett ❹

◻ Fishermen's Memorial State Park — Campground $

(☎401-789-8374; www.riparks.com; 1011 Point Judith Rd; tent sites RI residents/nonresidents $14/20; ◎May-Oct) Fishermen's Memorial State Park in Galilee is so popular that many families return year after year to the same site. There are only 180 campsites at Fishermen's, so it's wise to reserve early by requesting the necessary form from the park management or the Division of Parks & Recreation.

Block Island ❺

✖ Eli's — New American $$$

(☎401-466-5230; www.elisblockisland.com; 456 Chapel St, Old Harbor; mains $18-36; ◎from 5:30pm; ◢) The locally caught sea-bass special (tender fillets over scallions, grapes and beans) tastes so fresh and mildly salty and sweet that its memory will haunt you for weeks. For real. The room is cramped, crowded and casual with lots of pine wood and some well-conceived art.

◻ Atlantic Inn — Inn $$$

(☎401-466-5883; www.atlanticinn.com; High St, Old Harbor; d low season from $195-235, high season from $235-360; P) This 1879 establishment commands a gentle perch on a grassy hilltop, with ocean and town vistas. The gracefully appointed Victorian inn features a wide porch, a fine-dining restaurant and Adirondack chairs strewn across a spacious lawn. The 21 rooms vary in size, with some on the small side, but all are quaintly decorated with quilts and lace curtains.

Westerly ❻

✖ Shelter Harbor Inn — Historic Inn $$

(☎401-322-8883; www.shelterharborinn. com; 10 Wagner Rd; mains $14-26; P) Work up an appetite with a stroll along the inn's private beach, then order homey fare such as chicken pie or finnan haddie (smoked haddock). Traditional Rhode Island johnnycakes are always on the menu, too.

◻ Langworthy Farm — B&B $$

(☎401-322-7791; www.langworthyfarm.com; 308 Shore Rd, Westerly; r $130-185; P) Sitting at the head of the beach road to Misquamicut, handsome Langworthy Farm offers comfortable rooms, ocean views and wine tasting in its winery. A full country breakfast is included.

Quiet Corner

11

Known locally as 'the last green valley' between Boston and Washington, Connecticut's Quiet Corner offers some of the loveliest rural scenery in New England.

TRIP HIGHLIGHTS

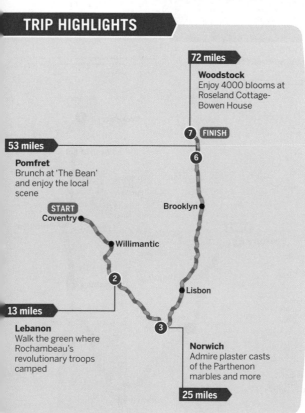

72 miles

Woodstock
Enjoy 4000 blooms at Roseland Cottage-Bowen House

7 **FINISH**

6

53 miles

Pomfret
Brunch at 'The Bean' and enjoy the local scene

START
Coventry

Willimantic

Brooklyn

2

Lisbon

13 miles

Lebanon
Walk the green where Rochambeau's revolutionary troops camped

3

Norwich
Admire plaster casts of the Parthenon marbles and more

25 miles

**3 DAYS
72 MILES / 116KM**

GREAT FOR...

BEST TIME TO GO
June to October for historic home openings.

ESSENTIAL PHOTO
Trumbull's house on Lebanon's village green.

BEST FOR FOODIES
Dinner and wine tasting at Sharpe Hill vineyard.

11 Quiet Corner

The Quiet Corner has the distinction of nurturing state hero Nathan Hale, the patriot-spy from Coventry whose only regret was that he had 'but one life to lose for his country,' and state heroine, abolitionist and Canterbury school teacher Prudence Crandall. Take this trip for a glimpse of New England past, when Washington plotted revolution on Lebanon's Green, and where today, local farms continue to welcome visitors with small-town friendliness.

1 Coventry

Begin where it all began, at the **Nathan Hale Homestead** (☎860-742-6917; www.ctlandmarks.org; 2299 South St, Coventry; adult/child under 6yr $10/free; ⏰11am-4pm Wed & Fri-Sun mid-May–Oct) on the edge of the **Nathan Hale State Forest**. Nathan, whose five brothers also served in the Revolutionary War, was already in the Continental army when his father built this rather fine red clapboard farmhouse in 1776. Inside, period furnishings re-create

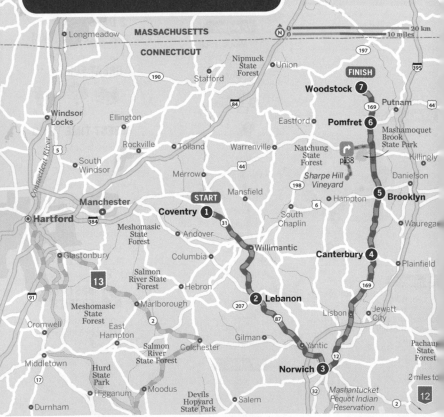

the domestic life of the early colony, along with a display of memorabilia of the schoolteacher turned patriot who was eventually pegged as a spy by the British and hanged at the age of 21. There are also tours of the heirloom gardens, guided walks around the 450-acre estate, Colonial cooking demonstrations and fall lantern tours.

 p139

The Drive >> Sweep round Lake Wangumbaug, past the Nathan Hale Cemetery and onto CT 31, which soon merges with CT 32 southwards. Loop through industrial Willimantic, once home to the American Thread Company and known as 'Thread City,' and stop for barbecued ribs if you're hungry. Cross the bridge, adorned with its giant bullfrogs, and pick up CT 289 south to Lebanon.

LINK YOUR TRIP

12 Connecticut Wine Trail

Meander south down CT 2 to the Jonathan Edwards Winery in North Stonington and join the Connecticut Wine Trail.

13 Lower River Valley

Head 20 miles west from Coventry to Hartford for this trip along the banks of the Connecticut River.

TRIP HIGHLIGHT

2 Lebanon

The best way to get acquainted with Lebanon's mile-long historic **Green** is to take a stroll around it on the walking path. On the eastern side, the butter-yellow **Jonathan Trumbull Jr House** (780 Trumbull Hwy; ⊙ noon-4pm Sat & Sun mid-May–mid-Oct; **P**) was home to Washington's military secretary, who hosted the great general in front of its eight fireplaces in March 1781. On the southwestern side of the Green you'll find **Governor Jonathan Trumbull House** (169 West Town St; ⊙1-6pm Fri, 11-5pm Sat & Sun mid-May–mid-Oct; **P**), the home of Trumbull's father, governor of Connecticut and the only Colonial governor to defy the Crown and support the War of Independence.

Next door, the strange little Palladian clapboard is actually the **Wadsworth Stable**, where Washington's horse stayed. A little beyond that is the two-room **Revolutionary War Office** (www.lebanontownhall.org/war-office.htm; 149 West Town St), where Washington met with Trumbull and the Comte de Rochambeau to coordinate military strategy.

The Drive >> Pick up CT 87 and head south along its leafy route, straight into Norwich. It's a short 11-mile drive.

TRIP HIGHLIGHT

3 Norwich

Money from the Quiet Corner's mills flowed into Norwich, accounting for the handsome Victorian houses set around the **Norwichtown Green**, the gorgeous Second Empire **City Hall** and the unique Romanesque Revival **Slater Memorial Museum** (✆860-887-2506; www.slatermuseum.org; 108 Crescent St, Norwich; adult/child $3/2; ⊙9am-4pm Tue-Fri, 1-4pm Sat & Sun), designed by Stephen Earle in 1886.

The museum was commissioned by William Slater, an educated and well-travelled man who aspired to make the great art of the Classical and Renaissance periods accessible to Norwich's citizens. With this in mind, he commissioned the 227 plaster casts that fill the museum's Beaux Arts interior on his grand tour in 1894–95. Ranging from the Parthenon Marbles to Michelangelo's *Pieta,* the casts were created via a now-illegal process from molds of the original. Visit the exhibit of Slater's grand tour before heading into the museum, which still forms part of the Norwich Free Academy.

 p139

The Drive >> From the Norwichtown Green, head down Washington St and Broadway, past grand Victorian mansions and the architecturally noteworthy City Hall, before picking up N Main St and heading out of town in a northeasterly direction to pick up the National Scenic Byway CT 169. Once en route, the scenery quickly becomes picturesque following low stone walls into deeply rural Canterbury.

JOY BROWN / SHUTTERSTOCK ©

④ Canterbury

Tiny Canterbury was at the forefront of the abolitionist cause some 30 years before the Civil War, thanks to Baptist schoolmistress Prudence Crandall. The **Prudence Crandall House Museum** (☎860-546-7800; http://friendsofprudencecrandall museum.org; 1 South Canterbury Rd; adult/child $6/free; ⊙10am-4pm Thu-Sun May-Nov) was the site of the academy, which Crandall opened in 1831.

When Crandall later accepted Sarah Harris, the daughter of a free African American farmer, among her students in the fall of 1832, many prominent townspeople withdrew their daughters from the school in protest. Rather than give in, Crandall changed her admissions policy and offered schooling to the free African American community. By April 1833, some 20 girls from Boston, Providence, New York and Philadelphia had enrolled. This caused an angry backlash; the school was vandalized, its well poisoned and, in July, Prudence was arrested. When the case against her was finally dismissed on September 9, 1834, the school was set on fire and Prudence reluctantly closed its doors.

The Drive » Leaving Canterbury's clapboard homesteads behind you, continue north on CT 169 to Brooklyn. To your right, sweeping views across paddocks and the distant valley open up and the country road is lined with farmyards and historic Dutch barns.

⑤ Brooklyn

By the time you hit Brooklyn, you're in the heart of the Quiet Corner, where admiring the scenery and stopping in at local farms and ice-cream stalls is the main activity.

Woodstock Roseland Cottage-Bowen House

First stop is the **Creamery Brook Bison Farm** (860-779-0837; www. creamerybrookbison.net; 19 Purvis Rd, Brooklyn; ☺hours vary, phone ahead), where you can take the equivalent of a Quiet Corner safari among the bison herd before stocking up at the farm shop: phone ahead so staff know you're coming. Next,

proceed to the **Meadow Stone Farm Shoppe** (☎860-774-4500; www.meadow stonefarm.com; 199 Hartford Rd, Brooklyn; ☺Mar-Dec, hours vary), where everything, from the goat's milk and cheeses to the specialty skin care products, is produced on the farm or with produce from the farm. If you want to see the soaps and cheeses

being made, call ahead to find out about production times.

✗ p139

The Drive ᐵ On your way out of Brooklyn, you'll pass the access road to the Golden Lamb Buttery on your left. Continue along CT 169, beneath the leafy canopy that creates the impression of driving through a verdant green tunnel. You'll pass fruit orchards on your right,

DETOUR:
SHARPE HILL VINEYARD

Start: ❻ Pomfret

In nearby **Abington**, up a winding country road buried deep in the forest, you'll find the Quiet Corner's most scenic vineyard, **Sharpe Hill** (☎860-974-3549; http://sharpehill.com; 108 Wade Rd, Pomfret; tastings $10-15; ⊙11am-5pm Fri-Sun). It's also arguably Connecticut's finest vineyard, with more than 250 medals for its signature Chardonnay Ballet of Angels and its St Croix Cabernet Franc. To appreciate the beautiful setting, consider spending the day here, walking up through the vineyard for spectacular views, tasting wine on the patio and then sitting down to a gourmet farm-to-table lunch or dinner in the gracious Fireside Tavern.

which belong to Lapsley Orchard farm, where you can PYO in season.

TRIP HIGHLIGHT

❻ Pomfret

With its expansive Colonial homes and hearty restaurants, Pomfret is considered the heart of the Quiet Corner, and is where many visitors choose to base themselves. Farming lives on in the vineyards, nurseries and orchards that surround it, while legends live on in **Mashamoquet Brook State Park** (☎860-928-6121; www.ct.gov/deep/mashamoquetbrook; 147 Wolf Den Dr, Pomfret Center). Here, local hero Israel Putnam, who led the troops at Bunker Hill in Boston, is said to have crawled into the den of a she-wolf that was ravaging local sheep, and shot it.

To follow in his footsteps, take the trail past the campground to Wolf Den. You can then continue on a 5-mile loop through thick woodland. Take a swimming costume along if you fancy bathing in the shallow pond.

🍴 🛏 p139

The Drive » The final stretch of CT 169 from Pomfret to Woodstock continues past farmland and the Roseland Lake, up through the modern buildings and grassy playing fields of South Woodstock, before arriving in Woodstock proper.

TRIP HIGHLIGHT

❼ Woodstock

The **Roseland Cottage-Bowen House** (☎860-928-4074; www.historicnewengland.org; 556 Rte 169; adult/student $10/5; ⊙11am-5pm Wed-Sun Jun 1-Oct 15) is proof that wealthy Americans had fancy summer homes even in the mid-1800s.

Beautifully preserved, this lovely Gothic Revival house sports pointed arches, crockets and stained-glass windows.

The garden is also a historic treasure, laid out according to the 1850 plan with some 4000 blooms bordered by formal boxwood parterres. Other follies include an aviary, a summerhouse, an icehouse and a vintage bowling alley.

After a stroll around the garden, head down to **Woodstock Orchards** (☎860-928-2225; 494 CT 169, Woodstock; ⊙9am-6pm) for a glass of fresh cider and to stock up on apples and berries before heading home. If you're in town around Labor Day, be sure to check out the enormous **Woodstock Fair** (www.woodstockfair.com; 281 Rte 169; adult/child $12/free; ⊙early Sep; 👪).

🍴 🛏 p139

Eating & Sleeping

Coventry ❶

🛏 Daniel Rust House   B&B $$

(☏860-742-0032; www.thedanielrusthouse.com; 2011 Main St; d $120-185; 🅿 😊 📶)
Serving travelers since 1800, the four period rooms brim with history. The finest is the Anna White room with its antique canopy bed, although the Mary Rose has a secret closet that was used to hide slaves traveling to freedom on the Underground Railroad.

Norwich ❸

🛏 Spa at Norwich Inn   Inn $$$

(☏860-425-3500; www.thespaatnorwichinn.com; 607 West Thames St; d/ste from $205/305; 🅿 📶 🏊) Set in 42 acres of woodland near the Public Golf Course, Norwich's elegant Georgian spa offers 36 treatment rooms, indoor and outdoor pools, tennis and golf. Be sure to book a room in the main house overlooking the flowering gardens.

Brooklyn ❺

🍴 Golden Lamb Buttery   Modern American $$$

(☏860-774-4423; www.thegoldenlamb.com; 499 Wolf Den Rd; mains lunch $12-17, prix-fixe dinner $75; ⏱noon-2.30pm Thu-Sat, 7pm sitting Fri & Sat; 🅿 🚹) Stop in for an atmosphere aplenty farm-to-table lunch, or, better still, dress to impress (jacket and tie for gents, please) and book ahead for the limited sitting, award-winning, prix-fixe, four-course gourmet dinner, with appetizers and a hayride thrown in.

Pomfret ❻

🍴 Vanilla Bean Cafe   Modern American $$

(www.thevanillabeancafe.com; 450 West Rd; mains $6.50-16; ⏱7am-3pm Mon & Tue, to 8pm Wed-Sun; 🚹) Families, cyclists and Sunday drivers regularly make the pilgrimage to 'The Bean' for creative casual dining, live music and artful surroundings.

🍴 We-Li-Kit Ice Cream   Ice Cream $

(☏860-974-1095; www.welikit.com; 728 Hampton Rd, Pomfret Center; scoops from $3.50; ⏱11am-8pm Apr-Oct; 🚹) Sit at trestle tables and slurp sundaes and homemade, farm-fresh ice cream with holidaymakers and locals. There's a bunch of wacky and wonderful flavors to choose from.

🛏 Chickadee Cottage   B&B $$$

(☏806-963-0587; 70 Averill Rd, Pomfret Center; cottages $175-210; 🅿 🐾) The spacious Carriage House here has its own deck, kitchenette and separate entrance, while the Lower Nest sleeps four. It also sits on the edge of the 500-acre Audubon preserve and neighbors the Air Line State Park scenic hiking and biking path.

Woodstock ❼

🍴 Mrs Bridge's Pantry   Tearoom $

(☏860-963-7040; 292 Rte 169, South Woodstock; items $4.50, tea service $14.50; ⏱11am-5pm; 🚹) Sit down to English tea with crumpets, scones and clotted cream in this quaint wooden teashop. Tea comes served in china cups and there's a light menu of British classics, such as beans on toast and ploughman's lunch.

🛏 Taylor's Corner   B&B $$

(☏888-974-0490; www.taylorsbb.com; 880 Rte 171; d from $105; 🅿 ❄ 📶) Taylor's Corner has just three antique-filled rooms overlooking lovely perennial-planted gardens. Features include real wood-burning fireplaces, wide-plank floorboards and curious beehive ovens.

Connecticut Wine Trail

12

Connecticut has established itself as a serious wine-growing region. Combine this vineyard tour of some of the best producers with gourmet dining in Greenwich and New Haven's stellar galleries.

TRIP HIGHLIGHTS

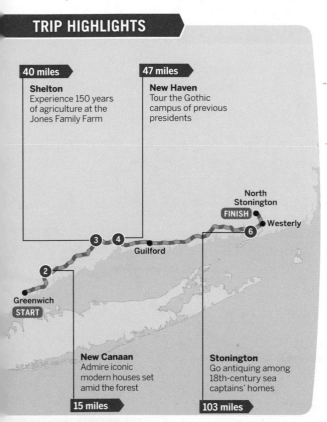

40 miles

Shelton
Experience 150 years of agriculture at the Jones Family Farm

47 miles

New Haven
Tour the Gothic campus of previous presidents

North Stonington
FINISH

Westerly

6

3 **4**

Guilford

2

Greenwich
START

New Canaan
Admire iconic modern houses set amid the forest

15 miles

Stonington
Go antiquing among 18th-century sea captains' homes

103 miles

---

5 DAYS
114 MILES / 183KM

GREAT FOR...

BEST TIME TO GO
August to October for the grape harvest.

ESSENTIAL PHOTO
Philip Johnson's glass cube amid the trees.

BEST FOR OUTDOORS
Picnicking at the Jonathan Edwards Winery.

---

12 Connecticut Wine Trail

Starting on Connecticut's moneyed Gold Coast, this tour wends its way between vineyards to encompass the compact downtown of Greenwich, with its high-end shops and notable museums; Philip Johnson's radical mid-century modern Glass House in New Canaan; and New Haven's neo-Gothic turrets. At its northern reaches, Stonington's 19th-century sea captains' homes cluster amid maritime vineyards, which produce some of the state's finest drops.

❶ Greenwich

In the early days, Greenwich was home to farmers and fishermen who shipped oysters and potatoes to nearby New York. But with the advent of passenger trains and the first cashed-up commuters, the town became a haven for Manhattanites in search of country exclusivity. Along **Greenwich Avenue**, high-end boutiques and gourmet restaurants line the route where the town's trolley once traveled.

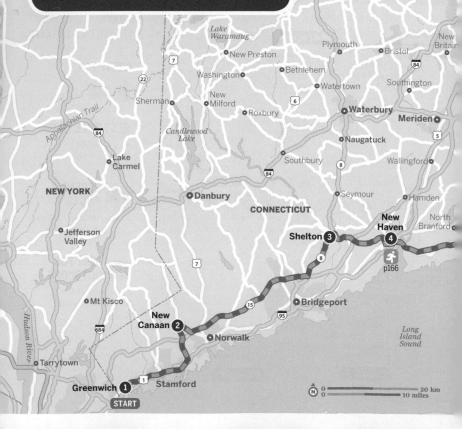

One of Greenwich's wealthiest 19th-century inhabitants was Robert Moffat Brucc, a textile tycoon who lived in what is now the **Bruce Museum** (☎203-869-0376; www. brucemuseum.org; 1 Museum Dr; adult/student & senior $7/6; ☺10am-5pm Tue-Sun). Now a variety of galleries house a natural science collection and a permanent display of impressionist works by the Cos Cob art colony, as well as hosting more than a dozen art exhibits a year.

✕ p147

The Drive » Head northeast along I-95, parallel to US 1, the old Boston–New York post road, until you come to the steel-and-glass towers of metropolitan Stamford. Then take exit 9 onto CT 106 and head inland through the suburbs to New Canaan.

TRIP HIGHLIGHT

❷ New Canaan

The only Gold Coast town without a shore-line, New Canaan is characterized by large

LINK YOUR TRIP

1 Coastal New England

From Stonington, continue north along I-95 across the Jamestown Bridge to Newport for more salty coastal scenery.

11 Quiet Corner

Continue north along scenic CT 169 to Canterbury for a laid-back tour of the Quiet Corner.

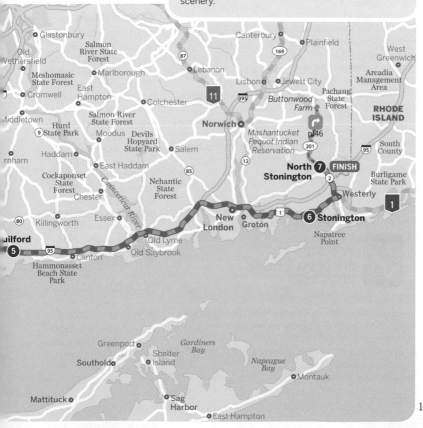

clapboard houses, grand Georgian mansions and, unusually, one of the most famous modern houses in the world: the 1949 **Philip Johnson Glass House** (📞866-811-4111; http://theglasshouse.org; 199 Elm St, New Canaan; tours from $25; 🕐11am-6pm Thu-Mon May 1-Nov 30). This icon of mid-century modern architecture, set in a dappled wood on 47 acres, was the home of late Pritzker Prize–winner Philip Johnson, and his art collector partner, David Whitney.

Almost totally transparent, the house offers stunning views of the autumnal countryside and Johnson's intriguing collection of contemporary art. Guided tours must be reserved; visitors assemble at the visitors centre across the street from the New Canaan train station. In addition to the house, the tour includes a look at Da Monsta, the concrete-and-Styrofoam gatehouse to the property.

🍴 p147

TOP TIP: FINDING THOSE WINERIES

It's worth bearing in mind that most wineries are tucked away down country roads, and finding your way can often be a challenge. A useful resource is the *Connecticut Wine Trail* (www.ctwine.com) brochure, which covers all the wineries in the state along with detailed driving directions.

The Drive » Leave bucolic New Canaan via CT 123 S and after 2 miles merge with the CT 15. Head north toward New Haven, skirting the suburbs of Norwalk, Westport and Trumbull, then take exit 8 onto CT 8 toward Waterbury. After 6 miles you'll arrive in Shelton.

TRIP HIGHLIGHT

❸ Shelton

Nestled in the White Hills of Shelton you'll find the 150-year-old, 400-acre **Jones Family Farm** (📞203-929-8425; www.jonesfamilyfarms.com; 606 Walnut Tree Hill Rd; 🕐10am-5.30pm Mon-Sat, 11am-5.30pm Sun mid-Dec–mid-Nov, noon-5pm Mon-Fri mid-Nov–mid-Dec), home of one of the premier wineries in the state. Jones Winery is known for using its own grapes or those from local vineyards. The vineyard's founder and resident winemaker, Jamie Jones, is now the sixth generational family member to operate the farm.

Aside from the winery and tasting room, there's berry picking in summer, a Heritage Farm Hike

in June, pumpkins and hayrides in fall and, of course, Christmas trees in November and December. You can also sign up for cooking classes and wine-education suppers at the Harvest Kitchen studio. Check the website for details.

The Drive » Rejoin CT 8 and cross the Housatonic River before taking exit 15 onto CT 34. After less than a mile, take the ramp onto CT 15 N, which weaves through New Haven's exclusive golf greens for 4 miles. Then take exit 59 onto CT 69 S, which takes you right into the center of New Haven.

TRIP HIGHLIGHT

❹ New Haven

New Haven is home to America's third-oldest university, Yale, and its leafy green is bordered by graceful Colonial buildings, statehouses and churches. The 1816 **Trinity Church** resembles England's Gothic York Minster, while the Georgian-style, 1812 **Center Church on the Green** is a fine example of New England Palladian. But nowhere is the city's history more palpable than at **Yale University** (📞203-432-2300; www.yale.edu/visitor; cnr Elm & Temple Sts; 🕐 visitor center 9am-4:30pm Mon-Fri, 11am-4pm Sat & Sun).

Pick up a free map of the campus from **Yale University Visitor Center** (📞203-432-2300; http://visitorcenter.yale.edu; 149 Elm

Stonington Jonathan Edwards Winery

St; ⊙9am-4:30pm Mon-Fri, 11am-4pm Sat & Sun) and take a stroll around the stately buildings, where alumni such as Presidents William H Taft, George HW Bush and Bill Clinton once studied.

In more recent years, New Haven has also built a reputation for itself as an arts mecca.

✗ 🛏 p39, p59, p147

The Drive ›› The 14-mile drive east from New Haven to Guilford is easy but uneventful. The highlight is crossing the New Haven harbor bridge before rejoining I-95 through the conurbations of East Haven and Branford before reaching Guilford.

⑤ Guilford

In the historic seaside town of Guilford, **Bishop's Orchards Winery** (☑203-453-2338; www.bishops orchards.com; 1355 Boston Post Rd; ⊙10am-7pm Mon-Sat, 11am-6pm Sun; 🚻) has been serving shoreline communities with fresh produce since 1871. Much more than just a winery, Bishop's is also a pick-your-own farm, where berries, peaches, pears, apples and pumpkins can be picked from June through October. The rich variety of produce means the Bishop's **market** (⊙year-round) is one of the

best in the area. If you have kids, they'll get a kick out of the llamas, alpacas and grazing goats.

The coastline around Guilford is wonderful, but much of it is built up. However, the nearby **Hammonasset Beach State Park** (☑203-245-2785; www.ct.gov/deep/ham monasset; 1288 Boston Post Rd; residents $9-13, nonresidents $15-22; ⊙8am-sunset; 🅿) provides a 1100-acre oasis, with a 2-mile pine-backed beach, boardwalk trails and excellent facilities for camping, picnicking and swimming.

✗ p147

DETOUR:
BUTTONWOOD FARM

Start: ❼ North Stonington

Beginning as early as mid-July, an astonishing number of interactive corn mazes begin cropping up on farms throughout New England. Travel north up CT 201 and you can get lost in the themed maze at **Buttonwood Farm** (📞860-376-4081; www. buttonwoodfarmicecream.com; 471 Shetucket Turnpike, Griswold; ⏰noon-9pm Mar-Oct; 👫), pick pumpkins from their patches, take hayrides and finish up with some of the farm's delicious homemade ice cream. In October, the maze is also open for night-time adventures – if you dare!

The Drive » Leave I-95 and pick up the old post road, US 1. This takes you through genteel Madison to the marshy doorstep of Hammonasset Beach State Park. Stop for a stroll or a picnic, then continue on US 1 for another 6 miles before rejoining I-95 for the remaining 28 miles to Stonington.

TRIP HIGHLIGHT

❻ Stonington

Stonington is one of the most appealing towns on the Connecticut coast. Compactly laid out on a peninsula, the town offers complete streetscapes of 18th- and 19th-century houses, many of which were once sea captains' homes.

The main thoroughfare, **Water Street**, features shops selling antiques and Quimper porcelain, colorfully painted dinnerware handmade in France since the 17th-century. At the southern end is the 'point,' with a park, a lighthouse and a tiny beach.

Situated on Stonington's south-facing slopes, **Stonington Vineyards** (📞860-535-1222; www. stoningtonvineyards.com; 523 Taugwonk Rd; tasting/tour $12/free; ⏰11am-5pm) produces some of the state's finest table wines, thanks to its glacial soils and maritime climate not unlike that of Bordeaux in France. As a result, you can expect creamy Chardonnays and award-winning Cabernet Franc.

🍴 🛏 p147

The Drive » Exit Stonington on US 1, which takes you through some very pretty rural countryside lightly dotted with handsome country homes. At Westerly, turn northward on US 2 for a further 5 miles, before turning right on Main St and heading into North Stonington.

❼ North Stonington

Heading northward away from the coast, you arrive at one of the most picturesque and scenically situated vineyards on the tour, the **Jonathan Edwards Winery** (📞860-535-0202; www.jedwards winery.com; 74 Chester Maine Rd, North Stonington; tastings $10-15; ⏰11am-5pm daily May-Dec, Wed-Sun Jan-Apr) in North Stonington. Housed in a lovingly renovated dairy barn on a hilltop overlooking the Atlantic, it is the perfect spot for a late-afternoon BYO picnic and wine tasting.

In winter, oenophiles warm themselves around the stone fireplace in the wood-paneled tasting room, while the knowledgeable and enthusiastic staff talk through a variety of wines, both from the Connecticut coast and the Edwards vineyards in Napa, CA.

Eating & Sleeping

Greenwich ❶

✕ Meli-Melo   Creperie $$

(☎203-629-6153; www.melimelogreenwich.com;
362 Greenwich Ave; crepes $8-16; ⏱7am-10pm
Mon-Fri, 8am-10pm Sat & Sun) For a quick and
delicious bite, you can't do better than Meli-Melo.
Meaning 'hodge-podge' in French, Meli-Melo
serves salads, soups and sandwiches, but its
specialty is undoubtedly buckwheat crepes. Try a
wild combination such as smoked salmon, chive
sauce, lemon and daikon ($11). The French onion
and French lentil soups are, appropriately, superb.

New Canaan ❷

✕ Sole   Italian $$

(☎203-972-8887; www.zhospitalitygroup.
com/sole; 105 Elm St; mains $14-28; ⏱noon-
9:30pm Mon-Sat, from 5pm Sun) Sit at the
marble-topped bar with a glass of Pinot Grigio
and watch the chef prepare wood-fired pizzas
and northern Italian dishes, such as Tuscan
bread salad or handmade potato gnocchi with
sausage, mushrooms and basil.

New Haven ❹

✕ Union
League Café   Modern French $$$

(☎203-562-4299; http://unionleaguecafe.
com; 1032 Chapel St; mains $23-38; ⏱11:30am-
9:30pm Mon-Sat) An upscale French bistro in the
historic Union League building. Expect a menu
featuring continental classics such as *cocotte de
joues de veau* (organic veal cheeks with sautéed
wild mushrooms; $25) along with nouvelle
cuisine. If your budget is tight, try a sinful dessert
like *crêpe soufflé au citron* (lemon crepes) washed
down with a glass from the exquisite wine list.

✕ ZINC   Modern American $$$

(☎203-624-0507; www.zincfood.com; 964
Chapel St; mains $12-28; ⏱noon-2:30pm & 5-9pm
Tue-Fri, 5-10pm Sat & Mon) Whenever possible,
this trendy bistro's ingredients hail from local
organic sources, but the chef draws inspiration
from all over, notably Asia and the Southwest.

There's a constantly changing 'market menu,' but
for the most rewarding experience, share several
of the small plates for dinner, such as the smoked
duck nachos or the *prosciutto Americano crostini.*
Reservations are advised.

⊨ Study at Yale   Hotel $$$

(☎203-503-3900; www.studyatyale.com; 1157
Chapel St; r from $209; P 🛜) The Study at
Yale manages to evoke a mid-century modern
sense of sophistication (call it '*Mad Men* chic')
without being over-the-top or intimidating. Ultra-
contemporary touches include in-room iPod
docking stations and cardio machines with built-
in TV. There's also an in-house restaurant and
cafe, where you can stumble for morning snacks.

Guilford ❺

✕ The Place Restaurant   Seafood $

(☎203-453-9276; www.theplaceguilford.com;
901 Boston Post Rd/US 1; mains $8-14; ⏱5-9pm
Mon-Fri, 1-10pm Sat & Sun Apr-Oct) Drive in, snag
a tree stump for a stool, crack open the cold beer
or wine you've brought with you and order up a
feast of littleneck clams, lobsters and charred
corn on the cob from the open-air fire pit.

Stonington ❻

✕ Noah's   Cafe $$

(☎860-535-3925; www.noahsfinefood.com; 113
Water St; mains $12-27; ⏱7.45am-9pm Tue-Sun;
👶) Noah's is a popular, informal place, with two
small rooms topped with original stamped-tin
ceilings. It's famous for its seafood (especially
chowder and scallops) and pastries, including
mouthwatering apple-spice and sour-cream
coffee cakes. Lunchtime is a family-friendly
affair, while dinner is more formal. Book ahead
at weekends.

⊨ Orchard Street Inn   B&B $$$

(☎860-535-2681; www.orchardstreetinn.
com; 41 Orchard St; d from $205-250; 🛜) This
unpretentious five-room inn is both quiet and
elegant, within easy walking distance of the
town center. Free use of bicycles is provided for
jaunts around town. There's a minimum two-
night stay on weekends.

Lower River Valley

13

From its spring-fed source near the Canadian border, the Connecticut River cuts a 410-mile trail southeast. Tour the valley for a glimpse of the state's first settlers and holidaying industrialists.

TRIP HIGHLIGHTS

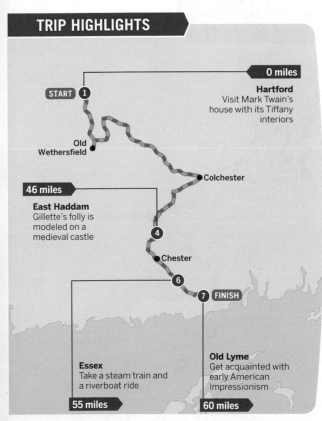

0 miles

START ①

Hartford
Visit Mark Twain's house with its Tiffany interiors

Old Wethersfield

● Colchester

46 miles

East Haddam
Gillette's folly is modeled on a medieval castle

④

● **Chester**

⑥

⑦ **FINISH**

Essex
Take a steam train and a riverboat ride

55 miles

Old Lyme
Get acquainted with early American Impressionism

60 miles

**4 DAYS
60 MILES / 96KM**

GREAT FOR...

BEST TIME TO GO
September to February for cruising and eagle-spotting.

 ESSENTIAL PHOTO
William Gillette's ruined Gothic folly.

 BEST FOR FAMILIES
Enjoy the summer steam train in Essex.

13 | Lower River Valley

Once the engine of 19th-century commerce, the Connecticut River — New England's longest waterway — now enchants visitors with its historic towns, artist colonies, nature conservancies and gracious country inns. River cruises and steam train rides allow for authentic glimpses into provincial Connecticut life. Even Hartford, the state capital, is rediscovering the river these days with new parks and walkways landscaped along its banks.

TRIP HIGHLIGHT

❶ Hartford

Despite the exodus of the insurance companies that earned Hartford its reputation as the 'filing cabinet of America,' those passing through will be surprised at how much the city has to offer. The standout **Wadsworth Atheneum** (☎860-278-2670; www. thewadsworth.org; 600 Main St; adult/child $15/5; ⏱11am-5pm Wed-Fri, from 10am Sat & Sun) houses 40,000 pieces of art in a castle-like

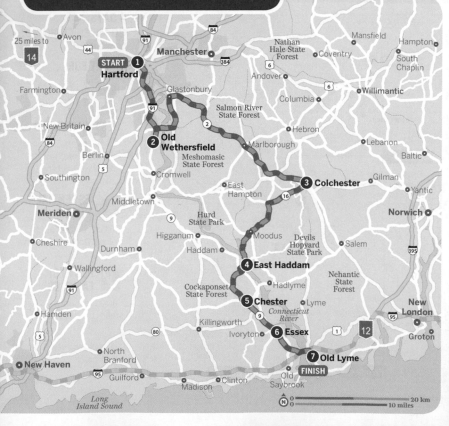

Gothic Revival building. These include some by Hartford native Frederic Church, alongside 19th-century impressionist works and a small but outstanding collection of surrealist art.

Other notable sites include **Mark Twain House** (860-247-0998; www.marktwainhouse.org; 351 Farmington Ave, parking at 385 Farmington Ave; adult/child $19/11; ⏰9:30am-5:30pm, closed Tue Jan-Mar; P), where novelist Samuel Langhorne Clemens (1835–1910) spent 17 years of his life writing the *Adventures of Tom Sawyer* and *Huckleberry Finn*. Architect Edward Tuckerman Potter embellished the house with turrets and gables, and some of the interiors were styled by Louis Comfort Tiffany. Next door to the Twain house is **Harriet Beecher**

LINK YOUR TRIP

 12 Connecticut Wine Trail

Travel west to Guilford along I-95 for a taste of Connecticut's Cabernet Sauvignon and New Haven culture.

 14 Litchfield Hills Loop

Head into the hills on US 44 for bucolic rural views, market towns and gourmet eats.

LOCAL KNOWLEDGE: WILD BILL'S NOSTALGIA CENTER

About 10 miles south of **Old Wethersfield** on the outskirts of Middletown, in the middle of nowhere significant, you'll find the wacky **Wild Bill's Nostalgia Center** (🎧860-635-1226; www.wildbillsonline.com; 1003 Newfield St, Middletown; ⏰10am-6pm). It's part museum, part curiosity barn filled with tons of mid-20th-century to present-day pop collectibles, knickknacks, junk, fun stuff, eccentric characters and even a homemade theme park under construction! Have a yarn with Wild Bill if he's in the house.

Stowe House (🎧860-522-9258; www.harrietbeecherstowe.org; 77 Forest St; adult/child $14/8; ⏰9:30am-5pm Mon-Sat, noon-5pm Sun; P). Built in 1871, the house reflects Stowe's ideas about decorating and domestic efficiency, which she expressed in her bestseller *American Woman's Home*. Stowe is most famous for her antislavery book, *Uncle Tom's Cabin*.

✗ p155

The Drive » Exit Hartford along Capitol Ave and Hudson, and merge onto the Colin Whitehead Hwy. Join I-91 S for a short 3.5-mile drive through Hartford's suburbs before taking exit 26 for Old Wethersfield.

➋ Old Wethersfield

A quick jaunt down I-91 will bring you to the historic district of Old Wethersfield. Despite sitting in the larger Hartford suburbs, Old Wethersfield is a living monument to the past, perfectly pre-served for more than 375 years. Wander around and you'll find hundreds of historic homes, as well as a number of interesting museums. The best way to get your bearings, however, is to start at the **Wethersfield Museum** (🎧860-529-7656; http://wethersfieldhistory.org; 200 Main St, Wethersfield; ⏰10am-4pm Tue-Sat, 1-4pm Sun).

The Drive » Accommodations in Hartford and Old Wethersfield tend to be underwhelming, expensive and business oriented. It's far better to push on across the river, via CT 3 N. The pretty, historic town of Glastonbury has some great B&B options (p155). From there, continue along CT 2 toward Colchester.

➌ Colchester

Rural Colchester, with its grazing fields and serried ranks of vines, is a certified Community Wildlife Habitat and listed on the National Register of Historic Places. However, the real reason to come to

Colchester is so you can visit **Cato Corner Farm** (📞860-537-3884; www.catocornerfarm.com; 178 Cato Corner Rd; 🕑10am-4pm Fri-Sun), where mother-and-son cheese makers Elizabeth and Mark craft dozens of aged farmhouse cheeses with raw milk from their herd of Jersey cows. Many of the cheeses, such as the Dairyere (a firm washed-rind cheese), are prizewinners.

Near the cheese shop is the notable **Priam Vineyards** (📞860-267-8520; www.priamvineyards.com; 11 Shailor Hill Rd; 🕑11am-6pm Wed-Sun mid-Mar–Dec), a 24-acre, solar-powered, sustainable vineyard growing French and American varieties, such as Cabernet Sauvignon, Riesling, Merlot, Cayuga and St Croix. In summer, visitors can take self-guided tours of the vineyards, picnic amid the vines and even enjoy live music concerts.

The Drive >> Leaving the interstate, turn southwest along Middletown Rd (CT 16) through farmland and alongside Babcock Pond until you reach CT 149, where you turn left and head directly south back toward the river. This part of the drive passes pleasantly through rural communities and historic towns along tree-lined roads.

- - - - - - - - - - - -

TRIP HIGHLIGHT
④ East Haddam

Looming on one of the Seven Sisters hills just above East Haddam is

Gillette Castle (📞860-526-2336; www.ct.gov/dep/gillette castle; 67 River Rd; adult/child $6/2; 🕑castle 10am-4:30pm late May–mid-Oct, grounds 8am-dusk year-round; 🅿), a turreted mansion made of fieldstone. Built in 1919 by eccentric actor William Gillette, who made his fortune in the role of Sherlock Holmes, the folly is modeled on the medieval castles of Germany's Rhineland and the views from its terraces are spectacular. The surrounding 125 acres are a designated state park and open year-round, but the interior is only open for tours from late May through mid-October.

With residents such as Gillette and banker William Goodspeed, East Haddam became a regular stopover on the summer circuit for New Yorkers, who traveled up on Goodspeed's steamship. To entertain them, he built the **Goodspeed Opera House** (📞860-873-8668; www.goodspeed.org; 6 Main St; tickets $45-70; 🕑performances Wed-Sun Apr-Dec) in 1876. It's now dedicated to preserving and developing American musicals, and you can still enjoy your intermission drinks on the balcony overhanging the river.

The Drive >> From East Haddam, cross the Connecticut River via the steel swing bridge and meander southeast through rural countryside for about 5 miles before merging with I-9 S

toward Old Saybrook. After 1.5 miles, take exit 6 for Chester.

- - - - - - - - - - - -

⑤ Chester

Cupped in the valley of Pattaconk Brook, Chester is one of the most charming river towns along the Connecticut River. Its quaint Main St is lined with good restaurants and thriving galleries and workshops, and most visitors come to simply browse the antique shops and indulge in some fine dining.

The **Connecticut River Artisans** (📞860-526-5575; www.ctriverartisans.org; 4 Water St; 🕑11am-5:30pm Tue-Sat, until 3pm Sun) co-operative offers one-of-a-kind craft pieces, including jewelry, pottery, folk art and clothing. Otherwise, drop in to have a coffee at local provender **Simon's Marketplace** (📞860-526-8984; www.simonsmarketplacechester.com; 17 Main St; items from $4; 🕑8am-6pm; 🖉 🚼) and pick up some tasty deli treats.

🍴 p155

The Drive >> Rejoin I-9 for the short 6-mile hop to Essex.

- - - - - - - - - - - -

TRIP HIGHLIGHT
⑥ Essex

Handsome, tree-lined Essex, established in 1635, features well-preserved Federal-period homes, legacies of rum and tobacco fortunes made in the 19th century. Today the town prides itself

Hartford Mark Twain House

TOP TIP: CHESTER–HADLYME FERRY

In summer you can cross the Connecticut River on the **Chester–Hadlyme Ferry** (www.ctvisit.com/listings/chesterhadlyme-ferry; car/pedestrian $5/2; ⊙7am-6:45pm Mon-Fri, 10:30am-5pm Sat & Sun Apr-Nov). The five-minute river crossing on the *Selden III* is the second-oldest ferry service in America, beginning in 1769. The ferry ride affords great views of Gillette Castle and is a fun way to link up with the Essex Steam Train, which runs between Chester and Essex.

on the oldest-known continuously operating waterfront in the country. That, and the **Connecticut River Museum** (☎860-767-8267; www.ctrivermuseum.org; 67 Main St; adult/child $9/6; ⊙10am-5pm Jun 1-Oct 10, Tue-Sun Oct 10-Jun 1; P ♿), next to the Steamboat Dock, where exhibits recount the area's history, including a replica of the world's first submarine, the *American Turtle*, built by Yale student David Bushnell in 1776.

The best way to experience the river is to take the **Essex Steam Train & Riverboat Ride** (☎860-767-0103; www.essexsteamtrain.com; 1 Railroad Ave; adult/child $19/10, incl cruise $29/19; ⊙May-Oct, dates vary; ♿), which transports you to Deep River on a steam train

and then runs you up to the Goodspeed Opera House at East Haddam in a riverboat. The train trip takes about an hour; with the riverboat ride, the excursion takes 2½ hours. In February look out for eagle-watching cruises, as bald eagles migrate to the river valley for the winter.

✖ 🛏 p89, p155

The Drive » For the final leg of the trip, rejoin I-9 for an uneventful drive south. Just the other side of the highway, Ivoryton offers some good accommodation options. Leave I-9 at exit 70 onto CT 156 E, which will loop round onto Shore Rd. Then follow the signs into Old Lyme.

- - - - - - - - - - - - -

TRIP HIGHLIGHT

➐ Old Lyme

Since the early 20th century, Old Lyme has

been the center of the Lyme Art Colony, which embraced and cultivated the nascent American impressionist movement. Numerous artists, including William Chadwick, Childe Hassam, Willard Metcalfe and Henry Ward Ranger, came here to paint, staying in the mansion of local art patron Florence Griswold.

Her house, which her artist friends decorated with murals (often in lieu of paying rent), is now the **Florence Griswold Museum** (☎860-434-4452; http://florencegriswoldmuseum.org; 96 Lyme St; adult/child $10/free; ⊙10am-5pm Tue-Sat, 1-5pm Sun; P) and contains a fine selection of both impressionist and Barbizon paintings. The estate consists of her Georgian-style house, the Krieble Gallery, the Chadwick studio and Griswold's beloved gardens. The neighboring **Lyme Academy of Fine Arts** (☎860-434-5232; www.lymeacademy.edu; 84 Lyme St; ⊙10am-4pm Mon-Sat) features rotating drawing, painting and sculpture exhibits by students.

🛏 p155

Eating & Sleeping

Hartford ❶

✖ Max Downtown — American $$$

(☎860-522-2530; www.maxrestaurantgroup.com/downtown; 185 Asylum St; mains $21-49; ⊙11:30am-2:30pm & 5-10pm Mon-Fri, 5-10pm Sat & Sun) With its swinging tunes, 'pre-Prohibition' cocktails and retro-luxe look, this is downtown's new hot spot for the professional and political classes. The menu includes classic chophouse fare, such as coffee-rubbed 'cowboy cut' beef-rib chop and peach-glazed sockeye salmon. Bookings are advisable.

Glastonbury ❷

✖ Plan B — Burgers $$

(☎860-430-9737; www.burgersbeerbourbon.com; 120 Hebron Ave, Glastonbury; mains $8-16; ⊙11:30am-midnight) The Glastonbury branch of this Connecticut burger chain is a rowdy joint with a cabinet of bourbons behind the bar, televised football games and red-leather booths. The burgers are 100% organic beef and come in a bewildering array of options. For the full blow-out, try one with truffle chips.

⊨ Connecticut River Valley Inn — B&B $$$

(☎860-633-7374; www.crvinn.com; 2195 Main St, Glastonbury; d from $220; P ❋ ⊜) This large Colonial clapboard sits proudly on Glastonbury's Main St and offers four handsome bedrooms, artfully decorated by host Pat Brubaker. But the best bit is the sumptuous homemade breakfast, which features baked muffins and lavender scones straight out of the oven, pancakes and hot salmon quiche.

Chester ❺

✖ Good Elephant Bistro — Vietnamese, French $$

(☎860-526-5301; www.goodelephantcafe.com; 59 Main St; meals $17-28; ⊙5-9pm Tue-Sun) In 2016 Chester's lauded L&E French bistro merged with the Good Elephant to expand its repertoire of contemporary French cuisine with aromatic French-Vietnamese dishes. It works. Come on Sunday for Vietnamese street food, Tuesday for an Asian twist on burger night, and any other night for foie gras, fresh seafood bursting with herbs and spices, and atmosphere aplenty.

✖ River Tavern — Bistro $$$

(☎860-526-9417; www.rivertavernrestaurant.com; 23 Main St; meals $20-34; ⊙11:30am-2:30pm & 5-9:30pm) This popular wood-accented bistro with a bar and dining-room menu dishes up impeccable food with a variety of inflections. The menu changes, but if it's in season you should definitely order shad, caught from the Connecticut River. Save room for Toshi's made-to-order date pudding with dark rum caramel sauce – order ahead.

Essex ❻

⊨ Griswold Inn — Inn $$

(☎860-767-1776; www.griswoldinn.com; 36 Main St; d/ste from $155/200; P ⊜) The landmark Griswold Inn is one of the oldest continually operating inns in the country and has been Essex's physical and social centerpiece since 1776. The inn's buffet-style Hunt Breakfast (served 11am to 1pm Sunday) is a tradition dating to the War of 1812, when British soldiers occupying Essex demanded to be fed.

Old Lyme ❼

⊨ Bee & Thistle Inn — Inn $$

(☎860-434-1667; www.beeandthistleinn.com; 100 Lyme St; r from $109-219; P ⊜) Occupying a handsome, Dutch Colonial farmhouse dating to 1756, this classy establishment has beautiful well-tended gardens that stretch down to the Lieutenant River. Most of its 11, plush, well-appointed rooms feature abundant antiques and a canopy or four-poster bed.

Litchfield Hills Loop

14

The Litchfield Hills is often described as 'the Hamptons for people who like privacy' for its sparkling lakes, enchanting forests, resident artists and old-moneyed Colonial farmhouses.

TRIP HIGHLIGHTS

0 miles

Norfolk
Listen to live music and picnic in a redwood music shed

1 START

Lakeville

West Cornwall

47 miles

Lake Waramaug
Sip low-oak Chardonnay overlooking the lake

FINISH
Litchfield

5

4

New Preston

6

Kent
Browse art galleries and admire the Kent waterfall

37 miles

Bethlehem
Amble through clouds of blooming peonies and roses

69 miles

**5 DAYS
77 MILES / 123KM**

GREAT FOR...

BEST TIME TO GO
August to October for harvest bounty.

ESSENTIAL PHOTO
Cornwall's picturesque covered bridge over the Housatonic.

BEST FOR FOODIES
Dine in style in Litchfield and Bethlehem.

Litchfield Church in the fall

14 Litchfield Hills Loop

With scenery to match the Green Mountains of Vermont, pre-Colonial villages worthy of any movie set, and the finest food, culture and music in Connecticut, the Litchfield Hills attracts a sophisticated crowd of weekending Manhattanites. But its hardwood forests, dappled river valleys and lakes, and abundant autumn fairs offer endless possibilities for intrepid walkers, anglers, antiquers and history buffs.

TRIP HIGHLIGHT

❶ Norfolk

Norfolk's bucolic scenery and cool summers have long attracted prosperous New Yorkers. They built many of the town's fine mansions, its well-endowed Romanesque Revival library and its arts-and-crafts-style town hall, now the **Infinity Music Hall & Bistro** (☏866-666-6306; www.infinityhall.com; 20 Greenwoods Rd W; ticket prices vary; ☺ box office 11am-9pm Wed-Sun).

Most opulent of all was **Whitehall**, the summer estate of Ellen and Carl Battell Stoeckel, passionate (and moneyed) music lovers who established the

Norfolk Music Festival (www.norfolkmusic.org; tickets $25-100; ☺Jul & Aug). These extravagant affairs – the couple thought nothing of recruiting and paying for a special train to transport a 70-piece New York philharmonic orchestra to their festival – were among the most popular summer events in New England. On her death in 1939, Ellen Stoeckel bequeathed the redwood 'Music Shed' to Yale University Summer School of Music, ensuring the tradition continues.

The Drive » Head west along the main, forest-lined route US 44 for Lakeville's twin town of Salisbury. From here it's a short, 1-mile drive along historic Main St to Lakeville's town center.

② Lakeville

The rolling farmland in this quiet and remote corner of the Litchfield Hills is home to millionaires and movie luminaries such as Meryl Streep. The Rockefellers favored the famous Hotchkiss preparatory school, and in Lakeville, Paul Newman raced the **Lime Rock Race Track** (www.limerock. com; 497 Lime Rock Rd; ⏰Apr-Nov), which he thought was the most beautiful racing track in America. Today the seven-turn, 1.5-mile circuit hosts vintage and historic automobile races, along with regular stock-car races.

Otherwise, head to the peaks of **Bear Mountain** or **Lion's Head** for eye-popping panoramas. Part of the Appalachian National Scenic Trail (www. appalachiantrail.com),

LINK YOUR TRIP

2 **Fall Foliage Tour**
Head north on CT 7 for leaf-peeping, walking and zip-lining in Massachusetts, Vermont and New Hampshire.

13 **Lower River Valley**
From Woodbury, take CT 84 for Mark Twain's hometown of Hartford and a leisurely drive down the Connecticut River Valley.

IMAGE SOURCE / GETTY IMAGES ©

you'll find the trailheads leading off Rte 41.

 p163

The Drive ≫ Exit Lakeville south on Sharon Rd before picking up the CT 112 E past the Lime Rock Race Track. From here, the drive swoops south through rolling farmland, dotted with big red-and-white barns and stables. After 5 miles, turn south on US 7 into West Cornwall.

- - - - - - - - - - - - - - - -

❸ West Cornwall

The village of West Cornwall is just one of six Cornwall villages in Connecticut, but it is the most famous thanks to its picturesque **covered bridge**. The bridge was known as the 'Kissing Bridge,' because horse-drawn carriages were able to slow down to a steady trot inside, thus allowing their passengers a brief bit of alone time.

Otherwise, the area attracts nature lovers, hikers and birders who come to hike, fish and

boat on the lazy Housatonic River. In winter the nearby **Mohawk Mountain Ski Area** (☏860-672-6100; www.mohawkmtn.com; 42 Great Hollow Rd, Cornwall) is the largest ski resort in the state, with 24 slopes and trails.

The Drive ≫ The 14-mile drive south along US 7 to Kent from West Cornwall is the most scenic stretch of the trip, especially in fall, when the thickly forested hillsides are ablaze. The road runs parallel to the Appalachian Trail and Housatonic River for most of the way, offering lots of opportunities to stop and stretch your legs along the river.

- - - - - - - - - - - - - - - -

`TRIP HIGHLIGHT`

❹ Kent

The area around Kent presents some of the loveliest rural scenery in the hills. At **Kent Falls State Park**, a waterfall tumbles 250ft over the rocky hillside. Hike the easy trail to the top, or just settle into a sunny picnic spot. Nearby, the

Sloane-Stanley Museum (☏860-927-3849; www.ericsloane.com/museum.htm; 31 Kent Cornwall Rd; adult/child $8/5; ⊙10am-4pm Wed-Sun May-Oct) houses a barn full of early American tools, collected by artist and author Eric Sloane, who painted the cloud-filled sky mural at the Smithsonian Air and Space Museum in Washington, DC. In autumn, the adjacent **Connecticut Industrial Museum** (☏860-927-0050; www.ctamachinery.com; 31 Kent Cornwall Rd; adult/child $3/1.50; ⊙10am-4pm Wed-Sun May-Oct; ⛷) is a fun, mostly outdoor child-

---

💬 LOCAL KNOWLEDGE: BANTAM CINEMA

Locals know that one of the best things to do on rainy days is book in to see a film at the **Bantam Cinema** (☏860-567-1916; www.bantamcinema.com; 115 Bantam Lake Rd, Bantam). Housed in a converted red barn on the shores of Lake Bantam, it's the oldest continuously operating movie theater in Connecticut and is a real Litchfield experience. The well-curated screenings focus on independent and foreign films, and the 'Meet the Filmmaker' series features guest directors, actors and producers, many of whom live here.

West Cornwall Covered bridge

friendly attraction with all manner of steam-powered locomotives.

✗ ⨭ p163

The Drive ≫ Take the CT 341 eastward out of Kent, climbing up out of the valley through more forested hills. After 10 miles, turn south toward Warren along CT 45. After a further 1.6 miles, Lake Waramaug will peek between the trees on your left.

- - - - - - - - - - -

TRIP HIGHLIGHT

❺ Lake Waramaug

Of the dozens of lakes and ponds in the Litchfield Hills, Lake Waramaug stands out. As you make your way around the northern shore of the lake

on North Shore Rd, you'll come to the **Hopkins Vineyard** (☎860-868-7954; www.hopkinsvineyard.com; 25 Hopkins Rd; ⏰10am-5pm Mon-Sat, 11am-5pm Sun Mar-Dec, 10am-5pm Fri-Sun only Jan-Mar). The wines here are made mostly from French-American hybrids and the low-oak Chardonnay frequently wins awards. The vineyard hosts wine tastings, and the view from the bar is worth the trip, particularly when the foliage changes in the fall. Be sure to arrive well before closing time for a tasting, and call ahead during the low season.

✗ ⨭ p163

The Drive ≫ Leaving Lake Waramaug along North and East Shore Rd, turn left onto US 202 toward Bantam. At Lake Bantam, take CT 209 and 109 around the western and southern edges of the lake and after 3.5 miles turn right onto CT 61 S into Bethlehem.

- - - - - - - - - - -

TRIP HIGHLIGHT

❻ Bethlehem

Bethlehem is Connecticut's 'Christmas Town' and every year thousands of visitors come for the **Christmas Fair** (www.ci.bethlehem.ct.us; ⏰Dec) and to have their Christmas mail hand-stamped in the village post office.

DETOUR: WOODBURY

Start: ⑥ Bethlehem (p161)

At the southern border of the Litchfield Hills, Woodbury is justifiably famous as the 'antiques capital' of Connecticut, boasting more than 30 dealerships and 20 stores along historic Main St. **Woodbury Antiques Dealers Association** (☎203-263-3775; www.antiqueswoodbury.com; 289 Main St S) publishes an online guide.

While you're in Woodbury, don't forget to stop by the **Good News Cafe** (☎203-266-4663; www.good-news-cafe.com; 649 Main St S/US 6; mains $14-22; ☺11:30am-10pm Mon & Wed-Sat, noon-10pm Sun; P🐾). Run by Carole Peck, considered the Alice Waters of the East Coast, the cafe is a magnet for celebrities and lovers of fine food who come for the locally sourced farm produce and inventive, seasonal menus.

The town's religious history extends to the founding of the first theological seminary in America by local resident Reverend Joseph Bellamy. His home, the **Bellamy-Ferriday House & Garden** (☎203-266-7596; www.ctlandmarks.org; 9 Main St North; adult/child $8/4; ☺noon-4pm Thu-Sun May-Sep, noon-4pm Sat & Sun Oct), a 1750s clapboard mansion, is open to the public and is a treasure trove of delftware, Asian art and period furnishings. Equally exquisite is the garden, the design of latter-day owner Caroline Ferriday, who designed it to resemble an Aubusson Persian carpet. Its geometrical box hedges are in-filled with frothing peonies, lilacs and heirloom roses.

The Drive » The final drive north to Litchfield passes through more bucolic scenery, dotted with country farmhouses and past the shores of Lake Bantam. Head north out of Bethlehem along CT 61, past the Bellamy-Ferriday House & Garden, then connect to CT 63 via Old Litchfield Rd, for a straight run into town.

- - - - - - - - - - - - -

⑦ Litchfield

The centerpiece of the region is Connecticut's best-preserved late-18th-century town. Founded in 1719, Litchfield prospered as a main thoroughfare between New York and Boston. The town itself converges on a long oval green, and is surrounded by swaths of protected land. In August, the **Litchfield Jazz Festival** (www.litchfieldjazzfest.com; ☺Aug), in nearby Goshen, draws a thousands-strong crowd.

Walk down **North Street** and **South Street** (with a free walking tour sheet from the information kiosk) and admire the great mansions. Washington slept at the **Sheldon Tavern** on North St on his way to confer with General Rochambeau. Down the street, **Bull House** was home to Ludlow Bull, the American Egyptologist who participated in the discovery of Tutankhamen's gold-filled tomb. On South St, New Jersey judge Tapping Reeve founded America's first law school, the **Reeve House & Litchfield Law School** (☎860-567-4501; www.litchfieldhistoricalsociety.org; 82 South St; adult/child $5/free; ☺11am-5pm Tue-Sat, 1-5pm Sun mid-Apr–Nov) in 1775. Admission to the small **Litchfield History Museum** (☎860-567-4501; www.litchfieldhistoricalsociety.org; 7 South St; adult/child $5/free; ☺11am-5pm Tue-Sat, 1-5pm Sun mid-Apr–Nov) is included in the ticket.

✕ 🛏 p163

Eating & Sleeping

Lakeville ②

🛏 Inn at Iron Masters   Motel $$

(📞860-435-9844; www.innatironmasters.com; 229 Main St/US 44; d from $159; 🅿 ❄ 🛜 🐾) At first glance the one-story Inn at Iron Masters, in Lakeville, looks suspiciously like a Florida motel, but the rooms are more elegant, the grounds feature gardens and gazebos, and there's a large common fireplace for chilly evenings.

Kent ④

✕ Gifford's   Modern American $$$

(📞860-592-0262; www.giffordsrestaurant.com; 9 Maple St; mains $18-34; ⏱5-9pm Wed-Sat, 4-8pm Sun) These specialty provenders know that without fresh, top-quality ingredients you can't have truly great food. Locally sourced seasonal vegetables and meats, including free-range, golden-hued chicken and Connecticut harvested clams, all feature. Stylish contemporary interiors and a delightful covered terrace make for a memorable dining experience.

✕ Fife 'n' Drum   Diner $$

(📞860-927-3509; www.fifendrum.com; 53 Main St; mains $8-24; ⏱11:30am-9pm Wed-Mon; 🅿) If you're a fan of 1950s Americana, you'll love this dark woodsy restaurant-cum-diner-cum-bar attached to an inn of the same name. It's delightfully olde-worldly, serving hearty comfort food to get you through a day's driving around the Litchfield Hills, or to put you to sleep (if you're the lucky one in the passenger seat) for said day's driving.

🛏 Inn at Kent Falls   Inn $$$

(📞860-927-3197; www.theinnatkentfalls.com; 107 Kent-Cornwall Rd/US 7; r $215-350; 🅿 🛜 🐾) This historic, highly acclaimed inn dates back to the early 1900s. Three generous lounges with open fireplaces and a grand piano, combined with plush, 'un-stuffy' guest rooms and suites that combine traditional style with modern touches, make for a home-away-from-home atmosphere. Freshly baked breads and pastries are included in the sumptuous country breakfast. In summer, guests love the outdoor pool.

Lake Waramaug ⑤

✕ Community Table   Modern American $$$

(📞860-868-9354; http://communitytablect.com; 223 Litchfield Turnpike/US 202; brunch $14-20, mains $18-32; ⏱5-9pm Mon & Tue, noon-2pm & 5-10pm Fri & Sat, 10am-2pm & 5-9pm Sun; 🅿) The name of this Scandinavian-inspired restaurant comes from the 300-year-old black walnut table, where you can sit down to Sunday brunch. Everything on the modern American menu is locally sourced.

🛏 Hopkins Inn   Inn $$

(📞860-868-7295; www.thehopkinsinn.com; 22 Hopkins Rd, Warren; r from $135, without bath from $125, apt from $150; 🅿 ❄ 🐾) The 19th-century Hopkins Inn boasts a well-regarded restaurant with Austrian-influenced country fare and a variety of lodging options, from simple rooms with shared bathrooms to lake-view apartments. Whatever the season, there's something magical about sitting on the porch gazing upon Lake Warramaug and the hills beyond.

Litchfield ⑦

✕ West Street Grill   Modern American $$$

(📞860-567-3885; http://weststreetgrill.com; 43 West St; mains $25-40; ⏱11:30am-9pm Wed-Sun) A Parisian-style bistro on Litchfield's historic green, this is one of the state's top restaurants. Over the years its inventive modern American cooking has earned it nods from *Gourmet* magazine and the *New York Times*. The shrimp salad with orange and fennel is delightful.

🛏 Tollgate Hill Inn   Inn $$

(📞866-567-1233; www.tollgatehill.com; 571 Torrington Rd/Rte 202; d/ste from $120/205; @ 🛜) About 2 miles east of town, this 1745 property used to be the main way station for travelers between Albany and Hartford. Divided between three buildings, including one of the oldest schoolhouses in Connecticut (which was relocated to here in 1920), rooms have a private deck and pull-out couch (great for families), while the suites afford a wood-burning fireplace, canopy bed, fridge and bar.

STRETCH YOUR LEGS NEWPORT

Start/Finish International Tennis Hall of Fame

Distance 4 miles

Duration 3.5 hours

Newport's status as a summer resort stretches back to the 19th century, when America's wealthiest industrialists erected mansions along Bellevue Ave. Admire their extravagant summer 'cottages,' which still line Newport's cliff tops, on this walk.

Take this walk on Trips

International Tennis Hall of Fame

To experience something of the 19th-century American aristocracy's approach to leisure, visit the **International Tennis Hall of Fame** (401-849-3990; www.tennisfame.com; 194 Bellevue Ave; adult/child $15/free; 10am-5pm). It lies inside the Newport Casino building (1880), which served as a summer club for Newport's wealthiest residents. If you've brought your whites, playing on one of its 13 grass courts ($130 for one or two people per 90 minutes) is a delightful throwback to earlier times; otherwise, have a drink lawnside at the **La Forge Casino Restaurant**.

The Walk » Stroll along lantern-lined Bellevue Ave past Newport's first 'cottage,' the Elizabethan folly of Kingscote on the right. Further on you'll pass the National Museum of American Illustration on the left, before arriving at Rosecliff.

Rosecliff

Further down Bellevue Ave stands the impressive **Rosecliff** (401-847-1000; 548 Bellevue Ave; adult/child $16/7; 9am-4pm Apr–mid-Oct, hours vary mid-Oct–Mar; P), built for Mrs Hermann Oelrichs, an heiress of the Comstock Lode silver discovery. Designed to look like the Grand Trianon at Versailles, its palatial ballroom and landscaped grounds quickly became the setting for some enormous parties. In June the **Newport Flower Festival** is held here.

The Walk » Continue straight along Bellevue Ave to reach Rough Point. In quick succession you'll pass the Astor's stucco mansion, Beechwood, on the left, along with William Vanderbilt's garishly opulent Marble House, with its white marble driveway and grand porte cochere.

Rough Point

While the splendor of the grounds alone is worth the price of admission to **Rough Point** (401-849-7300; www.new portrestoration.com; 680 Bellevue Ave; adult/child $25/free; 10am-2pm Thu-Sat mid-Apr–mid-May, 10am-3:45pm Tue-Sun mid-May–mid-

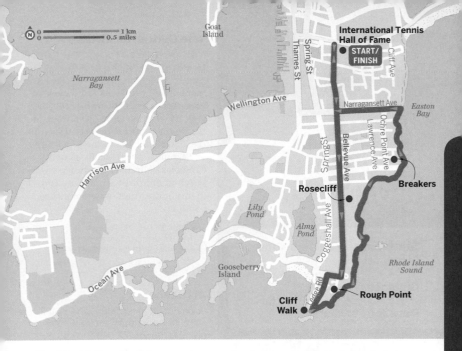

Nov; [P]), this faux-English manor house also contains Doris Duke's impressive art holdings, including medieval tapestries, furniture owned by French emperors, Ming-dynasty ceramics, and paintings by Renoir and Van Dyck. The house sits in a peerless location right on the point.

The Walk » To access the start of the Cliff Walk at Bailey's (Reject's) Beach, head right down to the end of Bellevue Ave. Before the avenue starts to merge with Ocean Ave, take a left down Ledge Rd to the trailhead.

Cliff Walk

In 1975, eager to protect their privacy, Newport's mansion owners sought to close Cliff Walk (www.cliffwalk.com), the public footpath that snakes along the cliff top overlooking their front lawns. The move was prevented by local fishermen and the 3.5-mile path was designated a National Recreation Trail. The best section runs from Ledge Rd near Rough Point to the Forty Steps

(each one named for someone lost at sea) on Narragansett Ave.

The Walk » Head down Ledge Rd, from Bellevue Ave, and pick up the Cliff Walk trail. The views are spectacular. The stretch between Ruggles Ave and Narragansett Ave is the most scenic, passing the Breakers, Vineland and French Gothic Ochre Court.

Breakers

Built at the behest of Cornelius Vanderbilt II, the **Breakers** (☎401-847-1000; www.newportmansions.org; 44 Ochre Point Ave; adult/child $21/7; ☺9am-5pm Apr–mid-Oct, hours vary mid-Oct–Mar; [P]) is the most magnificent of the Newport mansions. A 70-room Italian Renaissance megapalace, it was inspired by 16th-century Genoese palazzos, and more than 200 craftsmen were engaged to complete the lavish marquetry, mosaics and ornate sculptural details.

The Walk » Exit Cliff Walk up the Forty Steps, which brings you to Narragansett Ave. From here, it's a short walk back to Bellevue Ave. Turn right to return to the start and the International Tennis Hall of Fame for a drink.

165

STRETCH YOUR LEGS
NEW HAVEN

Start/Finish Yale Center for British Art

Distance 1.8 miles

Duration 2.5 hours

White-steepled churches, Colonial Revival buildings and neo-Gothic turrets form the stage-set for this exploration of New Haven's thriving arts scene, which includes Revolutionary canvases, rare manuscripts, community craftwork and avant-garde visual arts.

Take this walk on Trips

Yale Center for British Art

A Chapel St landmark, the **Yale Center for British Art** (☎203-432-2800; www.ycba. yale.edu; 1080 Chapel St; ☺10am-5pm Tue-Sat, noon-5pm Sun) was Louis Kahn's last commission and is the setting for the largest collection of British art outside the UK. Spanning three centuries from the Elizabethan era to the 19th century, and arranged thematically as well as chronologically, the collection gives an insight into British art, life and culture in prints, drawings, watercolors and paintings.

The Walk » This half-mile walk takes you past the New Haven Green. The Center Church's white spire is visible above the trees and the Gothic Revival Trinity Church is on your left. After Temple St, take the second right onto Orange St.

ArtSpace

Specializing in contemporary visual arts and community outreach, non-profit **ArtSpace** (☎203-772-2709; www. artspacenh.org; 50 Orange St; ☺noon-6pm Wed-Thu, to 8pm Fri & Sat) organizes the annual **City-Wide Open Studios** each fall. During the event it is possible to take a peek inside the workspaces of some of New Haven's up-and-coming artists. Check out the website for exact details.

The Walk » Retrace your steps to Church St and stroll northeast beside the green. On your right you'll pass the Federal Courthouse, the turreted City Hall and the Amistad Memorial. Continue onto Whitney Ave and then turn right on Audubon St.

Creative Arts Workshop

New Haven's Audubon Arts District is located between Church and Orange Sts. In its midst is the **Creative Arts Workshop** (☎203-562-4927; www.creative artsworkshop.org; 80 Audubon St; classes & workshops from $160; ☺9am-7pm Mon-Fri), a visual arts studio that operates both as a cultural resource center and as an art school. Classes are available.

In June, the workshop and the art district are abuzz with activity, hosting events for the two-week-long **Interna-**

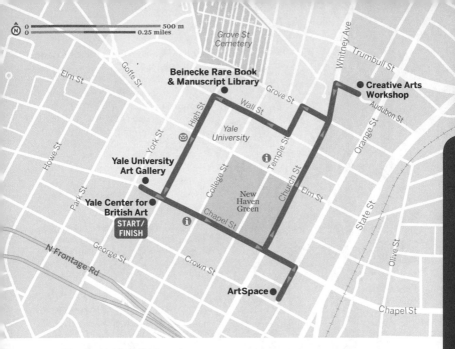

tional Festival of Arts & Ideas (www. artidea.org; ⊙Jun).

The Walk » Return to Whitney Ave, walk south and turn right on Grove St. Walk one block beside Timothy Dwight College, go left down Temple St and then right down Wall St. From here it's a pleasant tree-lined walk to Beinecke Plaza.

Beinecke Rare Book & Manuscript Library

On your stroll back, swing past the **Beinecke Rare Book & Manuscript Library** (📞203-432-2977; www.library.yale.edu/ beinecke; 121 Wall St; ⊙10am-7pm Mon-Thu, 9am-5pm Fri). This extraordinary piece of architecture is the largest building in the world designed for the preservation of rare manuscripts. The windowless cube has walls of Danby marble, which subdue the effects of light, while inside glass towers display sculptural shelves of books, including one of only 48 surviving Gutenberg Bibles (1455).

The Walk » Exit Beinecke Plaza westward onto High St. Walk southwest, passing Sterling Memorial Library on your right, and Dwight Hall on your left. At Chapel St, turn right and you'll find the modern exterior of the art gallery on your right.

Yale University Art Gallery

The oldest university art museum in the country, **Yale University Art Gallery** (📞203-432-0600; http://artgallery.yale. edu; 1111 Chapel St; ⊙10am-5pm Tue-Fri, to 8pm Thu, 11am-5pm Sat & Sun) was opened in 1832 with Colonel John Trumbull's collection of paintings depicting the American Revolution. Now it is home to 185,000 objects, including paintings, sculpture, silverware and artifacts from as far afield as Asia, South America and Africa.

The Walk » From the Yale University Art Gallery you can see the Yale Center for British Art across the street, where you started your walk.

Vermont

IF YOUR IDEA OF THE PERFECT ROAD TRIP INVOLVES SLOW-PACED MEANDERING
through verdant countryside, Vermont may feel like paradise. Stubborn mountain ridges and narrow country roads ensure an ever-present sense of adventure as you zigzag through one of America's most uniformly bucolic landscapes. The Green Mountain State's eclectic allure combines outdoor adventure, photogenic villages and locavore eating. Newcomers to Vermont invariably notice something different when they cross the state line. Perhaps it's the lack of billboards, or the enduring philosophy that 'small is beautiful', but it's also Vermont's independent-minded, creative spirit – from politicians who eschew traditional party labels to world-class theater artists and cult-status brewers operating from remote backcountry farms.

Stowe Maple trees in the fall
RON AND PATTY THOMAS / GETTY IMAGES ©

Vermont Pumpkins for sale at a garden center

Classic Trip

15 **Vermont's Spine: Route 100 3–4 Days**
Follow the Green Mountains north through the bucolic heart of Vermont. (p173)

16 **Cider Season Sampler 3–4 Days**
Sample Vermont's agricultural bounty during the state's most colorful season. (p183)

17 **Northeast Kingdom to Camel's Hump 3–4 Days**
Ramble down back roads between idyllic rural outposts and Vermont's highest peaks. (p191)

18 **Lake Champlain Byway 1–2 Days**
Discover Burlington's urban attractions and the slower-paced charms of Lake Champlain's islands. (p199)

19 **Southern Vermont Loop 2–3 Days**
Visit major historical landmarks and some of Vermont's prettiest villages. (p207)

✔️ DON'T MISS

Ben & Jerry's Factory Tour
Find out how two high-school pals created America's most celebrated ice cream on Trip 15

Boyden Valley Winery
Sip traditional varietals or maple-infused fruit wine at this award-winning winery with a gorgeous mountain backdrop. Stop in on Trip 16

Stowe
Vermont's most stunning mountain village is a mix of traditional New England architecture and awe-inducing setting. Visit on Trip 15

Magic Hat Brewery
Take an 'Artifactory' tour at Vermont's most creative microbrewery. Taste your favorite on Trip 18

Shelburne Museum
Learn about Vermont farm life and admire Americana in a village-like setting on Trip 18

Classic Trip

Vermont's Spine: Route 100

15

Yodeling pickles (yes, really), charming villages, idyllic landscapes and scoops of America's most famous ice cream make this one of New England's most iconic road trips.

TRIP HIGHLIGHTS

3–4 DAYS
130 MILES / 209KM

GREAT FOR...

BEST TIME TO GO

May to October for snow-free roads and sun-filled days.

ESSENTIAL PHOTO

The 360-degree views from the K1 Gondola above Killington.

BEST FOR FAMILIES

Poking around the Weston country store and taking a Ben & Jerry's Factory tour.

---

130 miles

9 FINISH

Stowe
A postcard-worthy New England village nestled in the Green Mountains

8

122 miles

Ben & Jerry's Factory
Watch how they make Chunky Monkey and Cherry Garcia

Waitsfield

Rochester

67 miles

5

West Bridgewater

Killington
Zip up the gondola for awe-inducing mountain views

3

38 miles

Weston
Hit the state's most famous country store

Wilmington

START

Classic Trip

15 Vermont's Spine: Route 100

Spanning the state from bottom to top, Vermont's revered Route 100 winds past the Northeast's most legendary ski resorts and through some of New England's prettiest scenery, with the verdant Green Mountains always close at hand. This drive takes you on a slow meander through the state, though you might speed up in anticipation of the Ben & Jerry's Factory tour beckoning on the final stretch of road.

❶ Wilmington

Chartered in 1751, Wilmington is the winter and summer gateway to Mt Snow, one of New England's best ski resorts and an excellent summertime mountain-biking and golfing spot. There are no main sights per se but the **Historic District** on W Main St is a prime example of 18th- and 19th-century architecture and is chock-full of restaurants and boutiques; the bulk of the village is on the National Register of Historic Places. This is an excellent base where you can stay overnight and grab a bite before your journey up north.

✕ p181

The Drive » Ski country (look for Mt Snow on your left) gives way to sleepy hamlets as you drive 26 miles north on VT 100 to the village of Jamaica.

❷ Jamaica

A prime dose of rural Vermont, with a country store and several antique shops, this artsy community tucked into the evergreen forest is also home to **Jamaica State Park** (☎802-874-4600; www.vtstateparks.com/htm/ jamaica.htm; 48 Salmon Hole Lane; adult/child $4/2; ☺ mid-May–mid-Oct), the best place in Vermont for riverside camping. The annual Whitewater Weekend held here in late September draws kayaking enthusiasts from all over New England to pit their skills against the

rampaging West River. There's good swimming right in the heart of the campground, but walkers can also head 3 miles upstream along a 19th-century railway bed to **Hamilton Falls**, a 50ft ribbon of water cascading into a natural swimming hole.

The Drive » Continue north 17 miles on VT 100 to Weston.

TRIP HIGHLIGHT

❸ Weston

Picturesque Weston is home to the **Vermont Country Store** (☎802-824-3184; www.vermontcountry store.com; 657 Main St/VT 100; ☺8:30am-7pm late May–mid-Oct, 9am-6pm rest of year), founded in 1946 and the state's most famous country store. It's a time warp from a simpler era, when

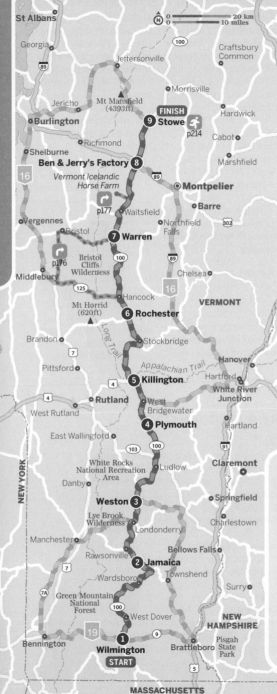

goods were made to last and quirky products with appeal had a home. Here you'll discover electronic yodeling plastic pickles, taffeta slips and three kinds of shoe stretchers (with customizable bunion and corn knobs) – in short, everything you didn't know you needed. Additionally, it carries small toys and games of yesteryear Americana (think vintage tiddlywinks or the classic 1960s board game Mystery Date), plus entire sections filled with candy jars and cases of Vermont cheese.

The Drive » Continue north on VT 100. At Plymouth Union, veer off to the right onto VT 100A for a few miles until you reach Plymouth Center. The drive is 22 miles.

❹ Plymouth

Gazing across the high pastures of Plymouth, you feel a bit like Rip

🔗 LINK YOUR TRIP

16 Cider Season Sampler

From Killington, head north on US 100 to enjoy fall's delicious delights.

19 Southern Vermont Loop

Branch off onto this circle tour of southern Vermont in Weston.

Classic Trip

Van Winkle – only it's the past you've woken up to. President Calvin Coolidge's boyhood home looks much as it did a century ago, with homes, barns, a church, a one-room schoolhouse and a general store gracefully arrayed among old maples on a bucolic hillside. At Plymouth's heart is the preserved **President Calvin Coolidge State Historic Site** (📞802-672-3773; http://historicsites.vermont.gov/directory/coolidge; 3780 Rte 100A, Plymouth Notch; adult/child $9/2; ⏱9:30am-5pm late May–mid-Oct). The village's

streets are sleepy today, but the museum tells a tale of an earlier America filled with elbow grease and perseverance. Tools for blacksmithing, wood-working, butter making and hand-laundering are indicative of the hard work and grit it took to wrest a living from Vermont's stony pastures. As a boy, Calvin hayed with his grandfather and kept the wood box filled.

Originally co-founded by Coolidge's father, the **Plymouth Artisan Cheese company** (📞802-672-3650; www.plymouthartisancheese.com; 106 Messer Hill Rd; ⏱10am-5pm May-Oct, to 4pm Nov-Apr) still produces a classic farmhouse cheddar known as granular curd cheese. Its distinctively sharp tang

and grainy texture are reminiscent of the wheel cheese traditionally found at general stores throughout Vermont. Panels downstairs tell the history of local cheese making, while a museum upstairs displays cheese-making equipment from another era.

The Drive ❯❯ Drive back along VT 100A and turn right to return to VT 100 N. The drive is 13 miles.

- - - - - - - - - - - -

TRIP HIGHLIGHT

❺ Killington

The largest ski resort in the east, Killington spans seven mountains, highlighted by 4241ft **Killington Peak**, the second highest in Vermont. It operates the largest snow-making system in North America and its numerous

---

DETOUR: MIDDLEBURY & LINCOLN GAPS

Start: ❻ Rochester (p177)

The 'gap roads' that run east–west over the Green Mountains offer some of the most picturesque views of the region. Ready to explore? Four miles north of Rochester, in Hancock, scenic VT 125 leads west over **Middlebury Gap**. Stops to look out for as you make the 15-mile crossing from Hancock to East Middlebury include beautiful **Texas Falls** (3 miles from Hancock), Middlebury Gap (6 miles), and the **Robert Frost Interpretive Trail** (10 miles), a pretty loop trail enlivened by plaques featuring Frost's poetry.

For a scenic loop back to the main route, continue west on VT 125 to East Middlebury, then take VT 116 north. Soon after crossing through the pretty village of **Bristol**, turn right on Lincoln Gap Rd and follow it 14 miles east to rejoin the main route at Warren.

The return trip also offers some nice stops. As you turn onto Lincoln Gap Rd, look for the parked cars at **Bartlett Falls**, where the New Haven River's raging waters cascade into one of Vermont's prettiest swimming holes. Later, after a crazy-steep climb (partly unpaved) to **Lincoln Gap**, stop at the 2428ft summit for lovely views and some nice trails, including the 5-mile round trip to the 4000ft summit of **Mt Abraham**.

DETOUR:
VERMONT ICELANDIC HORSE FARM

Start: ❼ Warren

Icelandic horses are one of the oldest, and some say most versatile, breeds in the world. They're also friendly and unbelievably affectionate creatures, and are fairly easy to ride even for novices – they tend to stop and think (rather than panic) if something frightens them. The **Vermont Icelandic Horse Farm** (☎802-496-7141; www.icelandichorses.com; 3061 N Fayston Rd, Waitsfield; 1-3hr rides $60-120, full day incl lunch $220, multiday treks $675-1695; ⊗by appointment; 🅿), 3 miles west of VT 100 (where the tarmac ends and becomes a dirt road), takes folks on one- to three-hour or full-day jaunts year-round; it also offers two- to five-day inn-to-inn treks (some riding experience required). The farm also runs **Mad River Inn** (☎802-496-7900, 800-832-8278; www.madriverinn.com; Tremblay Rd, Waitsfield; r incl breakfast & afternoon tea $105-175; ❄🛜), a pleasant inn a short trot away.

Head 9 miles north of Warren on VT 100 and follow the signs to the horse farm.

outdoor activities – from skiing and snowboarding in winter to mountain biking and hiking in summer – are all centrally located on the mountain. **Killington Resort** (☎800-621-6867, 802-422-6200; www.killington.com; 4763 Killington Rd; lift ticket adult/teen/senior weekend $96/82/74, midweek $94/80/72), the East Coast's answer to Vail, runs the efficient **K1-Express Gondola**, which in winter transports up to 3000 skiers per hour in heated cars along a 2.5-mile cable – it's the highest lift in Vermont. In summer and fall it whisks you to impeccable vantage points above the mountains: leaf-peeping atop the cascading rainbow of copper, red and gold in foliage season is truly magical.

The Drive » Enter the idyllic valley of the White River as you drive 24 miles north on VT 100 to Rochester.

❻ Rochester

This unassuming blink-and-you'll-miss-it town, with a vast village green lined by well-maintained, historic New England homes, is worth a stop to experience rural Vermont life minus the masses of tourists in other towns along VT 100.

Stop in at **Sandy's Books & Bakery** (☎802-767-4258; www.seasonedbooks.com; 30 North Main St; baked goods & light meals $3-10; ⊗7:30am-6pm Mon-Sat, to 3pm Sun; 🛜), a cafe and bookstore that serves as a local hangout. With homemade everything – granola, bagels, whole-wheat bread – Sandy's serves up mean dishes such as spinach and egg-filled biscuits, spanakopita, salads and soups. Tables are scattered between bookshelves, so it's a great spot for a java break and a browse of the

new and used books (or the locally made Vermont Soap). We dare you to resist the cookies.

🛏 p181

The Drive » Continue on VT 100 N. Roughly 10 miles past Rochester, the road enters a narrow and wild corridor of protected land. A little pullout on the left provides viewing access to pretty Moss Glen Falls. A mile or so later, the small ponds of Granville Gulf comprise one of the state's most accessible moose-watching spots (the best chance of seeing these big critters is at dawn or dusk). After 5 miles heading north, turn right onto Covered Bridge Rd and cross the bridge into Warren village.

❼ Warren

This sweet village is the southern gateway into Vermont's picturesque Mad River Valley. The river is popular with swimmers and kayakers, while the surrounding mountains are a mecca

Classic Trip

WHY THIS IS A CLASSIC TRIP
GREGOR CLARK, WRITER

After 20-plus years living in Vermont, I'm still smitten with VT 100. No other route so fully captures Vermont's four-season beauty, from the Green Mountains' fall colors to the Mad River's ski areas and sculpted-rock swimming holes; from the lonely moose country near Granville to the cozy village feel of Weston. For an unforgettable add-on, climb VT 108 from Stowe through Smugglers Notch at trip's end.

Top: Mountain accommodation in Stowe
Left: Hiking near East Middlebury
Right: Stowe

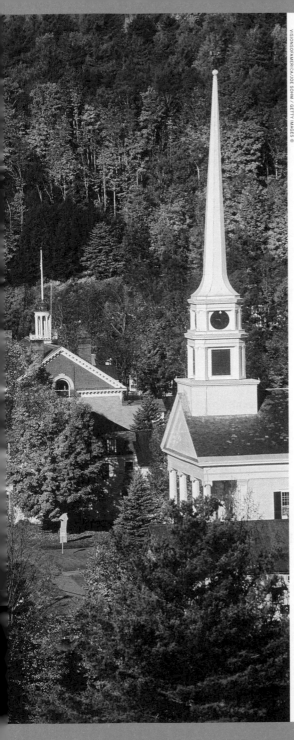

for skiers, who flock to the slopes at nearby **Sugarbush** (☎802-583-6300, 800-537-8427; www.sugarbush.com; 102 Forest Dr, Warren; adult/child lift ticket $93/73) and **Mad River Glen** (☎802-496-3551; www.madriverglen.com; VT 17, Waitsfield; lift ticket adult/child weekend $79/63, midweek $65/60).

Stop in at the **Warren Store** (☎802-496-3864; www.warrenstore.com; 284 Main St, Warren; sandwiches & light meals $5-9; h8am-7pm Mon-Sat, to 6pm Sun) in the village center, an animated community hangout with wavy 19th-century wood floors, a deli serving gourmet sandwiches and pastries, and a front porch ideal for sipping coffee while poring over the *New York Times*. The store upstairs sells an eclectic mix of jewelry, toys, Vermont casual clothing and knickknacks, while the sundeck below overlooks a pretty swimming hole framed by sculpted granite rocks.

✕ ⮕ p181

The Drive » Waitsfield, approximately 9 miles north of Warren off VT 100, has a handful of eating and sleeping options (p181). Continue on VT 100 through pretty farm country to Waterbury, then follow signs for Stowe, crossing the overpass over I-89 to reach Ben & Jerry's.

TRIP HIGHLIGHT

8 Ben & Jerry's Factory

No trip to Vermont would be complete without a visit to the **Ben & Jerry's Factory** (☎866-258-6877;

www.benjerrys.com; 1281 VT 100, Waterbury; adult/child under 13yr $4/free; ⏲9am-9pm Jul–mid-Aug, to 7pm mid-Aug–mid-Oct, 10am-6pm mid-Oct–Jun; ♿), the biggest production center for America's most famous ice cream. Sure, the manufacturing process is interesting, but a visit to the factory also explains how school pals Ben and Jerry went from a $5 ice-cream-making correspondence course to a global enterprise, and offers a glimpse of the fun, in-your-face culture that made these frozen-dessert pioneers so successful. You're treated to a (very) small free taste at the end, but if you need a larger dose make a beeline for the on-site scoop shop.

Quaintly perched on a knoll overlooking the parking lot, the Ben & Jerry's Flavor Graveyard's neat rows of headstones pay silent tribute to flavors that flopped, like Makin' Whoopie Pie and Dastardly Mash. Each memorial is lovingly inscribed with the flavor's brief life span on the grocery store of this earth and a poem in tribute. Rest in Peace, Holy Cannoli (1997–98)! Adieu, Miss Jelena's Sweet Potato Pie (1992–93)!

The Drive » Wipe that ice-cream smile off your face and replace it with an ear-to-ear grin as you ascend 9 miles up VT 100 to the magnificent ski village of Stowe.

- - - - - - - - - -

TRIP HIGHLIGHT

❾ Stowe

In a cozy valley where the West Branch River flows into the Little River and mountains rise to the sky in all directions, the quintessential Vermont village of Stowe (founded in 1794) bustles quietly. Nestled in the Green Mountain National Forest, the highest point in Vermont, **Mt Mansfield** (4393ft) towers in the background, juxtaposed against the town, making this *the* classic Vermont picture-postcard scene. With more than 200 miles of cross-country ski trails, some of the finest mountain biking and downhill skiing in the east and world-class hiking, this is a natural mecca for adrenaline junkies and active families. If shopping and cafe-hopping are more your style, the village center also makes a delightful spot for a leisurely stroll (p214).

In addition to winter snow sports, **Stowe Mountain Resort** (📞802-253-3000, 888-253-4849; www.stowe.com; 5781 Mountain Rd; lift ticket adult/child $115/95) opens from spring through to fall with **gondola sky rides** (adult/child $25/17; ⏲10am-4:30pm late Jun–mid-Oct), an **alpine slide** (adult/child $17/15; ⏲10:30am-4:30pm late Jun–mid-Oct, Sat & Sun only Sep & Oct) and a scenic auto **toll road** (per car $27; ⏲late May–mid-Oct) that zigzags to the top of Mt Mansfield.

If *The Sound of Music* is one of your favorite things, the hilltop Trapp Family Lodge boasts sprawling views and oodles of activities, such as hiking, horse-drawn sleigh and carriage rides, lodge tours detailing the family history (often led by a member of the Trapp family), summer concerts on their meadow and some frothy goodness at the on-site Trapp Family Brewery.

✕ 🛏 p181, p197

COVERED BRIDGES OF MONTGOMERY

A 38-mile drive north from Stowe via VT 100 and VT 118 takes you to the covered-bridge capital of Vermont. In an idyllic valley at the confluence of multiple watersheds, the twin villages of Montgomery and Montgomery Center share seven spans crisscrossing the local rivers. Especially beautiful – though challenging to find – is remote Creamery Bridge just off Hill West Rd, which straddles a waterfall with a swimming hole at its base.

Eating & Sleeping

Wilmington ❶

🍴 Wahoo's Eatery   American $

(📞802-464-0110; http://wahooseatery.com; VT 9; sandwiches & salads $6-9; ⏰11am-8pm mid-May–mid-Sep) 'We welcome your business and relish your buns': so reads the sign at this friendly, family-run roadside snack shack less than a mile east of Wilmington on VT 9. A long-standing local institution, it whips up quality burgers ($2 extra for grass-fed Vermont beef), along with hand-cut fries, handmade conch fritters, wraps, sandwiches, hot dogs, salads and ice cream.

Rochester ❻

🛏 Liberty Hill Farm   B&B $$

(📞802-767-3926; www.libertyhillfarm.com; 511 Liberty Hill Rd; r incl dinner & breakfast per adult/child/teen $132/62/75) With its magnificent red barn and White River Valley panoramas, this working farm just south of Rochester is a Vermont classic. Overnight stays include dinner and breakfast, served family-style and making ample use of produce from the on-site garden. Other highlights include lounging on the front porch, getting to know the farm animals and sampling the farm's ultra-fresh dairy products.

Warren ❼

🍴 Peasant   Modern American $$

(📞802-496-6856; www.peasantvt.com; 40 Bridge St, Waitsfield; mains $21-25; ⏰5:30-9pm Thu-Mon) Living up to its tagline 'a simple feast,' Peasant delivers seasonal farm-to-table treats that can vary from hearty cassoulet in the dead of winter to maple-glazed salmon with locally grown veggies in summer, all complemented by an ample choice of beer, wine and cocktails.

Look for it in a cozy slate-blue house in the village center.

🛏 Inn at Round Barn Farm   Inn $$$

(📞802-496-2276; www.roundbarninn.com; 1661 E Warren Rd, Waitsfield; r incl breakfast $175-330; 🐾📶🏊) This place gets its name from the adjacent 1910 round barn – among the few authentic examples remaining in Vermont. The decidedly upscale inn has antique-furnished rooms with mountain views, gas fireplaces, canopy beds and antiques. All overlook the meadows and mountains. In winter guests leave their shoes at the door to preserve the hardwood floors. The country-style breakfast is huge.

Stowe ❾

🍴 The Bistro at Ten Acres   Fusion $$$

(📞802-253-6838; http://tenacreslodge.com/bistro.php; 14 Barrows Rd; mains $19-32; ⏰5-10pm Wed-Sun) This immensely popular eatery in a plank-floored 1820s farmhouse blends cozy atmosphere with delicious food from New York–trained chef Gary Jacobson (think *steak frites*, slow-roasted duck, or lobster with bourbon-tarragon sauce and polenta). The attached bar serves a good selection of cocktails and draft beers, plus a cheaper burger-centric menu.

🛏 Trapp Family Lodge   Lodge $$$

(📞802-253-8511, 800-826-7000; www.trappfamily.com; 700 Trapp Hill Rd; r $191-610; @📶🏊🐾) With wide-open fields and mountain vistas, this hilltop lodge 3km southwest of town boasts Stowe's best setting. The Austrian-style chalet, built by Maria von Trapp of *Sound of Music* fame, houses traditional lodge rooms. Alternatively, you can rent one of the modern villas or cozy guesthouses scattered across the property. The 2700-acre spread offers stupendous hiking, snowshoeing and cross-country skiing.

Cider Season Sampler

16

Vermont in the fall is radiant, with farm stands overflowing and leaves showing the first hints of color. With pick-your-own berries, craft breweries and a burgeoning locavore movement, it's an epicure's delight.

TRIP HIGHLIGHTS

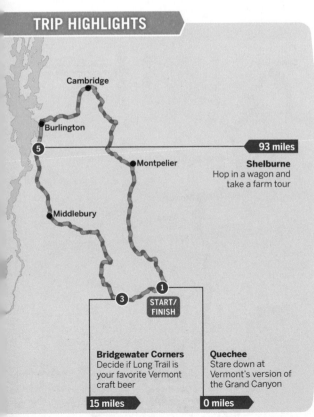

3–4 DAYS
229 MILES / 369KM

GREAT FOR...

BEST TIME TO GO

August to October, when apple-picking is at its prime.

ESSENTIAL PHOTO

Capture the orchards at Shelburne Farms in the early evening light.

BEST FOR FOODIES

Award-winning cheddar and crisp apples from Shelburne Farms, or divine meals with a waterfall view at Simon Pearce.

93 miles
Shelburne
Hop in a wagon and take a farm tour

Bridgewater Corners
Decide if Long Trail is your favorite Vermont craft beer

15 miles

Quechee
Stare down at Vermont's version of the Grand Canyon

0 miles

Cider Season Sampler

When most people think 'Vermont food and drink,' beer or maple syrup comes to mind. But these days, vineyards, makers of craft cider and locavore restaurants are also sprouting up around the state. Chefs, farmers and communities have begun working together in mutually supportive ways, revitalizing local culture as they build on Vermont's deep agricultural roots. Autumn, with its blaze of colors, is the best time to embrace the bounty.

TRIP HIGHLIGHT

❶ Quechee

Vermont's answer to the Grand Canyon, the **Quechee Gorge** is a 163ft-deep scar that cuts about 3000ft along the Ottauquechee River. View it from the bridge or work off those pancake breakfasts with a hike to the bottom – the 15-minute descent through pine forest is beautiful, following a trail on the south side of US 4.

In downtown Quechee Village, make a beeline

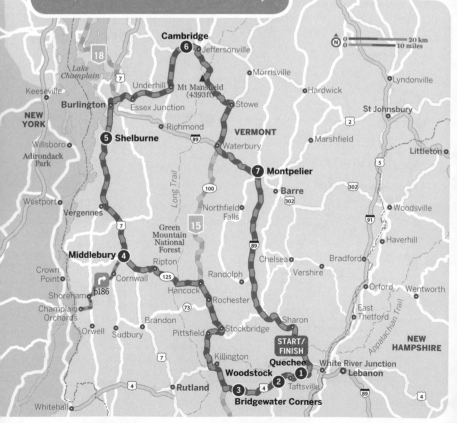

for **Simon Pearce Glass**
(☎802-295-2711; www.simon
pearce.com; 1760 Quechee
Main St; ⏱10am-9pm),
in the old woolen mill
cantilevered out over
the Ottauquechee River.
Pearce, an Irish glass-
blower, immigrated to
Quechee in 1981, drawn
by a vision of running
his entire operation self-
sufficiently with hydro
power. Three decades
later, he's built a small
empire. His flagship
Quechee store displays
pottery and glassware
and offers glassblowing
demonstrations daily.

✖ p189

The Drive » Follow US 4 west
for 7 miles to Woodstock.

- - - - - - - - - - - - - -

② Woodstock

Chartered in 1761, Wood-
stock has been the highly

LINK YOUR TRIP

15 **Vermont's Spine: Route 100**

Connect to VT 100 from
Cambridge via mountain-
hugging VT 108 through
Smugglers Notch.

18 **Lake Champlain Byway**

In Shelburne you can
connect with this scenic
journey up through
Vermont's Champlain
Islands.

dignified seat of scenic
Windsor County since
1766. The townspeople
built grand Federal and
Greek Revival homes
surrounding the oval
village green, and four
of Woodstock's churches
can claim bells cast by
Paul Revere. Senator Ja-
cob Collamer, a friend of
Abraham Lincoln's, once
observed, 'The good peo-
ple of Woodstock have
less incentive than others
to yearn for heaven.'

**Billings Farm & Mu-
seum** (☎802-457-2355;
www.billingsfarm.org; 5302
River Rd; adult/child $14/8;
⏱10am-5pm daily May-Oct, to
4pm Sat & Sun Nov-Feb, closed
Mar & Apr; 🚻) employs a
mix of 19th- and 20th-
century methods. Visitor
activities vary with the
seasons, from horse
and sleigh rides and the
afternoon milking of the
cows to demonstrations
of strawberry shortcake
made in a cast-iron
stove.

The **Marsh-Billings-
Rockefeller National**

ROBERT FROST'S VERMONT

In 1920 Robert Frost (1874–1963) moved from New
Hampshire to Vermont seeking 'a better place to
farm and especially grow apples.' For almost four
decades, Frost lived in the Green Mountain State,
growing apples and writing much of his poetry in
a log cabin in **Ripton**, a beautiful hamlet set in the
Green Mountains 12 miles west of VT 100, where he
kept a summer home. Today, tiny Ripton and the
surrounding area in the Green Mountain National
Forest have been officially designated **Robert Frost
Country**.

Historical Park (☎802-
457-3368; www.nps.gov/
mabi; 54 Elm St; mansion tours
adult/child $8/free, trails free;
⏱visitor center 10am-5pm
late May-Oct, tours 10am-4pm
late May-Oct) contains a
mansion with exhibits on
environmental conser-
vation and 20 miles of
trails. Combined tickets
with the Billings Farm &
Museum are available.

✖ p189

The Drive » Drive west on
US 4 for 8 miles to Bridgewater
Corners, following the curve of
the Ottauquechee a few miles
upstream.

- - - - - - - - - - - - - -

TRIP HIGHLIGHT

③ Bridgewater Corners

Located in an unassum-
ing spot right off the
road on the left, **Long
Trail Brewery** (☎802-672-
5011; www.longtrail.com; 5520
US 4 at VT 100A, Bridgewater;
⏱10am-7pm) is one of
Vermont's leading pro-
ducers of craft beer. On a
sunny day, it's delightful

to sit in its riverside beer garden, modeled after Munich's Hofbräuhaus. Inside is a cozy beer hall that's great for sampling brews. Check out the self-guided brewery tour on the 2nd floor – the small platform explaining the process is worth visiting if you want to know how that frothy goodness is produced.

The Drive » Take US 4 for 12 miles west through Killington, then head north 23 miles on VT 100 to Hancock. From here, scenic VT 125 snakes 20 miles west over the Green Mountains into Middlebury.

❹ Middlebury

Middlebury's original claim to fame was its prestigious liberal arts college, founded here in 1800. The pretty campus, dotted with buildings constructed of local marble and gray limestone, makes for a pleasant stroll, as does the pedes-trian bridge along the base of Otter Creek Falls in the heart of town.

Surrounded by fertile farm and orchard land, Middlebury is also a leader in Vermont's locavore movement and a major producer of craft beer and cider. On Wednesdays and Saturdays in summer, head down to the Marble Works, near the falls, to revel in the cornucopia of organic produce at the twice-weekly **farmers market**. Just under 2 miles north, you can stop in at **Woodchuck Cidery** (☎802-385-3656; www.woodchuck.com/ciderhouse; 1321 Exchange St; ⊙11am-6pm Wed-Fri, to 5pm Sat & Sun), Vermont's largest producer of hard cider, for free tastes (any four flavors from their dozen-plus lineup), or hop on over to **Otter Creek Brewing** (☎802-388-0727; www.ottercreek brewing.com; 793 Exchange St; ⊙11am-6pm), where you can watch the brewers at work while enjoying lunch and a six-beer sampler in the adjacent brewpub. If wine tasting is more your thing, continue 2 miles north on US 7 to New Haven's Lincoln Peak Vineyard (www.lincoln peakvineyard.com), one of the finest wineries in the state.

✕ 🏠 p189

The Drive » Head north 27 miles on US 7 into Shelburne, then take Harbor Rd 1.6 miles northwest to Shelburne Farms.

- - - - - - - - - - - - - -

TRIP HIGHLIGHT

❺ Shelburne

In 1886 William Seward Webb and Lila Vanderbilt Webb built a little place for themselves on Lake Champlain. The 1400-acre farm, designed by landscape architect Frederick Law Olmsted (who also designed New York City's Central Park), was both a country house for the Webbs and a working farm. These days, the century-old estate and National Historic Landmark exists as **Shelburne Farms** (☎802-985-8686; www.shelburnefarms.org; 1611 Harbor Rd; adult/child $8/5; ⊙9am-5pm mid-May–mid-Oct, 10am-5pm mid-Oct–mid-May; 🚻), a working farm and environmental education center.

Tours in a truck-pulled open wagon are a barrel of fun: you can admire the buildings

DETOUR: CHAMPLAIN ORCHARDS

Start: ❹ Middlebury

Wide-open farm country cascades toward Lake Champlain as you detour 16 miles southwest from Middlebury along VT 30 and VT 74 to **Champlain Orchards** (☎802-897-2777; www.champlainorchards. com; 3597 VT 74 W, Shoreham; 🚻). Here you can pick two dozen varieties of apples – including many New England heirlooms – or watch the pressing and bottling of ultra-fresh cider. The orchard is famous for its free 'while-you-pick' acoustic concerts and an annual October harvest celebration.

Vermont Pumpkin harvest

(inspired by European Romanticism), observe cheese making and learn about maple syrup and mustard production. Hikers can meander the walking trails and kids love the animals in the children's farmyard. In mid-September, drop by and celebrate autumn traditions at the annual **Harvest Festival**, featuring hay rides, a hay-bale maze, music and antique farm machines.

 p205

The Drive » Head north on US 7 through Burlington. Hop on VT 15, then VT 128 and VT 104 to Cambridge. The drive is 35 miles.

❻ Cambridge

Tucked into the stunningly beautiful Lamoille River valley at the foot of Mt Mansfield, **Boyden Valley Winery** (☎802-644-8151; www.boydenvalley.com; cnr VT 104 & VT 15; ☺10am-5pm Nov-May, to 6pm Jun-Oct) is one of Vermont's leading producers of dessert wines. Savor the views and check out the award-winning Gold Leaf, a Vermont-inspired concoction that uses maple syrup straight from the farm combined with local apples.

The Drive » For spectacular mountain scenery, take VT 108 south through Smugglers Notch to Stowe, then pick up VT 100 south to Waterbury and hop

---

VERMONT FRESH NETWORK

Fresh local food is never far away in the Green Mountain State, thanks to the Vermont Fresh Network (www.vermontfresh.net), a partnership between the state's restaurants and farmers. Restaurants commit to supporting local producers by buying direct from the farm, while 'farmers' dinners' throughout the year allow diners to meet the people who put the food on their table. For a full list of participating restaurants and upcoming events, see their website.

---

on I-89 east to Montpelier. The drive is 42 miles.

- - - - - - - - - - -

❼ Montpelier

With 9000 residents, Montpelier is America's smallest capital city and the only one without a McDonald's. It's home to the prestigious New England Culinary Institute (NECI; www.neci.edu), so stop here for a dose of Vermont history paired with fine food.

Adjacent to the gold-domed **State House** (www.vtstatehouse.org; 115 State St; ☺guided tours 10am-3:30pm Mon-Fri, 11am-2:30pm Sat Jul–mid-Oct, 9am-3pm Mon-Fri mid-Oct–Jun, self-guided tours year-round), whose front doors are guarded by a massive statue of American Revolutionary hero Ethan Allen, is the **Vermont History Museum** (☎802-828-2291; www.vermonthistory.org/visit/vermont-history-museum; 109 State St; adult/child $7/5; ☺10am-4pm Tue-Sat). Its

---

award-winning 'Freedom and Unity' (the state motto) exhibit walks you through 400 years of Vermont history. From your first few steps into an Abenaki wigwam, you're asked to consider the true meaning of this phrase. Controversies aren't brushed under the rug, either: a short film presents the early-20th-century debate over women's suffrage alongside footage from the 1999 statehouse hearings where citizens voiced their support for or opposition to civil unions. In a very Vermontish way, you're invited to ponder issues on your own regardless of any party line. The panoply of voices and imaginative presentations keep this exhibit fun and lively.

✗ p189

The Drive » From Montpelier, a straight 54-mile shot down I-89 returns you to your starting point at Quechee.

Eating & Sleeping

Quechee ❶

✘ Simon Pearce Restaurant
Modern American $$$

(☎802-295-1470; www.simonpearce.com; 1760 Quechee Main St; lunch mains $14-18, dinner mains $22-39; ◷11:30am-2:45pm & 5:30-9pm Mon-Sat, from 10:30am Sun) Be sure to reserve a window table overlooking the falls in Simon Pearce's dining room, which is suspended over the river in this converted brick mill. Local ingredients are used to inventive effect in such delicacies as crab and cod melt or seared chicken with roasted-corn mascarpone polenta. The restaurant's stemware is blown by hand in the adjacent glass workshop.

Woodstock ❷

✘ Worthy Kitchen
Pub Food $$

(☎802-457-7281; http://worthyvermont.com/worthy-kitchen; 442 E Woodstock Rd/US 4; mains $13-25; ◷4-10pm Mon-Fri, 11am-10pm Sat, 10am-9pm Sun) This laid-back brewpub serving farm-to-table comfort food has become a local favorite since opening in 2013. The ever-changing menu, scrawled on giant blackboards, features daily specials, such as burgers, buttermilk fried chicken, Caesar salad or mac-and-cheese with local Plymouth cheddar, all accompanied by a frequently rotating lineup of 18 microbrews (mostly from Vermont or elsewhere in New England).

Middlebury ❹

✘ American Flatbread
Pizza $$

(☎802-388-3300; http://americanflatbread.com/restaurants/middlebury-vt; 137 Maple St; flatbreads $13-22; ◷5-9pm Tue-Fri, noon-9pm Sat) In a cavernous marble-block building with a blazing fire that keeps things cozy in winter, this is one of Middlebury's most beloved eateries. The menu is limited to farm-fresh salads and custom-made flatbreads (don't call it pizza or they'll come after you with the paddle) topped with locally sourced organic cheeses, meat and veggies, accompanied by Vermont microbrews on tap.

⊨ Swift House Inn
Inn $$

(☎866-388-9925, 802-388-9925; www.swifthouseinn.com; 25 Stewart Lane; r incl breakfast $135-299; ☜) Two blocks north of the town green, this grand white Federal mansion (1814) is surrounded by fine formal lawns and gardens. Luxurious standard rooms in the main house and adjacent carriage house are supplemented by suites with fireplaces, sitting areas and Jacuzzis. Other welcome luxuries include a steam room and sauna, a cozy pub, a library and a sun porch.

Montpelier ❼

✘ Red Hen
Bakery $

(☎802-223-5200; www.redhenbaking.com; 961B US Rte 2, Middlesex; pastries from $3; ◷7am-4pm Mon, to 6pm Tue-Sat, 8am-6pm Sun) One of Vermont's finest bakeries, Red Hen is well worth the 6-mile trek west of Montpelier – and a perfect breakfast stop if you're headed toward Stowe, Waterbury or Burlington. Settle into its comfy seating area over sinfully delicious sweet rolls, blueberry-studded pastries and breakfast sandwiches on hearty Mad River Grain bread, or simply grab a loaf for the road.

✘ Threepenny Taproom
Pub Food $

(☎802-223-8277; www.threepennytaproom.com; 108 Main St; mains $10-16; ◷11am-late Sun-Fri, noon-late Sat) With the names of two dozen microbrews from Vermont and beyond scrawled on the blackboard every evening, this pub is a perennial late-night favorite. But it also has a fabulous lineup of snacks and light meals, including Vermont cheeses, salads, sandwiches, burgers, flatbreads and bistro classics, such as *moules frites* (mussels with French fries).

Northeast Kingdom to Camel's Hump

17

From the serenity of Vermont's 'Northeast Kingdom' to the dramatic beauty of the Green Mountains' highest peaks, this back-road ramble mixes off-the-beaten-track treasures with iconic Vermont villages.

TRIP HIGHLIGHTS

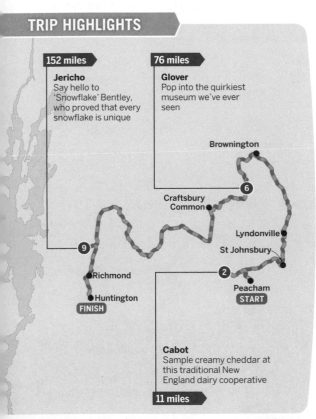

152 miles

Jericho
Say hello to 'Snowflake' Bentley, who proved that every snowflake is unique

76 miles

Glover
Pop into the quirkiest museum we've ever seen

Brownington

Craftsbury Common

Lyndonville

St Johnsbury

Richmond

Huntington
FINISH

Peacham
START

Cabot
Sample creamy cheddar at this traditional New England dairy cooperative

11 miles

3–4 DAYS
169 MILES / 272KM

GREAT FOR...

BEST TIME TO GO
May to October for warmish weather and snow-free roads.

ESSENTIAL PHOTO
Snap the papier-mâché creatures at the Bread & Puppet Museum.

BEST FOR OUTDOORS
Enjoy stunning vistas of bucolic rolling hills and peaceful, sparsely populated countryside.

Northeast Kingdom to Camel's Hump

Some say this is the real Vermont: historic villages frozen in time, narrow mountain passes and expanses of farmland stretching out to lush, maple-covered mountains. A word of warning: this trip is full of curves, lesser-known attractions and dirt roads without phone service. Translation? This trip is perfect for spontaneous explorers ready to embrace the quirky spirit of off-the-radar adventure that makes Vermont's back roads so enticing.

❶ Peacham

Surrounded by a dreamy landscape of high pastures and stone walls, Peacham is one of Vermont's quintessential historic villages. Originally a stop on the Bayley–Hazen Military Road – intended to help Americans launch a sneak attack on the British during the Revolutionary War – Peacham today retains a sleepy, lost-in-time quality. Take a self-guided **walking tour** using the free brochure from the town library, or browse the antiques and

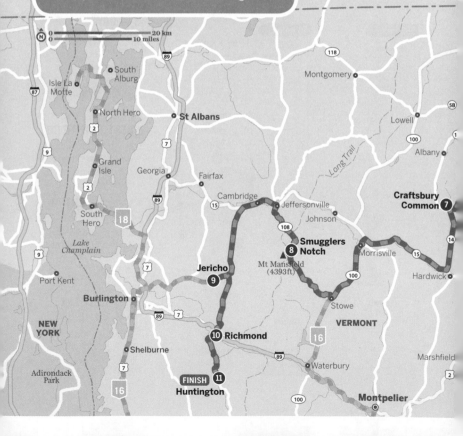

handicrafts at the **Peacham Corner Guild**.

The Drive ›› Head northwest over the mountains on unpaved Mack Mountain Rd; 7 miles out, a quick drive west on US 2 brings you to Danville Hill Rd, which plunges steeply down to Cabot. The drive is 11 miles.

TRIP HIGHLIGHT

❷ Cabot

Despite its nationwide distribution network, **Cabot Creamery** (☏800-837-4261; www.cabotcheese.com; 2878 Main St; tours adult/child $3/free; ◷9am-5pm mid-May–Oct, 10am-4pm Nov &

Dec, 10am-4pm Mon-Sat Jan–mid-May) remains basically true to its roots as a New England dairy cooperative. Its half-hour tour gives you a look at the cheese-making process (not to mention high-tech machinery painted like Holstein cows), after which you can pig out to your heart's content in the sample room.

The Drive ›› Backtrack 3.5 miles up Danville Hill Rd, then follow US 2 east for 14 miles into St Johnsbury.

❸ St Johnsbury

Home to the country's oldest art gallery (founded in 1871) still in its original form, the **St Johnsbury Athenaeum** (☏802-748-8291; www.stjathenaeum.org; 1171 Main St; ◷10am-5:30pm Mon, Wed & Fri, 2-7pm Tue & Thu, 10am-3pm Sat) is built around its crown jewel, Albert Bierstadt's 10ft-by-15ft painting *Domes of the Yosemite*. The rest of the collection consists of works by such Hudson

River School painters as Asher B Durand, Worthington Whittredge and Jasper Crospey.

✕ 🛏 p197

The Drive ›› Take exit 23 off I-91 north in Lyndonville, then continue north on US 5 and VT 5A to Lake Willoughby, 27 miles away. En route you'll pass near East Burke, home to a spectacular network of recreation trails and some enticing hilltop B&Bs (p197).

❹ Lake Willoughby

Sandwiched between Mt Hor and Mt Pisgah, whose cliffs plummet more than 1000ft to the waters below, this stunningly beautiful glacial-lake resembles a landlocked fjord. To appreciate the dramatic scenery, head for the good swimming beach at the lake's northern tip, or climb to one of the surrounding summits. The **South Trail** to Mt Pisgah (3.4 miles, three hours round-trip) and the easier **Herbert Hawkes Trail** to Mt Hor (1.9 miles,

❺ Brownington

Lake ❹ Willoughby

Glover ❻

p194

Lyndonville

St Johnsbury ❸

St Johnsbury

❷

❶ **Peacham**
START

Mcindoe Falls

§ **LINK YOUR TRIP**

16 **Cider Season Sampler**

For a taste of Vermont harvest season, join this trip in Cambridge (between Smugglers Notch and Jericho).

18 **Lake Champlain Byway**

From Richmond, follow I-89 west to Burlington for a scenic trip through the islands of Lake Champlain.

1½ hours round-trip) both begin just south of the great cleft along Lake Willoughby's southern shore.

The Drive ≫ Head briefly north of the lake on VT 5A, then turn left onto Schoolhouse Rd, continuing west into Brownington. The drive is 7 miles.

- - - - - - - - - - - - -

⑤ Brownington

Brownington's well preserved but little visited **Old Stone House Museum** (802-754-2022; http://oldstonehousemuseum. org; 109 Old Stone House Rd; adult/child $8/5; Wed-Sun mid-May–mid-Oct, self-guided tour of grounds 11am-5pm, 1hr guided Old Stone House tour 11:30am, 1:30pm & 3:30pm) is just one of many lovely 19th-century buildings reposing under the shade of equally ancient maple trees. The museum pays

tribute to educational trailblazer Alexander Twilight, the USA's first African American college graduate, who built Brownington's boarding school and ran it for decades.

The Drive ≫ Take VT 58 west, I-91 south and VT 16 south to Glover (13 miles), then turn left onto VT 122 and look for the Bread & Puppet Museum on your left within less than 1 mile.

- - - - - - - - - - - - -

TRIP HIGHLIGHT

⑥ Glover

A bright-turquoise school bus parked across from a barn with painted letters proclaiming 'Cheap Art Store' is your sign that you've stumbled upon the **Bread & Puppet Museum** (802-525-3031; http:// breadandpuppet.org/museum; 753 Heights Rd, Glover; donations welcome; 10am-6pm Jun-Oct, by appointment

Nov-May). For nearly 50 years, the internationally renowned Bread & Puppet Theater has been staging politically charged, avant-garde satirical spectacles starring gigantic papier-mâché puppets (some up to 20ft tall) borne through the fields on the company's hilltop farm. Vermont performances take place on weekends in July through August.

When no show is going on (the troupe tours nationally and internationally outside of summer), visit the museum in the cavernous old barn and admire freakishly impressive angels, devils, horses and other fantastic creatures from past performances, hauntingly crammed over two stories. Oh, and about that name? The director bakes bread

---

DETOUR:
HILL FARMSTEAD BREWERY

Start: ⑥ Glover

You know you're getting close when the asphalt disappears and you haven't had a phone signal for 30 minutes. Down two dirt roads in the middle of nowhere, **Hill Farmstead Brewery** (802-533-7450; www.hillfarmstead.com; 403 Hill Rd, Greensboro Bend; 4 tastes $5; noon-5pm Wed-Sat but call to confirm, tours by appointment) is, well, a farm on a hill, with a garage that holds a brewery and tasting nook. It produces a mere 300 to 400 gallons per week, and the output rarely leaves the state, yet Hill Farmstead has a cult following for its small-batch brews.

Produced by Shaun Hill, who's known for his creative concoctions and uncompromising adherence to quality, many of the beers have names based on the Hill family: Damon, a bourbon-barrel-aged Russian Imperial Stout, is the namesake of Shaun's childhood dog; the hoppy IPA, Edward, is named after Shaun's grandfather. No matter how you like your beer – bitter, malty, spicy – friendly staff will guide you to your favorite at the tiny bar.

Green Mountains Hiking in the woods

and shares it with the audience at each performance to create a sense of community.

🛏 p197

The Drive ›› Return to Glover and take VT 16 south for 2 miles, then head 13 miles west on Shadow Lake Rd, E Craftsbury Rd and S Craftsbury Rd into Craftsbury Common.

❼ Craftsbury Common

Welcome to Craftsbury Common, where you'll find what may be Vermont's most spectacular village green. White clapboard buildings surround a rectangular lawn that hasn't changed one iota since the mid-19th century. Nearby, the community-owned Craftsbury General Store (p197) has a well-stocked deli and a nice array of Vermont-made products, while the **Craftsbury Outdoor Center** (📞802-586-7767; www.craftsbury. com; 535 Lost Nation Rd, Craftsbury Common; trail pass adult/child $10/5; 👪) offers year-round outdoor activities (skiing, running, kayaking, canoeing and stand-up paddle surfing) on its 80 miles of trails and Big Hosmer Pond.

🍴 p197

The Drive ›› Take VT 14 south past Hardwick, then follow VT 15 west to Morrisville, looking on your left for the Fisher Covered Railroad Bridge, one of America's last covered railroad bridges. At Morrisville, turn south on VT 100 to Stowe, then climb 9 miles up VT 108 to Smugglers Notch. The drive is 36 miles in all.

❽ Smugglers Notch & Stowe

Tucked beneath Mt Mansfield (Vermont's highest peak), Smugglers Notch is Vermont's narrowest and most visually stunning paved mountain pass. As you crest the notch, the painted center line disappears in deference

LOCAL KNOWLEDGE: KINGDOM TRAILS

In 1997 a group of dedicated locals linked together 200-plus miles of single and double tracks and dirt roads to form the Northeast Kingdom's astounding, award-winning **Kingdom Trails network** (www.kingdomtrails.com; Welcome Center, 478 VT 114, East Burke (summer), Nordic Adventure Center, 2059 Darling Hill Road, Lyndonville (winter); day pass adult/child $15/7; ☺Welcome Center 8am-5pm Sun-Thu, 8am-6pm Fri & Sat May-Oct, Nordic Adventure Center 8:30am-4pm daily Nov-Apr; ⊞). Passing through century-old farms and soft forest floors dusted with pine needles, it offers one of New England's best mountain-biking experiences. In winter, the trails are ideal for cross-country skiing, snowshoeing and fat biking. Buy passes at the Kingdom Trails Welcome Center on VT 114 in East Burke, 5 miles east of I-91.

to a fairy-tale landscape of encroaching cliffs and boulders that squeeze the roadway down to a scant lane and a half. It's the trailhead for numerous (uphill!) hikes, including the scenic 1.2-mile scramble through the boulders to pretty **Sterling Pond**.

✕ 🛏 p197

The Drive » Descend through pretty mountain scenery along VT 108 to Jeffersonville, where you'll take VT 15 west for 24 miles to Jericho.

- - - - - - - - - - - -

TRIP HIGHLIGHT

⑨ Jericho

Jericho's photogenic **Old Red Mill** (☎802-899-3225; www.jerichohistoricalsociety.org/the-old-red-mill.html; Rte 15; ☺10am-5pm Mon-Sat Apr-Dec, 11:30am-4pm Sun Apr-Jun & Sep-Dec) sits

astride the Browns River gorge. Inside the mill, a nice display of Vermont crafts shares space with a free museum showcasing the captivating microphotography of native son 'Snowflake' Bentley, who provided groundbreaking evidence that no two snowflakes are identical. Out back, the **Browns River Trail** traverses a soft carpet of evergreen needles to a little sandy beach with big boulders and a deep pool for swimming.

The Drive » Return 2 miles east on VT 15, then take Browns Trace Rd 8 miles south through Jericho Center into Richmond.

- - - - - - - - - - - -

⑩ Richmond

Straddling the shores of the Winooski River, this pleasant village is worth a stop for its early-19th-century **Old Round Church** (☎802-434-2556; www.oldroundchurch.com; 25 Round Church Rd; ☺10am-4pm Sat & Sun late May–mid-Jun, daily mid-Jun–mid-Oct), one of Vermont's most unique structures. The graceful 16-sided edifice, used by multiple congregations over the years, is as elegant inside as outside.

The Drive » The main road (Huntington Rd) curves west just beyond the Old Round Church, then turns south toward Huntington, 7 miles away. In July and August, consider a brief detour off-route to **Owl's Head Blueberry Farm**, a scenic spot to pick your own berries.

- - - - - - - - - - - -

⑪ Huntington

Huntington's gorgeous valley is presided over by Vermont's most distinctively shaped peak, **Camel's Hump** (known to early French explorers as 'Le Lion Couchant' for its resemblance to a sleeping lion). It remains one of the state's wildest spots, the only significant Vermont peak not developed for skiing, and the summit is a hiker's dream: from Huntington Center, head east 3 miles, dead-ending at the trailhead for the 6-mile **Burrows to Forest City loop**. After climbing through forest, the final ascent skirts rock faces above the tree line, affording magnificent views.

Eating & Sleeping

St Johnsbury ❸

✖ Kingdom Taproom · Pub Food $

(☎802-424-1355; www.kingdomtaproom. com; 397 Railroad St; mains $8-14; ⊙4-10pm Mon-Thu, noon-midnight Fri & Sat, noon-8pm Sun) You'll find the Northeast Kingdom's largest selection of microbrews on tap at this recently opened pub in the heart of St Johnsbury. A bevy of Vermont beers such as 14th Star, Hill Farmstead, Fiddlehead and Lost Nation are offered on a rotating basis, along with mac-and-cheese, soups, salads, flatbreads and sandwiches.

⎮≃ Inn at Mountain View Farm · Inn $$

(☎802-626-9924, 800-572-4509; www. innmtnview.com; 3383 Darling Hill Rd, East Burke; r $215-245, ste $295-375, all incl breakfast & afternoon tea; ❄🛜) Built in 1883, this spacious, elegant farmhouse is set on a hilltop with stunning views, surrounded by 440 acres that are ideal for mountain biking, cross-country skiing or simply taking a long stroll on the hillside. There's also an on-site animal sanctuary, which is a rescue center for large farm animals; guests are encouraged to visit.

Glover ❻

⎮≃ Rodgers Country Inn · Inn $

(☎802-525-6677, 800-729-1704; http:// rodgerscountryinn.com; 582 Rodgers Rd, West Glover; s/d without bath incl breakfast $65/80, cabins per week $600) Not far from the shores of Shadow Lake, Jim and Nancy Rodgers offer five guest rooms in their 1840s farmhouse, plus two independent cabins. Hang out on the front porch and read, or take a stroll on this 350-acre former dairy farm. This inn appeals to people who really want to feel what it's like to live in rural Vermont.

Craftsbury Common ❼

✖ Craftsbury General Store · American $

(☎802-586-2440; http://craftsburygeneralstore. com; 118 S Craftsbury Rd, Craftsbury; sandwiches $7-10; ⊙7am-8pm, reduced hours in winter) The community-owned Craftsbury General Store serves sandwiches, pizzas and tasty deli treats. Don't miss the Wednesday-evening Globetrotting Dinners (4pm to 8pm), featuring cuisine from a different country every week.

Smugglers Notch & Stowe ❽

✖ Pie-casso · Pizza $$

(☎802-253-4411; www.piecasso.com; 1899 Mountain Rd, Stowe; mains $8-22; ⊙11am-10pm Sun-Thu, to 11pm Fri & Sat) Best known for its ample pizzas, from the sausage-and-pepperoni-laden Heart Stopper to the veggie-friendly Vienna with spinach, olives, sun-dried tomatoes and mozzarella, Pie-casso also serves everything from eggplant parmesan subs to fettuccine alfredo and penne with pesto. Gluten-free crusts using flour from nearby West Meadow Farm are also available.

⎮≃ Smugglers Notch State Park · Campground $

(☎802-253-4014; www.vtstateparks.com/ htm/smugglers.htm; 6443 Mountain Rd, Stowe; campsites $20-22, lean-tos $27-29; ⊙mid-May–mid-Oct) This 35-acre park, 8 miles northwest of Stowe, is perched up on the mountainside. It has 81 tent and trailer sites, and 20 lean-tos and walk-in sites.

⎮≃ Green Mountain Inn · Inn $$$

(☎802-253-7301; www.greenmountaininn.com; 18 Main St, Stowe; r/ste/apt from $179/289/299) The Stowe Recreation Path unfurls just a few steps from the door at this 180-year-old red-brick inn, which sits in the heart of downtown Stowe. How best to relax? Settle into a rocking chair on the front porch, enjoy afternoon cookies and tea, then head to the spa. The 104 rooms are classically decorated and come in a variety of configurations.

Lake Champlain Byway

18

Vermont's 'Great Lake' offers delights not found elsewhere in the state, from the sophistication of Burlington to the tranquil Champlain Islands, stretching like stepping stones to the Canadian border.

TRIP HIGHLIGHTS

53 miles

Isle La Motte
A pristine island home to the world's largest fossil reef

FINISH **7** ●South Alburg

●Winooski **3**

13 miles

Burlington
Vermont's biggest city boasts one of New England's best chocolatiers

1 **0 miles**

START

Shelburne
Visit an open-air museum that speaks volumes about Vermont history

1–2 DAYS
53 MILES / 85KM

GREAT FOR...

BEST TIME TO GO

June to October for long, summery days and abundant leaf-peeping opportunities.

ESSENTIAL PHOTO

Grab a shot at water's edge on Isle La Motte.

BEST FOR FOODIES

Sample the state's most famous beer export and indulge in Burlington's vibrant restaurant scene.

18 Lake Champlain Byway

Tucked between the Green Mountains and the Adirondacks of New York, beautiful Lake Champlain is the defining feature of northwest Vermont's landscape. Survey the lake from the stellar historical museum in Shelburne and the pedestrian-friendly waterfront in Burlington, then set off to discover the Champlain Islands, a 27-mile ribbon of largely undeveloped isles where simpler pleasures prevail: swimming, boating, apple picking, wine tasting, or rambling along sleepy farm roads and inter-island causeways.

TRIP HIGHLIGHT

❶ Shelburne

Feast your eyes on the stunning array of 17th- to 20th-century American artifacts – folk art, textiles, toys, tools, carriages and furniture – spread over the 45-acre grounds and gardens at **Shelburne Museum** (☎802-985-3346; www.shelburnemuseum.org; 6000 Shelburne Rd/US 7; adult/child/teen $24/12/14; ⏰10am-5pm daily May-Dec, 10am-5pm Wed-Sun Jan-Apr; ♿). This remarkable place is set up as a mock village, with 150,000 objects housed in 39 buildings. Highlights include a full-size covered bridge, a classic round barn, an 1871 lighthouse, a one-room schoolhouse, a railway station with a locomotive and a working blacksmith's forge.

The collection's sheer size lets you tailor your visit. Families are drawn to the carousel, the Owl Cottage children's center and the *Ticonderoga* steamship, while aficionados of quilts or, say, duck decoys can spend hours investigating their personal passion. Indeed, the buildings themselves are exhibits. Many were moved here from other parts of New England to ensure their preservation.

🛏 p205

The Drive » Continue north on US 7 for 4 miles until you reach South Burlington.

❷ South Burlington

One of the pioneers – and among the most famous – of Vermont's microbreweries is **Magic Hat Brewery** (☎802-658-2739; www.magichat.net; 5 Bartlett Bay Rd; ⏰10am-7pm Mon-Sat Jun–mid-Oct, to 6pm Mon-Thu, to 7pm Fri & Sat mid-Oct–May, noon-5pm Sun year-round), which started brewing in 1995. The 'Artifactory' exudes an infectious creative energy, with more than 20 varieties flowing from four dozen taps.

Guided 30-minute tours take you through the history of Vermont breweries and Magic Hat's role, how it makes its beer and keeps environmental impact as low as possible, and its involvement in the community (such as the annual Magic Hat Mardi Gras and its support for the performing arts). Guides will happily answer any question you have, such as who writes the sayings on the inside of each bottle cap. You can enjoy free tastes both before and after the tour. Must-tries are the trademark No 9 (pale ale with a hint of apricot), Circus Boy (lemongrass-infused Hefeweizen) and

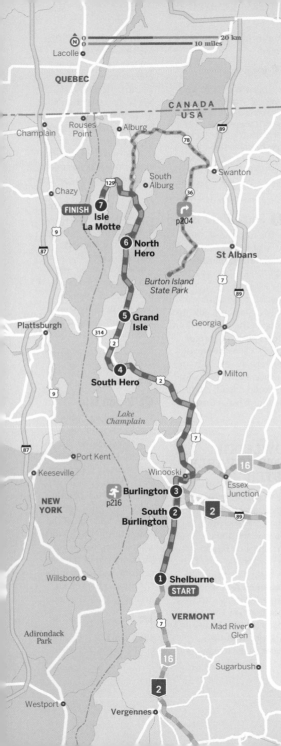

the whimsically changing lineup of seasonal brews and 'Reclusive Rarities'. (There's also a self-guided tour in case you miss one of the guided ones.)

The Drive » Continue north on US 7 for 4 miles to Burlington.

TRIP HIGHLIGHT

❸ Burlington

Perched above glistening Lake Champlain, Vermont's largest city would be a small city in most other states. Yet Burlington's diminutive size is one of its charms, with an easily walkable downtown (p216) and a gorgeous, accessible lakefront. With the University of Vermont (UVM) swelling the city (by 13,400 students) and a vibrant cultural and social life, Burlington has a spirited, youthful character. And when it comes to nightlife, this is Vermont's epicenter.

LINK YOUR TRIP

2 **Fall Foliage**
In Burlington, branch off to discover New England's blazing fall colors.

16 **Cider Season Sampler**
In Shelburne, hook up to the fall food-and-drink-filled loop.

Just before you reach the city center, a chocolate stop is in order. The aroma of rich melted cocoa is intoxicating as you enter the gift shop next to the glass wall overlooking the small factory at **Lake Champlain Chocolates** (☑802-864-1807; www.lakechamplainchocolates.com; 750 Pine St; ☺9am-6pm Mon-Sat, 11am-5pm Sun, hourly tours 11am-2pm Mon-Fri, tastings 11am-4pm Sat & Sun). Take the tour to get the history of the chocolatier and ample samples to taste-test the gooey goodness. Oh, and this shop is the only one with factory-seconds shelves containing stacks of chocolate at a discount. It tastes the same as the pretty stuff but for cosmetic reasons can't be sold at regular price. The cafe serves coffee drinks and its own luscious ice cream.

✕ ⊨ p205

The Drive ⟩⟩ Cast off for the Champlain Islands, cruising 10 miles north of Burlington on I-89 to exit 17, then west on US 2 for 9 miles. After Sand Bar State Park – a great picnic and swimming spot – cross the causeway and look for the photo-perfect parking island halfway across.

---

④ South Hero Island

Settle into the slower pace of island life at **Allenholm Orchards** (☑802-372-5566; www.allenholm.com; 111 South St, South Hero; ☺9am-5pm late May-Christmas Eve; ⊞), just outside the town of South Hero; grab a Creemee (that's Vermont-speak for soft-serve ice cream) or pick a few apples for the road ahead. About 3 miles west is **Snow**

LOCAL KNOWLEDGE: CHAMPLAIN'S LOVABLE LAKE MONSTER

Dinosaur relic or ice-age proto-whale? Tree trunk? Really really big fish? Lake Champlain's legendary lake monster – nicknamed 'Champ' – has long fascinated local residents. Known to the Abenaki as Tatoskok, Champ was even sighted by French explorer Samuel de Champlain back in the early 17th century. Indulge your curiosity at the Champ display in Burlington's **ECHO Lake Aquarium & Science Center** (☑802-864-1848; www.echovermont.org; 1 College St; adult/child $13.50/10.50; ☺10am-5pm; ⊞). For a more dependable sighting, attend a Vermont Lake Monsters baseball game, where a lovable green-costumed Champ mascot dances on the dugout roof between innings.

Farm Winery (☑802-372-9463; www.snowfarm.com; 190 W Shore Rd, South Hero; ☺11am-5pm daily May-Dec, 5-9pm Fri, 11am-5pm Sat & Sun Jan-Apr), Vermont's first vineyard, which boasts a sweet tasting room tucked away down a dirt road (look for the signs off US 2). Sample its award-winning whites or have a sip of ice wine in the rustic barn (three tastes are free), or drop by on Thursday evening for the free **concert series** (www.snowfarm.com; ☺6:30-8:30pm Thu mid-Jun–early Sep) on the lawn next to the vines – you can expect anything from jazz to folk to light rock and roll.

The Drive ⟩⟩ Continue north on US 2 for 8 miles.

---

⑤ Grand Isle

The **Hyde Log Cabin** (☑802-372-8339; http://historicsites.vermont.gov/road side_markers; US 2; adult/child $3/free; ☺11am-5pm Fri-Sun plus Mon holidays late May–mid-Oct; ⊠), the oldest (1783) log cabin in Vermont and one of the oldest in the US, is worth a short stop to see how settlers lived in the 18th century and to examine traditional household artifacts from Vermont.

⊨ p205

The Drive ⟩⟩ Continue north on US 2 for another 8 miles.

Vermont Apple orchard

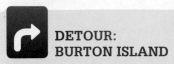

DETOUR:
BURTON ISLAND

Start: ❼ North Hero Island

For a deeper immersion in Lake Champlain's natural beauty, spend a night or two camping at **Burton Island State Park** (📞802-524-6353; www.vtstateparks.com/htm/burton.htm; 2714 Hathaway Point Rd, St Albans; day use adult/child $4/2; 🌐late May-early Sep; ♿), in the middle of the lake. Between Memorial Day and Labor Day, the *Island Runner* ferry (10 minutes) shuttles campers and their gear across a narrow channel from the mainland near St Albans to this pristine, traffic-free island with over two dozen lakefront lean-tos and campsites. Park facilities include boat rentals, a nature center with daily kids' activities and a store selling breakfast, lunch and groceries; the sign outside ('No shoes, no shirt, no problem!') epitomizes the island's laid-back vibe.

It's an easy 45-minute loop around the lake from North Hero to the ferry dock at Kill Kare State Park. Head 10 miles north on US 2 and then 10 miles east on VT 78 to get to Swanton; from there drive 10 miles south on VT 36 and turn right onto Hathaway Point Rd for the final 2.5 miles.

---

❻ North Hero Island

Boaters for miles around cast anchor at popular general store **Hero's Welcome** (📞802-372-4161; www.heroswelcome.com; 3537 US 2, North Hero; 🕑6:30am-8pm Mon-Fri, 7am-7pm Sat & Sun mid-Jun–early Sep, shorter hours rest of year). The store's amusing wall display of 'World Time Zones' – four clocks showing identical hours for Lake Champlain's North Hero, South Hero, Grand Isle and Isle La Motte – reflects the prevailing island-centric attitude. Pick up a souvenir, grab a sandwich or coffee and snap some pics on the outdoor terrace overlooking the boat landing.

🛏 p205

The Drive » From US 2, head west 4 miles on VT 129 to historic Isle La Motte.

TRIP HIGHLIGHT

❼ Isle La Motte

Pristine Isle La Motte is one of the most historic of all the Champlain Islands. Signs along its western shore signal its traditional importance as a crossroads for Native Americans; French explorer Samuel de Champlain landed here in 1609.

Tool around the loop road hugging the coast, stopping at **St Anne's Shrine** (📞802-928-3362; www.saintannesshrine.org; 92 St Anne's Rd; 🕑 shrine late May–mid-Oct, grounds year-round) on the site of Fort St Anne,

Vermont's oldest settlement. (Though it is welcoming to all, this is a religious place, so be respectful of those who come to pray.) The site features a striking granite statue of Samuel de Champlain, and its waterfront has spectacular views and a large picnic area.

Isle La Motte is also home to the 20-acre **Fisk Quarry Preserve** (www.ilmpt.org; West Rd; 🌐dawn-dusk), the world's largest fossil reef, 4 miles south of St Anne's Shrine. Half a million years old, the reef once provided limestone for Radio City Music Hall and Washington's National Gallery. Interpretive trails explain the history of the quarry.

Eating & Sleeping

Shelburne ❶

🛏 Inn at Shelburne Farms   Inn $$$

(📞802-985-8498; www.shelburnefarms.org/
staydine; 1611 Harbor Rd; r $270-525, without
bath $160-230, cottage $270-435, guesthouse
from $450; 😊 early May–mid-Oct; 🐾) One of
New England's top 10 places to stay, this inn,
7 miles south of Burlington off US 7, was once
the summer mansion of the wealthy Webb
family. It now welcomes guests, with rooms in
the gracious, welcoming country manor house
by the lakefront, as well as four independent,
kitchen-equipped cottages and guesthouses
scattered across the property.

Burlington ❸

🍴 Penny Cluse Cafe   Cafe $

(📞802-651-8834; www.pennycluse.com; 169
Cherry St; mains $9-14; 😊6:45am-3pm Mon-Fri,
8am-3pm Sat & Sun) In the heart of downtown,
one of Burlington's most popular breakfast spots
serves pancakes, biscuits and gravy, breakfast
burritos, omelets and tofu scrambles, along
with sandwiches, fish tacos, salads and the best
chile relleno you'll find east of the Mississippi.
Expect an hour's wait on weekends – best bet is
to put your name down, grab a coffee and take a
pre-meal wander.

🍴 Revolution
Kitchen   Vegan, Vegetarian $$

(📞802-448-3657; http://revolutionkitchen.
com; 9 Center St; mains $14-18; 😊5-10pm
Tue-Sat) Vegetarian fine dining? And romantic
atmosphere to boot? Yep, they all come together
at this cozy brick-walled restaurant that makes
ample and creative use of Vermont's abundant
organic produce. Asian, Mediterranean and Latin
American influences abound in house favorites
such as Revolution Tacos, crispy seitan piccata
and the Laksa Noodle Pot, and most items are
(or can be adapted to be) vegan.

🍷 Citizen Cider   Microbrewery

(📞802-497-1987; www.citizencider.com; 316
Pine St; 😊11am-10pm Mon-Sat, to 7pm Sun)

Tucked into an industrial-chic building with
painted concrete floors and long wooden
tables, this animated cidery is a home-grown
success story, using only Vermont apples to
make its ever-growing line of hard ciders. Taste-
test a flight of five for $7, including perennial
favorites such as the crisp, classic Unified
Press, or the Dirty Mayor, infused with ginger
and lemon peel.

🛏 Willard Street Inn   Inn $$

(📞802-651-8710; www.willardstreetinn.com;
349 S Willard St; r incl breakfast $159-279; 🐾)
Perched on a hill within easy walking distance
of UVM and the Church St Marketplace, this
mansion, fusing Queen Anne and Georgian
Revival styles, was built in the late 1880s. It has
a fine-wood and cut-glass elegance, yet radiates
a welcoming warmth. Many of the guest rooms
overlook Lake Champlain.

Grand Isle ❺

🛏 Grand Isle State Park   Campground $

(📞802-372-4300; www.vtstateparks.com/
htm/grandisle.htm; 36 East Shore South;
campsites $20-22, lean-tos $27-29, cabins $50;
😊mid-May–mid-Oct) Vermont's most popular
state-park campground straddles a pretty
stretch of Lake Champlain waterfront, with 117
tent and RV sites, 36 lean-tos and four cabins.

North Hero Island ❻

🛏 North Hero House   Inn $$

(📞888-525-3644, 802-372-4732; www.
northherohouse.com; 3643 US 2, North Hero;
r $125-250, ste $295-350; 🐾) This country
inn sits right across from the water, with
quilt-filled rooms, many with a private porch
and four-poster bed. Eating options include
a cozy restaurant serving New American
cuisine, Oscar's Oasis pub and the fantastic
outdoor Steamship Pier Bar & Grill, where
you can enjoy kebabs, burgers, lobster rolls
and cocktails smack on the pier, the water
glistening beside you.

Southern Vermont Loop

19

Crisscross the Green Mountains for a taste of everything southern Vermont has to offer, from Brattleboro's artsy counterculture to Bennington's white-steepled colonial heritage.

TRIP HIGHLIGHTS

2–3 DAYS
131 MILES / 211KM

GREAT FOR...

BEST TIME TO GO
May to October for great weather and autumnal colors.

 ESSENTIAL PHOTO
Capture the quintessential New England beauty of Grafton's clapboard homes, covered bridges and venerable old brick inn.

 BEST FOR OUTDOORS
Roam the trails on the grounds of Hildene, the Lincoln family estate.

63 miles

Manchester
Shop your heart out at the foot of beautiful Mt Equinox

104 miles

Grafton
Travel back in time to one of Vermont's prettiest historic villages

Weston

6

8

Townshend

2

Wilmington

Brattleboro
START/ FINISH

Bennington
Find out why Bennington was crucial to the American Revolution

40 miles

19 Southern Vermont Loop

Tidy white churches and inns surround village greens throughout historic southern Vermont, a region that's home to several towns that predate the American Revolution. This scenic loop takes in all the region's highlights: history-rich Bennington, the picture-postcard villages of Grafton and Weston, the upscale vacation mecca of Manchester, the imposing peak of Mt Equinox, the old stone home of Robert Frost and the opulent mansion of Abraham Lincoln's descendants.

❶ Brattleboro

Perched at the confluence of the Connecticut and West Rivers, Brattleboro is a little gem packed with independent shops, eateries and cultural venues such as the **Latchis Theater** (📞802-254-6300; http://theater.latchis.com; 50 Main St) and the **Brattleboro Museum & Art Center** (📞802-257-0124; www.brattleboromuseum.org; 10 Vernon St; adult/child $8/ free; ⊗11am-5pm Wed-Mon), housed in the town's 1915

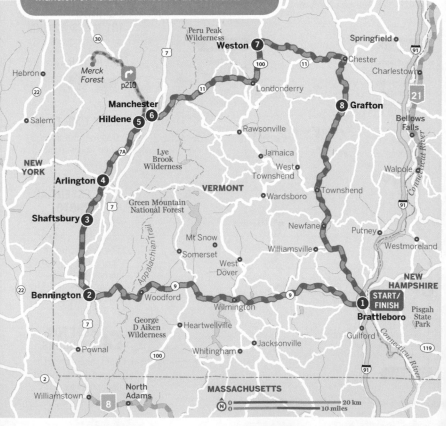

former railway station. An energetic mix of aging hippies and the latest crop of pierced and tattooed hipsters fuels the town's sophisticated eclecticism, keeping the downtown scene percolating and skewing its politics decidedly leftward.

✕ ⊨ p213

The Drive >> Take VT 9 west along the Molly Stark scenic byway for 40 miles to Bennington. After an ear-popping climb, 5 miles past the turnoff for the town of Marlboro, you'll come to the Hogback Mountain overlook; make sure to stop and admire the three-state views over Massachusetts, New Hampshire and Vermont.

LINK YOUR TRIP

8 **Mohawk Trail**
Explore New England's oldest scenic highway in Massachusetts. From Bennington, drive 13 miles south on US 7 to Williamstown.

21 **Connecticut River Byway**
Crisscross between Vermont and New Hampshire, following the banks of New England's mightiest river. From Brattleboro drive 23 miles north on I-91 to Walpole.

TRIP HIGHLIGHT

❷ Bennington

Bennington is divided into three sections: workaday town (Bennington proper), college town (North Bennington) and **Old Bennington**, which is where you'll find the main sights. The charming hilltop Colonial site is studded with 80 Georgian and Federal houses and the **Old First Church** (www.oldfirstchurch benn.org; cnr Monument Ave & VT 9; ☺10am-noon & 1-4pm Mon-Sat, 1-4pm Sun), built in 1806 in Palladian style. Its churchyard holds the remains of five Vermont governors, numerous soldiers of the American Revolution and poet Robert Frost (1874–1963), one of the best-known and best-loved American poets of the 20th century.

Up the hill to the north, the **Bennington Battle Monument** (☎802-447-0550; www.benningtonbattle monument.com; 15 Monument Circle, Old Bennington; adult/child $5/1; ☺9am-5pm mid-Apr–Oct) commemorates the crucial Battle of Bennington, fought during the American Revolution. Had Colonel Seth Warner and the local 'Green Mountain Boys' not helped weaken British defenses during this battle, the colonies might well have been split. The obelisk, built between 1887 and 1891, offers impressive views – an elevator whisks

you two-thirds of the way up the 306ft tower.

✕ p213

The Drive >> Head out of town along scenic VT 7A and drive 4 miles north to the Robert Frost Stone House. As the road winds along the valley, the southernmost section of the Green Mountains emerges on your left.

❸ Shaftsbury

When he moved his family to Shaftsbury, Robert Frost was 46 years old and at the height of his career. The **Robert Frost Stone House Museum** (☎802-447-6200; www.frostfriends.org; 121 VT 7A; adult/child $6/3; ☺10am-5pm Wed-Sun May-Oct) opens a window into the life of the poet, with one entire room dedicated to his most famous work, 'Stopping by Woods on a Snowy Evening,' which he penned here in the 1920s.

The Drive >> Drive 5 miles north along scenic VT 7A to Shaftsbury itself, then continue 6 miles further through bucolic farmland and wooded hollows to Arlington.

❹ Arlington

Arlington's tiny maple-syrup shop (the sweet stuff is made on-site) houses the **Norman Rockwell Exhibition** (☎802-375-6747; www.normanrockwellexhibit.com; VT 7A; ☺9am-5pm Mar-Christmas Eve), an homage to the artist, who lived in Arlington from 1939 to 1953. A section of the shop displays 500 of Rockwell's *Saturday Evening Post* covers and shows a short film about his life. (Exhibition hours vary; call to confirm.)

The Drive » Continue for 8 miles north along scenic VT 7A, passing the base of imposing Mt Equinox as you approach Hildene, on the southern outskirts of Manchester. The area is an excellent place for an overnight stay – oodles of B&Bs and hotels congregate in Manchester proper and along VT 7A as you approach town.

- - - - - - - - - - - - - -

❺ Hildene

Abraham Lincoln's wife, Mary Todd Lincoln (1818–82), and their son, Robert Todd Lincoln (1843–1926), came here during the Civil War;

as an adult Robert built **Hildene** (☎802-362-1788; www.hildene.org; 1005 Hildene Rd/VT 7A; adult/ child \$20/5, guided tours \$7.50/2; ⏱9:30am-4:30pm), a 24-room Georgian Revival mansion. Robert enjoyed the house until his death in 1926, and his great-granddaughter lived here until her death in 1975. Soon after, it was converted into a museum filled with Lincoln family personal effects and furnishings, including the hat Abraham Lincoln probably wore when he delivered the Gettysburg Address, and a brass cast of his hands, the right one swollen from shaking hands while campaigning for the presidency.

The surrounding grounds feature 8 miles of **walking trails**; an

exquisite flower garden designed to resemble a stained-glass Romanesque cathedral window; and a solar-powered barn where you can watch Hildene goat cheese being produced.

The Drive » Continue north on VT 7A for 2 miles to central Manchester.

- - - - - - - - - - - - - -

TRIP HIGHLIGHT

❻ Manchester

Manchester has been a fashionable resort town for almost two centuries. These days, the draws are the nearby skiing and hiking, the relaxed New England town vibe and the upscale outlet shopping (Manchester contains more than 100 shops, from Armani to Banana Republic).

DETOUR: MERCK FOREST

Start: ❻ Manchester

Encompassing more than 2700 acres of high-country farmland, meadow and forest, **Merck Forest & Farmland Center** (☎802-394-7836; www.merckforest.org; 3270 VT 315; ⏱visitor center 9am-4pm; 🚻) is a blissful place to experience Vermont's natural beauty and agricultural heritage. The park's centerpiece is a working organic farm with animals, vegetable gardens, renewable-energy installations and a sugar house where you can watch maple syrup being produced during sugaring season (generally mid-March to early April). It's hidden away on a gorgeous hilltop only 25 minutes from Manchester – but a world apart from the village hustle and bustle.

The center offers a wide range of **hikes**, environmental education programs and events such as sheepdog trials. It also rents out cabins and tent sites, which are spread all over the property. Sales of produce and syrup, coupled with voluntary contributions, help sustain the nonprofit foundation at the heart of it all.

To get here from Manchester, take VT 30 northwest 8 miles to East Rupert, then head 2 miles south on VT 315, looking for signs on your left at the top of the hill.

Shaftsbury Robert Frost Stone House Museum

Two families put the place on the map – the Lincolns and the Orvises. Franklin Orvis (1824–1900) established the Equinox House Hotel; his brother, Charles, founded the Orvis Company, makers of fly-fishing equipment with a worldwide following. Orvis Company products are showcased in the **American Museum of Fly Fishing** (📞802-362-3300; www.amff.com; 4070 Main St/VT 7A; adult/child $5/3; 🕙10am-4pm Tue-Sun Jun-Oct, Tue-Sat Nov-May), with fly collections and rods used by Ernest Hemingway, Bing Crosby and several US presidents.

Hikers can hit the trail for the dramatic climb to the summit of **Mt Equinox** (3848ft), which looms large just south of town. The five-hour hike (2918ft elevation gain) will reward you with exhilarating views; look for the trailhead behind the Equinox Hotel.

 p49, p213

The Drive » Follow VT 11 northeast for 15 miles towards Londonderry, then take VT 100 another 5 miles north into Weston.

---

7 Weston

Crowds flock to Weston for three main reasons: to browse the shelves at the **Vermont Country Store** (📞802-824-3184; www.vermontcountrystore. com; 657 Main St/VT 100; 🕙8:30am-7pm late May–mid-Oct, 9am-6pm rest of year); to attend the renowned summer theater festival at the **Weston Playhouse** (📞802-824-5288; www. westonplayhouse.org; 703 Main St; 🕙performances late Jun-early Sep), Vermont's oldest professional theater; or simply to bask in the glow of one of Vermont's most picturesque villages. From the gazebo at the center of Weston's circular town green, the views upstream to the town's waterfall and 19th-century mill are the stuff of tourist legend.

The Drive » Head 12 miles east on Weston–Andover Rd and VT 11 through the gorgeous stone village of Chester, then turn south on VT 35 and continue 7 miles south to Grafton.

TRIP HIGHLIGHT

8 Grafton

One of Vermont's prettiest villages, Grafton exudes a peaceful grace reminiscent of a bygone century. It's not that way by accident. In the 1960s the private Windham Foundation established a preservation program for the entire village, burying all electrical and telephone lines and restoring historic buildings and covered bridges. The town's most picturesque landmark is the Grafton Inn (p213) at the center of town. With its brick exterior and double porch, this venerable inn has played host to such notable guests as Rudyard Kipling, Theodore Roosevelt and Ralph Waldo Emerson. Stop in for a bite at the formal New England dining room or the casual tavern in the carriage house out back.

South of town, the **Grafton Ponds Outdoor Center** (📞802-843-2400; http://graftonponds.com; 783 Townshend Rd) offers year-round recreation on its network of mountain-biking, hiking and cross-country ski trails, along with canoeing, swimming, snow-tubing and adventure camps for kids. Along the same road you'll also find the **Grafton Village Cheese Company** (📞800-472-3866 x117; www.graftonvillage cheese.com; 533 Townshend Rd; 🕙hours vary), whose mouthwatering and nose-tingling cheddars regularly win awards at international cheese festivals.

 p213

The Drive » Continue 27 miles south along Grafton–Townshend Rd, VT 35 and VT 30 into Brattleboro, taking time to stop and admire the Georgian and Greek Revival architecture in postcard-worthy Newfane.

Eating & Sleeping

Brattleboro ❶

✕ TJ Buckley's
American $$$

(📞802-257-4922; http://tjbuckleysuptowndining. com; 132 Elliot St; mains $45; ☺5:30-9pm Thu-Sun year-round, plus 5:30-9pm Wed mid-Jun–early Oct) Chef-owner Michael Fuller founded this exceptional, upscale little eatery in an authentic 1927 diner more than 30 years ago. Ever since, he's been offering a verbal menu of four seasonally changing items, sourced largely from local farms. Locals rave that the food here is Brattleboro's best. The diner seats just 18 souls, so reserve ahead. No credit cards.

🛏 Latchis Hotel
Hotel $$

(📞800-798-6301, 802-254-6300; www. latchishotel.com; 50 Main St; r $99-190, ste $170-225, all incl breakfast; 📶) You can't beat the location of these 30 reasonably priced rooms and suites, in the epicenter of downtown and adjacent to the historic theater of the same name. The hotel's art-deco overtones are refreshing, and wonderfully surprising for New England.

Bennington ❷

✕ Pangaea
International $$

(📞802-442-7171; www.vermontfinedining.com; 1 Prospect St, North Bennington; lounge mains $8-12, restaurant mains $30; ☺lounge 5-10pm daily, restaurant 5-9pm Tue-Sat) Whether you opt for the tastefully decorated dining room, the intimate lounge or the small riverside terrace, you'll be served exceptional food here. The menu is full of fresh ingredients and international influences; try the Thai shrimp on organic udon noodles in a curry peanut sauce or the Herbes de Provence–rubbed Delmonico steak topped with gorgonzola. One of Vermont's finest restaurants.

Manchester ❻

✕ Perfect Wife
International $$

(📞802-362-2817; http://perfectwife.com; 2594 Depot St; mains tavern $12-22, restaurant $20-32; ☺restaurant 5-10pm Thu-Sat, tavern 4pm-late Tue-Sat Sep-May, both open Mon-Sat

Jun-Aug) In the hills east of town, this beloved eatery serves traditional favorites such as steak and sesame-crusted tuna alongside delicious international small plates in a cozy cobblestone-walled dining area. The adjoining Other Woman Tavern offers lower-priced pub fare and is an excellent evening hangout, with live music on Friday nights (folk, rock, blues and more).

🛏 Equinox
Resort $$$

(📞800-362-4747, reservations 877-854-7625; www.equinoxresort.com; 3567 Main St/VT 7A; r $299-489, ste $419-719; @📶☎) Manchester's most famous resort encompasses many worlds: cottages with wood-burning fireplaces, luxury town houses with full kitchens, the main house's elegant suites, and the Federal-style 1811 house's antique-filled rooms, canopied beds and oriental rugs. High-end extras abound: an 18-hole golf course, two tennis courts, a state-of-the-art fitness center, a full-service spa and endless activities, including falconry, archery and snowmobiling.

Grafton ❽

✕ Phelps Barn
Pub Food $$

(📞802-234-8718; www.graftoninnvermont. com/dining/phelps-barn; mains $11-19; ☺4-10pm Tue-Sun) Tucked into a historic carriage house, the Grafton Inn's casual on-site tavern serves light pub fare – burgers, fish and chips, steak frites – and a wide range of Vermont microbrews. Pop in on Thursday evening, when a burger and a pint go for $12, or on Flatbread Fridays, when it serves pizza cooked in 'Big Red,' the tavern's beloved pizza oven. There's also live music every Saturday night.

🛏 Grafton Inn
Inn $$

(📞802-234-8718; www.graftoninnvermont.com; 92 Main St; r incl breakfast $159-299; 📶) With a double porch that serves as Grafton's most picturesque landmark, this venerable inn has played host to such notable guests as Rudyard Kipling, Theodore Roosevelt and Ralph Waldo Emerson. While the original brick inn is quite formal, many of the 47 guest rooms and suites – scattered around houses within the village – are less so.

STRETCH
YOUR LEGS
STOWE

Start/Finish Quiet Path

Distance 2.5 miles

Duration Two to three hours

This walk takes you along the Quiet Path, a circular walk across bucolic farmland, then through the center of Stowe village. You'll cross a pedestrian covered bridge, visit local galleries and shops, and learn about Stowe's skiing and snowboarding history.

Take this walk on Trip

Quiet Path

The Quiet Path is a delightful, easy 1.8-mile walk that features mountain views and takes you past bucolic farmlands along the west branch of the Little River. Along the way, special plaques explain the ecosystem of the area. The loop is blissfully devoid of cyclists or anything else that moves quickly.

The Walk » Access the walk from the parking lot beneath the church on Main St. Follow the signs to the recreation path and veer right after the second bridge. The path loops around and returns to the start. Walk up the hill, turn right at the church, then right onto Mountain Rd.

Stowe Walkway

A pedestrian covered bridge (built 1972), the Stowe Walkway hugs the road across the Waterbury River. One of Stowe's most photographed spots, it's a mini, skinny version of the covered bridges you see across the state and features a sweet Stowe sign at the entrance.

The Walk » Cross the pedestrian bridge. At the other end, cross the street and turn left; your next stop is on your right.

Stowe Craft & Design

Stowe has no shortage of galleries and craft shops displaying work by artists of local and international renown. One of the best, in the heart of Stowe village, is **Stowe Craft & Design** (☎877-456-8388; www.stowecraft.com; 55 Mountain Rd, Stowe; ☺10am-6pm), with adventurous, eclectic and surreal works of art and craft.

The Walk » Follow Mountain Rd 300ft south to its junction with Main St, then cross Main St to reach your next stop.

Vermont Ski & Snowboard Museum

Located in an 1818 meeting house that was rolled to its present spot by oxen in the 1860s, the **Vermont Ski & Snowboard Museum** (☎802-253-9911; www.vtssm.com; 1 S Main St; $5; ☺noon-5pm Wed-

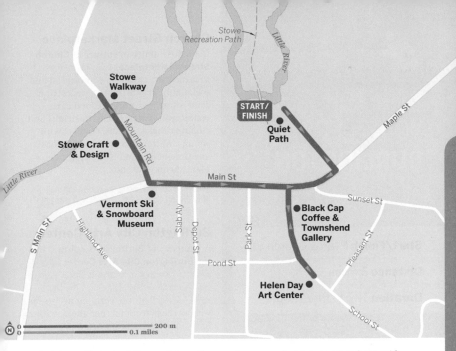

Sun) is a tribute to skiing and boarding, with more than 7500 cataloged items. It tells the tale of the famous 10th Mountain Division of skiing troops from WWII history, traces the evolution of equipment (75 years of Vermont ski lifts!) and gives you a chance to chuckle at 1970s slope-side fashion.

The Walk » Turn right out of the museum and walk down Main St — you'll pass oodles of shops and restaurants. Turn right onto School St and walk three blocks until you see your next stop on the right.

Helen Day Art Center

This gently provocative **community art center** (☏802-253-8358; www.helenday. com; 90 Pond St; ☉noon-5pm Wed-Sun) hosts rotating traditional and avant-garde exhibits. It also sponsors 'Exposed,' an annual, town-wide outdoor sculpture show running from mid-July to mid-October.

The Walk » Walk back down School St the way you came. At Main St, the next stop is on your right at the corner.

Black Cap Coffee & Townshend Gallery

What's art without coffee? After a browse through the **Townshend Gallery** (featuring rotating exhibits by mainly local artists), drop into **Black Cap Coffee** (☏802-253-2123; www.facebook. com/BlackCapCoffeeandBeer; 144 Main St; sandwiches $5.50-8.75; ☉7am-5pm; ☐) for a cuppa and a bite. It's located in an old house with a small but delightful front porch.

The Walk » To return to the beginning of the Quiet Path, cross Main St and walk down the hill (the church will be on your right) to the parking lot.

STRETCH YOUR LEGS
BURLINGTON

Start/Finish Pearl & Church Sts

Distance 3 miles

Duration Two to three hours

This walk takes you along Burlington's main drag and pedestrian hangout strip, ending with a stroll along the city's finest asset, Lake Champlain. You'll learn about the history of the city and the lake's ecosystem, and see where Burlington's residents sail, cycle and run a few steps from the center of town.

Take this walk on Trips

Church Street Marketplace

Get a dose of urban culture at **Church Street Marketplace** (www.churchstmarket place.com; 🚻), the city's commercial and social hub. This attractive pedestrian zone is lined with shops, food carts, restaurants, cafes, street musicians and climbing rocks that are popular with young children. It's packed with locals any time of day and is the epicenter of nightlife on weekends.

The Walk » Walk along the pedestrian mall. After College St, you will see your next stop on the right.

Burlington City Arts Center

A mainstay of Burlington's cultural life, the **Burlington City Arts Center** (📞802-865-7166; www.burlingtoncityarts.org/bca-center; 135 Church St; 🕙11am-5pm Sun & Tue-Thu, to 8pm Fri & Sat) features Vermont artists, as well as those from further afield, with a focus on contemporary art.

The Walk » From Church St, turn right onto Main St. You'll immediately see the lake looming in front of you. Walk downhill; the road dead-ends at your next stop.

Union Station

The brick beaux-arts-style structure (built in 1915) is **Union Station** (1 Main St), the former station for the Central Vermont railway; look for the quirky steel-winged monkeys looming on top of the building. Inside, admire the revolving local art; head downstairs to see murals detailing the history and development of Burlington, as well as a local artist's sculpture entitled *Train Ball*.

The Walk » Exit on the bottom floor and turn right. You'll pass the old platform, which looks like it could receive passengers anytime. Walk on the path following the tracks.

ECHO Lake Aquarium & Science Center

Nature-lovers, or those interested in green architecture, will definitely want to explore the **ECHO Lake Aquarium**

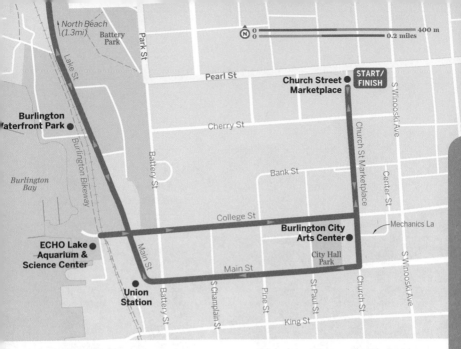

& Science Center (☎802-864-1848; www.echovermont.org; 1 College St; adult/child $13.50/10.50; ☉10am-5pm; ♿), a waterfront science museum that is LEED-certified for its state-of-the-art environmentally friendly design. Focusing on Lake Champlain's ecosystem, it features a moderate-sized aquarium with local fish and hands-on touch tanks. Don't miss the stand devoted to the lake's mythical sea creature, 'Champ.'

The Walk » Cross the roundabout and you'll see the boathouse off to the left and the boardwalk up ahead, both part of your next stop.

Burlington Waterfront Park

Refreshingly unencumbered by the souvenir stands that crowd the more developed waterfronts, the park has a low-key promenade with four-person swinging benches and swaths of grassy spots. Its marina contains **Splash at the Boathouse** (☎802-658-2244; www.

splashattheboathouse.com; College St, at Lake Champlain; ☉11am-10pm mid-may,–Sep), an outdoor restaurant and bar on a floating dock that's perfect for watching the sun set over the lake and the Adirondack Mountains beyond with a cocktail (it's best for the drinks and views, not the food).

The Walk » Walk down the boardwalk and continue past the sailing club to the Burlington Recreation Path, a paved path that takes you along the lake. As you follow the shoreline 1.3 miles to North Beach, the elevation increases slightly to give you excellent views from above.

North Beach

This wide stretch makes you feel like you've landed on a small ocean. Wriggle your feet in the sand, breathe in the crisp air and, if it's summer, dive in.

The Walk » Return to the Burlington Recreation Path and walk back to the waterfront park. Then walk east along College St back to the Church St Marketplace.

New Hampshire

THE BEST THING ABOUT A TRIP THROUGH THE GRANITE STATE? The whole place is one big scenic attraction. You don't have to drive through miles of suburbia to get to the good stuff because most of it *is* the good stuff: lofty peaks, shimmering lakes, crashing waterfalls and powerful rivers. After crossing the state line, everything's within a half-day's trip.

In the north, the word 'presidential' best describes the scenery. Mt Washington anchors the magnificent Presidential Range, replete with trails and high granite summits. It's all about lake views and water fun at Lake Winnipesaukee, where wildlife roams in nearby hills. Vistas are gentler along the Connecticut River and in towns near Mt Monadnock, regions that draw artists and families with their museums and covered bridges.

Crawford Notch State Park View of Mt Washington

White Mountain National Forest Peabody River

20 **White Mountains Loop 3 Days**
Hike to waterfalls, gorges and summits in the shadow of Mt Washington. (p223)

21 **Connecticut River Byway 2 Days**
Follow New England's great river to farms, museums and an irresistible chocolate shop. (p231)

22 **Lake Winnipesaukee 2 Days**
This family-friendly lakeside loop features trails, wildlife, drive-in movies and ice-cream shops. (p239)

23 **Monadnock Villages 2 Days**
Discover the sun-dappled trails and artsy villages of the Mt Monadnock region. (p247)

24 **Woodland Heritage Trail 2 Days**
Explore northern New Hampshire's theme parks, rivers, forests and logging history. (p255)

 DON'T MISS

Kancamagus Highway
Drive past majestic vistas of granite peaks and watch out for moose on Trip **20**

Moat Mountain Smokehouse & Brewing Co
After hiking up Mt Washington, swap lies about the trail at this North Conway pub on Trip **20**

Burdick Chocolate
A decadent dessert here is a must, but the quiche may be the best you've ever tasted. Try it on Trip **21**

Hiking Mt Monadnock
If Thoreau liked it twice, the view must be good. Conquer America's most popular summit for yourself on Trip **23**

Wildlife Watching
Learn about local wildlife from folks who are helping it thrive, at Squam Lakes Natural Science Center and Loon Center on Trip **22**

White Mountains Loop

20

Adventure calls from every trailhead on this notch-linking loop that swoops along the Kancamagus Hwy, climbs the slopes of Mt Washington and passes the mighty flumes of Franconia Notch.

TRIP HIGHLIGHTS

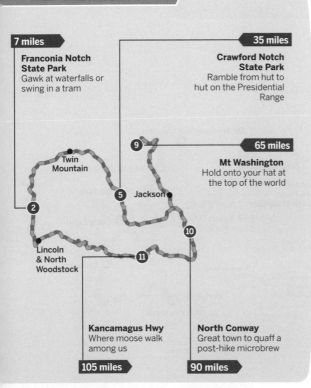

7 miles

Franconia Notch State Park
Gawk at waterfalls or swing in a tram

35 miles

Crawford Notch State Park
Ramble from hut to hut on the Presidential Range

Twin Mountain

9

65 miles

Mt Washington
Hold onto your hat at the top of the world

5 Jackson

2

10

Lincoln & North Woodstock

11

Kancamagus Hwy
Where moose walk among us

105 miles

North Conway
Great town to quaff a post-hike microbrew

90 miles

3 DAYS
135 MILES / 217KM

GREAT FOR...

BEST TIME TO GO
Visit from May to October for warm days and full foliage.

ESSENTIAL PHOTO

Capture presidential peaks from the CL Graham Overlook.

BEST FOR HISTORY

Bretton Woods, where the World Bank was created.

Presidential Range View of Mt Washington from Mt Washington Auto Road

223

20 White Mountains Loop

Hikers, lace up your boots and grab your walking sticks. The White Mountain National Forest, with an assist from the Appalachian Mountain Club, is home to one of the most impressive trail networks in the nation. What will you experience? Waterfalls crashing through gorges, streams rippling past an abandoned settlement and mountain huts serving up meals and beds for weary ramblers. Not a hiker? Locomotive rides through leafy terrain and a fairy-tale theme park bring the adventure to you.

❶ Lincoln & North Woodstock

Outdoor shops, an adventure outfitter and a gob-smacking array of pancake houses line the Kancamagus Hwy on its run through Lincoln and nearby North Woodstock. Start at the **White Mountains Visitor Center** (☏National Forest 603-745-3816, visitor info 603-745-8720; www.visitwhitemountains. com; 200 Kancamagus Hwy, North Woodstock; ☺visitor info 8:30am-5pm, National Forest desk 9am-3:30pm daily late May-Oct, Fri-Sun only rest

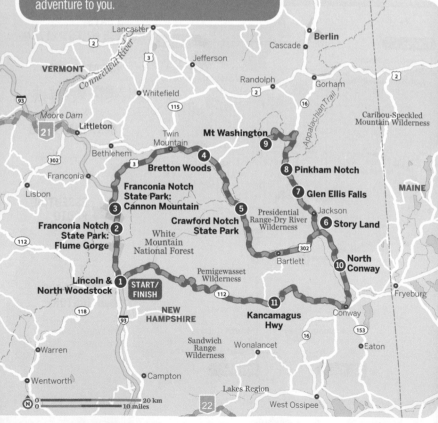

of year), where a life-size stuffed moose and free cups of coffee set the mood for adventure. This is also the place to grab brochures and trail maps and purchase a White Mountain National Forest Recreation Pass ($5 per week), which is required for extended stops at national forest trailheads.

Want to leave the planning to others? Try **Alpine Adventures** (☏603-745-9911; www.alpinezipline.com; 41 Main St/ Kancamagus Hwy, Lincoln; zips from $64; ⊙9am-4pm Mon-Fri, to 5pm Sat & Sun; 👪) a few doors down. These knowledgeable folks lead backwoods safaris and zip-line tours.

🛏 p229

LINK YOUR TRIP

21 Connecticut River Byway

Drive toward Littleton on I-93 north from Franconia Notch to start a pastoral drive along the Connecticut River.

22 Lake Winnipesaukee

Leave the mountains behind and discover New Hampshire's beautiful lakes region; from Lincoln, it's a 45-minute drive to Weirs Beach via I-93 and NH 104.

The Drive >> Drive 4 miles north on I-93 to exit 34A and follow the signs half a mile further to Flume Gorge.

TRIP HIGHLIGHT

2 Flume Gorge

Expect crowds at **Flume Gorge** (☏603-745-8391; www.flumegorge.com; I-93, exit 34A; adult/child $16/13; ⊙9am-5pm early May-late Oct), a natural granite sluice with 90ft walls in Franconia Notch State Park. But don't let elbow jostling keep you away – the verdant, moss-covered cliffs and rushing stream are worth it. The trail has a sturdy walkway, making it accessible for everyone. If you plan to ride the Cannon Mountain Aerial Tramway, buy the Discovery Pass (adult/child $29/23), which covers the flume and the tram at a reduced rate.

Take a walk or a bike ride on the 8-mile **Recreation Trail** beside the Pemigewasset River or stroll 500ft to the **Basin**, the first of several waterfalls accessed from the Basin parking lot north of the Flume Gorge Visitor Center.

The Drive >> Follow US 3 for 1 mile north to join I-93, then continue 4.5 miles north to exit 34B. Here in the heart of Franconia Notch State Park, I-93 and US 3 merge into a single highway, flanked closely on either side by the Kinsman and Franconia mountain ranges.

---

3 Cannon Mountain

A short drive north, the **Cannon Mountain Aerial Tramway** (☏603-823-8800; www.cannonmt.com; 260 Tramway Dr, off I-93, exit 34B; round-trip adult/child $17/14; ⊙9am-5pm late May–mid-Oct; 👪) whisks you to a look-out point so lofty that you'll feel you've sprouted wings.

Every New Hampshirite mourns the **Old Man of the Mountain**, a rock formation that remains the state symbol despite its collapse in May 2003. Near the Tramway Valley Station, the departure point for the tram, you'll find the **Old Man of the Mountain Museum** (I-93, exit 34B; ⊙noon-5pm Wed-Mon late May–mid-Oct), where there are forensically accurate diagrams of 'the Profile's' collapse, and tributes to this beloved bit of state history.

The Drive >> Follow I-93 north to exit 35, taking US 3 north to Twin Mountain, where you'll pass a prison-striped moose at the police station. Fill up the tank at Foster's Crossroads, then follow US 302 east. The drive is 17 miles.

---

4 Bretton Woods

In July 1944, the Mt Washington Hotel (p229) hosted the Bretton Woods International Monetary Conference. This history-making summit established the

World Bank and helped stabilize the global economy as WWII ended. World leaders were determined to avoid the disastrous economic fallout that occurred after WWI. Today, spend a sumptuous night in one of the resort's 200 rooms or simply stop by to wander past the historic photographs beside the lobby.

🛏 p229

The Drive » Follow US 302 south 4 miles to the park.

`TRIP HIGHLIGHT`

❺ Crawford Notch

The Pond Loop and Sam Tilley trails are two easy riverside hikes in this **state park** (📞603-374-2272; www.nhstateparks.org; 1464 US 302, Harts Location; adult/child $4/2; ☺visitor center late May–mid-Oct, park year-round unless posted otherwise) at the base of the White Mountains. For details about local trails, stop by the **AMC**

Highland Center (www.amc-nh.org; Crawford Notch; ☺24hr), one of the country's best launch pads for outdoor exploration. There's an information desk, a dining room and a small outdoor retail shop. Overnight lodging is also available, and hikers can link to the AMC's popular hut-to-hut trail system from here. The huts are lodge-like dorms offering meals, bunks and stellar views. The Highland Center is just north of the park.

The Conway Scenic Railroad's Notch Train stops at the nearby 1891 **Crawford Depot & Visitor Center** (www.outdoors.org; ☺9am-5pm Jun–mid-Oct), which contains a small but good collection of train-related history.

🛏 p229

The Drive » Continue east on US 302 for 16 miles, passing Dry River Campground and the Crawford Notch General Store. Turn left at NH 16, and continue a quarter mile to Story Land.

❻ Story Land

With its bright, off-kilter facade, **Story Land** (📞603-383-4186; www.storylandnh.com; 850 NH 16, Glen; $33; ☺9am-6pm daily Jul & Aug, to 5pm rest of season, Sat & Sun only late May–early Jun & Sep–mid-Oct; 🚻), a quarter mile north of US 302, is like a Venus flytrap, luring families in for a closer look, then preventing escape with scenes of kiddie-minded fun just beyond its protective wall. What's inside this roadside theme park? Shows, games and 23 rides based on fairy tales and make-believe. This popular place gets a thumbs-up from kids and parents alike.

The Drive » Drive north on NH 16. In 2 miles, take a photo break at the covered bridge in tiny Jackson. Continue 8 miles to the trailhead for Glen Ellis Falls.

❼ Glen Ellis Falls

Only a stone's throw off NH 16, stop at Glen Ellis Falls for a few snapshots. This easy walk brings you 0.3 miles to a 60ft waterfall, one of the prettiest in the region. Most can make the hike without breaking a sweat.

The Drive » Continue north almost 1 mile to the visitor center.

✓ **TOP TIP: HIKER SHUTTLE**

Need transportation before or after a strenuous one-way hike? Use the **AMC hiker shuttle** (📞reservations 603-466-2727; www.outdoors.org/lodging/lodging-shuttle.cfm; one-way trip AMC members/nonmembers $19/23; ☺daily Jun–mid-Sep, Sat & Sun mid-Sep–mid-Oct) system for your pick-up or drop-off. One-way rides are best reserved in advance.

White Mountain National Forest Swift River

8 Pinkham Notch

Hikers tackling Mt Washington should stop by the **Pinkham Notch Visitor Center** (☎603-466-2721; http://www.outdoors.org/lodging/lodges/pinkham/pinkham-notch-visitor-center.cfm; 361 NH 16; ◷6:30am-10pm May-Oct, to 9pm Nov-Apr) for information, maps and a diorama that spotlights area trails. The 4.2-mile **Tuckerman Ravine Trail** to the summit starts behind the visitor center. Appropriate preparation for this brutal climb – which can be deadly in bad weather – is imperative.

🛏 p229

The Drive » Drive 3 miles north to the entrance to the Auto Rd.

TRIP HIGHLIGHT

9 Mt Washington

Welcome to Mt Washington, New England's highest peak and the site of the world's second-highest recorded wind gust: 231mph (and the highest ever observed by humans). The heavy chains wrapped around the **Auto Road Stage Office** at the summit attest that winter here is no laughing matter.

Up top, stop in for souvenirs, refreshments, views from the lookout tower and a visit to the recently opened **Extreme Mt Washington** (☎800-706-0432; www.mountwashington.org/visit-us; Mt Washington summit; ticket $5, incl with Mt Washington Cog Railway or Auto Road ticket; ◷variable, depending on weather) museum, where you can contemplate Mt Washington's claim as 'home of the world's worst weather' and learn how scientists track climate conditions year-round despite hurricane-force winds and Arctic temperatures. If you time it right, the winding **Mt Washington Auto Road** (📞603-466-3988; www.mountwashingtonautoroad.com; off NH 16, Gorham; car & driver $29, extra adult/child $9/7, guided tour adult/child $36/16; ⏰7:30-6pm mid-Jun–Aug, shorter hours mid-May–mid-Jun, Sep & Oct) will be open, but there will still be snow and ice at the summit. Aspiring athletes take note: a handful of runners have reached the top, a 7.6-mile climb, in less than one hour (!) during the annual Mt Washington Road Race.

The Drive » Backtrack to the junction of NH 16 and US 302. Follow US 302/NH 16 southeast for 5 miles to North Conway, stopping at the Intervale Scenic Vista for views, brochures and restrooms.

- - - - - - - - - - - -

TRIP HIGHLIGHT

⑩ North Conway

North Conway is the perfect mountain town: lively pubs, top-notch breakfast joints and numerous quaint inns. Shopaholics can pop into one of the 60-plus outlet stores (including LL Bean). North Conway is also home to the **Conway Scenic Railroad** (📞800-232-5251, 603-356-5251; www.conwayscenic.com; 38 Norcross Circle; Notch Train coach/1st class/dome car $62/76/90, Valley Train coach/1st class/dome/dining

car from $17/21/25.50/36.50; ⏰mid-Jun–Oct; 🚻), which runs half-day train trips up into Crawford Notch. On sunny days they may attach the open-air coach car, a restored Pullman with no glass in the windows that's perfect for shutterbugs.

What happens when you push the red button inside the mock observatory building at the **Mt Washington Weather Discovery Center** (📞603-356-2137; www.mountwashington.org; 2779 White Mountain Hwy; adult/child $2/1; ⏰10am-5pm Thu-Mon)? We won't spoil the surprise, but you might want to hold on tight. This small but fascinating museum examines wild weather events and explains the unique weather conditions atop Mt Washington.

✕ 🛏 p49, p229

The Drive » US 302 splits from NH 16 south of downtown. Follow NH 16 heading south for 2.5 miles, taking it through Conway, then hop onto NH 112, which is better known as the Kancamagus Hwy.

- - - - - - - - - - - -

TRIP HIGHLIGHT

⑪ Kancamagus Hwy

Roll down the windows and slip on your shades. It's time to drive. This 34.5-mile byway, named for a peace-seeking Sagamon chief, rolls

through the **White Mountain National Forest** unhampered by commercial distractions or pesky stoplights – although you do need to gauge your speed and watch for wildlife. Stop by the **Saco Ranger District Office** (📞603-447-5448; 33 Kancamagus Hwy, Conway; ⏰8am-4:30pm Tue-Sun, 9am-4:30pm Mon) for maps, information and a recreation pass ($5 per week) if you plan to park and explore.

Fifteen miles west, pull over at **Sabbaday Falls** for an easy climb to flumes cascading through granite channels and small pools. After the falls, the road starts rising and leafy maples are replaced by dark conifers. The serene view at **Kancamagus Pass** (elevation 2855ft) can be beat only by Mt Washington. For camera-ready panoramas, stop at the **CL Graham Wangan Grounds Overlook** just east of the pass, or the **Pemi Overlook** just west.

The **Lincoln Woods Trail** (NH 112/Kancamagus Hwy, 5 miles east of I-93) at the parking area further west follows the Pemigewasset River for 2.9 miles. Kids enjoy the suspension bridge beside the visitor center.

The Drive » From here, drive west on NH 112 to return to Lincoln and North Woodstock.

Eating & Sleeping

Lincoln & North Woodstock

🛏 The Notch Hostel   Hostel $

(📞603-348-1483; http://notchhostel.com; 324 Lost River Rd, North Woodstock; dm $30, d $60-90; 🛜📺) Exactly what the North Woodstock/Lincoln area needed, this gorgeous new hostel, opened in 2015, is the brainchild of outdoor enthusiasts (and newlyweds) Serena and Justin. A class act all around, it welcomes guests with multiple outdoor decks, a spacious kitchen, a mountain-themed library, a newly built sauna for chilly winter nights and a cozy vibe throughout.

Bretton Woods ❹

🛏 Omni Mt Washington Hotel & Resort   Hotel $$$

(📞603-278-1000; www.omnihotels.com; 310 Mt Washington Hotel Rd; r $149-549, ste $769-959; ❄@🛜🏊) Open since 1902, this grand hotel maintains a sense of fun – note the moose's head overlooking the lobby and the framed local wildflowers in many of the guest rooms. Also offers 27 holes of golf, red-clay tennis courts, an equestrian center and a spa. There's a $25 daily resort fee.

Crawford Notch ❺

🛏 AMC Highland Lodge   Lodge $$

(📞front desk 603-278-4453, reservations 603-466-2727; www.outdoors.org/lodging/lodges/highland; NH 302; per adult/child/teen r from $158/48/92, without bath from $109/48/92, all incl breakfast & dinner; 🛜) This cozy Appalachian Mountain Club (AMC) lodge is set amid the splendor of Crawford Notch, an ideal base for hiking the trails criss-crossing the Presidential Range. The grounds are beautiful, rooms are basic but comfortable, meals are hearty and guests are outdoor enthusiasts. Discounts available for AMC members. The information center, open to the public, has loads of information about regional hiking.

Pinkham Notch ❽

🛏 Joe Dodge Lodge   Lodge $

(📞603-466-2727; www.outdoors.org/lodging/lodges/pinkham; 361 NH 16; r adult/child/teen incl breakfast $80/28/61, incl breakfast & dinner $105/41/78) The AMC camp at Pinkham Notch incorporates this lodge, with dorms housing more than 100 beds. Reserve bunks in advance. Discounts are available for AMC members.

North Conway ❿

🍴 May Kelly's Cottage   Irish, American $$

(📞603-356-7005; www.maykellys.com; 3002 White Mountain Hwy; mains $9-24; ⏰4-9pm Tue-Thu, noon-10pm Fri & Sat, noon-8pm Sun) Irish conviviality and friendliness? May Kelly's is the real deal. Local-attic decor, helpful servers, mountain views, sandwiches and hearty mains such as the Ploughman's Dinner (top sirloin steak, Irish potato cake, brown bread and baked beans) make it a local favorite.

🍴 Stairway Cafe   Breakfast $

(📞603-356-5200; www.stairwaycafe.com; 2649 White Mountain Hwy; mains $7-14; ⏰7am-3pm) The all-day breakfast treats are scrumptious at this brightly decorated, six-table upstairs cafe, from blackboard specials including homemade cinnamon muffins to lobster Benedict. Omelets come with grilled red Maine potatoes, veggie baked beans or homemade apple sauce, and there's a range of artisanal wild-game sausages (try the venison-merlot-blueberry or wild boar–cranberry-shiraz varieties). Lunch offerings include burgers, wraps and salads.

🛏 Golden Gables   Motel $$

(📞888-422-5346, 603-356-2878; www.goldengablesinn.com; 1814 White Mountain Hwy; r $75-199; ❄🛜🏊) The balconies with mountain views close the deal at this stylish motel. It has a back lawn perfect for letting the kids run free.

Connecticut River Byway

21

Crossing back and forth between New Hampshire and Vermont, this drive follows the roaring southbound flow of the mighty Connecticut River, linking white-clapboard villages, farms and historical museums.

TRIP HIGHLIGHTS

0 miles

Littleton
The world's longest candy counter sells gummy eggs!

1 START

● Orford

3 ── **59 miles**

Montshire Museum of Science
Touch the tooth of a mastodon

● Claremont

127 miles ── **8** FINISH

Walpole
Dawdle over a double-shot mocha at Burdick Chocolate

2 DAYS
127 MILES / 204KM

GREAT FOR...

BEST TIME TO GO
April to November for spring flowers, summer greenery and fall foliage.

ESSENTIAL PHOTO
The Cornish Windsor Covered Bridge linking Vermont and New Hampshire.

BEST FOR FOODIES
Dig into fancy chocolates and savory fare at Burdick Chocolate in Walpole.

Littleton Walking trails

21 | Connecticut River Byway

Taking this leisurely, winding road trip through the Connecticut River's Upper Valley is like earning a liberal arts degree in one weekend. There's the Colonial history of the Fort at No 4, natural sciences at the Montshire Museum and a mini-session in the arts among the sculpture-dotted grounds of Saint-Gaudens. Along the way, you'll be greeted by lush farms and maple-covered hillsides rolling down to meet New England's longest river.

TRIP HIGHLIGHT

1 Littleton, NH

Littleton may be off the beaten path, but it's an inspirational place to start this trip. The White Mountains hover to the southeast. The Am-monoosuc River churns through town. A towering steeple overlooks Main St. And the world's longest candy counter beckons with a rainbow's array of sweets at **Chutters** (☎603-444-5787; www.chutters.com; 43 Main St; ☉9am-5pm Mon-Thu, to 7pm Fri & Sat, 10am-5pm Sun).

At the eastern end of Main St, the **Littleton Chamber of Commerce Welcome Center** (☎603-444-6561; www.littletonareachamber.com; 2 Union St; ☉9am-5pm Mon-Fri) provides a walking-tour brochure with a stop at the **Littleton Grist Mill**. Built in 1797, it's back in service as a mill after renovations initiated in the 1990s. The adjacent Ammonoosuc drops 144ft as it crashes through town. The **covered bridge** here, built in 2004, looks like it's barely hanging onto the riverbank – but it's perfectly safe for walking.

🍴 🛏 p237

The Drive » Take I-93 north to exit 44 and NH 135 south. This bucolic road passes fields, red barns and cattle-crossing signs as it hugs the river. Snap a photo of the covered bridge in Woodsville, then continue south on NH 10. In Orford, look left for the impressive Seven Ridge Houses, built in the Bullfinch

SHOPPING & STROLLING LITTLETON, NH

Lined with 19th- and early-20th-century buildings, Littleton's Main St is a delightful place to stroll, with some attractive, independently owned stores. For outdoor gear and clothing, step into **Lahout's** (☎603-444-5838; www.lahouts.com; 245 Union St; ☉9:30am-5:30pm Mon-Sat, 10am-4:30pm Sun), America's oldest ski shop. A few doors down, the **League of New Hampshire Craftsmen** (☎603-444-1099; http://littleton.nhcrafts.org; 81 Main St, lower level; ☉10am-6pm Mon-Sat, to 5pm Sun) runs a gallery that sells jewelry, pottery and other New Hampshire–made arts and crafts. For lunch and a slice of local life, grab a seat at the Coffee Pot (p237) on Main St, or head round the corner to the 18th-century grist mill by the Ammonoosuc River, where you can soak up river views over sandwiches at Miller's Cafe & Bakery (p237) or craft brews and pizza at Schilling Beer Co (p237).

style by local craftspeople between 1773 and 1839. Cross the bridge to Fairlee (VT) and continue south along US 5, following the Connecticut River down to East Thetford. The drive is 58 miles.

2 Cedar Circle Farm, East Thetford, VT

With its vast fields stretching out towards the banks of the Connecticut River and bins overflowing with homegrown organic produce, **Cedar Circle Farm** (📞802-785-4737; www.cedarcirclefarm.org; 225 Pavilion Rd, East Thetford; 🕙10am-6pm Mon-Sat, to 5pm Sun; 🚻) is like a roadside farm stand on steroids. Wander through the lush fields of produce, pick your own berries, flowers and pumpkins, lounge in an Adirondack chair by the river, or simply stop in at the cafe to pick up a snack for the road ahead. Summer and fall events include dinners

LINK YOUR TRIP

3 Ivy League Tour

Cross the river near the Montshire museum to tour Dartmouth College.

23 Monadnock Villages

From Walpole, take NH 12 to Keene to join our trip through the Mt Monadnock region.

in the field, workshops on canning and freezing, and strawberry (June) and pumpkin (October) festivals.

The Drive » Follow US 5 south for 11 miles to Norwich, VT, then take Montshire Rd to the Montshire Museum.

TRIP HIGHLIGHT

❸ Montshire Museum, Norwich, VT

Rub the tooth of a mastodon. View current images from the Hubble telescope. Watch leafcutter ants at work. But whatever you do at the **Montshire** (📞802-649-2200; www.montshire.org; 1 Montshire Rd, Norwich; adult/child $16/13 late Jun–early Sep, $14/11 rest of year; ⏰10am-5pm; 🚻), don't park your car near the planet Neptune – it's part of the model solar system that stretches the length of the parking lot and beyond (and Neptune is way, way out there).

Located on a 110-acre site beside the Connecticut River, this kid-friendly museum offers exhibits covering ecology, technology and the natural and physical sciences. It's also the regional visitor center for the **Silvio Conte National Fish & Wildlife Refuge** – look for the life-size moose and the displays that highlight local flora and fauna. In summer, water-focused and sensory exhibits in the Montshire's outdoor Science Park will fascinate younger kids.

🛏 p237

The Drive » Cross the river back to Hanover, NH, taking NH 10 past the strip-mall wasteland of West Lebanon, where you pick up NH 12A south to Saint-Gaudens; the drive is 18 miles. (For variety, the river can be tracked along US 5 in Vermont between a village or two, with regular bridges connecting New Hampshire and Vermont until you reach Walpole.)

❹ Saint-Gaudens National Historic Site, Cornish, NH

In the summer of 1885, the sculptor Augustus Saint-Gaudens rented an old inn near the town of Cornish and came to this beautiful spot to work. He returned summer after summer and eventually bought the

Cornish Saint-Gaudens National Historic Site

place in 1892. The **estate** (📞603-675-2175; www.nps. gov/saga; 139 Saint Gaudens Rd, Cornish; adult/child $7/ free; 🕐 buildings 9am-4:30pm, grounds 9am-dusk Jun-Oct, visitor center only 8:45am-4:15pm Mon-Fri Nov-May), where he lived until his death in 1907, is now open to the public.

Saint-Gaudens is best known for his public monuments, including the Robert Gold Shaw Memorial across from the state house in Boston. Recasts of his greatest sculptures dot the beautiful grounds. Visitors can also tour his home and wander the studios, where artists-in-residence sculpt. Exhibit buildings are closed in winter, but the visitor center is usually open from 9am to 4:15pm weekdays.

The Drive » Head 1.5 miles south on NH 12A to reach the 1866 Cornish Windsor Covered Bridge.

❺ Cornish-Windsor Covered Bridge

Built in 1866, this 449ft long beauty is the longest wooden covered bridge in the United States. Even better, you can still drive across it! One bit of trivia, in case you were wondering: the whole thing belongs to the state of New Hampshire, so you won't actually cross into Vermont until you touch the riverbank on the far side.

The Drive » Cross the covered bridge into Windsor, VT, then take US 5 north to the Old Constitution House at 16 N Main St.

❻ Windsor, VT

Affectionately known as the 'Birthplace of Vermont,' Windsor is home to the Old Constitution House State Historic Site (http://historicsites.vermont.gov/directory/old_constitution). This small museum occupies the former tavern where a devoted band of Vermonters – rejecting the competing claims of New York and New Hampshire to their territory – officially declared Vermont's independence in July 1777. The groundbreaking constitution signed here was the first in the New World to outlaw slavery, create a free public education system for both men and women, and give every man (regardless of property ownership) the right to vote.

Vermont held its ground as an independent republic for 14 years (eat your heart out, Texas!) before finally joining the union as the 14th state in 1791. Visitors can tour the museum here and learn about Vermont's early history on weekends from Memorial Day to Columbus Day.

The Drive » Bop back into New Hampshire via the Cornish–Windsor Bridge and turn right to follow the Connecticut River downstream. Not quite 1 mile south, bear left onto Town House Rd at the fork for two more covered bridges, then continue south for another 17 miles on NH 12A, which soon rejoins NH 12, to Charlestown.

❼ Fort at No 4, Charlestown, NH

Named for a 1700s land grant, the original fort was built in the 1740s to protect pioneer farmers from Native Americans and the French. The original fort, which was no longer needed by the late 1770s and no longer exists, was reconstructed in the 1960s as a **living history museum** (☎603-826-5700; www.fortat4.org; 267 Springfield Rd/NH 11, Charlestown; adult/child/teen $10/6/8; ⏱10am-4:30pm Mon-Sat, to 4pm Sun May-Oct), with a layout based on a detailed drawing sketched in 1746.

Visitors can explore the different rooms of the fort, wander the riverside grounds and watch historical re-enactors, whose activities vary from weekend to weekend. Check the Fort at No 4 Facebook page for current activities.

The Drive » Views of rolling mountains and hills, as well as fields, railroad tracks, river views and a sugar house, decorate the 14-mile drive on NH 12 south to Walpole.

TRIP HIGHLIGHT

❽ Walpole, NH

Locals descend from surrounding villages to dine at Burdick Chocolate (p237). Originally a New York City chocolatier, Burdick opened this sophisticated chocolate shop and cafe to showcase its desserts. These carefully crafted treats look like they attended finishing school – no slovenly lava cakes or naughty whoopee pies here. But you'll find more than just rich chocolate indulgences. The adjoining bistro serves creative new American dishes, plus artisanal cheeses and top-notch wines; the creamy quiche is fantastic.

Purchase local art and crafts across the street at the **Walpole Artists Cooperative** (☎603-756-3020; www.walpoleartisans.org; 52 Main St; ⏱10am-5pm Wed-Sat, 11am-4pm Sun), then cross Westminster St for a gander at **Ruggles & Hunt** (☎603-756-9607; www.rugglesandhunt.com; 8 Westminster St; ⏱11am-6pm Mon-Sat, noon-5pm Sun), an eclectic boutique with toys, women's clothes and home furnishings.

✕ p237

Eating & Sleeping

Littleton, NH ❶

✕ Coffee Pot

Diner $

(☎603-444-5722; http://thecoffeepotrestaurant.com; 30 Main St; mains $3-11; ⊙6:30am-4pm Mon-Fri, to 2pm Sat, to noon Sun) Sit at the counter and you'll be gabbing with locals before you even order your eggs. A friendly spot for getting the Littleton lowdown.

✕ Miller's Cafe & Bakery

Sandwiches $

(☎603-444-2146; www.millerscafeandbakery.com; 16 Mill St; mains $7-11; ⊙9am-3:30pm Mon & Tue, 8am-3:30pm Wed-Sun; 🛜) With friendly service, free wi-fi and a two-level deck overlooking the Ammonoosuc River, this cafe-bakery in Littleton's historic mill district is an agreeable spot for morning coffee or afternoon soups, salads and sandwiches.

✕ Schilling Beer Co

Pizza, Pub Food $$

(☎603-444-4800; http://schillingbeer.com; 18 Mill St; pizzas & bar snacks $10-16; ⊙3-10pm Mon-Thu, noon-11pm Fri & Sat, noon-10pm Sun) In a historic mill by the Ammonoosuc River, this relatively new microbrewery (opened in 2013) serves delicious crunchy-crusted, wood-fired pizzas along with bratwurst and a nice selection of home brews, from Konundrum sour pale ale to Erastus Belgian abbey-style Tripel. The post-and-beam-style main room, looking out at a covered bridge, makes for a convivial setting, as does the riverside deck.

🛏 Littleton Motel

Motel $

(☎603-444-5780; www.littletonmotel.com; 166 Main St; r $68-108, ste $98-158; ⊙May-Oct; ❄🛜🐾) Why, yes, I would like to stay in New Hampshire's oldest motel. But don't worry – the 20 rooms at this old-school motor inn, which opened in 1948, have refrigerators, microwaves, air-con and wi-fi.

Norwich, VT ❸

🛏 Norwich Inn

Inn $$

(☎802-649-1143; www.norwichinn.com; 325 Main St; r $159-299; 🛜) Just across the Connecticut River in Norwich, VT, this is both a historic inn and a microbrewery. Rooms in the main house are decorated with Victorian antiques and traditional country furniture, and the two adjacent buildings include modern furnishings and gas fireplaces in each room. At least four of its beers (its signature ales have won multiple awards) are on tap at its brewpub, Jasper Murdock's Alehouse, and the wine list includes more than 2000 wines from its on-site wine cellar.

Walpole, NH ❽

✕ Burdick Chocolate

Cafe $

(☎603-756-2882; www.burdickchocolate.com/chocolateshop-cafe-walpole.aspx; 47 Main St; pastries from $5; ⊙7am-5pm Mon, to 8pm Tue-Thu, to 9pm Fri & Sat, 9am-5pm Sun) Locals descend from surrounding villages to dine at this fabulous eatery. Originally a New York City chocolatier, Burdick relocated to this tiny gem of a New Hampshire village and opened a sophisticated cafe to showcase its desserts.

✕ The Restaurant at Burdick's

Bistro $$

(☎603-756-9058; www.47mainwalpole.com/the-restaurant.html; 47 Main St; mains $15-24; ⊙11:30am-2:30pm & 5:30-9pm Tue-Sat, 10am-2pm Sun) This spectacular restaurant in tiny Walpole has a full menu of French-themed dishes, such as onion soup, *steak frites*, *croque monsieur* and *salade lyonnaise* (frisee lettuce salad with bacon, poached duck egg and grain-mustard vinaigrette), accompanied by artisanal cheeses and top-notch wines.

Lake Winnipesaukee

22

This trip loops around the state's largest lake, past wildlife preserves, trails, museums and a drive-in – there's something for toddlers, teens, the kids in-between and good ol' mom and dad.

TRIP HIGHLIGHTS

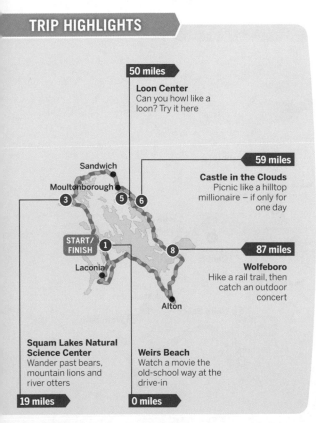

50 miles

Loon Center
Can you howl like a loon? Try it here

59 miles

Castle in the Clouds
Picnic like a hilltop millionaire – if only for one day

Sandwich

Moultonborough

3 **5** **6**

START/ FINISH **1**

Laconia

8

87 miles

Wolfeboro
Hike a rail trail, then catch an outdoor concert

Alton

Squam Lakes Natural Science Center
Wander past bears, mountain lions and river otters

19 miles

Weirs Beach
Watch a movie the old-school way at the drive-in

0 miles

2 DAYS
125 MILES / 201KM

GREAT FOR...

BEST TIME TO GO

June to September: school's out and the weather is warm.

ESSENTIAL PHOTO

The Weirs Beach Boardwalk – it's a classic!

✓ BEST FOR WILDLIFE

Visit Squam Lakes Natural Science Center for critter-watching and live animal demos.

22 Lake Winnipesaukee

Weirs Beach drive-in has shown movies on the big screen since 1949. Across the lake, Bailey's Bubble has scooped ice cream for generations of appreciative families. Summer camps in the area have thrived for decades, too. There's something special about this mountain-ringed lake, a place that summons people back year after year. But it's not just the beauty. It's the little moments of family fun and summer camaraderie that make it truly magical.

TRIP HIGHLIGHT

❶ Weirs Beach

Word of warning: if you're traveling with kids, they're going to want to stay here all day. With its colorful distractions – video arcades, slippery waterslides, souvenir stands and a bustling boardwalk – Weirs Beach is the lake region's center of tacky fun. Escape the hoopla on the **Winnipesaukee Scenic Railroad** (☏603-745-2135; www.hoborr. com; 211 Lakeside Ave; adult/ child 1hr $16/12, 2hr $18/14), whose '20s and '30s train cars travel to the lake's southern tip at Alton Bay and back – kids love the ice-cream-parlor car. The train depot is also the departure point for MS *Mt Washington*.

After a day on the beach, unwind with a movie at the **Weirs Drive-In** (☎603-366-4723; http://weirsdrivein.com; 76 Endicott St/US 3; ⏰7-11pm mid-May–early Sep; ♿). Opened in 1949 and in continual operation since then, the WDI is a revered institution. Note that every car will be charged, at a minimum, for two adults.

The Drive » Continue north on US 3/Endicott St, which runs parallel to the lake. Soon after passing the high-flying ropes course at Monkey Trunks (www.monkeytrunks.com), US 3's local name changes to Daniel Webster Hwy. Meredith is located 5 miles north of Weirs Beach.

LINK YOUR TRIP

3 Ivy League Tour
Follow I-93 to the Ivies for guided tours about history and traditions.

20 White Mountains Loop
From Holderness, drive north to the Notches for trains, hiking and cascades.

CRUISING ON MS MT WASHINGTON

Boasting 183 miles of coastline, Lake Winnipesaukee is prime cruising territory. The classic **MS Mt Washington** (☎603-366-5531; www.cruisenh.com; 211 Lakeside Ave, Weirs Beach; adult/child regular cruise $30/15, Sunday brunch cruise $47/24) steams out of Weirs Beach on a relaxing 2½-hour scenic lake cruise, departing twice daily in July, August and late September to mid-October (reduced schedule May, June and early September).

Special trips include the Sunday champagne brunch cruise and the evening sunset, fall foliage and theme cruises (tribute to Elvis, Lobsterfest etc) running throughout summer and fall ($48 to $55). The boat stops in Meredith on Monday and in Wolfeboro daily from Tuesday to Saturday.

---

② Meredith

Upscale Meredith is a lively lakeside town with attractive Colonial and Victorian homes flanking a commercial center. In Meredith village, boutiques, art and craft stores, galleries and restaurants line US 3 and Main St.

Just south of the village roundabout, stop in at **Mill Falls Marketplace** (http://millfalls.com/shop; 312 Daniel Webster Hwy/US 3; ⏰from 10am daily), a restored linen mill that houses a dozen shops and restaurants. Climb to the top floor and settle in at **Waterfall Cafe** (☎603-677-8631; http://millfalls.com/dine; Mill Falls Marketplace, 312 Daniel Webster Hwy/US 3; mains $5-10; ⏰6:30am-1pm), a cozy spot where you can enjoy omelets, buttermilk pancakes,

eggs Benedict, salads and sandwiches against the backdrop of a spectacular wall mural depicting Lake Winnipesaukee and the surrounding rolling hills.

The Winnipesaukee Scenic Railroad and the MS *Mt Washington* boat (Monday only) both stop in Meredith.

✗ p245

The Drive » From Meredith, continue 5 miles north on woodsy, easy-driving US 3. Don't be surprised if you see lots of motorcyclists. Squam Lake soon nudges into view to the northeast.

TRIP HIGHLIGHT

③ Holderness

The site of the movie *On Golden Pond,* Squam Lake and Holderness remain placid and peaceful, perfect for a pair of waders and fly-fishing, or

241

for plopping your butt in a beach chair and soaking up the sun. If you hike in the shady forests, you'll frequently surprise deer, moose or even a black bear or two.

It's all about the wildlife at **Squam Lakes Natural Science Center** (☎603-968-7194; www.nhnature.org; 23 Science Center Rd, off NH 113; adult/child $19/14, boat tours $25/21; ⏰9:30am-5pm May-Oct; 👪), where four nature paths weave through the woods and around the marsh. The 0.75-mile **Gephardt Trail** is a highlight, leading past large trailside enclosures that hold bobcats, mountain lions, river otters and raptors. (Most of the animals were orphaned or injured and unable to live on their own in the wild.) The center also offers 90-minute tours of the lake and educational live animal demonstrations.

✕ 🛏 p245

The Drive » From the nature center, follow NH 113 northeast for 5 miles. About a quarter-mile after the 'Rockywold Deephaven Camps' sign, look for the 'West Rattlesnake Trail' sign. Park in one of the pull-offs on either side of the road. The trail is on the lakeside.

FRASER HALL / ROBERTHARDING ©

❹ West Rattlesnake Trail

The West Rattlesnake Trail climbs to a rocky outcrop atop Rattle-snake Mountain that yields stunning views of Squam Lake. It's less than a mile to the top, making this a good hike for families. (Just watch younger kids on the rocks.)

The Drive » NH 113 twists past cottages, pine trees and rock walls, offering glimpses of Squam Lake to the southeast before entering Center Sandwich. From this white clapboard village, pick up NH 109 south for 4.5 miles to NH 25/Whittier Hwy. Turn right onto NH 25 and follow it about half a mile to Blake Rd and turn left. Follow Blake Rd to Lees Mill Rd and turn right.

TRIP HIGHLIGHT

❺ Loon Center

Loons may be water birds, but their closest relatives are actually penguins, not ducks or geese. Known for their unique and varied calls (the wail sounds like a howling wolf), loons experienced a sharp decline in the 1970s.

The Loon Preservation Committee monitors the birds and works to restore a strong, healthy population. At the secluded **Loon Center** (☎603-476-5666; www.loon.org; 183 Lees Mill Rd, Moultonborough; ⏰9am-5pm daily Jul–mid-Oct, Mon-Sat mid-

Holderness Jetty on Squam Lake

May–Jun, Thu-Sat mid-Oct–mid-May; [icon]), wildlife enthusiasts can learn about the birds' plumage, habitat and distinctive calls and watch an award-winning video. There are also details about protecting the birds. Kid-friendly activities include interactive games, a scavenger hunt and a junior biologist's guide.

The center sits within the 200-acre **Markus Wildlife Sanctuary** (www. loon.org/loon-center-markus -sanctuary.php; 183 Lee's Mill Rd, Moultonborough; [icon] dawn-dusk). The sanctuary's **Loon Nest Trail** is a haven for birds: the 1.7-mile path

winds through the forest and past a marsh to the shores of Lake Winnipesaukee. The best time for loon spotting is nesting season, in June and July.

The Drive » Follow Lees Mill Rd to Lee Rd. Turn right and continue to NH 109. Turn right. Continue 1.2 miles to the junction of NH 109 and the start of NH 171/Old Mountain Rd. Drive about 2 miles on NH 171. The entrance to Castle in the Clouds will be on the left.

- - - - - - - - - -

TRIP HIGHLIGHT

⑥ Castle in the Clouds

Perched on high like a king surveying his

territory, the arts and crafts–style **Castle in the Clouds** ([icon]603-476-5900; www.castleintheclouds. org; 455 Old Mountain Rd/NH 171, Moultonborough; adult/child $16/8; [icon]10am-5:30pm daily early Jun-late Oct, Sat & Sun May-early Jun) wows with its stone walls and exposed-timber beams, but it's the views of lakes and valleys that draw the crowds – in autumn the kaleidoscope of rust, red and yellow beats any postcard. The 5500-acre estate features gardens, ponds and a path leading to a small waterfall. Admission includes the castle and stories about the eccentric millionaire Thomas Plant, who built it.

From late June to early September, make reservations for the Monday-morning 'Walks and Talks,' about anything from birds to wild food, or for the Thursday-evening 'Jazz at Sunset' performances.

The Drive » Return to NH 109 south, following a woodsy route that tracks Lake Winnipesaukee (although you won't always be able to see the water). After Melvin Village, cross Mirror Lake on a pinch of land before hitting the outskirts of Wolfeboro. The drive is 10 miles.

⑦ Libby Museum

At the age of 40, Henry Forrest Libby, a local doctor, began collecting things. In 1912 he built a home for his collections, which later became the eccentric little **Libby Museum** (☏603-569-1035; www.thelibbymuseum.org; 755 N Main St/NH 109, Winter Harbor; adult/child $2/1; ☺10am-4pm Tue-Sat, noon-4pm Sun Jun-Aug, Sat & Sun only Sep–mid-Oct). Starting with butterflies and moths, the amateur naturalist built up a private natural-history collection that now includes numerous stuffed mammals and birds. Other collections followed, including Abenaki relics and early-American farm and home

implements. The museum sits in a lovely spot across from Winter Harbor on Lake Winnipesaukee.

The Drive » Drive 3.2 miles southeast on NH 109 to downtown Wolfeboro.

- - - - - - - - - - - -

TRIP HIGHLIGHT

⑧ Wolfeboro

The self-proclaimed 'Oldest Resort in America' is a nice place to wander for a few hours. The waterfront is picturesque, with a grassy lakeside park, and in summer there are lots of free concerts and art events. (It's also garnered fame as the site of Republican presidential candidate Mitt Romney's summer home.)

Stretch your legs on the **Cotton Valley Rail Trail**, which runs for 6 miles along a former railroad track. It passes two lakes, climbs through Cotton Valley and winds through forests and fields. The trail starts behind the **Wolfeboro Chamber of Commerce** (☏800-516-5324, 603-569-2200; www.wolfeborochamber.com; 32 Central Ave; ☺10am-3pm Mon-Fri, 10am-noon Sat, longer hours late May–mid-Oct), inside the former train depot, which carries a fantastic map detailing the walk. Before leaving, buy a scoop of ice cream downtown from **Bailey's**

Bubble (☏603-569-3612; www.baileysbubble.com; 5 Railroad Ave; ice cream from $3; ☺noon-8pm Sun-Thu, to 9pm Fri & Sat mid-May–early Sep), where they've served generations of families.

✴ ⛺ p245

The Drive » Leave NH 109 in Wolfeboro, picking up NH 28 east just south of downtown. Summer camps dot the 10-mile drive to Alton, where you pick up NH 11 north and drive for 20 miles, passing the Mt Major Trail and then Ellacoya State Beach before swinging into Laconia.

- - - - - - - - - - - -

⑨ Laconia

Plunked between I-93 and Weirs Beach, busy Laconia has the largest population in this region. There aren't any noteworthy sites, but the community does have a variety of restaurants and a number of local motels. In nearby Gilford, it's fun to sit on the upstairs porch at **Patrick's Pub** (☏603-293-0841; www.patrickspub.com; 18 Weirs Rd, Gilford; mains $10-20; ☺11:30am-midnight Sun-Thu, to 12:30am Fri & Sat) and sip a beer while watching airplanes swoop into Laconia Municipal Airport next door.

✴ ⛺ p245

The Drive » To complete the loop, return to Weirs Beach by taking US 3 heading north for 7 miles.

Eating & Sleeping

Meredith ➋

✖ Lakeside Deli & Grille   Sandwiches $

(☎603-677-7132; www.facebook.com/
LakesideDeliGrille; 2 Pleasant St; soups &
sandwiches $5-12; ⏱11am-4pm Sun-Thu, to
8pm Fri & Sat) For a delicious lunch with prime
Lake Winnepesaukee views, hit the front porch
of this deli just east of downtown, beloved for
its homemade soups, and fish tacos with fresh
haddock and chipotle mayo.

Holderness ➌

✖ Walter's Basin   American $$

(☎603-968-4412; www.waltersbasin.com;
859 US 3; sandwiches $9-19.50, mains $15-26;
⏱11:30am-9pm Sun-Thu, to 9:30pm Fri & Sat)
Lake trippers are encouraged to dock their boats
and come in for a meal at this casual waterfront
spot. Located on Little Squam Lake near the
bridge, the friendly restaurant features stuffed
haddock, elk meatloaf, blueberry-glazed salmon
and lobster macaroni and cheese.

🛏 Manor on Golden Pond   B&B $$$

(☎800-545-2141, 603-968-3348; www.
manorongoldenpond.com; 31 Manor Dr, off US 3;
r $280-410, cottage $410, ste $480, all incl
breakfast; ⏱closed 1 week at Christmas &
1 week early spring; 🛜🐾) This luxurious
B&B is perched on Shepard Hill, overlooking
serene Squam Lake. Elegant rooms (some with
fireplaces and Jacuzzis), gourmet breakfasts
and a lovely private beach make this one of the
lake region's finest retreats. Children under 12
years are not welcome here.

Wolfeboro ➑

✖ Wolfetrap Grill
& Rawbar   Seafood $$

(☎603-569-1047; www.wolfetrapgrillandrawbar.
com; 19 Bay St; mains $15-26; ⏱11am-late mid-
May–Sep) Nantucket meets new Hampshire at
this airy eatery tucked away on Back Bay, an inlet
of Lake Winnipesaukee. Inside tables are covered

with parchment paper – ready for you to attack
and get messy with shellfish (oysters, clams,
shrimp, lobster) – while the deck has loungey
chairs overlooking the water. The bar keeps
going, as the bartenders say, 'till the wolf howls'.

🛏 Wolfeboro Inn   Inn $$$

(☎603-569-3016; www.wolfeboroinn.com;
90 N Main St; r $199-319, ste $259-359, all incl
breakfast; @🛜) The town's best-known lodging
is right on the lake with a private beach. One of
the region's most prestigious resorts since 1812,
it has 44 rooms across a main inn and a modern
annex. Rooms have modern touches including
flat-screen TVs, new beds and contemporary
furnishings: it feels less historic but oh-so-
luxurious. Facilities include a restaurant and
pub, **Wolfe's Tavern** (☎603-569-3016; www.
wolfestavern.com; 90 N Main St; lunch mains $11-
20, dinner mains $13-30; ⏱7am-9pm).

Laconia ➒

✖ Union Diner   Diner $

(☎603-524-6744; www.theuniondiner.com; 1331
Union Ave; mains $5-10; ⏱6am-3pm Mon-Wed, to
8pm Thu-Sat, to 1pm Sun) Escape the waterfront
hubbub at this classic American diner 3 miles
south of Weirs Beach, housed in a converted
1950s railway dining car with oak-mahogany
woodwork and decorative tile floors. Grab a booth
or a counterside stool and treat yourself to early-
bird breakfast specials or a lunch of homemade
meatloaf, lobster stew, or roast turkey with
stuffing and cranberry sauce. Yum!

🛏 Proctor's Lakehouse
Cottages   Apartment $$

(☎603-366-5517; www.lakehousecottages.com;
1144 Weirs Blvd/US 3; cottage $170-320, ste
$170-300; 🛜🐾) This family-owned collection
of cottages and suites, all with kitchens, are
blissful. The more modern suites clustered
in the main structure feature porches, while
cottages exude old-school New England. All
have views of the lake (there's a tiny beach
and deck), and every unit comes with its own
lakeside grill.

Monadnock Villages

23

Driving between the villages encircling Mt Monadnock is like gliding through a 19th-century landscape painting – one brought vividly to life with hikers, blooming rhododendrons and abundant wildlife.

TRIP HIGHLIGHTS

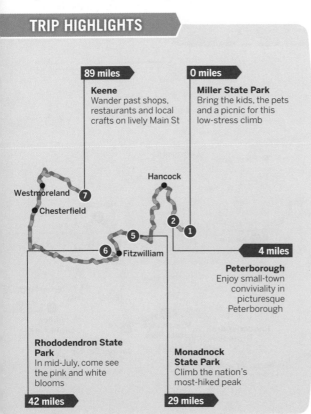

89 miles

Keene
Wander past shops, restaurants and local crafts on lively Main St

0 miles

Miller State Park
Bring the kids, the pets and a picnic for this low-stress climb

Hancock

Westmoreland **7**

Chesterfield

5

2 **1**

6 Fitzwilliam

4 miles

Peterborough
Enjoy small-town conviviality in picturesque Peterborough

Rhododendron State Park
In mid-July, come see the pink and white blooms

42 miles

Monadnock State Park
Climb the nation's most-hiked peak

29 miles

2 DAYS
89 MILES / 143KM

GREAT FOR...

BEST TIME TO GO
April through October for festivals, foliage and hiking.

📷 **ESSENTIAL PHOTO**

From Kimball Farm, photograph Mt Monadnock, then order your ice cream.

✓ **BEST FOR OUTDOORS**

A hike to the summit of Mt Monadnock – it's a classic!

23 Monadnock Villages

Striking peaks, birch-lined streams, white-painted villages – no wonder artists and writers such as Henry David Thoreau, Willa Cather and Thornton Wilder have found inspiration here. But the camaraderie found in the towns, with their attractive communal spaces, surely added oomph to their oohs and ahs. This convivial spirit continues today, from the shared sense of adventure on the White Dot Trail to the ice-cream fans toughing out the winds on a chilly day at Kimball Farm.

TRIP HIGHLIGHT

❶ Miller State Park

If Mt Monadnock is the main course, then **Pack Monadnock** is the appetizer. Just 4 miles east of Peterborough, this 2290ft mountain is the heart of **Miller State Park** (☎603-924-3672; www.nhstateparks. org; 13 Miller Park Rd, Peterborough; adult/child $4/2; ⏱9am-5pm late May-Oct, limited access Nov-late May). Established in 1891, the park is New Hampshire's oldest, and a good one to visit if you're traveling with young children and

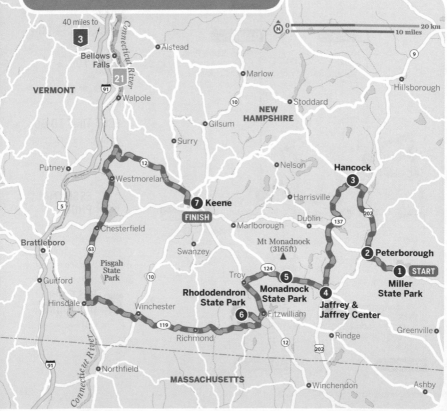

pets. Two separate trails, the **Womack Trail** and the **Marion Davis Trail**, lead 1.4 miles from the parking lot to the summit, where you can climb a **fire tower** (built in 1939) for sweeping views. Short on time? Drive the 1.3-mile paved road to the top.

The Drive » Take NH 101 west for 4 miles into Peterborough.

TRIP HIGHLIGHT

❷ Peterborough

This charming village of red-brick houses and tree-lined streets, with the idyllic Nabasuit River coursing through its historic center, is a particularly nice place for an extended stop. Its atmosphere is enhanced by the artistic influence of the nearby MacDowell Colony (www.macdowell colony.org).

LINK YOUR TRIP

3 Ivy League Tour
Head north from Keene to Hanover via NH 12 and I-91 for a tour of New England's most legendary colleges.

21 Connecticut River Byway
Swoop west from Keene on NH 12 to join the beautiful valley of the Connecticut River.

Pop into the **Mariposa Museum** (☎603-924-4555; www.mariposamuseum.org; 26 Main St; adult/child $6/4; ⏰11am-5pm Tue-Sun; 👶) for folk art and folklore from around the world. It's a 'please touch' kind of place, and kids are encouraged to try on costumes and play the musical instruments. The indie bookstore **Toadstool Bookshop** (☎603-924-3543; www. toadbooks.com; 12 Depot Sq; ⏰10am-6pm Mon-Fri, to 5pm Sat, to 4pm Sun) has a welcoming vibe, a good selection of books and a small cafe, **Aesop's Tables** (☎603-924-1612; 12 Depot Sq; sandwiches & salads $5-11; ⏰7:30am-4pm Mon-Fri, 9am-4pm Sat).

✕ 🛏 p253

The Drive » From Peterborough, drive 9 miles northwest on US 202/NH 123, along a woodsy route also popular with motorcyclists.

❸ Hancock

In the first half of the 1800s, wandering artists would paint colorful landscape murals on bedroom walls in homes and inns throughout New England. Rufus Porter, an inventor who started *Scientific American* magazine, was one of the most famous of these traveling artists; unfortunately, many of his stencils and paintings were subsequently covered, and ruined, by

wallpaper. Two murals are still visible inside the Hancock Inn (p253), a three-story B&B in the heart of town. The inn is the oldest in New Hampshire and has been in continuous operation since 1789 – when George Washington was president! Although the murals are in guest rooms, you can enjoy a Porter-style mural – with a cocktail – in the inn's sitting room before a meal at the restaurant.

🛏 p253

The Drive » NH 137 winds past marshes, stone walls and lichen-covered rocks on its way to NH 101, which is 6.5 miles south. Continue south on NH 137 for 7 miles to Jaffrey or, if you need to break for a meal, turn left and continue to Peterborough, then head south to Jaffrey on US 202.

❹ Jaffrey & Jaffrey Center

Jaffrey Center, 2 miles west of Jaffrey, is another tiny, picture-perfect village of serene lanes, 18th-century homes and a dramatic white-steepled meetinghouse. All of its historic sites are clustered around the wee historic district, located on both sides of Gilmore Pond Rd off NH 124. The most intriguing sights include the frozen-in-time **Little Red School House** and the **Melville Academy**, which houses a one-room museum of rural artifacts (both are open 2pm to 4pm on summer weekends). Willa Cather, a frequent visitor to Jaffrey, is buried in the **Old Burying Ground** behind the meeting-house, with a quote from *My Antonia* gracing the headstone.

Jaffrey is perhaps best known as the home of Kimball Farm, an ice-cream shop that is favored by Mt Monadnock hikers.

 p253

The Drive ⟫ From Jaffrey, drive 2 miles west on NH 124, passing through Jaffrey Center, and turn right on Dublin Rd. Pass a church camp and follow the signs to the park.

- - - - - - - - - - - -

TRIP HIGHLIGHT

❺ Monadnock State Park

Roughly 125,000 people climb the commanding 3165ft **Mt Monadnock** (☏603-532-8862; www. nhstateparks.org; 116 Poole Rd, Jaffrey; adult/child 6-11yr

$4/2) every year, helping it earn the honor of the most-climbed peak in the US. Henry David Thoreau climbed it twice, in 1858 and 1860. Displays inside the visitor center explain that *monadnock* comes from the Abenaki word meaning 'special' or 'unique.' The word is now used geologically to describe a residual hill that rises alone from a plain.

Twelve miles of un-groomed **ski trails** lure cross-country skiers in winter, while more than 40 miles of **hiking paths** draw the trail-hungry hordes in summer. Numerous combinations of trails lead to the summit. The **White Dot Trail**, which joins the White Cross Trail, is the most direct route, running from the visitor center to the bare-topped peak; it's a 4-mile round-trip and takes about 3½ hours. On clear days, you can gaze 100 miles across all six New England states.

LOCAL KNOWLEDGE: KIMBALL FARM

After a hike to the summit of Mt Monadnock, everyone knows that the best reward is ice cream from **Kimball Farm** (☏603-532-5765; kimballfarm.com/jaffrey; 158 Turnpike Rd/NH 124; mains $6-29; ⏱11am-10pm May-Oct). Consider the 40 flavors, order at the window, then find a seat at a picnic table out front. Perennial favorites include maple walnut, vanilla peanut butter, raspberry chocolate chip and coffee Oreo. Take note: the scoops are huge.

The park's seasonal Gilson Pond Campground is well placed for a sun-rise ascent.

🛏 p253

The Drive ⟫ Return to NH 124 and follow it 4.5 miles west, then bear left onto Troy Rd/Monadnock St and continue 2.5 miles west to join NH 12 near Troy. Turn left onto southbound NH 12 and drive 4 miles to Fitzwilliam, whose town green is surrounded by lovely old houses and a towering steeple. Follow NH 119 about 1 mile west, then turn right on Rhododendron Rd and drive for 2 miles.

- - - - - - - - - - - -

TRIP HIGHLIGHT

❻ Rhododendron State Park

The 16-acre rhododendron grove in this serene **park** (☏603-532-8862; www. nhstateparks.org; 424 Rock-wood Pond Rd, US 119W, Fitzwilliam; adult/child $4/2; ☼year-round unless otherwise posted; 👶) is the largest in New England. It makes for a nice stroll in mid-July, when thick stands of the giant plant (*Rhododendron maximum*) bloom white and pink along the 0.6-mile **Rhododendron Trail** circling the grove. The blooms can last for weeks and the final blossoms may occur as the leaves are turning. Listen for songbirds in the foliage while on the trail. The trail is also accessible by people with disabilities.

Hikers can hook onto the adjacent **Wildflower Trail**, where they may see

Monadnock State Park View from Mt Monadnock

PICK-YOUR-OWN FARMS

Sun-warmed raspberries, plump blueberries, oversized pumpkins – if you want to pick it, New Hampshire probably has it. Pick-your-own farms dot the state, and it's fun and delicious for all ages. Some of our favorites include **Monadnock Berries** (☎603-242-6417; www.monadnockberries.com; 545 West Hill Rd, Troy), a pretty farm with blueberries, raspberries, gooseberries and currants to pick, and **Butternut Farm** (www.butternutfarm.net; Farmington), where you can pick apples, peaches, plums, nectarines, blueberries and – of course – pumpkins.

The sheer number of pick-your-own farms in New Hampshire is mind-boggling: chances are, there's a location near you. Pick Your Own (www.pickyourown.org/NH.htm) lists farms throughout the country and includes a section on New Hampshire; the website is unwieldy but generally up to date. Better yet, ask a local or your innkeeper for the closest and best in your area. Offerings vary by the season and many are only open May to October, so be sure to call ahead.

mountain laurel blooms in June and berries in the fall. More ambitious ramblers can link from the Rhododendron Trail to the **Little Monadnock Mountain Trail**, which climbs to the 1883ft summit of Little Monadnock Mountain. On the way it joins the 117-mile **Meta-Comet–Monadnock Trail** (nicknamed the M&M Trail), which continues to the summit of Mt Monadnock.

The Drive ≫ Drive west on NH 119, crossing NH 32 before heading into Winchester. Continue west on NH 119, passing one entrance to Pisgah State Park. Turn right on NH 63 for a bucolic spin past cows and red barns. Cross NH 9 to begin a particularly scenic drive past Spofford Lake, pine trees and the startlingly impressive Park Hill Meeting House. Turn right on NH 12 at Stuart & Johns Sugar House and drive toward Keene. The drive is 47 miles.

TRIP HIGHLIGHT

➐ Keene

Keene is like the hub of a giant wheel, with a half-dozen spokes linking to dozens of outlying villages that encircle the city, providing an endless supply of scenic loops. You really can't go wrong with any of them.

Keene itself is a great place to explore, particularly along its pleasant and lively Main St, which is lined with indie shops and cozy eateries. For local crafts, foodstuffs and gifts, stop by **Hannah Grimes Marketplace** (www.hannahgrimesmarketplace; 42 Main St; ☺10am-6pm Mon-Sat, to 4pm Sun).

Main St is crowned by a small tree-filled plaza (Central Sq) with a fountain at one end. The elegant, red-brick **Keene State College** (☎603-358-

2276; www.keene.edu; 229 Main St) anchors the western end of Main St and accounts for one-quarter of the town's population, as well as its youthful, artistic sensibility. The spacious, skylit halls at the **Thorne-Sagendorph Art Gallery** (☎603-358-2720; www.keene.edu/tsag; Wyman Way; ☺noon-5pm Sat-Wed, to 7pm Thu & Fri) showcase rotating exhibits of regional and national artists. The small permanent collection includes pieces by national artists who have been drawn to the Monadnock region since the 1800s.

In the evening, see what's doing at the 80-year-old **Colonial Theater** (☎603-352-2033; www.thecolonial.org; 95 Main St), which offers a diverse lineup of entertainment.

✕ ⮂ p253

Eating & Sleeping

Peterborough ❷

✕ Waterhouse
Modern American $$

(☎603-924-4001; www.waterhousenh.com; 18 Depot St; mains $12-25; ☺11:30am-9pm Mon-Sat, to 2:30pm Sun; ✐) For riverside charm, step into Waterhouse's bright wood-floored dining room and grab a table beside the floor-to-ceiling windows directly overlooking the rushing Nabanusit. The lunch menu abounds in revisited American classics such as BLTs, fish and chips, burgers and tuna melts, while dinner offerings expand to include steak and seafood.

⌂ Little River Bed & Breakfast
B&B $$

(☎603-924-3280; www.littleriverbedandbreakfast. com; 184 Union St; r $119-149; ☜) One mile west of the village center on the gorgeous Nubanusit River, this 19th-century farmhouse once served as housing for artists at the nearby MacDowell Colony. Innkeepers Paula and Rob Fox have converted it into a cozy B&B with four immaculate guest rooms and tasty breakfasts featuring homemade granola and muffins.

Hancock ❸

⌂ Hancock Inn
Inn $$$

(☎603-525-3318, 800-525-1789; www. hancockinn.com; 33 Main St; r incl breakfast $178-395; ☜) New Hampshire's oldest inn has 15 rooms, each with its own unique charms. Room prices vary according to size and features: some of the coolest include dome ceilings (in rooms that used to be part of a ballroom), fireplaces and private patios. The cozy dining room is open to the public for dinner nightly.

Jaffrey & Jaffrey Center ❹

✕ Sunflowers
Cafe $$

(☎603-593-3303; www.sunflowerscatering. com; 21 Main St, Jaffrey; breakfast & lunch mains $5-14, dinner mains $12-28; ☺7-10:30am, 11am-2pm & 5-8pm Mon & Wed-Sat, 9am-3pm Sun) In the heart of Jaffrey (2 miles east of Jaffrey

Center), this cozy cafe with its cheerful blue and yellow facade is the perfect place to greet the day with cinnamon rolls, scones, quiches and omelets. It's just as tempting later in the day for creative salads, baked haddock dinners, steaks and gourmet mac 'n' cheese.

Monadnock State Park ❺

⌂ Gilson Pond Campground
Campground $

(☎603-532-2416, reservations 877-647-2757; 585 Dublin Rd/NH 124; tent sites $25; ☺May-Oct) Well placed for a sunrise ascent up the mountain, this state park campground has 35 peaceful, well-shaded sites. From November through April, when Gilson Pond is closed, camping is available at the nearby park headquarters on a first-come, first-served basis.

Keene ❼

✕ Luca's Mediterranean Café
Italian $$

(☎603-358-3335; 10 Central Sq; lunch mains $9-14, dinner mains $15-27; ☺restaurant 11:30am-2pm Mon-Fri, 5-9pm Mon-Sat year-round, plus 5-9pm Sun May-Dec) Luca's Café serves excellent thin-crust pizzas, tasty salads and gourmet sandwiches at lunch, while dinner sees a tempting array of pastas, grilled fish and pan-seared beef tenderloin. The adjacent gourmet Italian **food market** (panini $7; ☺9am-7pm Mon-Sat) morphs into a casual spaghetti house each weekend.

⌂ Fairfield Inn & Suites Keene Downtown
Hotel $$

(☎603-357-7070; www.fairfieldinnkeene.com; 30 Main St; r $104-279, ste $129-329; ❄☜) In a picture-perfect Main St location, this venerable century-old hotel (formerly known as the Lane Hotel) has 40 attractive rooms, each uniquely furnished in a classic style, ensuring you won't get the cookie-cutter experience. There are plenty of creature comforts (individual climate control, high-speed internet connection) and a good restaurant on the 1st floor.

Woodland Heritage Trail

24

Embrace the solitude on this loop through the North Woods, where the stories of entrepreneurs, immigrants, lumberjacks and one very effective conservationist are as fascinating as the scenery.

TRIP HIGHLIGHTS

13 miles

Weeks State Park
Visit the hilltop home of a famous conservationist

43 miles

Milan Hill State Park
Sleep in a yurt and climb a fire tower

Groveton

6

4

2

START/ FINISH

8

Jefferson
Hunt for elves and St Nick at Santa's Village

3 miles

Gorham
If you don't see a moose then your eyes aren't open

75 miles

2 DAYS
89 MILES / 143KM

GREAT FOR...

BEST TIME TO GO
June to October for warm weather, fall foliage and open-for-business attractions.

ESSENTIAL PHOTO
Stark Covered Bridge, which anchors a picturesque village.

BEST FOR HISTORY
Learn about logging at Northern Forest Heritage Park.

24 Woodland Heritage Trail

Why is northern New Hampshire so wild? Because a forward-thinking US senator from the Granite State, John W Weeks, introduced a bill in 1909 that birthed the modern national forest system. This trip makes the most of Weeks' vision by circling the White Mountain National Forest's rugged Kilkenny District, plunked dramatically between the Connecticut and Androscoggin Rivers and the Presidential Range.

❶ Fort Jefferson Fun Park

This trip starts with guns a' blazin' at **Fort Jefferson Fun Park** (☎603-586-4592, 603-586-4510; www.fortjeffersonfun park.com; 1492 Presidential Hwy/US 2, Jefferson; all-day ride pass $12.95; ⏰10am-5pm late May-early Sep), an Old West theme park east of Jefferson that, well, doesn't have much to do with New Hampshire's logging past. But hey, everybody likes cowboys, right? Younger kids will most enjoy the low-key

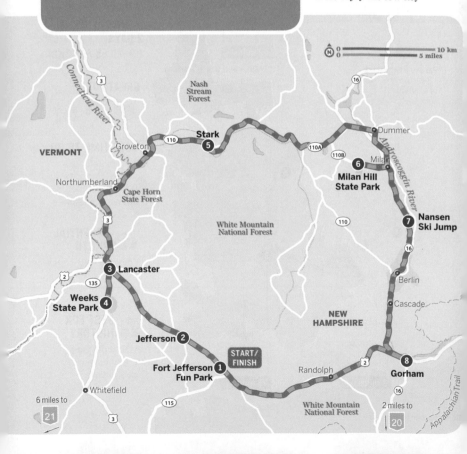

rides, which include a roller coaster, a raft coaster, go-karts and some waterslides. Stop by the appropriately named Water Wheel (p261) for maple syrup, New Hampshire gifts and a hearty meal.

The Drive » From the Water Wheel, look both ways for logging trucks, then turn right on US 2 and head to Jefferson, 3 miles away.

TRIP HIGHLIGHT

❷ Jefferson

Just west of mountain-ringed Jefferson is another theme park, **Santa's Village** (☎603-586-4445; www.santasvillage.com; 528 Presidential Hwy/US 2; $31; ⏰9:30am-6pm daily mid-Jun–Aug, to 5pm Sat & Sun late May–mid-Jun & Sep–mid-Oct). Look for Santa's 26 elves as you enjoy the kiddie-focused rides, a Ferris wheel and the *Jingle Bell*

LINK YOUR TRIP

20 White Mountains Loop

From Gorham, drive south to Mt Washington, New England's highest peak.

21 Connecticut River Byway

Vistas are bucolic on the Connecticut River Byway, which rolls south from Lancaster.

Express train. Kids can even visit Santa himself, usually found relaxing at home. The attached **water park**, Ho Ho H20, is open on warm days. The park opens weekends in December for holiday visits.

🍴 🛏 p261

The Drive » Continue west 7 miles from Santa's Village to Lancaster, passing clapboard homes, logging trucks and commanding views of the Presidential Range.

❸ Lancaster

Photo op! Substitute your face for Paul Bunyan's at the **Great North Woods Welcome Center** (☎603-788-3212; www.northern gatewaychamber.org; 25 Park St; ⏰10am-4pm Mon-Sat) in downtown Lancaster. Here you can pick up maps and brochures before wandering past the boutiques and antique stores lining nearby Main St.

NEW HAMPSHIRE'S FAVORITE STONE

New Hampshire will forever be known as 'the granite state.' This refers not merely to the tough, take-no-bullshit attitude of the locals but also to the state's enormous granite quarries, which still yield vast amounts of this very solid stone. They've also played a pivotal role in some of the country's most important structures: New Hampshire granite was used in Boston's Quincy Market, the Brooklyn Bridge, the Pentagon and even the Library of Congress.

The Drive » Follow US 3 for 3 miles south out of downtown Lancaster. The Weeks State Park entrance is on the left, across the street from a scenic pull-off.

TRIP HIGHLIGHT

❹ Weeks State Park

Named for US senator John Weeks, **Weeks State Park** (☎603-788-4004; www.nhstateparks.org; 200 Weeks State Park Rd, off US 3, Lancaster; adult/child $5/3; ⏰10am-5pm Wed-Sun mid-Jun–Aug, Sat & Sun only late May–mid-Jun & Sep–mid-Oct) sits atop Mt Prospect. Weeks was a Lancaster native who introduced legislation in 1909 that helped to stem the degradation of local lands caused by unregulated logging, with legislation that became known as the Weeks Act. By authorizing the federal government to purchase land at the head of navigable streams, the Act kick-started the national forest system, adding more than 19 million

DENSTANONEYE / GETTY IMAGES ©

acres of land to the nation's holdings.

The park encompasses the 420-acre **Weeks estate**, where you can explore the Weeks home and enjoy 360-degree mountain views from the property's stone **fire tower**.

The Drive » From Lancaster, drive north on US 3, also known as the Daniel Webster Hwy, through Coos Junction, passing bogs and paralleling the railroad tracks. In Groveton, 10 miles north, snap a photo of the covered bridge before continuing east on NH 110 for 21 miles to Stark.

LIVE FREE OR DIE

New Hampshire is the most politically conservative state in New England, with a libertarian streak that runs deep. It's tough and rugged, and its citizens still cling with pride to the famous words uttered by General John Stark, victor at the crucial Battle of Bennington: 'Live Free or Die!' The famous saying graces local license plates and appears all over the state.

⑤ Stark

Fans of George RR Martin's novel *A Game of Thrones* can't be blamed if they ask directions to Winterfell, the northern holdfast of the Stark family that sits on the fringes of the lonely Wolfswood. But there aren't any wildling or wargs in this roadside village (that we saw, anyway), just the impossibly picturesque **Stark Covered Bridge**. This white, 134ft Paddleford truss bridge – constructed in 1862 and subsequently rebuilt and

Stark Stark Covered Bridge in the fall

strengthened – spans the Upper Ammonoosuc River. It's flanked by the white **Union Church** (1850) and a white schoolhouse, making for an eye-catching photo. General John Stark was a famous commander during the American Revolution.

Two miles east, pull over for the **Camp Stark Roadside Marker**, which describes the WWII prisoner-of-war camp located nearby, where prisoners were put to work cutting pulpwood. It was the only war camp in New Hampshire.

The Drive » Continue east 2.7 miles. Make a sharp left onto NH 110A at the junction of NH 110 and NH 110A. Drive just over 3.5 miles (you'll pass 110B, a cut-through) to NH 16 and a view of the mighty Androscoggin River. Turn right and follow NH 16 south towards Berlin for 4 miles. Turn right at 110B for a short drive to Milan Hill State Park.

- - - - - - - - - - - - -

TRIP HIGHLIGHT

⑥ Milan Hill State Park

How often do you get to spend the night in a purple yurt? Yep, that's an option at **Milan Hill State Park** (📞603-449-2429; www.nhstateparks.org;

72 Fire Tower Rd, Milan; day-use adult/child $4/2; ☺year-round; 🐾), also known for its cross-country skiing and snowshoe trails. The 45ft **fire tower** provides expansive views of New Hampshire's mountains, as well as of mountain ranges in Vermont, Maine and Canada. The park is pet-friendly, so bring Fido for a walk or picnic. The park is open year-round but only staffed seasonally; no day-use fee is collected in the low season.

The park is just south of New Hampshire's **13 Mile Woods Scenic Area**,

LOCAL KNOWLEDGE: BOOM PIERS

Driving south on NH 16 from Milan to Gorham, it's hard to miss the compact clusters of wood that rise from the middle of the river. Are they beaver dams? Small islands? Nope, those eye-catching clusters are boom piers, artificial islands that were used by lumbermen to separate logs by owner during the annual log drives. (Stamps that identified the owners were hammered into the end of the logs.) The log drives ended in 1963.

which stretches along NH 16 and the Androscoggin River a few miles north and is known to be a popular strip for free-ranging moose.

🛏 p261

The Drive » Continue south on NH 16 from Milan for 4 miles, keeping your eyes open for moose, particularly in the morning and early evening. The road hugs the western side of the birch-lined Androscoggin River, a log-carrying highway in the first half of the 20th century.

----

❼ Nansen Ski Jump

South of Milan, on the way to Gorham, pull over at the historic marker describing the **Nansen Ski Jump**, which is visible on the adjacent hill as you look north. This 171ft ski jump, first used in 1936, was the site of Olympic ski-jump trials in 1938. It was last used in 1982.

The Drive » Continue another 11 miles south on NH 16 to reach Gorham.

TRIP HIGHLIGHT

❽ Gorham

Gorham is a regional crossroads, linking roads flowing in from the North Woods, from Mt Washington and North Conway, and from the Rangeley Lakes region of northwestern Maine. Stop here for one of the area's best restaurants, Libby's Bistro (p261). Housed in an old bank building, it has a relaxed, speakeasy feel and uses local produce, seasonal vegetables and New Hampshire seafood. Original wall safes speak of the building's banking past.

By this point, you've probably seen several moose-crossing signs dotting the route. If you still haven't seen an actual moose, join a moose safari with **Gorham Moose Tours** (📞877-986-6673, 603-466-3103; www.gorhammoosetours.org; 69 Main St; adult/child $25/15; 🕐variable hours). These determined folks know where the moose are and have a 95% moose-spotting success rate (and, yes, they've done the math!).

🍴 🛏 p261

The Drive » Complete the loop by returning to Fort Jefferson Fun Park, just west of the junction of US 2 and NH 115.

Eating & Sleeping

Jefferson ②

✕ Water Wheel American $

(☏603-586-4313; www.waterwheelnh.com; 1955 Presidential Hwy/US 2; mains $7-12; ⊙6am-2pm daily Jun-Aug, Thu-Mon Sep-May) A red water wheel marks the spot at this down-home eatery where decorative bears hang from the wooden rafters. Portions are hearty, and breakfast is served all day.

🛏 Evergreen Motel Motel $

(☏603-586-4449; www.evergreenmotelnh.com; 537 Presidential Hwy/US 2; r incl breakfast $45-95; 🖥🛜🐾) This 18-room mom-and-pop establishment is across the street from Santa's Village. There's also a complimentary 18-hole miniature golf course on-site. Snowmobilers can ride to their doors from the Corridor 5 route.

🛏 Jefferson Inn B&B $$

(☏800-729-7908, 603-586-7998; http://jeffersoninn.com; 6 Renaissance Lane/US 2; r $115-155, ste $145-195, all incl breakfast; ❄🛜🐾) Eleven homespun rooms – think quilts, old brooms and washboards on the wall – fill this attractive Victorian house perched on a hill above the Presidential Hwy. Four rooms have air-con and two rooms are pet-friendly.

Milan Hill State Park ⑥

🛏 Milan Hill State Park Campground Campground $

(☏603-449-2429; www.nhstateparks.org; 72 Fire Tower Rd, Milan; tent & RV sites/yurts from $23/50; ⊙mid-May–mid-Oct) Four furnished yurts, each sleeping four people, are on offer at this state-park campground. There are also six campsites, three of them available by reservation.

Gorham ⑧

✕ Saladino's Italian Market Italian $

(☏603-466-2520; www.saladinositalianmarket.com; 152 Main St; mains $7-10; ⊙10am-6pm Wed-Fri) Run by a friendly family with Sicilian roots, Saladino's deli cranks out tasty, filling Italian subs, panini and salads, along with take-out Italian dinners such as lasagna, spaghetti with meatballs and eggplant Parmesan.

✕ Libby's Bistro & Saalt Pub International $$

(☏603-466-5330; www.libbysbistro.org; 111 Main St/NH 16; mains $12-23; ⊙bistro from 5-9pm Fri & Sat, pub 5-9pm Wed-Sun) A labor of love for acclaimed chef Liz Jackson, this 20-year-old bistro serves a seasonally changing, globally inspired menu that draws heavily on locally sourced ingredients. In the pub, expect more casual fare.

🛏 Mt Madison Inn Motel $$

(☏800-516-1778, 603-466-3622; www.mtmadisonmotel.com; 365 Main St; r $79-169, ste $119-164; ❄🛜🐾🐶) The recently upgraded king and queen rooms at this 32-room motel have all been re-carpeted and come with microwaves, coffee makers and refrigerators. A few rooms are pet-friendly; pets are $8 per pet per night. Other amenities include a heated pool and hot tub.

🛏 Top Notch Inn Motel $$

(☏800-228-5496, 603-466-5496; www.topnotchinn.com; 265 Main St; r $99-169, house $199-259, cottage $259-319; ⊙mid-May–late Oct; ❄🛜🐾🐶) In addition to standard motel rooms, the inn has five 'no-kids' rooms (aka Country Rooms) that are also pet-free. The three-room Pinkham House, a restored farmhouse, sleeps up to eight people, and the Mt Moriah Cottage up to 10. Laundry facilities are available.

STRETCH
YOUR LEGS
PORTSMOUTH

Start/Finish Colby's Breakfast & Lunch

Distance 1.5 miles

Duration Four hours

This easy stroll reveals the abundant charms of Portsmouth's vibrant historic district. Fuel up at the city's favorite breakfast joint, then set off to discover Colonial churches and mansions, a pretty waterfront park and one of New England's premier history museums.

Take this walk on Trip

Colby's Breakfast & Lunch

If you get to **Colby's** (☎603-436-3033; 105 Daniel St; mains $4-13; ⊘7am-2pm) after 8am on the weekend, there's going to be a wait, so give 'em your name and enjoy a cup of free coffee on the patio. Once in, egg lovers can choose from a multitude of Benedicts, and there's always the huevos rancheros and the chalkboard specials.

Colby's owners are serious about preserving their eatery's intimate appeal. In 2012, management posted a 'No Politicians, No Exceptions' sign on the door in the days before New Hampshire's presidential primary – campaign staff and candidates were disrupting business in the 28-seat restaurant.

The Walk ⟩⟩ Turn left out of Colby's and walk a block and a half to Market Sq.

Market Square

A public gathering place since the mid-1700s, this lively square, anchored by the 1854 **North Church**, is still the heart of Portsmouth. Nearby are open-air cafes, colorful storefronts and tiny galleries with banjo-playing buskers for entertainment on warm summer nights. There's public wi-fi here, and an information kiosk is open in summer.

The Walk ⟩⟩ Stroll down Pleasant St, passing the granite US Custom House, built in 1860. Next, on the left, is Governor John Langdon's House, where the three-term governor hosted George Washington in 1789. Bear left on Gates St and follow it to Marcy St, where you'll turn right and continue one block to find the meetinghouse on your right.

South Ward Meetinghouse

The towering **meetinghouse** (280 Marcy St), completed in 1866, replaced a parish meetinghouse that had been on the site since 1731. The 1st floor of the new building held a school, and the 2nd floor was used for meetings. Black citizens celebrated Emancipation Day here in January 1882.

The Walk ⟩⟩ From the front of the meetinghouse, cross Marcy St and walk down Hunking St.

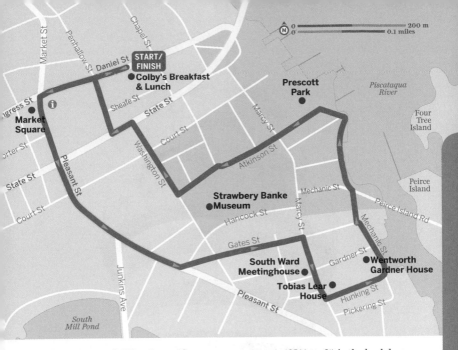

Tobias Lear & Wentworth Gardner Houses

Tobias Lear House (📞603-436-4406; http://wentworthlear.org; 50 Mechanic St; 🕐11am-4pm Thu-Mon Jun-Oct), built in 1740, was in the Lear family for 120 years. The fifth Tobias Lear served as private secretary to President George Washington, who visited Lear's mother here in 1789. Around the corner is the 1760 **Wentworth Gardner House** (📞603-436-4406; http://wentworthlear.org; 50 Mechanic St; adult/child $6/3; 🕐11-4pm Thu-Mon Jun–Oct), one of the finest Georgian houses in the USA. Elizabeth and Mark Hunking Wentworth were among Portsmouth's wealthiest citizens, so no expense was spared in building the home, which was a wedding gift for their son.

The Walk » Turn left on Mechanic St and follow it past the windswept headstones at Point of Graves to Prescott Park.

Prescott Park

Overlooking the Piscataqua River, this leafy **park** (www.cityofportsmouth.com/prescottpark; 105 Marcy St) is the backdrop for a summer **arts festival** (www.prescottpark.org; 🕐Jun-early Sep; 🚻), with free music, dance and theater. The design of the shoreside **Sheafe Warehouse** (c 1705) made it easy for flat-bottomed boats to load and unload cargo.

The Walk » Cross Marcy St and enter the parking lot of the Strawbery Banke Museum.

Strawbery Banke Museum

Spread across 10 acres, the **museum** (📞603-433-1100; www.strawberybanke.org; 14 Hancock St; adult/child 5-17yr $20/10; 🕐10am-5pm May-Oct) is a blend of period homes dating to the 1690s. Costumed guides recount tales that took place among the 38 historic buildings. The museum includes **Pitt Tavern** (1766), a hotbed of Revolutionary sentiment, and **Goodwin Mansion**, a grand 19th-century house from Portsmouth's most prosperous time.

The Walk » Follow Washington St northwest to State St, turn left, walk a few steps then turn right onto Penhallow St and return to Daniel St.

Maine

YOU KNOW THERE'S SOMETHING SPECIAL ABOUT A STATE when its most prominent citizens donate their land for the enjoyment of all. Governor Percival Baxter provided the wilderness for Baxter State Park while John D Rockefeller and his neighbors donated land for Acadia National Park.

For travelers, a coastal drive north from Portland swooshes past the legendary LL Bean flagship store, shipbuilding villages, Acadia National Park and first-in-the-nation sunrises. And we haven't even mentioned the lighthouses and lobster shacks. Inland, scenic byways hug rivers, lakes, forests and mountains. If you're lucky, you'll spy a moose; even if you don't, we're pretty certain you'll relish the quirky towns, charming inns, locavore dishes and excellent local brews you'll encounter.

Lubec West Quoddy Light
DANITA DELIMONT / GETTY IMAGES ©

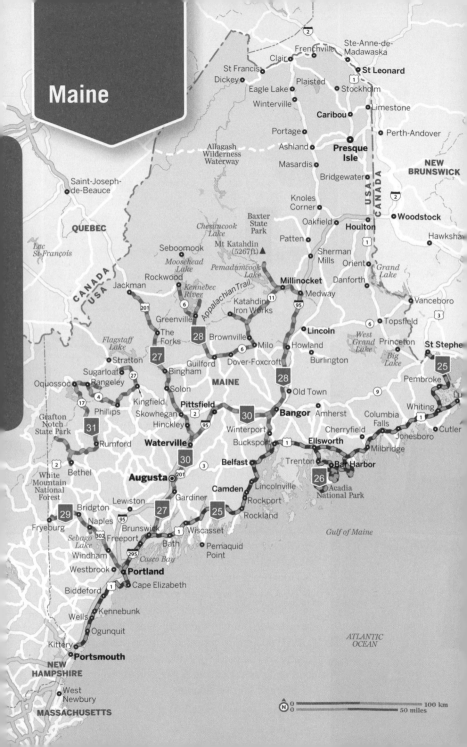

Maine Eagle Lake

 DON'T MISS

Lighthouse Hike
You'll earn your view of the coast after a hike across granite blocks to the Rockland Breakwater Lighthouse. View it on Trip 25

Heavenly Views
Lie on the sand and ponder the universe during the Stars over Sand Beach program at Acadia National Park. Enjoy it on Trip 26

Gifford's Ice Cream Stand
Fuel up for the North Woods with a scoop of Maine Blackberry or Caramel Caribou from Gifford's. Try it on Trip 27

Moose Safari
Haven't spotted a moose? Increase your odds on a Northwoods Outfitters safari. Try your luck on Trip 28

Museums & Murals
View works by American masters at the Portland Museum of Art, and snap photos of Maine-inspired murals down the street. Take them all in on Trip 30

Classic Trip

Maritime Maine

25

US 1 between Kittery and Calais is a route meant for lingering: fog-wrapped lighthouses, oceanfront picnic tables, seafaring artifacts in dusty museums, and one sprawling outdoors store.

TRIP HIGHLIGHTS

78 miles

Bath
Seafaring artifacts are a link to Maine's maritime past

265 miles

Quoddy Head State Park
Crashing waves, an eerie foghorn and a lonely lighthouse

FINISH
Calais

11

Camden

9

127 miles

Rockland Breakwater Lighthouse
A granite walkway leads to the distant beacon

7

3

Ogunquit

Kittery
START

Cape Elizabeth
Snap photos of the lighthouse and wander past WWII bunkers

42 miles

5 DAYS
285 MILES / 459KM

GREAT FOR...

BEST TIME TO GO

Summer is great, but you'll shake the crowds in September and October.

ESSENTIAL PHOTO

Stand on the rocks for a photo of Pemaquid lighthouse.

BEST FOR HISTORY

Exhibits on seafaring are captivating at the Maine Maritime Museum.

Scarborough Canoe on a lake

269

25 Maritime Maine

The rugged complexity of the Maine coast hits home at Rockland's visitor center, where a giant state map – complete with lighthouses – sprawls across the floor. Islands, peninsulas, harbors – no wonder this state has such a strong maritime heritage. And it's this heritage that makes the trip memorable. The sunrises and rocky coasts are lovely, but it's the stories about lighthouse keepers, brave captains and shipyard Rosie the Riveters that make this coastal drive truly unique.

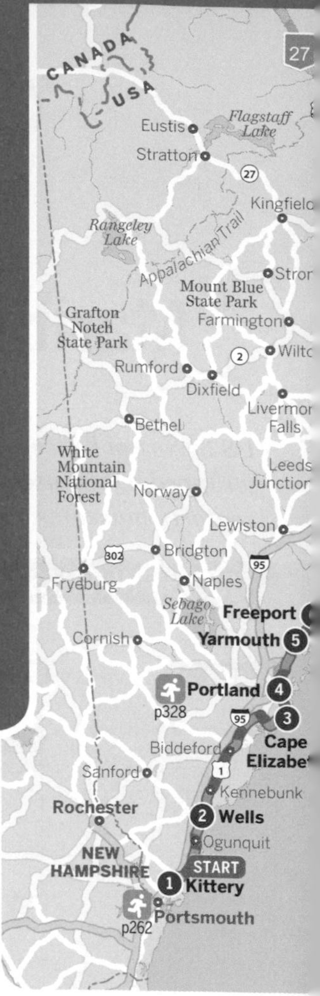

❶ Kittery

The drive to **Fort Foster Park** (http://fortfoster.
weebly.com/; Pocahontas Rd;
car/walk-in $10/5; ⏰10am-
8pm daily Jun-Aug, Sat &
Sun May & Sep; 👪) twists
past blooming flowers,
Victorian homes and tan-
talizing ocean glimpses.
The seaside park is a nice
place to walk some trails,
have a picnic, and play
in rocky tide pools. Look
out to sea for **Whaleback
Ledge** (1831), the first
lighthouse on this trip.

To get here from US 1,
take ME 103 for 5 miles,
then cross a small chan-
nel to Gerrish Island.

Follow Pocahontas Rd
through the woods.

From Kittery, you can
pop across to Portsmouth
(p262) for a walking tour.

The Drive » Continue north
on US 1. There's a nice but
potentially crowded sand beach
at Ogunquit. Seven miles north
of Ogunquit, turn right onto
Laudholm Farm Rd.

❷ Wells

Wildlife-lovers, bird-
watchers and families en-
joy wandering the 7 miles
of trails at the 2250-acre
**Wells National Estuarine
Research Reserve** (📞207-
646-1555; www.wellsreserve.
org; 342 Laudholm Farm Rd;
adult/child $5/1; ⏰trails
7am-sunset, nature center
10am-4pm), a protected
coastal ecosystem. No
pets permitted. Down the
road, the **Rachel Carson
National Wildlife Reserve**
(📞207-646-9226; www.fws.
gov/refuge/rachel_carson;
321 Port Rd; ⏰dawn-dusk)
holds more than 14,000
acres of protected coastal

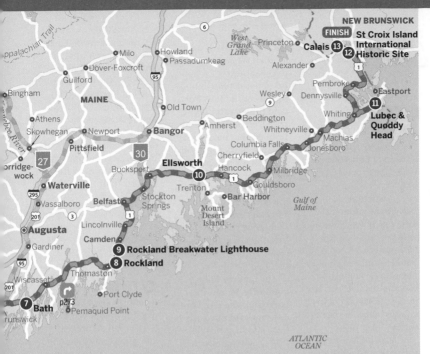

areas, with four trails
scattered along 50 miles
of shoreline. The 1-mile,
pet-friendly Carson Trail
meanders along tidal
creeks and salt marshes.

The Drive ≫ Follow US 1
north, passing through Saco. In
Scarborough, turn right onto
ME 207. Follow it almost 3 miles
to ME 77 and turn left. Drive just
over 7 miles, passing Two Lights
Rd, to Shore Rd. Turn right.

LINK YOUR TRIP

27 **Old Canada Road**
From Bath, drive
to Brunswick to wander
a museum about Arctic
explorers, then continue
the route north along the
stunning Kennebec River.

30 **Mainely Art**
In Rockland, join a
cultural loop of Maine's
artistic heritage and
contemporary culture.

Classic Trip

TRIP HIGHLIGHT

❸ Cape Elizabeth

Good photo opportunities abound at **Fort Williams Park** (www.fortwilliams.org; 1000 Shore Rd; ☺ sunrise-sunset), where you can explore the ruins of the fort, which was a late-19th-century artillery base, and check out WWII bunkers and gun emplacements (a German U-boat was spotted in Casco Bay in 1942). The port actively guarded the entrance to the bay until 1964.

A favorite feature of the park is the **Portland Head Light**, the oldest of Maine's 52 functioning lighthouses. Commissioned by George Washington in 1791, it was staffed until 1989, when machines took over. The keeper's house is now the **Museum at Portland Head Light** (☎207-799-2661; www.portlandheadlight. com; 1000 Shore Rd; adult/child $2/1; ☺ museum 10am-4pm Jun-Oct), which traces the maritime and military history of the region.

✕ p277

The Drive » Drive north 1 mile on Shore Rd, then turn right onto Preble St. Drive another mile, then turn right on Broadway then left onto Breakwater Dr. Just ahead, turn right onto Madison St.

❹ Portland

Maine's largest city and port is graced by a handful of handsome lights, including the 1875 **Portland Breakwater Light**, with Corinthian columns. Dubbed the 'Bug Light' because of its tiny size, it sits in a small park in South Portland with a panoramic view of downtown across the harbor. You can't enter the Bug Light, but you can traipse over the stone breakwater and walk around the light's exterior.

The **Liberty Ship memorial**, across the park from the Bug Light, describes the site's history as a shipyard during WWII, when more than 30,000 people, including about 3750 women, were employed here to build cargo vessels, called Liberty Ships.

✕ 🛏 p277, p311, p319

The Drive » Follow I-295 north and take exit 17. DeLorme cartographic company will be on your right off the ramp (signed 'Global Village'). You can also follow US 1 north from Portland.

❺ Yarmouth

On your way to the stores of Freeport, geography boffins shouldn't miss a visit to the DeLorme cartographic company (now owned by Garmin) – its lofty office atrium is home to a giant rotating globe named **Eartha** (www.delorme.com/about/ eartha.aspx; 2 DeLorme Dr; ☺8am-6pm Mon-Fri). Eartha has a diameter of 41.5ft and has been acknowledged by the Guinness Book of Records as the world's largest revolving and rotating globe. The detail on it is impressive (it took two years to build), as is the opportunity for visitors to stop by for a look.

The Drive » Follow US 1 north 4.5 miles past outlet stores and motels to LL Bean. There's a large parking lot on the left between Howard Pl and Nathan Nye St.

❻ Freeport

A century ago Leon Leonwood Bean opened a shop here to sell equipment and provisions to hunters and fishers. His success lured other retailers and today nearly 200 stores line US 1, leading to traffic jams in summer.

Fronted by a 16ft hunting boot, the large flagship **LL Bean store** (☎877-755-2326; www.llbean. com; 95 Main St; ☺24hr) is a Maine must-see. In 1951 Bean himself removed the locks from the doors, deciding to stay open 24 hours a day, 365 days a year. With almost three million visitors annually, the store is one of the state's most popular tourist attractions. There's a 3500-gallon aquarium and trout pond, a stuffed moose, and eateries – not to mention outdoor clothing and gear, spread over a small campus of stores (one dedicated to hunting and fishing, another to bike, boat and ski, another to home furnishings – all open 24 hours).

Two 'Bootmobiles' travel the country on a mission to inspire people to get outside. The **LL Bean Outdoor Discovery School** (☏888-552-3261; www.llbean.com/ods; 95 Main St) offers an array of courses, from instore bike-maintenance clinics to first aid, plus fantastic excursions, tours and classes locally and across the state – from archery to snowshoeing by way of fly-fishing and bird-watching.

 p277

The Drive » Follow US 1 north 18 miles through Brunswick to Bath. Pass Middle St, then turn right on Washington St and drive 1.2 miles to the museum.

- - - - - - - - - -

TRIP HIGHLIGHT

7 Bath

This quaint Kennebec River town was once home to more than 20 shipyards producing more than a quarter of early America's wooden ships. Bath Iron Works, founded in 1884, is still one of the largest and most productive shipyards in the nation.

On the western bank of the Kennebec, the **Maine Maritime Museum** (☏207-443-1316; www.mainemaritimemuseum.org; 243 Washington St; adult/child $15.50/10; ☉9:30am-5pm) preserves the town's traditions with paintings,

models and exhibits that tell the tale of the last 400 years of seafaring. Landlubbers and old salts alike will find something of interest, whether it's an 1849 ship's log describing the power of a hurricane or a hands-on tugboat pilot's house. On the grounds, look for the partial remains of the *Snow Squall,* a three-mast 1851 clipper ship that foundered near the Falkland Islands, and a life-size sculpture of the *Wyoming,* the largest wooden sailing vessel ever built.

In summer, the museum offers a variety of **boat cruises**, taking in assorted lighthouses and bird-rich bays (per person $32 to $50, including museum admission). It also has a trolley tour that gives an insider's perspective of the Bath Iron Works.

The Drive » Return to US 1 and continue north 40 miles, taking a moment to ogle the long line at Red's, a popular lobster shack in Wiscasset known for its lobster rolls. Continue north to Rockland.

- - - - - - - - - -

8 Rockland

This thriving commercial port boasts a large fishing fleet and a proud year-round population. Settled in 1769, it was once an important shipbuilding center and a transportation hub for river cargo. Today, tall-masted ships still fill the harbor because Rockland (along with nearby Camden) is a center for Maine's **windjammer cruises** (☏800-807-9463; www.sailmainecoast.com; ☉cruises late May–mid-Oct), which are multiday sailings on wind-powered schooners.

A map of Maine's coast, with all of its lighthouses,

DETOUR: PEMAQUID POINT

Start: just beyond 7 Bath

Maine's most famous lighthouse these days is the 1827 **Pemaquid Point Light**, which was featured on the special-edition Maine quarter. It's perched dramatically above rock-crashing surf in **Pemaquid Lighthouse Park** (☏207-677-2494; www.facebook.com/pemaquidlighthouse; 3115 Bristol Road, Pemaquid Point; adult/child $2/free; ☉sunrise-sunset). The keeper's house now serves as the **Fisherman's Museum** (admission incl with park entry; ☉10:30am-5pm May-Oct). Staffed by volunteers (so with occasionally irregular hours), it displays fishing paraphernalia and photos. From Damariscotta, between Wiscasset and Waldoboro, follow ME 130 south.

Classic Trip

WHY THIS IS A CLASSIC TRIP
CAROLYN BAIN, WRITER

There's undeniable buzz in joining the coast-cruising crowds at iconic lighthouses and lobster shacks, but it's fun to uncover lesser-known gems. On my final day in Maine I found myself back in Kittery, where my research had begun. The malls didn't hold my interest; a local suggested Chauncey Creek Lobster Pier. After a fine lobster roll and an eyeful of pretty scenery, I bid a fond farewell to Maine.

Top: Lobster roll
Left: Picnic tables by the water, Maine
Right: Portland Head Light, Cape Elizabeth

THOMAS NORTHCUT / GETTY IMAGES ©

spreads across the floor of the **Penobscot Bay Regional Chamber of Commerce** (📞207-596-0376; www.mainedreamvacation.com; 1 Park Dr; 🕐9am-5pm Jun-Oct, 9am-4pm Mon-Fri Nov-May) beside Rockland Harbor. Ask for the list that identifies the lighthouses on the map. The chamber of commerce shares a roof with the **Maine Lighthouse Museum** (📞207-594-3301; www.mainelighthouse museum.org; 1 Park Dr; adult/child $8/free; 🕐10am-5pm Mon-Fri, to 4pm Sat & Sun Jun-Oct, 10am-4pm Thu-Sat Nov-May; 🚹), which exhibits vintage Fresnel lenses, foghorns, marine instruments and ship models.

✗ 🛏 p277, p319

The Drive ❯❯ Follow Main St/US 1 north just over 1 mile from downtown to Waldo Ave. Turn right and drive half a mile. Turn right onto Samoset Rd, following it to a small parking lot.

- - - - - - - - - - - -

TRIP HIGHLIGHT

❾ Rockland Breakwater Lighthouse

Feeling adventurous? Tackle the rugged stone breakwater that stretches almost 1 mile into Rockland Harbor from Jameson Point at the harbor's northern shore. Made of granite blocks, this 'walkway' – which took 18 years to build – ends at the **Rockland Breakwater Lighthouse** (www.rocklandharborlights. org; Samoset Rd). Older kids should be fine; just

Classic Trip

watch for slippery rocks and ankle-twisting gaps between stones. Bring a sweater, and don't hike if a storm is on the horizon.

The Drive » US 1 hugs the coast as it swoops north past the artsy enclaves of Rockport, Camden and Belfast, curving east through Bucksport before landing in Ellsworth, about 60 miles from Rockland.

⑩ Ellsworth

Cooks and coffee-lovers, this stop's for you. In old-school Ellsworth, pull over for **Rooster Brother** (☎207-667-8675; www.roosterbrother.com; 29 Main St; ⊙ store 9:30am-5:30pm Mon-Sat, coffee from 7:30am), a kitchenware boutique that also sells amazing roasted coffee. Step downstairs from the retail store for a coffee sample – but be careful, you'll likely end up buying a full cup or a pound to go. Check out the excellent fresh cookies, especially the super-tasty ginger and molasses. Wine, chocolate, cheese and fresh bread are also for sale.

🍴 🛏 p277

The Drive » From Ellsworth, drive east on US 1. Consider taking ME 182, the most direct route north, but it's a more scenic option to follow US 1 south onto the Schoodic Peninsula. ME 182 hooks back onto US 1

at Cherryfield. From here, enter 'Down East' Maine, an unspoiled region dotted with traditional fishing villages. For a good meal and convenient lodging, stop in Machias (p277).

TRIP HIGHLIGHT

⑪ Lubec & Quoddy Head State Park

Lubec is a small fishing village that makes its living off transborder traffic with Canada and a bit of tourism. South of town, a walking trail winds along towering, jagged cliffs at the 541-acre **Quoddy Head State Park** (☎207-733-0911; www.maine.gov/quoddyhead; 973 S Lubec Rd, Lubec; adult/child $4/1), a moody place when the mist is thick and the foghorn blasts its lonely wail. The tides here are also dramatic, fluctuating 16ft in six hours. Look for whales migrating along the coast in summer. The park is also the site of the 1858 **West Quoddy Light**, which looks like a barber's pole.

The Drive » Return to US 1 north, passing Pembroke and Perry. About 3 miles north of Perry look for a pull-off on the left marking the 45th parallel, the halfway point between the North Pole and the equator. Continue 8.5 miles north.

⑫ Saint Croix Island International Historic Site

The site of one of the first European settlements in the New

World is visible from this **historic park** (www.nps.gov/sacr; 84 St Croix Dr, Calais; ⊙ dawn-dusk), 8 miles south of Calais. In 1604, a company of settlers sailed from France to establish a French claim in North America. They built a settlement on a small island in Passamaquoddy Bay, between Maine and New Brunswick, Canada. The settlers were ill-prepared for winter, and icy waters essentially trapped them on the island with limited food until spring. Many perished. The settlement was abandoned in 1605 and a new home was established in Port Royal, Nova Scotia. A short trail at the park winds past bronze statues and historic displays; a visitor center is staffed from mid-May to mid-October.

The Drive » Return to US 1 and drive 5 miles north to a rest area on your right. If you end up in Canada – or pass the local high school – you've gone too far.

⑬ Calais

Maine's northernmost lighthouse is **Whitlocks Mill Light** (www.stcroixhistorical.com; US 1), visible from a rest area 3.5 miles south of Calais. To spot the lighthouse, look for the sign, walk down to the fence and look north.

Eating & Sleeping

Cape Elizabeth ③

✕ Lobster Shack at Two Lights
Seafood $$

(☏207-799-1677; www.lobstershacktwolights.com; 225 Two Lights Rd; mains $5-25; ⏰11am-8pm Apr-Oct) Crack into a lobster dinner, lobster roll or chowder bowl at this well-loved Cape Elizabeth seafood shack, with killer views of the crashing Atlantic from both indoor and outdoor seating areas. It's about 7.5 miles south of downtown Portland.

Portland ④

🛏 Pomegranate Inn
B&B $$$

(☏207-772-1006; www.pomegranateinn.com; 49 Neal St; r $159-389; ❄🖥) Whimsy prevails at this eight-room inn, a historic home transformed into a showcase for antiques and contemporary art. Common spaces are a riot of colors and patterns; guest rooms come with hand-painted, oversized flower patterns and a wild mix of antique and contemporary furniture. Somehow everything fits together beautifully.

Freeport ⑥

✕ Harraseeket Lunch & Lobster Co
Seafood $$

(☏207-865-4888; www.harraseeketlunchand lobster.com; 36 Main St, South Freeport; mains $5-30; ⏰11am-7:45pm May, Jun, Sep & Oct, to 8:45pm Jul & Aug) Head down to the marina to feast on lobster at this iconic red-painted seafood shack. Come early to beat the crowds. Finish with a slice of blueberry pie. BYOB. Cash only.

🛏 Recompence Shore Campground
Campground $

(☏207-865-9307; www.freeportcamping.com; 134 Burnett Rd; campsites $28-52; ⏰May-Oct; 🖥) Adjacent to the Wolfe's Neck Woods State Park, this fabulous, family-oriented, 626-acre campground has waterfront and wooded sites spread over a working saltwater farm. The farm is part of a nonprofit organization dedicated to promoting sustainable agriculture and outdoor recreation; it's open for the public to check out the animals and walk the trails.

Rockland ⑧

✕ Primo
Italian $$$

(☏207-596-0770; www.primorestaurant.com; 2 Main St/ME 73; mains $32-45; ⏰dinner Wed-Sun mid-May–Oct) In a sprawling Victorian house a mile from downtown sits Primo, widely considered one of the best restaurants in Maine. Awarded chef Melissa Kelly has reached celebrity status for her creative ways with New England ingredients – think scallops atop local wild leek and fiddlehead ferns, or farm-raised chicken with ricotta *gnudi* (dumplings). The menu, truly a farm-to-table ode, changes daily.

🛏 Lindsey Hotel
Boutique Hotel $$

(☏207-596-7950; www.lindseyhotel.com; 5 Lindsey St; r $129-249; 🖥) There's a sophisticated seafaring theme at this newly revitalized, nine-room boutique hotel on a side street just steps from Main St. The building started as a sea captain's home but has had other incarnations; check out the 'snack vault' and the handsome oak-paneled breakfast room.

Ellsworth ⑩

✕ Helen's Restaurant
American $$

(☏207-255-8423; www.helensrestaurantmachias.com; 111 Main St/US 1, Machias; mains $8-30; ⏰6am-8pm Mon-Sat, 7am-2pm Sun) Helen's is the kind of friendly locals' joint where waitresses call you 'hon,' but their food makes your standard American diner fare look like mud in comparison. Fresh haddock is moist and flakey, salads are made with local goats cheese, the hot roast beef sandwich comes on homemade bread, and the blueberry pie is the envy of restaurants across the state.

🛏 Machias River Inn
Motel $$

(☏207-255-4861; www.machiasriverinn.com; 103 Main St/US 1, Machias; r $84-165; ❄🖥🖳) Next to Helen's Restaurant, this roadside lodge exceeds expectations with 39 clean, spacious rooms. Most have great views of the Machias River out back. Bikes are available for hire.

Classic Trip

Acadia National Park

26

For adventurers, Mt Desert Island is hard to beat. Mountain hiking. Coastal kayaking. Woodland biking. Bird-watching. When you're done exploring, unwind by stargazing on the beach.

TRIP HIGHLIGHTS

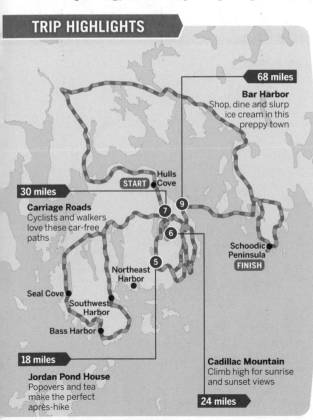

68 miles

Bar Harbor
Shop, dine and slurp ice cream in this preppy town

30 miles

Carriage Roads
Cyclists and walkers love these car-free paths

Hulls Cove
START

9

7

6

5

Schoodic Peninsula
FINISH

Northeast Harbor

Seal Cove

Southwest Harbor

Bass Harbor

18 miles

Jordan Pond House
Popovers and tea make the perfect après-hike

Cadillac Mountain
Climb high for sunrise and sunset views

24 miles

---

3 DAYS
112 MILES / 180KM

GREAT FOR...

BEST TIME TO GO
May through October for good weather and open facilities.

ESSENTIAL PHOTO
Capture that sea-and-sunrise panorama from atop Cadillac Mountain.

BEST FOR OUTDOORS
Hike a 'ladder trail' up a challenging cliff.

26 Acadia National Park

Drivers and hikers alike can thank John D Rockefeller Jr and other wealthy landowners for the aesthetically pleasing bridges, overlooks and stone steps that give Acadia National Park its artistic oomph. Rockefeller in particular, before donating the lands, worked diligently with architects and masons to ensure that the infrastructure – for both carriage roads and motor roads – complemented the surrounding landscape. Today, park explorers can put Rockefeller's planning to good use – tour the wonderful Park Loop Rd by car, but be sure to explore on foot and by bike wherever you can.

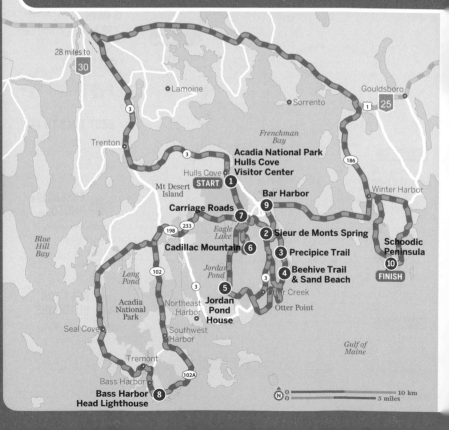

① Hulls Cove Visitor Center

Whoa, whoa, whoa. Before zooming into Bar Harbor on ME 3, stop at the **park visitor center** (☎207-288-3338; www.nps.gov/acad; ME 3; ⏱8:30am-4:30pm mid-Apr–Jun, Sep & Oct, 8am-6pm Jul & Aug) to get the lay of the land and pay the admission fee. Inside, head directly to the large diorama, which provides a helpful overview of Mt Desert Island (MDI). As you'll see, Acadia National Park shares the island with several nonpark communities, which are tucked here and there beside Acadia's borders.

From the visitor center, the best initiation to the park is to drive the 27-mile **Park Loop Road**, which links the park's highlights in the eastern section of MDI. It's one way (traveling clockwise) for most of its length.

LINK YOUR TRIP

25 | **Maritime Maine**
Enjoy Bass lighthouse? Hop on US 1 for more photogenic beacons.

30 | **Mainely Art**
Take US 1 south to Rockland for galleries, museums and local artists.

TOP TIP: PARK SHUTTLES

With millions of visitors coming to the park each summer, traffic and parking can be a hassle. On arrival, drive the Park Loop Rd straight through for the views and the driving experience. Then leave the driving to others by using the **Island Explorer** (www.exploreacadia.com; ⏱late Jun–Oct), free with park admission. Shuttles run along eight routes that connect visitors to trails, carriage roads, beaches, campgrounds and in-town destinations. They can even carry mountain bikes.

The Drive » From the visitor center, turn right onto the Park Loop Road, not ME 3 (which leads into Bar Harbor). Take in a nice view of Frenchman Bay on your left before passing the spur to ME 233. A short distance ahead, turn left to begin the one-way loop on Park Loop Rd.

② Sieur de Monts Spring

Nature-lovers and history buffs will enjoy a stop at the Sieur de Monts Spring area at the intersection of ME 3 and the Park Loop Rd. Here you'll find a nature center and the summer-only branch of the **Abbe Museum** (☎207-288-3519; www.abbemuseum.org; ME 3 & Park Loop Rd; adult/child $3/free; ⏱10am-5pm late May–mid-Oct), which sits in a lush, nature-like setting. Twelve of Acadia's biospheres are displayed in miniature at the **Wild Gardens of Acadia** (Park Loop Rd & ME 3), from bog to coniferous woods to meadow. Botany enthusiasts will appreciate the plant labels. There are also some amazing stone-step trails here, appearing out of the talus as if by magic.

The Drive » If you wish to avoid driving the full park loop, you can follow ME 3 from here into Bar Harbor. Push on for the full experience – you won't regret it.

③ Precipice Trail

What's the most exciting way to get a bird's-eye view of the park? By climbing up to where the birds are. Two 'ladder trails' cling to the sides of exposed cliffs on the northeastern section of Park Loop Rd, dubbed Ocean Drive. If you're fit and the season's right, tackle the first of the ladder trails, the steep, challenging 1.6-mile Precipice Trail, which climbs the east face of Champlain Mountain on iron rungs and ladders. (Note that the trail is typically closed late spring to mid-August because it's a nesting area for peregrine falcons. If it is closed, you might catch volunteers and staff monitoring the birds through scopes from the trailhead parking lot.) Skip the trail on rainy days.

The Drive › Continue south on Park Loop Rd. The Beehive Trail starts 100ft north of the Sand Beach parking area.

④ Beehive Trail & Sand Beach

Another good ladder trail is the Beehive Trail. The 0.8-mile climb includes ladders, rungs, narrow wooden bridges and scrambling – with steep drop-offs. As with the Precipice Trail, it's recommended that you descend via a nearby walking route, rather than climbing down.

Don't let the crowds keep you away from Sand Beach. It's home to one of the few sandy shorelines in the park, and it's a don't-miss spot. But you don't have to visit in the middle of the day to appreciate its charms. Beat the crowds early in the morning, or visit at night, especially for the **Stars over Sand Beach** program. During these free one-hour talks, lie on the beach, look up at the sky and listen to rangers share stories and science about the stars. Even if you miss the talk, the eastern coastline along

Ocean Dr is worth checking out at night, when you can watch the Milky Way slip right into the ocean.

The Drive › Swoop south past the crashing waves of Thunder Hole. If you want to exit the loop road, turn right onto Otter Cliff Rd, which hooks up to ME 3 north into Bar Harbor. Otherwise, pass Otter Point then follow the road inland past Wildwood Stables.

TRIP HIGHLIGHT

⑤ Jordan Pond House

Share hiking stories with other nature-lovers at the lodge-like **Jordan Pond House** (☏207-276-3316; www.acadiajordanpondhouse. com; Park Loop Rd; ☺11am-9pm mid-May–mid-Oct), where afternoon tea has been a tradition since the late 1800s. Steaming pots of Earl Grey come with hot popovers (hollow rolls made with egg batter) and strawberry jam. Eat on the broad lawn overlooking the lake. On clear days the glassy waters of 176-acre Jordan Pond reflect the image of Mt Penobscot like a mirror. Take the 3.2-mile nature trail around the pond after finishing your tea.

The Drive › Look up for the rock precariously perched atop South Bubble from the pull-off almost 2 miles north. Continue north to access Cadillac Mountain Rd.

TRIP HIGHLIGHT

⑥ Cadillac Mountain

Don't leave the park without driving – or hiking – to the 1530ft summit of Cadillac Mountain. For panoramic views of Frenchman Bay, walk the paved half-mile **Cadillac Mountain Summit loop**. The summit is a popular place in the early morning because it's long been touted as the first spot in the US to see the sunrise. The truth? It is, but only between October 7 and March 6. The crown is passed to northern coastal towns the rest of the year because of the tilt of the Earth. But, hey, the sunset is always a good bet.

The Drive › Drunk on the views, you can complete the loop road and exit the park, heading for your accommodations or next destination. But consider finding a parking lot and tackling walking trails, or heading to Bar Harbor to hire bikes.

TRIP HIGHLIGHT

⑦ Carriage Roads

John D Rockefeller Jr, a lover of old-fashioned horse carriages, gifted Acadia with some 45 miles of crisscrossing carriage roads. Made from crushed stone, the roads are free from cars and are popular with cyclists, hikers and equestrians. Several of them fan out from Jordan Pond House, but if the lot is too crowded, continue north to the parking area at **Eagle Lake** on US 233 to link to the carriage road network. If you're planning to explore

Acadia National Park Woodland trails

by bike, the Bicycle Express Shuttle runs to Eagle Lake from the Bar Harbor Village Green from late June through September. Pick up a Carriage Road User's Map at the visitor center.

The Drive » Still in the mood for cruising? Before you head for the bright lights of Bar Harbor, take a detour: drive ME 233 toward the western part of MDI, connecting to ME 198 west, then drop south on ME 102 toward Southwest Harbor. Pass Echo Lake Beach and Southwest Harbor, then bear left onto ME 102A for a dramatic rise up and back into the park near the seawall.

- - - - - - - - - - - - -

⑧ Bass Harbor Head Lighthouse

There is only one lighthouse on Mt Desert Island, and it sits in the somnolent village of Bass Harbor in the far southwest corner of the park. Built in 1858, the 36ft lighthouse still has a Fresnel lens from 1902. It's in a beautiful location that's a favorite of photographers. The lighthouse is a coast-guard residence, so you can't go inside, but you can take photos. You can also stroll to the coast

Classic Trip

on two easy trails near the property: the **Ship Harbor Trail**, a 1.2-mile loop, and the **Wonderland Trail**, a 1.4-mile round-trip. These trails are spectacular ways to get through the forest and to the coast, which looks different from the coast on Ocean Dr.

The Drive » For a lollipop loop, return on ME 102A to ME 102 through the village of Bass Harbor. Follow ME 102 then ME 233 all the way to Bar Harbor.

- - - - - - - - - - - - -

TRIP HIGHLIGHT

9 Bar Harbor

Tucked on the rugged coast in the shadows of Acadia's mountains, Bar Harbor is a busy gateway town with a J Crew joie de vivre. Restaurants, taverns and boutiques

are scattered along Main St, Mt Desert St and Cottage St. Shops sell everything from books to camping gear to handicrafts and art. For a fascinating collection of natural artifacts related to Maine's Native American heritage, visit the **Abbe Museum** (☏207-288-3519; www. abbemuseum.org; 26 Mount Desert St; adult/child $8/free; ◷10am-5pm May-Oct, shorter hours rest of year). The collection holds more than 50,000 objects, such as pottery, tools, combs and fishing instruments spanning the last 2000 years, including contemporary pieces. (There's a smaller summer-only branch in Sieur de Monts Spring.)

Done browsing? Spend the rest of the afternoon,

or early evening, exploring the area by water. Sign up in Bar Harbor for a half-day or sunset sea-kayaking trip. Both **National Park Sea Kayak Tours** (☏800-347-0940; www.acadiakayak.com; 39 Cottage St; 4hr tour $52; ◷late May–mid-Oct) and **Coastal Kayaking Tours** (☏20 7-288-9605; www.acadiafun. com; 48 Cottage St; 2½/4hr tours $39/49; ◷May-Oct) offer guided trips along the jagged coast.

✕ ⛺ p287

The Drive » There's another part of the park you haven't yet explored. To reach it involves a 44-mile drive (north on Rte 3 to US 1, following it about 17 miles to ME 186 south). ME 186 passes through Winter Harbor and then links to Schoodic Point Loop Rd. It's about an hour's drive one way. Alternatively, hop

WHY THIS IS A CLASSIC TRIP
CAROLYN BAIN, WRITER

New England's only national park turned 100 in 2016, and what a grand centenarian it is. The Park Loop Rd is a brilliant way to get oriented, but getting off the well-worn path brings rewards, too. I loved finding lobster shacks on the 'Quietside' and driving the 'other' loop road on the Schoodic Peninsula. And I gave silent thanks to those who generously gifted the park to the people.

Left: Bass Harbor Head Lighthouse
Right: Boardwalk around Jordan Pond

on a Downeast Windjammer ferry from the pier beside the Bar Harbor Inn.

- - - - - - - - - -

⑩ Schoodic Peninsula

The Schoodic Peninsula is the only section of Acadia National Park that's part of the mainland. It's also home to the Park Loop Rd, a rugged, woodsy drive with splendid views of Mt Desert Island and Cadillac Mountain. You're more likely to see a moose here than on MDI – what moose wants to cross a bridge?

Much of the drive is one way. There's an excellent new **campground** near the entrance, then a picnic area at **Frasier Point**. Further along the loop, turn right for a short ride to **Schoodic Point**, a 440ft-high promontory with ocean views.

The full loop from Winter Harbor is 11.5 miles and covers park, town and state roads. If you're planning to come by ferry, you could rent a bike beforehand at **Bar Harbor Bicycle Shop** (📞207-288-3886; www.barharborbike.com; 141 Cottage St; rental per day $25-50; ☺year-round) – the Park Loop Rd's smooth surface and easy hills make it ideal for cycling.

In July and August, the Island Explorer Schoodic shuttle bus runs from Winter Harbor to the peninsula ferry terminal and around the Park Loop Rd. It does not link to Bar Harbor.

ISLAND VISIT PLANNER

Acadia National Park

Orientation & Fees

Park admission is $25 per vehicle (including passengers), $20 per motorcycle and $12 for walk-ins and cyclists. Admission is valid for seven days.

Camping

There are two great rustic campgrounds on Mt Desert Island, with nearly 500 sites between them. Both are densely wooded and near the coast; reservations are essential (except in winter at Blackwoods). **Seawall** (📞877-444-6777; www.recreation.gov; 668 Seawall Rd, Southwest Harbor; campsites $22-30; ☺late May–Sep) is 4 miles south of Southwest Harbor on the 'Quietside' of Mt Desert Island, while **Blackwoods** (📞877-444-6777; www.recreation.gov; ME 3; campsites $30; ☺year-round) is closer to Bar Harbor (5 miles south, on ME 3).

Bar Harbor & Mt Desert Island

Before your trip, check lodging availability via the **Acadia Welcome Center** (📞800-345-4617, 207-288-5103; www.acadiainfo.com; 1201 Bar Harbor Rd/ME 3, Trenton; ☺9am-5pm Mon-Sat, 10am-4pm Sun late May–mid-Oct, 9am-5pm Mon-Fri mid-Apr–May & mid-Oct–Nov) website, run by the Bar Harbor Chamber of Commerce. Staff can mail you a copy of the visitor guide. Otherwise, stop by the welcome center itself for lodging brochures, maps and local information. It's located north of the bridge onto Mt Desert Island. There is a second **visitors center** (📞800-345-4617, 207-288-5103; www.barharborinfo.com; cnr Main & Cottage Sts; ☺8am-8pm mid-Jun–Sep, 9am-5pm Sep–mid-Jun) in Bar Harbor itself.

Eating & Sleeping

Bar Harbor ❾

✕ Mount Desert Island Ice Cream
Ice Cream **$**

(☎207-801-4006; www.mdiic.com; 325 Main St; ice cream $4-6; ☉mid-Apr–Oct, hours vary) A cult hit for innovative flavors such as stout beer with fudge, chocolate with wasabi, and blueberry-basil sorbet, this ice-cream counter is a post-dinner must. The small, original outlet is at 7 Firefly Lane, by the Village Green.

✕ Mache Bistro
French **$$**

(☎207-288-0447; www.machebistro.com; 321 Main St; mains $18-32; ☉from 5:30pm Tue-Sat May-Oct) A strong contender for Bar Harbor's best midrange restaurant, Mache serves contemporary, French-inflected fare in a stylishly renovated cottage. The changing menu highlights the local riches – think sustainably harvested scallops on fennel salad, rosemary-grilled quail, and wild blueberry trifle. Specialty cocktails add to the appeal. Reservations are suggested, but the bar is open to walk-ins.

✕ 2 Cats
Breakfast **$$**

(☎207-288-2808; 130 Cottage St; mains $7-20; ☉7am-1pm; ⚶) It's the most important meal of the day, so 2 Cats channels all its attention to breakfast. On weekends, crowds line up for banana-pecan pancakes, smoked-trout omelets, tofu scrambles and homemade muffins at this sunny, arty little cafe. Pick up a kitty-themed gift in the gift shop.

✕ Havana
Latin American **$$$**

(☎207-288-2822; www.havanamaine.com; 318 Main St; mains $25-37; ☉from 5pm May-Oct) First things first: order a rockin' Cuba libre or mojito. Once that's done, you can take your time with the menu and the epic global wine list. Havana puts a Latin spin on dishes that highlight local produce, and the kitchen output is accomplished. Signature dishes include crab cakes, paella and a deliciously light lobster *moqueca* (stew). Reservations recommended.

🛏 Acadia Inn
Hotel **$$**

(☎207-288-3500; www.acadiainn.com; 98 Eden St; r $89-209; ☉Apr–early Nov; ❄🛜♿) This traditional 95-room hotel with helpful staff sits beside a trail leading into the park. The good-sized rooms are smart and comfortable, there's a laundry and a heated pool, and the park shuttle stops here in summer. It's a good choice if you don't mind being out of the town center.

🛏 Moseley Cottage Inn & Town Motel
B&B, Motel **$$**

(☎207-288-5548; www.moseleycottage.net; 12 Atlantic Ave; B&B $175-295, motel $139-185; ❄🛜) This two-faced option is down a quiet street just steps from Main St, and covers its bases very well. There are nine large, charming, antique-filled B&B rooms in a traditional 1884 inn (options with fireplace and private porch), plus a small collection of cheaper motel-style units next door. All are of a consistently high standard.

🛏 Aysgarth Station Inn
B&B **$$**

(☎207-288-9655; www.aysgarth.com; 20 Roberts Ave; r $85-170; ❄🛜) On a quiet side street, this 1895 B&B has six cozy rooms with homey touches. Request the Tan Hill room, which is on the 3rd floor, for a view of Cadillac Mountain, or the Chatsworth room for its private deck.

🛏 Bass Cottage Inn
Inn **$$$**

(☎207-288-1234; www.basscottage.com; 14 The Field; r $220-400; ☉mid-May–Oct; ❄🛜) If most Bar Harbor B&Bs rate about a '5' in terms of stylishness, this Gilded Age mansion deserves an '11.' The 10 light-drenched guest rooms have an elegant summer-cottage chic, all crisp white linens and understated botanical prints. Tickle the ivories at the parlor's grand piano or read a novel beneath the Tiffany stained-glass ceiling of the wood-paneled sitting room.

Old Canada Road

27

The Kennebec River offers a stunning backdrop for photographers, a link to the past for history students, a white-water mecca for rafters and a source of inspiration for, well, everyone.

TRIP HIGHLIGHTS

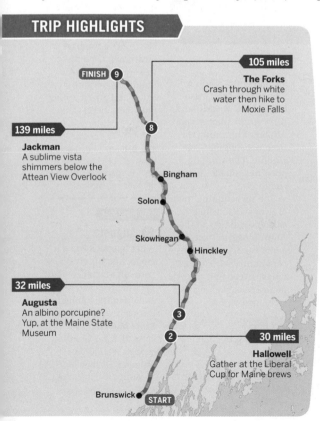

105 miles

The Forks
Crash through white water then hike to Moxie Falls

139 miles

Jackman
A sublime vista shimmers below the Attean View Overlook

32 miles

Augusta
An albino porcupine? Yup, at the Maine State Museum

30 miles

Hallowell
Gather at the Liberal Cup for Maine brews

FINISH 9

8

Bingham

Solon

Skowhegan

Hinckley

3

2

Brunswick

START

2 DAYS
139 MILES / 224KM

GREAT FOR...

BEST TIME TO GO
July to October for top rafting and hiking.

ESSENTIAL PHOTO
From the Attean View Overlook, take a sunset shot of Attean Lake and distant mountains.

 BEST FOR OUTDOORS

White-water rafting trips launch onto the Kennebec and Dead Rivers near The Forks.

27 Old Canada Road

The Old Canada Road is a 'hands-on' museum for history buffs. Stretching north from Hallowell to the Canadian border along US 201, it tracks the Kennebec River for most of the drive, passing farms, old ports, private timberlands and rafting companies – all of the industries that have sustained the region over the last few centuries. You're also following the trail of Benedict Arnold, who marched this way for George Washington during the Revolutionary War.

❶ Brunswick

What better place to start a road trip than a museum dedicated to an intrepid explorer? On the campus of Bowdoin College, the **Peary-MacMillan Arctic Museum** (☎207-725-3416; www.bowdoin.edu/arctic-museum; Hubbard Hall, 9500 College St, Bowdoin College campus; ⊙10am-5pm Tue-Sat, 2-5pm Sun) displays memorabilia from the expeditions of Robert Peary and Donald MacMillan, who were among the first explorers to reach the North Pole – or a spot pretty darn close to it. Exhibits include an oak-and-rawhide sledge used to carry the expedition to the pole and Peary's journal entry reading 'The pole at last!' Also notable are MacMillan's B&W Arctic photos and displays examining the Inuit people and Arctic wildlife. The stuffed polar bears look...not so cuddly.

The surrounding town of Brunswick, which sits on the banks of the Androscoggin River, is a handsome, well-kept community with a pretty village green and historic homes tucked along its tree-lined streets.

✗ ⊨ p295, p319

The Drive ❯❯ Follow US 201 north past meadows, fruit stands, old Chevy pickup trucks and Dunkin' Donuts (they're everywhere!) on this 30-mile stretch.

TRIP HIGHLIGHT

❷ Hallowell

Hallowell, a major river port for many years, thrived on the transportation of granite, ice and timber. There's a nice view of the town and the Kennebec River from the **Kennebec-Chaudière International Corridor Information Panel**, located at a small pull-off south of town and describing the 233-mile international heritage trail between Quebec City and coastal Maine. Hallowell dates from 1726, and it's a sociable place, dubbed 'the New Orleans of the North.' The compact downtown is home to numerous historic buildings, antique stores, cafes, and an easygoing pub, the Liberal Cup.

✗ ⊨ p295

The Drive ❯❯ From Hallowell, follow US 201 just 1.5 miles north to downtown Augusta and the State Capitol complex.

TRIP HIGHLIGHT

❸ Augusta

What happens when a moose and his rival lock horns in mortal combat? Their interlocked racks end up in the Cabinet of Curiosities at the **Maine State Museum** (☎207-287-2301; www.mainestatemuseum.org; 230 State St; adult/child $2/1; ⊙9am-5pm Tue-Fri, 10am-4pm Sat; [♿]) in Augusta, the state

capital. The museum, a four-story ode to all things Maine, is situated around a multistory mill that churns by waterpower. The newest permanent exhibit, At Home in Maine, looks at homes throughout the years; in the mod 1970s house you can watch a family filmstrip and dial a rotary phone. Groovy!

Across the parking lot, take a tour (guided or self-guided) of the **State House** (☎207-287-1692; http://legislature.maine.gov/lio; cnr State & Capitol Sts; ⊙8am-5pm Mon-Fri), built in 1832 and enlarged in 1901. It was designed by Boston architect Charles Bulfinch, the same architect behind the nation's Capitol building in Washington, DC.

The Drive » On the 19-mile drive to Winslow you'll cross the river and pass a barn or two, a taxidermy shop, pine trees, creeks and small churches.

LINK YOUR TRIP

28 **Great North Woods**
From Jackman, take ME 6 east to Rockwood to tour Maine's largest lake.

30 **Mainely Art**
Visit the Bowdoin College Museum of Art in Brunswick, then stroll through galleries along the coast.

④ Waterville & Winslow

The oldest blockhouse fortification in the US is located at the **Fort Halifax State Historic Site**, in a small park on the banks of the Kennebec River in Winslow. The log blockhouse is all that remains of a larger palisaded garrison built by British Americans in 1754, designed to guard against attacks by the French and their allied Native American tribes. In 1987 the blockhouse's logs came apart during a flood and floated downstream. They were recovered, and the fortification was rebuilt. It sits in pretty Fort Halifax Park on US 201, a mile south of the Winslow-Waterville Bridge (well hidden among gas stations).

✖ p295

The Drive >> Cross the Winslow-Waterville Bridge and continue on US 201 north through downtown Waterville. From here it's a 9-mile drive. Look out for logging trucks as the road approaches Hinckley.

⑤ LC Bates Museum

Any road-trip guidebook worth its stripes includes at least one eccentricity. This guide earns its stripes – and its spots and feathers – with the nicely nonconformist **LC Bates Museum** (🎵207-238-4250; www.gwh.org; US 201, Hinckley; adult/child $3/1; 🕙10am-4:30pm Wed-Sat, 1-4:30pm Sun Apr-Sep, shorter hours rest of year). Housed in a 1903 brick school building on the Good Will-Hinckley educational complex south of Hinckley, the museum embraces the concept of the 20th-century Cabinet of Curiosities with a huge assortment of natural, geologic and artistic artifacts. On the 1st floor, look for an amazing array of taxidermied birds. The basement holds stuffed mammals (including one of the last caribou shot in Maine), rocks, minerals and fossils. There are treasures here, and staff members are glad to point out the more interesting finds and answer questions. Nature trails meander through the forest out back.

The Drive >> The Kennebec stays in the picture on the 10-mile drive to Skowhegan, former home of Margaret

JOSEPH DEVENNEY / GETTY IMAGES ©

BENEDICT ARNOLD SLEPT HERE

About 12 miles north of Bingham, on the left side of the road, a small stone memorial marks the spot where Benedict Arnold and his soldiers left the Kennebec River in October 1775 during the Revolutionary War. Arnold, at the time still loyal to America, had been placed in command of 1100 men by George Washington. His mission? To follow the Kennebec and Dead Rivers north to defeat the British forces at Quebec. The soldiers used bateaux to travel up the Kennebec and encountered numerous difficulties along the way. Many men were lost through desertion and illness. A weakened force of about 500 reached Quebec, where they were ultimately defeated.

Moscow Driving past the Kennebec River

Chase Smith, the first woman elected to both the US House of Representatives and Senate.

- - - - - - - - - - -

⑥ Skowhegan

At Skowhegan's hard-to-resist **Gifford's Ice Cream Stand** (☎207-474-2257; www.giffordsicecream.com; 307 Madison Ave/US 201; cones from $3; ⊘mid-Mar–mid-Oct), every ice-cream flavor sounds delicious, from Maine Wild Blueberry to Caramel Caribou to Moose Tracks with peanut-butter cups and fudge. If you don't pull over for a scoop, you'll never hear the end of it from your kids or your

co-pilot. But don't worry, these creamy concoctions are delicious. Plus: if you need a real leg-stretch, there's a mini-golf course here too.

The Drive » From Skowhegan, drive 10 miles north to the junction of US 201 and ME 43, which marks the start of the Old Canada Road National Scenic Byway – a particularly lovely stretch of the longer Old Canada Road.

- - - - - - - - - - -

⑦ Robbins Hill Scenic Area

Take a picnic and your camera to the overlook at Robbins Hill near the start of the national by-

way. Look west for views of Saddleback Mountain, Mt Abraham and other mountains in Maine's Rangeley Lakes region. Signboards detail the history of the communities along the Old Canada Road, from the region's agricultural beginnings in the late 1700s to the effects of the railroad to the arrival of the timber industry.

The Drive » Pass white clapboard houses in Solon and another roadside pull-off, this one overlooking the Kennebec River. Here you'll find informational plaques about the railroad and the logging industries, including a picture of

293

NORTH WOODS RIVER-RAFTING TRIPS

Some of the best white water in America rushes through Maine's North Woods. From early May to mid-October, dozens of companies run organized rafting trips on the Kennebec, Dead and Penobscot Rivers. Bingham and The Forks serve as bases for rafting companies, and trips range in difficulty from Class II to Class V. For a one-day trip on the Kennebec, expect to pay between $69 and $129, with prices at their highest in July and August.

Recommended rafting companies, all with lodges for accommodation and meals, plus offering other outdoor activities (including river tubing, fishing, wildlife spotting and winter snowmobiling):

Crab Apple Whitewater (☎800-553-7238; www.crabapplewhitewater.com; Lake Moxie Rd, The Forks; rafting $70-120)

Northern Outdoors (☎800-765-7238; www.northernoutdoors.com; 1771 US 201, The Forks; rafting $69-129)

Three Rivers Whitewater (☎207-663-2104; www.threeriverswhitewater.com; 2265 US 201, The Forks; ⊘rafting $79-119)

---

the last American log drive here in 1976. Continue past anglers' cabins, rafting businesses and brewpubs.

TRIP HIGHLIGHT

❽ The Forks

After passing through Bingham and Moscow, US 201 follows a gorgeous stretch of river into The Forks. At this dot on the map, the Dead River joins the Kennebec River, setting the stage for excellent white-water rafting. At the junction of US 201 and Lake Moxie Rd, there's a small rest area with picnic tables, an information kiosk and a footbridge over the Kennebec River. From here, drive 2 miles east on Lake Moxie Rd to the trailhead for the easy

walk (0.6 miles one way) to the dramatic **Moxie Falls**. At 90ft, this is one of the highest waterfalls in the state.

✗ p295

The Drive » On this 20-mile push, you'll ascend Johnson Mountain before reaching the Lake Parlin overlook, where there are details about the American moose – which can reach speeds of 35mph.

TRIP HIGHLIGHT

❾ Jackman

Jackman knows how to throw out the welcome mat. Just south of town, the **Attean View Overlook** greets road-trippers with a dramatic view of Attean Lake and distant mountains – a landscape that sweeps into Canada.

The lake and overlook are named for Joseph Attean, a Penobscot Indian leader who guided Henry David Thoreau on trips through the Maine woods in 1853 and 1857. Attean died during a log drive on July 4, 1870. Legend says that his boots were hung from a pine knot near where his body was found, a tradition for river drivers killed while working the waterway. Today, Jackman is a good base for outdoor fun, including fishing, canoeing, hiking, biking, snowmobiling and cross-country skiing. Its ATV trails are considered some of the state's best.

🛏 p295

Eating & Sleeping

Brunswick ❶

✗ Tao Yuan   Asian $$

(📞207-725-9002; www.tao-yuan.me; 22
Pleasant St; dishes $7-18; ⏱5-9pm Tue-Sat,
4-8pm Sun) A young, lauded chef (a James
Beard 'Rising Star' nominee) is behind this high-
quality pan-Asian eatery, where accomplished
dishes dazzle palates with fresh flavor. Small
plates range from dumplings and pork buns to
fresh tangy salads (the Asian slaw is a treat).
Come hungry for the chef's tasting menu
(15 courses for $68, or $48 on Wednesday).
Reservations recommended.

⌂ Black Lantern   B&B $$

(📞207-725-4165; www.blacklanternbandb.com;
57 Elm St, Topsham; r $95-140; 🛜) Looking like
something from a postcard, this mid-19th-
century home houses three pretty, affordable
guest rooms, plus a lovely garden that stretches
down to the river's edge. It's in Topsham, just
a mile from downtown Brunswick, across the
Androscoggin River.

Hallowell ❷

✗ Slates Restaurant
& Bakery   Modern American $$

(📞207-622-4104; www.slatesrestaurant.
com; 165 Water St/US 1; lunch $6-20, dinner
mains $12-29; ⏱3:30-8pm Mon, 11am-8:30pm
Tue-Thu, 11am-9pm Fri & Sat, 10am-2pm Sun)
Inside this big yellow house on the main street,
the crowd-pleasing menu includes crabmeat
crepes, grilled pesto pizzas and beef tenderloin
au poivre. At lunchtime, chicken pie and crab
cakes are a hit. The bakery next door serves
breakfast goodies, breads, sandwiches and
coffee from 7am daily.

⌂ Maple Hill Farm B&B   B&B $$

(📞207-622-2708; www.maplebb.com; 11 Inn
Rd; r $105-219; ❄🛜) Hosted by former Maine
state senator Scott Cowger, this laid-back
B&B sits 3 miles west of Hallowell amid acres
of rolling hayfields and forests crisscrossed
by hiking trails. The eight rooms are bright
and comfortable, and much of their energy is
powered by solar panels and a wind turbine.

Waterville & Winslow ❹

✗ Big G's   American $

(📞207-873-7808; www.big-g-s-deli.com; 581
Benton Ave, Winslow; mains under $9; ⏱6am-
7pm) The sandwiches are *huge* and inexpensive
(trust us, you only need half a portion), making
Big G's a good stop for travelers on a budget.
Grab your sandwich to go and take it down to
the river for a picnic. Breakfast is available till
noon.

The Forks ❽

✗ Kennebec River
Pub & Brewery   Pub Food $$

(📞207-663-4466; www.northernoutdoors.com;
1771 US 201; dinner mains $10-30; ⏱7am-9pm
Jan–mid-Mar & May–mid-Oct, 4-9pm Nov)
After a day of rafting, enjoy a burger or steak
and a 'Let 'er Drift' summer ale. The brewpub
is inside the main lodge at the Northern
Outdoors Adventure Resort and serves up a
full day's worth of hearty eats to white-water
rafters (from May to mid-October), hunters (in
November, evenings only) and snowmobilers
(January to mid-March).

Jackman ❾

⌂ Bishops Country Inn Motel   Motel $

(📞207-668-3231; www.bishopsmotel.com;
461 Main St; d $79-105; ❄🛜) The plain but
spacious rooms here work well for gear-laden
adventurers and come with microwave,
refrigerator and flat-screen TV. Peak season
here is winter (January to March), when
snowmobilers hit town to revel in Jackman's
surrounding forest trails.

Great North Woods

28

Welcome to the highlands, a land of superlatives where you can hike Maine's highest mountain, canoe its largest lake and ogle the stomping grounds of America's spookiest author – if you dare.

TRIP HIGHLIGHTS

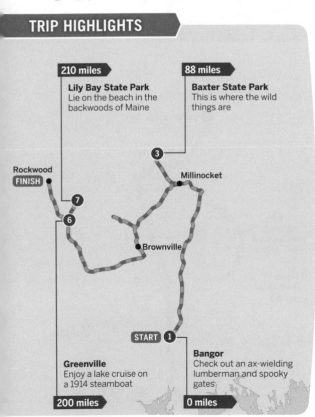

210 miles

Lily Bay State Park
Lie on the beach in the backwoods of Maine

88 miles

Baxter State Park
This is where the wild things are

Rockwood
FINISH

Millinocket

Brownville

START **1**

Bangor
Check out an ax-wielding lumberman and spooky gates

Greenville
Enjoy a lake cruise on a 1914 steamboat

200 miles

0 miles

3 DAYS
250 MILES / 402KM

GREAT FOR...

BEST TIME TO GO

July and August brings warm weather and no blackflies.

ESSENTIAL PHOTO

Capture Mt Katahdin rising behind Baxter State Park's southern entrance.

BEST FOR OUTDOORS

Hike through the vast virgin wilds of Baxter State Park.

28 Great North Woods

Texts. Tweets. Twenty-four hours of breaking news. If you need a respite from the modern world, grab your map – a paper one! – and drive directly to the Maine highlands, part of the sprawling North Woods. What will you find? Silence and solitude. Water and pines. The unfettered wildness of Baxter State Park. And access to 175,000 acres of private forest thrown open for public recreation.

TRIP HIGHLIGHT

❶ Bangor

Bangor is the last city on the map before the North Woods. So it seems appropriate that a towering **statue of Paul Bunyan** (Main St btwn Buck & Dutton Sts) stands near the center of downtown. The 31ft statue has watched over Bangor since the 1950s, but the ax-wielding lumberman isn't getting much love these days. His view of the Penobscot River is now blocked by a casino, and a new multi-

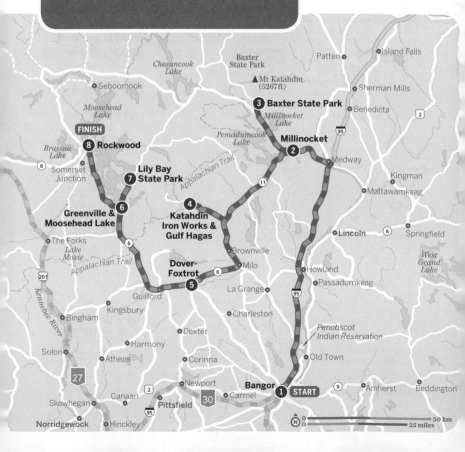

TOP TIP:
BAXTER STATE PARK PRACTICALITIES

» No pets are permitted inside the park boundaries.

» Bring insect repellent. Blackflies and no-see-ums bite in the spring and mosquitoes appear in June. Green deer flies and black moose flies can also bite in the middle of summer.

» Pack warm clothes, even in summer, as well as water, a flashlight and rain protection.

» There are no treated water sources inside the park, so bring your own or carry purifying tablets.

» Cell phones and iPads don't work in the park. Handheld GPS devices work with reasonable accuracy, but always hike with a map and compass. Vehicle GPS units can be less reliable. Use written directions after Millinocket Lake, near the south entrance. (See www.baxterstateparkauthority.com/maps/directions.htm.)

purpose arena has risen behind him.

But Paul's not the only star in town. Stephen King, the mega-selling author of horror novels such as *Carrie* and *The Shining,* resides in an appropriately Gothic red Victorian **house** (West Broadway), off Hammond St. You can't go inside, but you can snap a photo of his splendidly creepy wrought-iron front fence that's adorned with spiderwebs and bats. The house is in a residential neighborhood, so please keep your shrieking to a minimum.

 p303, p319

The Drive » The 60-mile drive on I-95 north to exit 244 for Millinocket isn't that interesting. But it's efficient, and the rest of the drive will blow this ho-hum stretch from your memory. From exit 244, drive northwest on ME 11/157.

- - - - - - - - - - - - -

2 Millinocket

Baxter State Park is far, far off the beaten path, and many of its rules and policies differ from those at other Maine state parks – so do a bit of planning before driving out here. The town of Millinocket, with its motels, inns and eateries, works well as a base camp. Eighteen miles from the park, it's also the closest town to the southern entrance. For park information and a copy of *Windnotes,* the helpful park visitor guide, stop by the **Baxter State Park Authority Headquarters** (☎207-723-5140; www.baxterstatepark authority.com; 64 Balsam Dr/ ME 157; ☺8am-4pm daily mid-May–mid-Oct, Mon-Fri mid-Oct–mid-May); **it's just beside the McDonald's.**

 p303

The Drive » The drive from Millinocket to Baxter State Park takes in bogs, birches and pine trees and then some very narrow roads. Gape at Katahdin from the 'Keep Maine Beautiful' sign, then continue to Togue Pond Gate.

LINK
YOUR
TRIP

 27 Old Canada Road

Head west to US 201 from Rockwood for rafting and riverside history.

 30 Mainely Art

In Bangor, kickstart a loop of Maine's finest art and culture with a visit to the University of Maine Museum of Art.

TRIP HIGHLIGHT

❸ Baxter State Park

In the 1930s, Governor Percival Baxter began buying land for **Baxter State Park** (☎207-723-5140; www.baxterstatepark authority.com; per car per day $14, Maine residents free), using his own money. By the time of his death in 1969, he had given, in trust, more than 200,000 acres to the park as a gift to the people of Maine. **Mt Katahdin** is the park's crowning glory. At 5267ft it is Maine's tallest mountain and the northern endpoint of the 2190-mile Appalachian Trail.

Baxter also left an endowment fund for the support and maintenance of the park. His greatest desire was for the land to remain wild and to serve as a 'sanctuary for beast and birds.' To ensure that his vision is followed, the park is kept in a primitive state and there is very little infrastructure inside its boundaries. And what a difference that makes. Baxter is Maine at its most primeval: the wind whips around dozens of peaks, black bears root through the underbrush, and hikers go for miles without seeing another soul.

🛏 p303

The Drive » From Millinocket, follow ME 11 south for about 25 miles. Turn right onto Katahdin Iron Works Rd, and drive 6.3 miles on a dirt road. If you get to Brownsville Junction on ME 11, you missed Katahdin Iron Works Rd.

❹ Katahdin Iron Works & Gulf Hagas

A reminder of a time when blast furnaces and charcoal kilns smelted iron all day, the **ironworks** (www.maine.gov/katahdinironworks; ☀9am-sunset) was built in 1843. Eventually the costs of operating in such isolation made the facility unable to compete with

---

BAXTER STATE PARK

Admission

In order to protect the park from overuse, day-use is limited by the capacity of trailhead parking lots. Parking lots for the most popular Katahdin-access trailheads fill very early (by 6:30am) on sunny summer weekends.

Parking space at the most popular day-use parking lots is reservable ($5) under the park's Day Use Parking Reservation (DUPR) system – see the website www.baxterstateparkauthority.com. Reservations can be made up to two weeks before your visit.

Baxter's two main gates are **Togue Pond Gate** in the south, and **Matagamon Gate** in the north. Both are generally open 6am to 10pm from mid-May to mid-October.

Togue Pond is 18 miles from Millinocket; there's a visitor center (offering canoe rental) just south of the gate. The less-popular access point at Matagamon is 26 miles from the town of Patten.

There is a $14 admission fee per vehicle per day (free for Maine residents).

Hiking

Read the park's website thoroughly. To hike, you need a car-parking reservation. A few spots may be available on a first-come, first-served basis, but don't count on that on a summer weekend. Make a DUPR online.

For an easy day in the southern part of the park, try the mile-long walk to Katahdin Stream falls or the pleasant 2-mile nature path around Daicey Pond. See the park's website for maps and details about hiking Mt Katahdin.

Bangor Paul Bunyan statue, by artist J. Norman Martin

foundries in Pennsylvania and other states, and it closed in 1890.

From here, Katahdin Iron Works Rd leads another 6.5 miles to the trailhead for **Gulf Hagas** (☏207-435-6213; www.northmainewoods.org; access from Katahdin Iron Works Rd; day-use adult/child $12/free; ⏰6am-9pm May–early Oct), dubbed the Grand Canyon of Maine. The gorge features a stunning 500ft drop studded with waterfalls over the course of its 3 miles. Carved over five million years by water eroding the slate bedrock, the gulf is a national natural landmark and is surrounded by some of Maine's oldest white pines. An 8-mile rim-trail hiking loop is remote and challenging, so come very prepared.

Gulf Hagas is within the KI-Jo Mary Multiple-Use Forest, which is owned and managed by private timber interests but allows public use. Pay the entrance fee at the checkpoint across from Katahdin Iron Works. Visit the North Maine Woods website for maps as well as details about access and trails at Gulf Hagas.

The Drive >> From Brownville, south of Brownsville Junction, continue south on ME 11. Take ME 6 west to Dover-Foxcroft.

---

❺ Dover-Foxcroft

It's a bit of a haul between the ironworks and Greenville. This route swings below the private logging roads of the North Woods. Take a break for **Butterfield's Ice Cream** (www.butterfields icecream.com; 946 W Main St; cones from $3; ⊙11:30am-8pm Mon-Sat, noon-8pm Sun mid-Apr–Sep, to 9pm daily Jun–Aug) in Dover-Foxcroft. Walk up to the window, choose your scoop, grab a seat and enjoy your licks beside the smiling cow.

The Drive >> Follow ME 6 west through Guilford and Abbot Village. North of Monson, look for a pull-off on your right beside the Appalachian Trail. From this trailhead it's 112 miles north to Katahdin. This trailhead marks the southern start of a very remote section of the trail. The pull-off is about 11 miles south of Greenville.

TRIP HIGHLIGHT

❻ Greenville & Moosehead Lake

Silver-blue and dotted with islands, Moosehead Lake sprawls over 120 sq miles of North Woods wilderness. Named, some say, after its shape from the air, it's one of the state's most glorious places. Greenville is the region's main settlement.

Owned and maintained by the Moosehead Marine Museum, the steamboat **SS Katahdin** (☎207-695-2716; www.katahdincruises.com; Lily Bay Rd, Greenville; 3hr cruise adult/child $35/5; ⊙mid-Jun–mid-Oct) was built in 1914. It still makes the rounds on Moosehead Lake from Greenville's center, just like it did in Greenville's heyday. The lake's colorful history is preserved in the **Moosehead Marine Museum** (www.katahdin cruises.com/museum; 12 Lily Bay Rd; entry by donation; ⊙10am-4pm Tue-Sat, noon-4pm Sun & Mon mid-Jun–mid-Oct), next to the dock. For moose-spotting safaris, white-water rafting, ATV tours, guided fishing trips and canoe adventures, stop by **Northwoods Outfitters** (☎20 7-695-3288; www.maine outfitter.com; 5 Lily Bay Rd; ⊙8am-7pm) in the center of town. It also rents and sells outdoor gear.

The **Moosehead Lake Region Chamber of Commerce** (☎207-695-2702; www.mooseheadlake.org; 480 Moosehead Lake Rd/ME 15; ⊙9am-5pm) runs a useful visitor center south of downtown.

✗ �🛏 p303

The Drive >> Tantalizing glimpses of Moosehead Lake peek through the trees on the 8-mile drive from Greenville on Lily Bay Rd, culminating in grand views from Blair Hill

---

TRIP HIGHLIGHT

❼ Lily Bay State Park

To camp on the shores of Moosehead Lake, pitch your tent at one of the 90 campsites at this lovely, 925-acre **park** (☎207-695-2700; www.maine.gov/lilybay; 13 Myrle's Way, Greenville; adult/child $6/1). Relax on the sandy beach, bird-watch and stroll the 2-mile shoreline trail.

The Drive >> Return to Greenville, then drive 20 miles north on ME 6, passing the Lavigne Memorial Bridge and marker, memorializing a local son who died in WWII.

---

❽ Rockwood

The distinctive **Mt Kineo** is a 1769ft rhyolite mountain rising from the bottom of Moosehead Lake. For a good silhouette of its steep, towering face, which juts more than 700ft above the lake, pull over in the village of Rockwood north of Greenville. From Rockwood, return to Greenville or continue 26 miles through the woods on a lovely ribbon of road with lake views to US 201 near Jackman.

Eating & Sleeping

Bangor ❶

✘ Fiddlehead — Modern American $$

(📞207-942-3336; www.thefiddleheadrestaurant.
com; 84 Hammond St; mains $17-35; ⏱4-9pm
Tue-Fri, 5-10pm Sat, 5-9pm Sun) **The young chef
at this downtown place has been earning raves
(and a packed dining room) for her international
spin on local, seasonal ingredients. Think
okonomiyaki (Japanese pancake) with Maine
shrimp, seared halibut with *char siu* pork, and
rose-petal crème brûlée. Exposed brick walls,
cool cocktails, and a bar crowded with hipsters
make this a definite hot spot.**

Millinocket ❷

✘ River Drivers Restaurant & Pub — Pub Food $$

(📞207-723-8475; www.neoc.com/riverdrivers;
30 Twin Pines Rd, Millinocket Lake; mains lunch
$8-14, dinner $18-29; ⏱lunch & dinner Jan, Feb
& Jun-Aug, shorter hours rest of year) **At this
relaxed, family-friendly restaurant at NEOC Twin
Pines Camp, enjoy sandwiches, seafood, steak
and pasta with a great view of Mt Katahdin.
It's open year-round, but it's worth checking
opening hours online (or on the restaurant's
Facebook page) in advance. It's signed off the
road to Baxter State Park.**

🛏 NEOC Twin Pines Camp — Cabin $$

(📞800-634-7238, 207-723-5438; www.neoc.
com; 30 Twin Pines Rd, Millinocket Lake; 4-person
cabin $245-529; 🛜🐾) **En route to Baxter State
Park, the New England Outdoor Center offers
a delectable slice of rural Maine, with creature
comforts in abundance in a glorious lakeside
setting. Spread over the property are 22 comfy
cabins and stylish lodges with all mod cons
(including full kitchen); some can sleep up to
14. Prices vary with type of accommodation and
number of guests.**

Baxter State Park ❸

🛏 Baxter State Park Campgrounds — Campground $

(📞207-723-5140; www.baxterstateparkauthority.
com; tent sites $30, dm $11, cabins $55-130)
**The park has 11 campgrounds, a handful of
bunkhouses and basic cabins sleeping up to six,
and numerous backcountry sites, including some
sites with lean-tos and bunkhouses. Reserve your
spot well in advance.**

Greenville & Moosehead Lake ❻

✘ Auntie M's — American $

(📞207-695-2238; 13 Lily Pond Rd, Greenville;
mains under $10; ⏱5am-3pm) **Eat breakfast all
day at this cozy eatery near the center of town.
Burgers, wraps and Mexican pizza are served
at lunch. It also sells bag lunches ($6.50) with a
sandwich and snacks, perfect for those heading
out into the woods. Cash only.**

🛏 Moose Mountain Inn — Motel $

(📞207-695-3321; www.moosemountaininn.
com; 314 Rockwood Rd/ME 15, Greenville; r
$60-120; ❄🛜☕🐾) **Owned by Northwoods
Outfitters, this no-frills two-story motel offers
15 simple rooms with refrigerators, microwaves
and flat-screen TVs. It's north of Greenville, en
route to Rockwood.**

🛏 Blair Hill Inn — B&B $$$

(📞207-695-0224; www.blairhill.com; 351 Lily Bay
Rd, Greenville; r $299-499; ⏱late May–mid-Oct;
🛜) **The Chicago socialite who commissioned
this dreamy hilltop cottage in the late 1800s
had it cleverly built atop a 20ft-high stone
foundation, thus providing views of the lake
from almost every window. Today it's a 10-room
B&B, whose smallest detail whispers good taste:
plush, white down comforters, fluffy robes, in-
room fireplaces and a sleek wooden bar.**

Lakes Tour

29

Bright blue lakes dapple the landscape like drops from Mother Nature's paintbrush, luring travelers with sandy beaches, excellent kayaking, small-town strolling and New England's favorite state fair.

TRIP HIGHLIGHTS

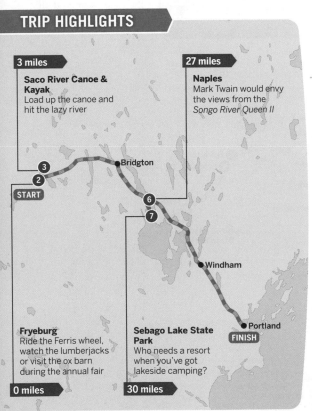

3 miles

Saco River Canoe & Kayak
Load up the canoe and hit the lazy river

27 miles

Naples
Mark Twain would envy the views from the *Songo River Queen II*

Bridgton

3
2
START

6
7

Windham

Portland
FINISH

Fryeburg
Ride the Ferris wheel, watch the lumberjacks or visit the ox barn during the annual fair

0 miles

Sebago Lake State Park
Who needs a resort when you've got lakeside camping?

30 miles

**2 DAYS
60 MILES / 97KM**

GREAT FOR...

BEST TIME TO GO
To enjoy swimming and boating, visit from May to October.

ESSENTIAL PHOTO
Stake your position on the Naples causeway for sweet pics of Long Lake.

BEST FOR FAMILIES
Spend a lazy afternoon canoeing the Saco River near Fryeburg.

29 Lakes Tour

US 302 in southeast Maine is the quickest link between North Conway's outlet stores and the LL Bean store just north of Portland, but the road is also the lifeline for the stunning Lakes Region. Filled with glacier-made lakes and ponds, this summer hot spot is home to the state's most popular campground as well as a beloved paddle wheeler and the family-friendly Saco River. Lovely B&Bs encourage lingering with water views and scrumptious breakfasts.

❶ Fryeburg Visitor Information Center

Just east of the Maine state line, this state-run **visitor center** (📞207-935-3639; www.mainetourism.com; 97 Main St/US 302, Fryeburg; ⊙9am-5:30pm Nov-Apr, 8am-6pm May-Oct) can prepare you for an adventure anywhere in the Pine Tree State. It's well stocked with brochures, and the staff is very helpful. Want to stretch your legs? A 4.2-mile section of the new **Mountain Division Trail** begins just behind the visitor center. If all

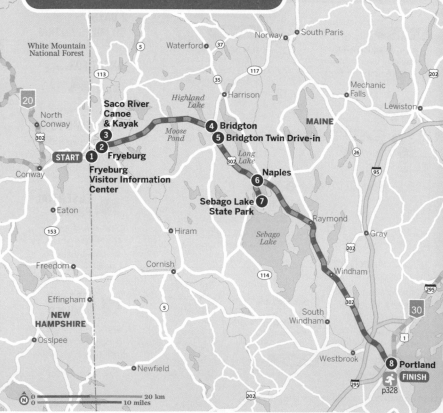

goes to plan, the hiking and biking trail will eventually extend 52 miles from Fryeburg to Portland.

The Drive ›❯ From the visitor center, follow US 302 east into downtown.

- - - - - - - - - - - -

TRIP HIGHLIGHT

❷ Fryeburg

Sitting prettily on the banks of the Saco River, Fryeburg is best known for hosting the annual **Fryeburg Fair** (☑207-935-3268; www.fryeburgfair.com; 1154 Main St, Fryeburg; adult/child $10/free, parking $5; ⊙early Oct), an eight-day state agricultural fair that started in 1851. Today it attracts more than 300,000 people. Events and attractions include everything from livestock and flower

LINK YOUR TRIP

20 **White Mountains Loop**

Take US 302 west to North Conway, NH, to hop a train ride to the Presidential Range.

30 **Mainely Art**

For cultural inspiration, join this gallery-filled route, starting with the American landscapes at the Portland Museum of Art.

shows to a whoopee pie contest, a pig scramble (local pigs only, please), a horse-pulling contest and Woodsmen's Day, when male and female lumberjacks chisel poles of timber with their chainsaws and hurl their mighty axes.

The rest of the year, the big draw is the Saco River. If you want to feel the sand under your feet after hiking through the White Mountains in next-door New Hampshire, relax on **Weston's Beach**. To get there, take a left onto ME 113/River Rd just before entering Fryeburg from the visitor center. Parking is ahead on the right after crossing the river.

🛏 p311

The Drive ›❯ Follow ME 5 north for half a mile from the junction of US 302 and ME 5, where signs advertising chowder suppers and community dinners tempt weary travelers.

- - - - - - - - - - - -

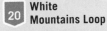

TRIP HIGHLIGHT

❸ Saco River Canoe & Kayak

Ready to get out on the water? The friendly folks at **Saco River Canoe & Kayak** (☑207-935-2369; www.sacorivercanoe.com; 1009 Main St, Fryeburg), who've run self-guided trips for more than 40 years, will set you up on the family-friendly Saco River. The river flows about 120 miles

from Saco Lake in New Hampshire's upper White Mountains through Crawford Notch and into Maine. In Maine, the Saco runs parallel to US 302 as it makes its way to the Gulf of Maine southwest of Portland. The river is particularly pleasant around Fryeburg, with leafy banks and sandy shores, mountain views and gentle conditions. Trips can range from one hour to several days. Canoe and kayak rentals run from $30 to $45 per day, depending on watercraft and season. Delivery and pick-up services are charged separately, and cost $6 to $16 per trip (minimum charge from $10). Service to the nearby Swans Fall access point is free.

The Drive ›❯ US 302 passes Christmas-tree farms and diamond-blue lakes on its 15-mile run east to Bridgton.

- - - - - - - - - - - -

❹ Bridgton

Bridgton is prime digs for a weekend getaway. Main St runs for 1.5 miles past a museum, a movie house, an inviting park and an eclectic array of indie shops. The well-regarded **Rufus Porter Museum** (☑207-647-2828; www.rufusportermuseum.org; 121 Main St; suggested donation $10; ⊙noon-4pm Jun–early Sep), in new main-street digs, looks at the work of

SHOPS OF BRIDGTON

Welcoming proprietors and an eclectic mix of shops in close proximity make downtown Bridgton a great spot for an hour or two of shopping. A few stores are included below; check websites for hours not listed, which vary seasonally.

Bridgton Books (📱207-647-2122; 140 Main St; 🕑9:30am-5:30pm Mon-Sat, 11am-4:30pm Sun) A large inventory of new and used books in this independent bookstore, and helpful staff.

Gallery 302 (📱207-647-2787; www.gallery302.com; 112 Main St; 🕑seasonal hours) Sixty-member artists co-op displays and sells art in all its forms.

Harry Barker's Emporium (📱207-647-4500; www.harvesthills.org; 142 Main St; 🕑10am-5pm) In partnership with Harvest Hills Animal Shelter, Harry Barker (get it?) sells an eclectic mix of antiques and vintage items from over 20 vendors. Inventory changes daily.

Renys (📱207-647-3711; www.renys.com; 151 Main St; 🕑8am-8pm Mon-Sat, 9am-5pm Sun) A discount mini department store in Maine with 14 locations. Look for clothing, housewares and a bit of this and that.

19th-century Renaissance man Rufus Porter. Porter is recognized throughout New England for the landscape murals he painted in hundreds of houses in the region between 1825 and 1845. Also an inventor, he sold the concept of the revolving rifle to Samuel Colt in 1844, and created *Scientific American* magazine.

Take a moment to walk through the photogenic Bob Dunning Memorial Bridge – built by district craftsmen in 2007 to honor a local conservationist. It marks the northern entrance to **Pondicherry Park** (access from Depot St), a 66-acre woodland park filled with trails and wildlife. The park sits behind the **Magic Lantern** (📱207-647-5065; www.magiclanternmovies.

com; 9 Depot St; adult/child $7.50/6; 🕑Tue-Sun), a beloved community movie house – and the site of a tannery in the 1800s – that anchors downtown. Congenial staff, a pub with a 23ft screen and three new, themed theaters make this a pleasant spot to catch a blockbuster, an indie flick or the big game.

 p311

The Drive » From downtown Bridgton drive 1 mile east on US 302.

- - - - - - - - - - - -

⑤ Bridgton Twin Drive-In

One of just six drive-ins remaining in the state, **Bridgton Twin Drive-in** (📱207-647-8666; 383 Portland Rd/US 302; adult/child $7.50/5; 🕑mid-Apr–Sep; 👪) has been going strong

for 60 years. It shows movies on two screens, and is a popular choice with families. Visit its Facebook page to see what's playing.

The Drive » US 302 rolls east out of Bridgton, turning in a more southerly direction as it approaches Naples, 8 miles to the south.

- - - - - - - - - - - -

TRIP HIGHLIGHT

⑥ Naples

Restaurants and shops cluster around the Causeway in downtown Naples, which sits on a spit of land between Long Lake and Brandy Pond. A walk along the Causeway affords grand views of bright blue Long Lake. The big draw here, beyond the eateries and bars with lake views, is the red-and-white **Songo River Queen II**

Maine Saco River

(☎207-693-6861; www.
songoriverqueen.net; US 302;
tours adult/child 1hr $15/8,
2hr $25/13; ⊙ noon, 2:30pm,
4pm late Jun–early Sep, Sat &
Sun only late May–late Jun &
Sep–mid-Oct), a 93ft paddle
wheeler with a covered
upper deck. The boat
churns up the east coast
of the lake, then comes
back down the west side
(or vice versa). You'll get
a look at Mt Washington
and the Presidential
Range during the cruise.
The *Songo* holds 350
people, so reservations
are not typically needed.

If a cruise feels too
placid, there are other
options to get out on the
lake. **Captain Dingley's**
(☎207-693-5253; www.captain
dingleys.com; 845 Roosevelt
Trail; ⊙ late May–early Sep)
has lots of water toys for
rent – stand-up paddle-
boards ($50 per day), and
skis and tubes for use
with your own boat. With-
out a boat? Don't worry –
book the Captain's for les-
sons in waterskiing and
wakeboarding.

✕ p311

The Drive » From the
Causeway, turn left onto ME 114
and drive 2 miles south. Turn
left onto State Park Dr and take
a woodsy cruise to the park
entrance.

TRIP HIGHLIGHT

❼ Sebago Lake State Park

With 250 campsites
scattered throughout the
woods beside the sandy
shores of Sebago Lake, this
1500-acre **state park** (☎20
7-693-6231; www.maine.gov/
sebagolake; 11 Park Access Rd,
Casco; adult/child $8/1; ⊙ year-
round, camping late May–early
Sep; ♿) is a popular and
scenic place to swim, picnic and camp on the way
to Portland. Sebago Lake
is Maine's second-largest
lake at 45 sq miles. Visitors can enjoy the beaches
(Songo Beach is a pearl),
grills and picnic tables,
and if the beach gets too
crowded, just step into
the woods, where you can
wander several miles of
easy to moderate trails or
bike the roadways. There's
also a nature center. In
summer, rangers lead
talks, hikes and canoe
trips; look for details on
the bulletin board at the
park entrance. Pets are not
allowed on the beaches
or in the campground.

🛏 p311

The Drive » Continue
southeast on US 302, passing
through Windham. Suburbia
and development creep in as
Portland approaches.

❽ Portland

Well, hello there. Is that
a brew house at the east-
ern end of US 302, on
the fringes of downtown
Portland? Yes? Cheers,
we say! And welcome
to the **Great Lost Bear**
(☎207-772-0300; www.
greatlostbear.com; 540 Forest
Ave; ⊙11:30am-11:30pm
Mon-Sat, noon-11pm Sun; 🛜),
a fun and quirky place
in a fun and quirky city.
Decked out in Christmas
lights and flea-market
kitsch, this rambling
bar and restaurant is
a Portland institution.
Seventy-eight taps serve
primarily Northeastern
brews, including 40
from Maine, making the
GLB one of America's
best regional beer bars.
Atmosphere is family-
friendly (at least early
in the evening), with a
massive menu of burg-
ers, quesadillas and
other bar nibbles. The
perfect fuel stop before
further explorations of
Portland's museums,
mansions and working
wharves (p328).

✕ 🛏 p277, p311, p319

Eating & Sleeping

Fryeburg ❶

🛏 Oxford House Inn   B&B $$

(📞207-935-3442; www.oxfordhouseinn.com; 548 Main St; r $119-185; 🕑year-round) Enjoy Saco River views from this century-old house with four stylish rooms. The owners are chefs and the highly regarded on-site restaurant serves contemporary American dishes (dinner mains $26 to $34) from a seasonal menu; much of the produce is sourced from Weston Farms, behind the property. A cozy, inviting pub, Jonathan's, is on the lower level.

Bridgton ❹

✗ Campfire Grille   American $$

(📞207-803-2255; www.thecampfiregrille.com; 646 N High St/US 302; mains $10-23; 🕑 noon-9pm Mon-Wed, to 10pm Thu, to 11pm Fri, 11am-11pm Sat, 11am-9pm Sun) Tucked between US 302 and Beaver Pond – with views of the latter – this easygoing eatery serves pub-grub dishes with gourmet flair: burgers, steaks, flatbread pizzas etc. The $7 weekday lunch special is great value.

🛏 Noble House Inn   B&B $$

(📞207-647-3733; www.noblehousebb.com; 81 Highland Rd; r $145-275; ❄🛜) Did you say bottomless cookie jar? Yup, and that's just one of the details that make the nine-room Noble House Inn so inviting. Breakfasts are baked from scratch and typically sourced from locally grown, organic ingredients. Wildlife carouses on the lawn or in the adjacent pine grove, while Highland Lake beckons across the street.

🛏 Bear Mountain Inn   B&B $$

(📞207-583-4404; www.bearmtninn.com; 364 Waterford Rd, Waterford; r $100-325; ❄🛜🐾) Eight miles north of Bridgton (take ME 37), this charming inn sits on a 25-acre site on a hill overlooking Bear Pond (kayaks and canoes are available for guest use). The deck, with lake view and BBQ grill, is a guest favorite. The 11 rooms have rustic-chic flair; there's a separate lakefront home that sleeps eight, and a sweet, pet-friendly cottage.

Naples ❻

✗ Rick's Cafe   American $$

(📞207-693-3759; www.rickscafenaples.com; US 302; mains $10-24; 🕑11:30am-9pm late May–early Sep) In the thick of the Causeway action, Rick's is good for camaraderie, drinks and lake views (with a side order of live music Thursday to Saturday night).

Sebago Lake State Park ❼

🛏 Sebago Lake State Park Campground   Campground $

(📞park 207-693-6231, reservations 207-624-9950; www.campwithme.com; 11 Park Access Rd, Casco; sites $35, with hookup $45) Campsites are in hot demand due to their proximity to the swimmable lakes, picnic grounds and trails of the state park. The 250-site campground starts accepting reservations on February 1 at 9am. All sites become first-come, first-served after mid-September. Prices do not include the reservation fee ($5 per site per night) or the 9% state lodging tax. Maine residents get a $10-per-site discount.

Portland ❽

✗ Susan's Fish & Chips   Seafood $

(📞207-878-3240; www.susansfishnchips. com; 1135 Forest Ave/US 302; mains $10-20; 🕑11am-8pm; 🚻) Pop in for fish and chips and plenty of deep-fried seafood at this no-fuss, family-friendly eatery on US 302. It's low on pretensions, high on good cheer, and set up in a former garage with under-the-sea decor.

✗ Green Elephant   Vegetarian, Asian $$

(📞207-347-3111; www.greenelephantmaine. com; 608 Congress St; mains $12-17; 🕑11:30am-2:30pm & 5-9:30pm Mon-Sat, 5-9pm Sun; 🌱) Even carnivores shouldn't miss the vegetarian fare at this Zen-chic, Thai-inspired cafe (with lots of vegan and gluten-free options, too). Start with the crispy spinach wontons, then move on to one of the stir-fry, noodle or curry favorites such as tofu tikka masala or Malaysian *char guay teow*.

Mainely Art

30

Up the river, into the woods and down the coast. On this drive you'll view the work of Maine's finest painters inside art museums and lovely galleries, then cruise past the landscapes that inspired them.

TRIP HIGHLIGHTS

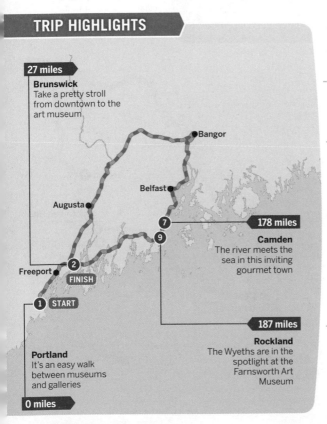

27 miles

Brunswick
Take a pretty stroll from downtown to the art museum

Bangor

Belfast

Augusta

178 miles

Camden
The river meets the sea in this inviting gourmet town

Freeport

FINISH

START

187 miles

Rockland
The Wyeths are in the spotlight at the Farnsworth Art Museum

Portland
It's an easy walk between museums and galleries

0 miles

3 DAYS
239 MILES / 384KM

GREAT FOR...

BEST TIME TO GO
May through October is high season for art walks.

ESSENTIAL
PHOTO

Capture all of island-dotted Penobscot Bay from the top of Mt Battie in Camden Hills State Park.

BEST FOR
CULTURE

Galleries, museums and a mural keep Portland cutting-edge.

Camden View of the harbor

313

30 Mainely Art

Art museums in Maine spotlight native sons and daughters and other American masters who found inspiration here. It's a talented bunch that includes Winslow Homer, George Bellows, Edward Hopper, Louise Nevelson and the Wyeths. But really injecting energy into the contemporary art scene are the fantastic special exhibits that explore the issues of our day, from conservation to urban planning to social networking, in unexpected but thought-provoking work.

TRIP HIGHLIGHT

❶ Portland

Is it art? Is it graffiti? Does it matter as long as it catches your eye? Whatever its classification, the **mural** (Free St) splashed across the back wall of the Asylum nightclub, east of Center St, captures the artistic spirit of Portland. At press time, the vibrant mural, painted by eight Maine-based street artists, was a postcard for the city, but facing the threat of demolition: the Asylum club is planning expansion and a name

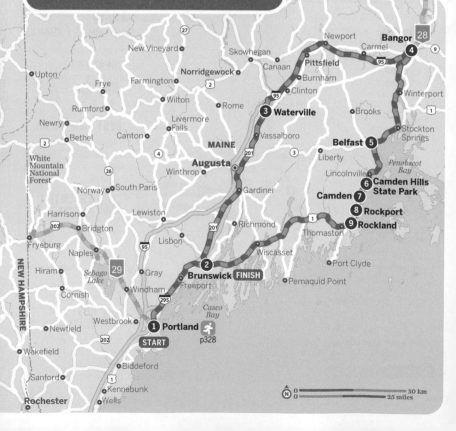

change (to Free Street Live), but promises to dedicate exterior space to street artists once renovations are finalized. Stay tuned.

Things are a bit more formal at the nearby **Portland Museum of Art** (20 7-775-6148; www.portland museum.org; 7 Congress Sq; adult/child $15/free, 4-8pm Fri free; ⏱11am-6pm Sat-Wed, to 8pm Thu & Fri, closed Mon & Tue Oct-May), founded in 1882. This well-respected museum houses an outstanding collection of American works. Maine artists, including Winslow Homer, Edward Hopper, Louise Nevelson and Andrew Wyeth, are particularly well represented. You'll also find a few paintings by European masters. From here, some of the city's coolest highlights (p328) are within easy walking distance.

✖ 🛏 p277, p311, p319

LINK YOUR TRIP

28 Great North Woods

From Bangor, a short drive on I-95 leads to the North Woods and Mt Katahdin.

29 Lakes Tour

Hop on US 302 in Portland and head north for a bright-blue lake-dappled landscape.

TOP TIP: GALLERY GUIDE & ART NEWS

For a list of galleries and studios throughout the state, pick up the free **Maine Gallery & Studio Guide** at art museums and galleries. It's available online at www.mainegalleryguide.com. An up-to-date listing of openings is provided at the **Cafe des Artistes blog**, maintained by the *Bangor Daily News* at http://cafedesartistes.bangordailynews.com.

The Drive » If you want to make good time, hop on I-295 and drive 25 miles north to Brunswick. For LL Bean and the outlet stores, make a detour onto US 1 at Freeport.

TRIP HIGHLIGHT

❷ Brunswick

Tidy Brunswick, with its well-kept central green and dramatic perch over the Androscoggin River, is a landscape painting come to life. The view stays inspiring on the Bowdoin College campus, where stately buildings surround a tree-dotted quad. The dramatic glass entrance pavilion at the **Bowdoin College Museum of Art** (📞207-725-3275; www.bowdoin.edu/art-museum; 9400 College St, Bowdoin College campus; ⏱10am-5pm Tue-Sat, 1-5pm Sun) injects this pastoral scene with a bit of modernity, and sets a compelling tone for further exploration. The 20,000-piece collection is particularly strong in the works of 19th- and 20th-century European and American painters,

with some surprising antiquities, too.

✖ 🛏 p295, p319

The Drive » For inspiring views of the Kennebec River and time on the historic Old Canada Road, follow US 201 north. The quickest route for the 50-mile drive is I-295 north to I-95 north.

❸ Waterville

Another bucolic college campus, another outstanding art collection – this time, it's the **Colby College Museum of Art** (📞207-859-5600; www.colby. edu/museum; 5600 Mayflower Hill Dr; ⏱10am-5pm Tue-Sat, noon-5pm Sun), fresh from a marvelous expansion and the addition of a 26,000-sq-ft glass pavilion. The space displays works from a nearly 500-piece collection gifted to Colby by long-time benefactors Peter and Paula Lunder. It is one of the largest gifts of art to a liberal-arts college; highlights of the collection are numerous, with works by James McNeill Whistler, Winslow Homer and Georgia

O'Keeffe, among others, and a focus on American and contemporary art.

The Drive » From Waterville, I-95 swoops along the edges of the Maine highlands as it angles north and then east on its 55-mile swing to Bangor.

❹ Bangor

The small **University of Maine Museum of Art** (☏207-561-3350; www.umma.umaine.edu; 40 Harlow St; ◷10am-5pm Mon-Sat) in Bangor is the northernmost art museum on the Maine Art Museum Trail (www.maineartmuseums.org). It's not the largest or most impressive collection in the state, but Bangor is a pleasant gateway for exploring the moody Maine highlands to the north and the mid-coast art towns just south. The university's collection spotlights mid-century modern American artists as well as contemporary pieces by David Hockney, Roy Lichtenstein, Andy Warhol and others. The special exhibits can really shine, so check the online calendar to see what's on display.

✖ p303, p319

The Drive » This 45-mile jaunt south on US 1A west to US 1 south passes the Paul Bunyan statue in downtown Bangor then tracks the Penobscot River, passing the informative **Penobscot Marine Museum** in Searsport.

JAMES LEMASS / GETTY IMAGES ©

❺ Belfast

There aren't any art museums in Belfast, but this working-class community with Scots-Irish roots does have an inviting downtown with 12 or so galleries and studios. The oceanfront town is also the site of the nation's oldest shoe store, **Colburn Shoe** (79 Main St), which opened in 1832! Stop by **High Street Studio & Gallery** (☏207-338-8990; www.facebook.com/HighStreetStudioGallery; 149 High St; ◷10am-5pm Mon-Thu, to 8pm Fri, to 4pm Sat) for bright paintings by a trio of local women, plus painting classes. The art-deco **Colonial Theatre** (☏207-338-5087; www.colonialtheatre.com; 163 High St; adult/child $8.50/5.50) has shown movies since 1912, luring moviegoers with a neon sign and a rooftop elephant. On the way out of town, see what's happening at **Waterfall Arts** (☏207-338-2222; www.waterfallarts.org; 256 High St; ◷10am-5pm Tue-Fri, hours vary for events), a non-profit contemporary arts center that hosts exhibitions, lectures, art classes, musical performances, film screenings and more.

Portland Portland Museum of Art

The Drive » Follow US 1 south for 16 miles, mostly along the coast, passing Ducktrap and Lincolnville.

- - - - - - - - - -

⑥ Camden Hills State Park

A favorite hike in **Camden Hills State Park** (📞207-236-3109; www.maine.gov/camdenhills; 280 Belfast Rd/US 1, Camden; adult/child $6/1; ⏱9am-sunset), the half-mile climb up **Mt Battie** offers outstanding views of Penobscot Bay. Feeling sluggish? You can drive up the mountain, too.

🛏 p319

The Drive » Drive 2 miles south on US 1 to downtown Camden.

- - - - - - - - - -

TRIP HIGHLIGHT

⑦ Camden

Camden and its picture-perfect harbor, framed against the mountains of Camden Hills State Park, is one of the prettiest sites in the state. The Megunticook River crashes dramatically into the sea beside the public landing, behind US 1 in the center of town. At the landing you'll also find the helpful **Penobscot Bay Regional Chamber of Commerce**

(📞207-236-4404; www.mainedreamvacation.com; 2 Public Landing; ⏱9am-5pm Jun-Oct, 9am-4pm Mon-Fri Nov-May). Camden offers windjammer cruises (www.sailmainecoast.com) – anything from two-hour rides to multiday journeys up the coast. There are also galleries, fine seafood restaurants and back alleys for exploring. Enjoy good meals at **Fresh & Co** (📞207-236-7005; www.freshcamden.com; 1 Bayview Landing; mains $21-32; ⏱11:30am-2:30pm & from 5pm Thu-Tue Jul & Aug, shorter hours rest of year) or **Francine Bistro** (📞207-230-0083; www.

MID-COAST ART WALKS

If it's a Friday night in July or August, and you're driving along Maine's mid-coast, you're going to drive past an art walk:

Bath 4pm to 7pm, third Friday of the month, June to September; www.visitbath.com/events/artwalk.

Belfast 5:30pm to 8pm, fourth Friday of the month, May to October; http://belfastartwalk.com.

Brunswick 5pm to 8pm, second Friday of the month, May to October; www.artwalkmaine.org/brunswick.

Portland 5pm to 8pm, first Friday of the month, year-round; www.liveworkportland.org/arts/walk.

Rockland 5pm to 8pm, first Friday of the month, May to November; www.artsinrockland.org.

For a list of art walks throughout the state, visit www.artwalkmaine.org.

francinebistro.com; 55 Chestnut St, Camden; mains $16-29; ☺5:30-10pm Tue-Sat).

🛏 p319

The Drive » By the time you get your seatbelt buckled you're already in Rockport, just a 2-mile drive south on US 1.

🔞 Rockport

Photographers flock to Rockport, a sleepy harborside town, for more than just the picturesque coast. Rockport is the home of the world-renowned **Maine Media Workshops** (☎20 7-236-8581; www.mainemedia.edu; 70 Camden St), one of the world's leading instructional centers in photography, film and digital media. The institute offers hundreds of workshops and master classes throughout the year. Student and faculty works are displayed in a gallery at 18 Central St.

But let's not forget the most important attraction in town: the granite statue of **Andre the Seal** (Rockport Marine Park, Pascal Ave), about half a mile off US 1 via Main St. Andre was a crowd-pleasing showboat who swam to the harbor every summer from Boston, from the 1970s until his death in the mid-'80s. He was the subject of a children's book, *Andre the Seal,* and a 1994 movie.

The Drive » Leave Andre behind as you turn left onto Pascal Ave, following it to US 1. Rockland is 6 miles to the south.

TRIP HIGHLIGHT

🔞 Rockland

Rockland is a cool little town. Its commercial port adds vibrancy, and its bustling Main St is a window into the city's sociocultural diversity, with working-class diners, bohemian cafes and high-end bistros beside galleries and old-fashioned storefronts.

Just off Main St, the **Farnsworth Art Museum** (☎207-596-6457; www.farnsworthmuseum.org; 16 Museum St; adult/child $15/free; ☺10am-5pm Jun-Oct, closed Mon Jan-Apr, May, Nov & Dec, plus Tue Jan-Mar) is one of the country's best small regional museums, with works spanning 200 years of American art. The 'Maine in America' collections spotlight artists who have lived or worked in the state. Exhibits about the Wyeths – Andrew, NC and Jamie – are housed in galleries throughout the museum and in the Wyeth Center, a former Methodist church across the garden.

The wonderful **Archipelago Fine Arts** (☎20 7-596-0701; www.thearchipelago.net; 386 Main St; ☺9:30am-5:30pm Mon-Fri, to 5pm Sat, 11am-4pm Sun) sells jewelry, paintings and arts and crafts by artists living on Maine's islands and coast. It works in partnership with the Island Institute (www.islandinstitute.org), an organization whose goal is to support Maine's remote coastal and island communities.

✕ 🛏 p277, p319

The Drive » From Rockland, continue south along the coast on US 1 to loop back to Brunswick.

Eating & Sleeping

Portland ❶

✕ Fore Street   Modern American $$$
(☎207-775-2717; www.forestreet.biz; 288
Fore St; small plates $12-15, mains $28-38;
⊙5:30-10pm Sun-Thu, to 10:30 Fri & Sat) Fore
Street is the lauded, long-running restaurant
many consider to be the originator of today's
food obsession in Portland. Chef-owner Sam
Hayward has turned roasting into a high art:
chickens turn on spits in the open kitchen as
chefs slide iron kettles of mussels into the
wood-burning oven. Local, seasonal eating is
taken very seriously and the menu changes
daily.

🛏 Danforth Inn   Boutique Hotel $$$
(☎207-879-8755; www.danforthinn.com; 163
Danforth St; r $199-469; P❄🛜) Staying at
this ivy-shrouded West End boutique hotel feels
like being a guest at an eccentric millionaire's
mansion. Shoot pool in the wood-paneled
game room (a former speakeasy) or climb into
the rooftop cupola for views across Portland
Harbor. The nine rooms are decorated with flair,
in a sophisticated mix of antique and modern.

Brunswick ❷

🛏 Brunswick Inn   B&B $$
(☎207-729-4914; www.brunswickinnparkrow.
com; 165 Park Row; r $139-259; 🛜) Overlooking
Brunswick's town green, this elegant guesthouse
has 16 rooms ranging from small to spacious.
Each is uniquely designed in an airy, farmhouse-
chic style, a mix of worn woods and modern
prints. There's a self-contained garden cottage
that's ideal for families. Enjoy drinks by the
fire in the bar, or on the porch overlooking the
Town Mall.

Bangor ❹

✕ Friars' Bakehouse   Bakery $
(☎207-947-3770; 21 Central St; sweets $2-8;
⊙8:30am-2pm Tue-Thu, to 5pm Fri) A couple of
Franciscan friars in long brown robes preside over
this tiny bakery, serving soups and sandwiches
at lunch. Biting into one of their crunchy-topped
blueberry muffins is practically a...spiritual
experience. Tables are shared, in keeping with the
'love thy neighbor' spirit. No credit cards, no cell
phones. Take home a bag of whoopie pies.

Camden Hills State Park ❻

🛏 Camden Hills
State Park   Campground $
(☎207-624-9950; www.campwithme.com; 280
Belfast Rd/US 1, Camden; campsites $35-45;
⊙mid-May–mid-Oct; 🛜) The park's appealing
campground has hot showers and wooded sites,
some with electric hookups. There's also wi-fi.
Reserve online through Maine's government
reservations portal.

Camden ❼

🛏 Norumbega   B&B $$$
(☎207-236-4646; www.norumbegainn.com;
63 High St; r & ste $199-639; 🛜) Looking like
something out of a slightly creepy fairy tale,
this 1886 turreted stone mansion was built to
incorporate elements of the owner's favorite
European castles. Today, it's Camden's poshest
and most dramatically situated B&B, perched
on a hill above the bay, with 11 distinctive rooms
and suites.

Rockland ❾

✕ Suzuki Sushi Bar   Japanese $$
(☎207-596-7447; www.suzukisushi.com; 419
Main St; sushi $4-9, mains $14-25; ⊙5-9pm
Tue-Sat) The super-fresh seafood of the Maine
Midcoast is put to exquisite use at Suzuki's,
which sets itself apart from many sushi bars.
Firstly because the sushi chefs are women (in
a field dominated by men); but also, they offer
no fried food and no grilled food. Sashimi and
sushi dominate the menu, though noodles and
donburi are also available.

Moose & Mountains: Western Maine

31

This trek feels akin to flying. Leafy byways soar up the sides of mountains. Pristine forests float beneath lofty overlooks. And bumpy frost-heaves add turbulence on the back roads.

TRIP HIGHLIGHTS

68 miles

Height of Land
Enjoy sweeping views of Mooselookmeguntic Lake

93 miles

Rangeley Lakes Trails Center
Nordic skiing and hiking on wooded lakeside trails

FINISH
Sugarloaf

Oquossoc

6

4

Small Falls

Houghton

2

Mexico

START **1**

Grafton Notch State Park
Inspire your inner artist at beautiful Screw Auger Falls

18 miles

Bethel
A stylish base camp for multi-season adventure

0 miles

2 DAYS
160 MILES / 257KM

GREAT FOR...

BEST TIME TO GO
June through March is good for hiking, leaf-peeping and skiing.

 ESSENTIAL PHOTO
Frame a shot of Mooselookmeguntic Lake from the Height of Land overlook.

 BEST FOR WILDLIFE
ME 16 between Rangeley and Stratton is a local moose alley.

31

Moose & Mountains: Western Maine

The first time you see a moose standing on the side of the road, it doesn't seem unusual. You've been prepped by all of the moose-crossing signs. But then it registers. 'Hey, that's a moose!' And you simultaneously swerve, slam on the brakes and speed up. Control these impulses. Simply slow your speed and enjoy the gift of wildlife. Then share your good fortune on Facebook, of course.

TRIP HIGHLIGHT

❶ Bethel

If you glance at the map, tiny Bethel doesn't look much different from the other towns scattered across this alpine region. But look more closely. The town is cocooned between two powerful rivers, and several ski resorts and ski centers call the community home. Four state and national scenic byways begin within an 85-mile drive.

Of the ski resorts, **Sunday River** (☏800-543-2754; www.sundayriver.com; ME 26;

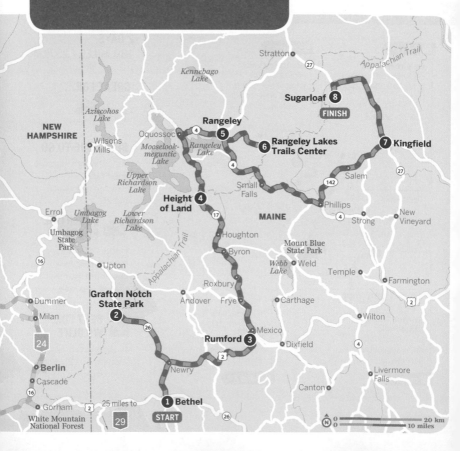

full-day lift ticket adult $89, child $59-69; 🎿) is the biggest draw, luring skiers with eight interconnected peaks, 135 trails and a host of winter activities. From July until early October, the resort opens 25 mountain-bike trails and runs trips up to North Peak on its fast-moving **Chondola** (☏800-543-2754; www.sundayriver.com; ME 26; round-trip adult/child $15/10; ⊘10am-4pm Thu-Mon Jul & Aug, Fri-Sun Sep). There's also a six-line **zipline tour** (☏800-543-2754; www.sundayriver.com; ME 26; tickets $59-69; ⊘9am, 10am, 11:30pm & 2pm Thu-Mon Jul & Aug, Fri-Sun Sep). Several outdoor centers, including the **Bethel Nordic Ski Center** (☏207-824-6276; www.caribourecreation.com; 21 Broad St; day pass adult/child $20/13; ⊘mid-Dec–Mar), are base camps for cross-country skiing and snowshoeing, with 'fat biking'

LINK YOUR TRIP

24 Woodland Heritage Trail

Take US 2 west to learn the history of logging on the Androscoggin River.

29 Lakes Tour

Follow the Pequawket Trail Scenic Byway along ME 113 to a riverside beach in Fryeburg and more lakes beyond.

SCENIC BYWAYS IN THE LAKES & MOUNTAINS REGION

Grafton Notch Scenic Byway From Bethel, follow US 2 north, then turn left at Newry and take ME 26 through Grafton Notch State Park.

Pequawket Trail Scenic Byway Follow the Androscoggin River west from Bethel on US 2. Turn south onto ME 113 at Gilead and follow it to Fryeburg.

State Route 27 Scenic Byway From stop 7, in Kingfield, follow ME 16/27 to Sugarloaf, then continue north on ME 27 to Canada.

Rangeley Lakes National Scenic Byway Drive east on US 2 from Rumford to Mexico, then turn north on US 17. The byway begins about 15 miles north, just beyond the town of Byron.

Read more at www.exploremaine.org/byways.

(on mountain bikes with wide tires) growing in popularity.

🍴 🛏 p327

The Drive » Follow ME 5/ ME 26/US 2 north from Bethel, tracking the Sunday River about 6 miles north. Keep left on NH 26 as it leaves ME 5/US 2 and becomes Bear River Rd, which leads to the park 11 miles west.

- - - - - - - - - - - -

TRIP HIGHLIGHT

❷ Grafton Notch State Park

Sitting astride the Grafton Notch Scenic Byway within the Mahoosuc Range, this rugged **park** (☏207-824-2912; www.maine.gov/graftonnotch; ME 26; adult/child $4/1) is a stunner. Carved by a glacier that retreated 12,000 years ago, the notch is a four-season playground, chock-full of waterfalls, gorges, lofty viewpoints

and hiking trails, including 12 strenuous miles of the **Appalachian Trail**. Peregrine falcons build nests in the cliffs, helping the park earn its spot on the Maine Birding Trail (www.mainebirdingtrail.com); the best viewing is May to October. Cross-country skiers and snowshoers enjoy the park in winter. If you're short on time, simply wander the path beside **Screw Auger Falls**, off the main parking lot. This 23ft waterfall crashes dramatically through a narrow gorge. If you have more time, try the 2.4-mile round-trip hike up to **Table Rock overlook** or the 2.2-mile **Eyebrow Loop Trail**. There are excellent picnicking opportunities within the park – the Spruce Meadow picnic area is signed off ME 26.

The Drive » Return to US 2 north. On the 16-mile drive, you'll pass stone walls and antique stores, and enjoy the Androscoggin River tagging along on your right.

③ Rumford

How do you know you've arrived? When the giant, ax-wielding **Paul Bunyan** says, 'Hey there.' According to legend, the red-shirted lumberman was born in Maine but was later sent west by his parents. Today, he stands tall beside the information center of the **River Valley Chamber of Commerce** (📞207-364-3241; www.rivervalleychamber. com; 10 Bridge St; ⏰9am-5pm Jun-Oct, 10am-2pm Nov-May). Walk a few steps beyond the information center building for a fantastic view of the wild and woolly **Rumford Falls**. The highest falls east of Niagara, they drop 176ft over a granite ledge. The small park here holds a black marble memorial honoring local son and former US senator Edmund Muskie, who authored the Clean Water Act.

The Drive » Leave Rumford and US 2, picking up ME 17 north in Mexico. From here ME 17 runs parallel to pines, farms, meadows and the rocky Swift River. Snap a photo of the river barreling through metamorphic rock at the Coos Canyon Rest Area in Byron, then head north, picking up the Rangeley Lakes National Scenic Byway north of Houghton.

④ Height of Land

The entrance to this photogenic **overlook** sneaks up on you – it's on the left as you round a bend on Brimstone Mountain, just after a hiker warning sign. But don't slam on your brakes and swerve across the grass divider if you miss the turn (we saw this happen), because there's another entrance just north. But you *should* pull over. The expansive view of island-dotted **Mooselookmeguntic Lake**, the largest of the Rangeley Lakes, as it sweeps north towards distant mountains is astounding. Views of undeveloped forest stretch for up to 100 miles; you can even see the White Mountains in New Hampshire. The dogged **Appalachian Trail** runs alongside the viewpoint, and an interpretive sign shares a few details abut the 2190-mile footpath.

The Drive » Drive north to the village of Oquosocc, then turn right onto ME 4/16. Take a photo at the Rangeley Scenic Overlook, where there is a panoramic view of Rangeley Lake. This overlook is about 5.5 miles from Height of Land. From here, continue east.

⑤ Rangely

An adventure hub, with tidy inns and down-home restaurants,

KENNETH H THOMAS / GETTY IMAGES ©

Rangeley makes a useful base for skiing, hiking, white-water rafting and mountain biking in the nearby mountains. Snowmobilers can zoom across 150 miles of trails. For information, stop by the **Rangeley Lakes Chamber of Commerce** (📞207-864-5364; www.rangeleymaine. com; 6 Park Rd; ⏰10am-4pm Mon-Fri, to 2pm Sat), which has handouts about restaurants, lodging options, local trails and moose-watching. Just behind the visitor center, the **Lakeside Park** (Park Rd; ⏰5am-10pm) is a nice spot to enjoy a picnic by the lake. On rainy days,

Height of Land View of Mooselookmeguntic Lake

ask at the chamber about the local museums.

✕ 🛏 p327

The Drive ❱❱ ME 4 breaks from ME 16 in downtown Rangeley. From the chamber of commerce, follow ME 4 east. Turn left onto Dallas Hill Rd, then in 2.5 miles bear right on Saddleback Mountain Rd and continue another 2.5 miles.

TRIP HIGHLIGHT

➏ Rangely Lakes Trails Center

A green yurt marks your arrival at the **Rangeley Lakes Trails Center** (☎20 7-864-4309; www.rangeley lakestrailscenter.com; 523 Sad-dleback Mountain Rd; day pass $9-19), a four-season trail system covering gorgeous woodland terrain beside Saddleback Lake. Here there are more than 34 miles of trails for cross-country skiing and snow-shoeing during snow season (rental equipment available inside the yurt, along with hot soup!). In summer, the cross-country trails double as hiking trails, and the snowshoe trails allow single-track biking. The yurt is closed in summer, but trail maps are available from an informa-tion board (or from the chamber of commerce in Rangeley).

The Drive ❱❱ Follow ME 4 southeast, passing another Rangeley Lake overlook. Continue southeast. You'll pass another Appalachian Trail crossing before entering prime moose country. Follow ME 12 east to NE 16/27 north.

➐ Kingfield

If you enjoy hiking and cross-country skiing, but not backpacking, consider a hut-to-hut trip through **Maine Huts & Trails** (☎207-265-2400; www.mainehuts.org; 496 Main St; per person incl meals $90-130), a wonderful non-profit organization based in Kingfield, which oper-ates four ecolodges along

LOCAL KNOWLEDGE:
HERE A MOOSE, THERE A MOOSE

Moose-crossing signs are as ubiquitous as logging trucks in these parts. But spotting one of these chunky beasts, which can reach a height of 7ft at the shoulder and weigh anywhere from 1000lb to 1400lb, is trickier. You'll most likely see them eating on the side of the road in the morning, in the evening and between noon and 2pm. According to a handout from the Rangeley Lakes Chamber of Commerce, these are some of the top moose-spotting sites in the area:

Route 4 Phillips to Rangeley.

Route 16 Rangeley to Stratton; Wilsons Mills to the New Hampshire border.

Route 17 Between the Height of Land overlook and the Rangeley Lake overlook.

Route 16/27 Stratton to Carrabassett Valley.

When driving these routes stay extra vigilant and slow down, particularly at night. Moose don't always leap out of the way like deer, and in the dark your vehicle's headlights won't always reflect off the animals' eyes, due to their height. If you come upon a moose standing in the road, do not get out of the car (they can charge the vehicle) or drive around it. Wait for the moose to mosey off the road.

an 80-mile trail system near Sugarloaf (with more huts planned). Choose a dorm bed or a private bunk room and enjoy three meals (including a packed lunch) and pretty plush off-the-grid relaxation. Pillows and blankets are provided, but not bedding. Winter and summer are peak popularity for the huts; in the off-season you can still stay overnight, but without meal service (and with reduced prices). There is no vehicle access to the lodges (two are less than 2 miles from a trailhead).

The Drive » From Kingfield, NH 16 joins ME 27, unfurling beneath the pines, with the Carrabassett River tumbling merrily alongside.

- - - - - - - - - - - - -

❽ Sugarloaf

The Rangeley area's most popular **ski resort** (☏207-237-2000, 800-843-5623; www.sugarloaf.com; 5092 Access Road, Carrabassett Valley; full-day lift ticket adult $86, child $60-70), Sugarloaf has a vertical drop of 2820ft, with 162 trails and glades, and 13 lifts. This is Maine's second-highest peak (4237ft). Summer activities

include lift rides, zip lines and golf. The resort village complex has an enormous mountain lodge, an inn and rental condos. Nearby towns of Kingfield and Stratton are also good bases.

Near Sugarloaf's slopes, the **Sugarloaf Outdoor Center** (☏207-237-6830; www.sugarloaf.com; ME 27/ME 16, Carrabassett Valley; day pass adult/child $21/13; ◷9am-5pm Sun-Fri, to 8pm Sat Dec-Mar) has 56 miles of groomed cross-country trails, plus guided snowshoeing safaris and public ice-skating on an NHL-size rink.

Eating & Sleeping

Bethel ❶

✖ Good Food Store
Sandwiches $

(📞207-824-3754; www.goodfoodbethel.com; 212 Mayville Rd/ME 26; salads & sandwiches under $8; ⏱ store 9am-8pm, takeout 11am-6pm) Buy super sandwiches, salads and heat-and-eat meals at this gourmet organic market and wine shop. The homemade cookies and dried fruit are fantastic. Barbecue by Smokin' Good BBQ (www.smokingoodbarbecue.com) is sold here Thursday through Sunday, from a food trailer in the parking lot.

✖ DiCocoa's Market & Bakery
Cafe $

(📞207-824-6386; www.cafedicocoa.com; 125 Main St; mains $5-13; ⏱7am-4pm; 🍴) This funky orange bungalow is a morning must for espresso-based drinks. It also serves whole-grain baked goods, croissants, lunchtime wraps, soups and stews. The ganache-dipped eclairs are worth an indulgence.

✖ Cho Sun
Asian $$

(📞207-824-7370; www.chosunrestaurant.com; 141 Main St; mains $17-27; ⏱5-9pm Tue-Sun) Korea meets rural Maine at this unassuming Victorian house, whose interior has been transformed into an Asian oasis of bamboo and paper lanterns. Try flavor-filled dishes from the owner's native South Korea, like bibimbap (rice pot with meat and veggies) or kimchi stew. There's also a high-quality sushi bar and a (booze) bar.

🛏 Chapman Inn
B&B $$

(📞207-824-2657; www.chapmaninn.com; 2 Church St; dm $35, r $59-139; ❄🐾) Run by a friendly, globe-trotting retiree, this roomy downtown guesthouse has character in spades. The 10 private rooms are done up in florals and antiques, with slightly sloping floors attesting to the house's age. The cozy common space is stocked with Monopoly and other rainy-day games.

Rangely ❺

✖ Red Onion
American $$

(📞207-864-5022; www.rangeleyredonion.com; 2511 Main St; mains $8-18; ⏱11am-9pm; 🍴) A big plate of chicken parmesan spaghetti after a day on the slopes has been a Rangeley tradition for four decades. This boisterous Italian-American joint is also known for its pizzas and its 1970s wood-paneled bar.

🛏 Loon Lodge
Inn $$

(📞207-864-5666; www.loonlodgeme.com; 16 Pickford Rd; r $110-165; 🐾) Hidden in the woods by the lake, this century-old log-cabin lodge has eight rooms, most with a backwoods-chic look, with wood-plank walls and handmade quilts (no TV). There's a formal dining room on-site, plus the intimate, friendly Pickford Pub, serving classics such as burgers, fish and chips, and steak.

🛏 Rangeley Inn & Tavern
Inn $$

(📞207-864-3341; www.therangeleyinn.com; 2443 Main St; r $110-230) Behind the inn's pretty powder-blue facade, you can relax by the fire and admire the mounted bear in the lobby. Rooms are simple and old-fashioned in this creaky turn-of-the-20th-century lodge, with floral wallpaper and brass beds. There's also a motel-style lodge on the property.

STRETCH YOUR LEGS PORTLAND

Start/Finish Portland Museum of Art

Distance 2 miles

Duration Four hours

This walk takes in museums and a magically transformed landmark before dropping to the bars and boutiques of the hard-charging Old Port District. Re-energize along the working wharves, then head to the West End for a sun-dappled finale among the mansions.

Take this walk on Trips

25 29 30

Portland Museum of Art

Paintings by Winslow Homer and other Maine artists are highlights at the **museum** (207-775-6148; www.portlandmuseum.org; 7 Congress Sq; adult/child $15/free, 4-8pm Fri free; 11am-6pm Sat-Wed, to 8pm Thu & Fri, closed Mon & Tue Oct-May), which anchors the city's Arts District. The collection sprawls across three separate buildings. Most pieces are in the postmodern Charles Shipman Payson Building, designed by the firm of IM Pei. Don't miss the flying staircase in the 1801 Federal-style McClellan House in the back.

The Walk » Leave the museum and turn right onto Free St. You'll pass the Children's Museum. Turn left on Oak St and return to Congress St. Turn right and follow Congress two blocks. The Wadsworth-Longfellow House is on the left.

Wadsworth-Longfellow House

The revered American poet Henry Wadsworth-Longfellow (1807–82) grew up in this Federal-style **house** (207-774-1822; www.mainehistory.org; 489 Congress St; guided tour adult/child $15/3; noon-4pm May, 10:30am-4pm Mon-Sat, noon-4pm Sun Jun-Oct), built in 1785 by his Revolutionary War–hero grandfather. The house has been impeccably restored to look as it did in the 1800s, complete with original furniture and artifacts. The ticket price includes admission to the Maine Historical Society Museum next door, which has rotating exhibits about life in Maine over the past few centuries.

The Walk » Continue along Congress St, walking past Monument Sq and the bronze statue dedicated to Portland's Civil War. Turn right onto Exchange St.

Press Hotel

From old Portland to new: the **Press Hotel** (207-808-8800; www.thepresshotel.com; 119 Exchange St; r $169-369; P) is a clever, creative conversion of the building that once housed the offices and printing plant of Maine's largest

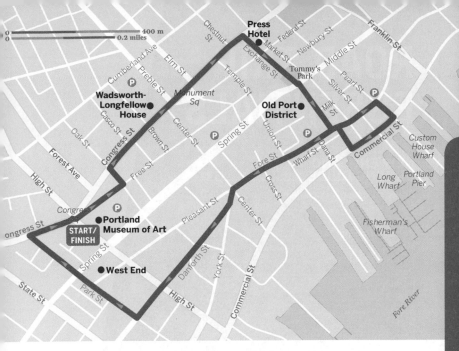

newspaper. The press theme shines in whimsical details – a wall of vintage typewriters, old headlines revived on hallway wallpaper, letterpress artwork behind the reception desk. Drop by for a coffee or microbrew in Inkwell, the lobby bar, and pop downstairs to check out the mini art gallery that features works by local artists.

**The Walk ›› ** A walk down Exchange St towards the waterfront takes you through a pretty little green pocket known as Tommy's Park – look out for the hot-dog vendor here, a fixture for the past decade.

Old Port District

Handsome 19th-century brick buildings line the streets of Old Port, with the city's most enticing stores, pubs and restaurants. By night, flickering gas lanterns add to the atmosphere. Wander down Exchange St and its offshoots for fresh seafood, local microbrews and tiny galleries. To sign up for a sightseeing boat tour or order lobster to ship home, walk down to the wharves.

**The Walk ›› ** Follow Fore St west to its junction with Danforth St, where there's a statue of movie director and native son John Ford. Continue west on Danforth St.

West End

Portland's loveliest neighborhood is a hillside enclave of brick town houses, elegant gardens and stately mansions; some date from the neighborhood's founding in 1836. Be sure to walk past the **Victoria Mansion** (☏207-772-4841; www.victoriamansion.org; 109 Danforth St; adult/child $15/5; ⊙10am-3:45pm Mon-Sat, 1:15-4:45pm Sun May-Oct). This Italianate palace, whose exterior would work well in a Tim Burton movie, dates to 1860. If you have time, delving further west into the neighborhood brings rewards, including the scenic Western Promenade, a grassy pathway with fine views over the harbor, especially around sunset.

**The Walk ›› ** Return to the art museum by taking Park St northwest to Congress St.

ROAD TRIP ESSENTIALS

New England Driving Guide

Scenic, generally well-maintained roads make New England a delightful road-trip destination. Let us answer all your driving-related questions, including where to park your car.

Driving Fast Facts

→ **Right or left?** Drive on the right

→ **Legal driving age** 16

→ **Manual or automatic?** Most rental cars come with automatic transmission

→ **Top speed limit** 75mph (on interstate in rural Maine)

→ **Best bumper sticker** 'Wicked Cool Bumpah Stickah'

DRIVER'S LICENSE & DOCUMENTS

All drivers must carry a driver's license, the car registration and proof of insurance. If your license is not in English, you will need an official translation or an International Driving Permit (IDP).

INSURANCE

Liability All drivers are required to obtain a minimum amount of liability insurance, which would cover the damage that you might cause to other people and property in case of an accident. Liability insurance can be purchased from rental-car companies for about $12 per day.

Collision For damage to the rental vehicle, a collision damage waiver (CDW) is available from the rental company for about $18 a day.

Alternative sources Your personal auto insurance may extend to rental cars, so it's worth investigating before purchasing liability or collision from the rental company. Additionally, some credit cards offer reimbursement coverage for collision damages if you rent the car with that credit card; again, check before departing. Most credit-card coverage isn't valid for rentals of more than 15 days or for exotic models, SUVs, vans and 4WD vehicles.

RENTING A CAR

Rental cars are readily available at regional airports and in major towns. Rates usually include unlimited mileage. Dropping off the car at a different location from where you picked it up usually incurs an additional fee. It always pays to shop around between rental companies, utilizing price-comparison websites.

Renting a car without a major credit card is difficult, if not impossible. Without one, some agencies simply will not rent vehicles, while others require prepayment, a deposit slightly higher than the cost of your rental, pay stubs, proof of round-trip airfare and more.

The following companies operate in New England:

Alamo (☑844-341-8645; www.alamo.com)

Avis (☑800-633-3469; www.avis.com)

Budget (☑800-218-7992; www.budget.com)

Dollar (☑800-800-3665; www.dollar.com)

Enterprise (☑844-362-0812; www.enterprise.com)

Road Trip Websites

American Automobile Association (AAA; ☑emergency roadside assistance 800-222-4357, member services 800-922-8228; www.aaa.com; annual membership from $56) Provides maps and other information, as well as travel discounts and emergency assistance for members. Members get discounts on car rentals, air tickets, hotels and attractions, as well as emergency road service and towing. AAA has reciprocal agreements with automobile associations in other countries. Bring your membership card from your country of origin.

Gas Buddy (www.gasbuddy.com) Find the cheapest gas in town.

New England Travel Planner (www.newenglandtravelplanner. com) Routes, reviews and other travel resources.

Traffic.com (www.traffic.com) Real-time traffic reports, with details about accidents and traffic jams.

Hertz (☑800-654-3131; www.hertz.com)
National (☑877-222-9058; www.national car.com)
Rent-A-Wreck (☑877-877-0700; www.rent awreck.com) Rents cars that may have more wear and tear than your typical rental vehicle but are actually far from wrecks.
Thrifty (☑800-847-4389; www.thrifty.com)

BORDER CROSSING

Generally, crossing the US–Canada border is straightforward. The biggest hassle is usually the length of the lines. All travelers entering the USA are required to carry passports, including citizens of Canada and the USA.

MAPS

Detailed state highway maps are distributed free by state governments. You can call or write to state tourism offices in advance to request maps, or you can pick them up at highway tourism information offices (welcome centers) when you enter a state on a major highway.

Another excellent resource is DeLorme (www.delorme.com), which publishes individual state road atlases. These contain large-format maps with topographic detail and exhaustive coverage of backcountry roads. The scale ranges from 1:65,000 to 1:135,000. The New England box set includes all six states for $61.95, or you can buy individual state atlases for $19.95 to $22.95 each.

ROADS & CONDITIONS

New England roads are very good – even the warren of hard-packed dirt roads that crisscross Vermont. A few hazards to be aware of:

➡ Some of the region's big, old cities can be difficult to navigate. Boston in particular is notorious for its scofflaw drivers and maddening maze of one-way streets. Park your car and use alternative means to get around.

➡ Traffic is heavy around urban areas during rush hour (7am to 9am and 4pm to 7pm Monday through Friday).

➡ Some roads across northern mountain passes in Vermont, New Hampshire and Maine are closed during the winter, but good signage gives you plenty of warning.

Toll Roads

You are likely to encounter tolls for some roads, bridges and tunnels while driving around New England, including the following:

➡ Blue Star Turnpike (New Hampshire Turnpike; I-95)
➡ Claiborne Pell Newport Bridge (Rhode Island)
➡ Frederick E Everett Turnpike (Central New Hampshire Turnpike)
➡ Maine Turnpike (I-95)
➡ Massachusetts Turnpike (I-90)
➡ Mt Equinox Skyline Dr (Vermont)
➡ Mt Mansfield Auto Toll Rd (Vermont)
➡ Mt Washington Auto Rd (New Hampshire)
➡ Spaulding Turnpike (New Hampshire)
➡ Sumner Tunnel (Massachusetts)
➡ Ted Williams Tunnel (Massachusetts)
➡ Tobin Bridge (Mystic River Bridge; Massachusetts)

Road Distances (miles)

	Boston, MA	Provincetown, MA	Portsmouth, NH	Portland, ME	Bar Harbor, ME	Burlington, VT	Brattleboro, VT	Norwich, VT/ Hanover, NH	Hartford, CT
Provincetown, MA	114								
Portsmouth, NH	58	171							
Portland, ME	108	221	51						
Bar Harbor, ME	267	380	210	159					
Burlington, VT	217	330	207	209	334				
Brattleboro, VT	120	220	124	175	354	151			
Norwich, VT/Hanover, NH	127	240	116	167	346	96	69		
Hartford, CT	101	206	150	201	380	236	85	152	
Providence, RI	50	120	106	157	336	265	137	175	86

ROAD RULES

The maximum speed limit on most New England interstates is 65mph, but some have a limit of 55mph, and one stretch of I-95 in rural Maine has a limit of 75mph. On undivided highways, the speed limit will vary from 30mph to 55mph. Police enforce speed limits by patrolling in police cruisers and in unmarked cars. Fines vary by state but can run into hundreds of dollars.

Other road rules include the following:

➡ Driving laws are different in each of the New England states; all except New Hampshire require the use of seat belts.

➡ In every state, children under four years of age must be placed in a child safety seat secured by a seat belt.

➡ Most states require motorcycle riders to wear helmets whenever they ride. In any case, use of a helmet is highly recommended.

➡ All six New England states prohibit texting while driving, while Vermont, New Hampshire and Connecticut have banned handheld cell-phone use by drivers.

PARKING

Public parking is readily available in most New England destinations, whether on the street or in parking lots. In rural areas and small towns, it is often free of charge. Bigger towns and cities typically have coin- or credit-card-fed parking meters, which will limit the amount of time you can leave your car (usually two hours or more).

Parking can be a challenge in urban areas, especially Boston. Street parking is limited, so you will probably have to pay for parking in a private lot or garage.

New England Playlist

Sweet Baby James James Taylor

The Impression that I Get The Mighty Mighty Bosstones

Farmhouse Phish

New Hampshire Matt Pond PA

Good Times Roll The Cars

FUEL

Gas stations are ubiquitous and many are open 24 hours a day. Small-town stations may be open only from 7am to 8pm or 9pm.

Prices vary, tending to be more expensive in remote rural areas with limited competition, or in states with high fuel taxes (Connecticut's taxes are the highest; New Hampshire's are the lowest). Some stations offer specially discounted prices one day per week; watch for signs advertising this.

Most stations require that you pay before you pump. More modern pumps have credit-/debit-card terminals built into them, so you can pay with plastic right at the pump. At 'full-service' stations, an attendant will pump your gas for you; no tip is expected.

SAFETY

New England does not present any particular safety concerns for drivers. That said, travelers are advised to always remove valuables and lock all car doors, especially in urban areas.

Driving can be tricky in big cities, where narrow streets, clogged traffic and illogical street layouts can make unfamiliar drivers miserable. New England drivers are notoriously impatient. Beware the 'Boston left', where the first left-turning vehicle jumps out in front of oncoming traffic.

Be extra cautious driving at night on rural roads, which are often not well lit and may be populated by deer, moose and other creatures that can total your car if you hit them the wrong way. In winter, snow tires or all-season tires are a must, especially for mountain driving.

RADIO

Maine WCYY (94.3FM), based in Portland, specializes in alternative rock, with a good mix of oldies and newbies.

Massachusetts Boston is blessed with two public radio stations – WGBH (89.7FM) and WBUR (90.9FM) – broadcasting news, classical music and radio shows.

New Hampshire The Freewaves (91.3FM) is run by the students of the University of New Hampshire, offering indie, classical, jazz and folk.

Vermont WRUV (90.1FM) – also known as Burlington's Better Alternative – is a nonprofit student- and volunteer-run radio station,

Driving Problem-Buster

What should I do if my car breaks down? Call the service number provided by the rental-car company and it will make arrangements with a local garage. If you're driving your own car, it's advisable to join the American Automobile Association (AAA), which provides emergency assistance.

What if I have an accident? If any damage is incurred, you'll have to call the local police (☑911) to come to the scene of the accident and file an accident report, for insurance purposes.

What should I do if I get stopped by the police? Always pull over to the right at the first available opportunity. Stay in your car and roll down the window. Show the police officer your driver's license and automobile registration. For any violations, you cannot pay the officer issuing the ticket; rather, payment must be made by mail or by internet.

How do the tolls work? Most tolls are payable in cash only. Tollbooths are usually staffed, so exact change is not required. Alternatively, consider purchasing an E-ZPass for the state you will be traveling in (this is not transferable to other states).

What if I can't find anywhere to stay? In summer and autumn, it's advisable to make reservations in advance. Most towns have tourist information centers or chambers of commerce that will help travelers find accommodation in a pinch.

Driving Tips

Yes, driving really is the best way to see New England. Just watch out for the following:

➡ Traffic jams are common in and around New England's larger cities during morning and evening commute hours.

➡ Municipalities control parking by signs on the street, stating explicitly where you may or may not park. A yellow line or yellow-painted curb means that no parking is allowed there.

➡ In urban areas, New England drivers can be aggressive, speedy and unpredictable, particularly around Boston.

playing a mix of music at the DJs' discretion, but absolutely no songs that were ever in the Billboard Hot 100.

FERRY CROSSINGS

Several ferry companies serve New England's offshore islands. Park your car in port ($10 to $20 per day) – or, if you want to bring your vehicle along, book well in advance and expect to pay high prices.

Block Island Ferry (✆401-783-4613; www. blockislandferry.com) Operates car ferries and high-speed passenger ferries between Point Judith, RI, and Block Island, RI.

Downeast Windjammer (www.downeast windjammer.com; adult/child $30/20, bikes $6) Passenger-only ferry between Bar Harbor, ME, and Winter Harbor, ME, allowing exploration of the island and mainland sections of Acadia National Park.

Hy-Line Cruises (✆508-778-2600; www. hylinecruises.com; Ocean St Dock) Operates ferries from Hyannis, MA, to Nantucket and Martha's Vineyard.

Steamship Authority (✆508-477-8600; www.steamshipauthority.com; South St Dock) Operates ferries from Hyannis, MA, to Nantucket, and from Woods Hole, MA, to Martha's Vineyard.

New England Travel Guide

GETTING THERE & AWAY

While the two most common ways to reach New England are by air and car, you can also get here easily by train and bus. Boston is the region's hub for air travel, but some international travelers fly into New York City to do some sightseeing before heading up to New England. Flights, cars and tours can be booked online at lonely planet.com/bookings.

AIR

Because of New England's location on the densely populated US Atlantic seaboard between New York and eastern Canada, air travelers have a number of ways to approach the region.

Depending on where you will be doing the bulk of your exploring, several airports in the region receive national and international flights. It's also feasible to fly into one of New York's major airports.

Bangor International Airport (BGR; ☑866-359-2264; www.flybangor.com; 287 Godfrey Blvd) This international airport in Maine is served by regional carriers associated with American Airlines, Delta Air Lines and United Airlines.

Bradley International Airport (BDL; ☑860-292-2000; www.bradleyairport.com; Windsor Locks) Twelve miles north of Hartford in Windsor Locks, Connecticut (I-91 exit 40), this airport is served by American Airlines, Southwest Airlines, Delta Air Lines, United Airlines and JetBlue.

Burlington International Airport (BTV; ☑802-863-2874; www.btv.aero; 1200 Airport Dr, South Burlington) Vermont's major airport.

Green Airport (PVD; ☑888-268-7222; www.pvdairport.com; 2000 Post Road, War-

wick) Located 20 minutes south of Providence, Rhode Island.

Logan International Airport (BOS; ☑800-235-6426; www.massport.com/logan) The major gateway to the region is in Boston, and it offers many direct flights from major airports in the US and abroad.

Manchester-Boston Regional Airport (MHT; ☑603-624-6556; www.flymanchester. com) A quiet alternative to Logan, Manchester Airport is just 55 miles north of Boston in New Hampshire.

Portland International Jetport (PWM; ☑207-874-8877; www.portlandjetport.org; 1001 Westbrook St) Serves coastal Maine.

BUS

You can get to New England by bus from all parts of the US and Canada, but the trip will be long and may not be much cheaper than a discounted flight. Bus companies usually offer special promotional fares.

Greyhound (☑800-231-2222, international customer service 214-849-8100; www.grey hound.com) The national bus line, serving all major cities in the USA.

Peter Pan Bus (☑800-343-9999; www. peterpanbus.com) The regional bus company, serving 54 destinations in the northeast as far north as Concord, NH, and as far south as Washington, DC, as well as into western Massachusetts.

Go Bus (www.gobuses.com; Alewife Brook Pkwy; one way $18-42; ☎; Ⓣ Alewife), **Lucky Star Bus** (www.luckystarbus.com; South Station; one way $25; ☎) and **Megabus** (www. megabus.com; South Station; one way $10-30; ☎) offer inexpensive bus fares between New York City and Boston.

CAR & MOTORCYCLE

Interstate highways connect New England with other points throughout the USA and Canada.

I-95 runs northeast along the Atlantic seaboard from New York City, Philadelphia, Washington, DC, and points south all the way up to the Canadian border, offering the quickest access to coastal areas of Connecticut, Rhode Island, Massachusetts, New Hampshire and Maine.

I-89 runs from Boston northwest through New Hampshire and Vermont, providing the best region-wide links for travelers from Montreal and points west in Canada.

Interior regions of Connecticut, Massachusetts, Vermont and New Hampshire can also be reached via I-91, which runs north–south up the Connecticut River Valley, and I-90, which runs east–west through Massachusetts from Boston, continuing west to Albany, NY, Cleveland, Chicago and beyond.

TRAIN

Amtrak (☑800-872-7245; www.amtrak. com) is the main rail passenger service in the US. Services along the Northeast Corridor (connecting Boston, Providence, Hartford and New Haven with New York and Washington, DC) are some of the most frequent in Amtrak's system. Amtrak's high-speed *Acela Express* makes the trip from New York City to Boston in three hours.

Other Amtrak services to New England include the following:

➡ The *Ethan Allen* is an express train linking New York City and Albany to Rutland, VT.

➡ The *Vermonter* runs from Washington, DC, and New York City, through New Haven and Hartford in Connecticut, Springfield and Amherst in Massachusetts, and then on to St Albans in Vermont.

➡ The *Lake Shore Limited* departs from Boston, stopping at Worcester, Springfield and Pittsfield before crossing into New York and continuing west.

Connecticut is also served by commuter trains from New York City, operated by **Metro-North** (☑212-878-7000, 877-690-5116; www.mta.info) and **Shore Line East** (☑800-255-7433; www.shorelineeast.com).

DIRECTORY A–Z

ACCOMMODATION

New England provides an array of accommodations, but truly inexpensive options are rare. Reservations are recommended, especially in high season.

B&Bs, Inns & Guesthouses

Options range from small, family-run B&Bs to rambling old inns that have sheltered travelers for several centuries. Accommodations and amenities can vary widely, from the very simple to the luxurious (and prices vary accordingly). Many inns require a minimum stay of two or three nights on weekends, and advance reservations or bills paid by check or in cash (not by credit card). Some inns do not welcome children under a certain age.

Many B&Bs are booked through agencies, such as Inns of New England (www.innsofnewengland.com), which books B&Bs and inns in all five New England states.

Camping

With few exceptions, you'll have to camp in established campgrounds (there's no bivouacking on the side of the road). Make reservations well in advance (especially in July and August) for the best chance of getting a site. Most campgrounds are open from mid-May to mid-October.

Rough camping is occasionally permitted in the Green Mountain National Forest or the White Mountain National Forest, but it must be at established sites. State-park sites usually offer services such as flush toilets, hot showers and dump stations for RVs. Campsites at these places cost between $15 and $30. Private campgrounds are usually more expensive ($25 to $40) and less spacious than state parks, but

Book Your Stay Online

For more accommodation reviews by Lonely Planet authors, check out lonelyplanet.com/hotels. You'll find independent reviews, as well as recommendations on the best places to stay. Best of all, you can book online.

Efficiencies

An 'efficiency,' in New England parlance, is a room in a hotel, motel or inn with cooking and dining facilities: stove, sink, refrigerator, dining table and chairs, cooking utensils and tableware. Efficiency units are located throughout New England. They cost slightly more than standard rooms.

they often boast recreational facilities such as playgrounds, swimming pools, game rooms and miniature golf.

The following resources provide camping information:

Connecticut Department of Environmental Protection (☎860-424-3000; www.ct.gov/dep) Has a large section on outdoor recreation in Connecticut.

Maine Bureau of Parks and Land (☎207-287-3821; www.parksandlands.com) Offers camping in 12 state parks.

Massachusetts Department of Conservation and Recreation (☎617-626-1250; www.mass.gov/eea) Offers camping in 29 state parks.

Rhode Island Division of Parks & Recreation (☎401-222-2632; www.riparks.com) For a listing of all of Rhode Island's state beaches.

Vermont State Parks (☎888-409-7579; www.vtstateparks.com) Complete camping and parks information.

Cottages & Cabins

Cottages and cabins are generally found on Cape Cod, Nantucket, Martha's Vineyard and in New England's woods. They are two- or three-room vacation bungalows with basic furnishings, bathroom and kitchen. Rates vary greatly, from $80 to $700 per night, depending upon the location, season and size.

Hostels

Hosteling isn't as well developed in New England as it is in other parts of the world. But some prime destinations, including Boston, Cape Cod, Bar Harbor, Martha's Vineyard and Nantucket, have hostels that allow you to stay in $150-per-night destinations for $30 to $60 per night.

US citizens/residents can join **Hostelling International USA** (☎240-650-2100; www.hiusa.org). Non-US residents should buy a HI membership in their home countries. If you are not a member, you can still stay in US hostels for a slightly higher rate.

Hotels & Resorts

New England hotels, mostly found in cities, are generally large and lavish, except for a few 'boutique' hotels (which are small and understatedly lavish). Resorts often offer a wide variety of guest activities, such as golf, horseback riding, skiing and water sports. Prices start from $100 per night.

Motels

Motels, located on the highway or on the outskirts of most cities, range from 10-room places in need of a fresh coat of paint to resort-style facilities. Prices cost $65 to $150 per night. Motels offer standard accommodations: a room with a private entrance, private bathroom, cable TV, heat and air-con. Some have small refrigerators, and many provide a simple breakfast, often at no extra charge.

ELECTRICITY

120V/60Hz

Sleeping Price Ranges

The following price ranges refer to a double room with bathroom in high season. Unless otherwise indicated, breakfast is not included. Rates do not include taxes, which cost 5.2% to 12% depending on the state.

Category	Cost
$	less than $100
$$	$100–250
$$$	more than $250

FOOD

Eating in New England is a treat, whether feasting on fresh seafood, munching berries from the bush or dining at one of the region's top, chef-driven restaurants.

The finest dining and most innovative cooking takes place in New England's cities, especially Boston, Portland, Providence, Portsmouth and Burlington. At high-end restaurants, reservations for dinner are usually recommended, especially during peak tourist seasons and on weekends. Reservations are not usually needed for lunch.

Except in the most rural areas or the smallest towns, vegetarians will have no problem finding animal-free eats. Other dietary restrictions are also usually accommodated.

INTERNET ACCESS

Many hotels, restaurants and public spaces offer wireless access for free or for a small fee. Cybercafes and libraries offer inexpensive online computer access. If you bring a laptop with you from outside the US, it's worth investing in a universal AC and plug adapter.

LGBT TRAVELERS

Out and active gay communities are visible across New England, especially in cities such as Boston, Portland, New Haven and Burlington, which have substantial LGBT populations. Provincetown, MA, and Ogunquit, ME, are gay meccas, especially in summer. Northampton, MA, and Burlington, VT, also have lively queer communities.

MONEY

ATMs and Cash

Automatic teller machines (ATMs) are ubiquitous in towns throughout New England. Most banks in New England charge at least $2 per withdrawal. The Cirrus and Plus systems both have extensive ATM networks that will give cash advances on major credit cards and allow cash withdrawals with affiliated ATM cards.

If you're carrying foreign currency, it can be exchanged for US dollars at Logan International Airport in Boston. Many banks do not change currency, so stock up on dollars when there's an opportunity to do so.

Credit Cards

Major credit cards are widely accepted throughout New England, including at car-rental agencies and at most hotels, restaurants, gas stations, grocery stores and tour operators. However, some restaurants and B&Bs – particularly those handled through rental agencies – do not accept credit cards. We have noted in our reviews when this is the case.

Visa and MasterCard are the most common credit cards. American Express and Discover are sometimes not accepted.

Tipping

Many service providers depend on tips for their livelihoods, so tip generously for good service.

Eating Price Ranges

The following price ranges refer to a standard main course. Unless otherwise stated, a service charge and taxes are not included.

Category	Cost
$	less than $15
$$	$15–25
$$$	more than $25

Baggage carriers $1 per bag

Housekeeping $2 to $5 per day, $5 to $10 per week

Servers and bartenders 15% to 20%

Taxi drivers 15%

Tour guides $5 to $10 for a one-hour tour

OPENING HOURS

The following is a general guideline for operating hours. Shorter hours may apply during low seasons, when some venues close completely. Seasonal variations are noted in the listings.

Banks & Offices 9am or 10am–5pm or 6pm Monday to Friday; sometimes 9am–noon Saturday

Bars & Pubs 5pm–midnight, some until 2am

Restaurants Breakfast 6am–10am, lunch 11:30am–2:30pm, dinner 5pm–10pm daily

Shops 9am–7pm Monday to Saturday; some open noon–5pm Sunday, or until evening in tourist areas

PUBLIC HOLIDAYS

New Year's Day January 1

Martin Luther King Jr Day Third Monday of January

Presidents' Day Third Monday of February

Easter March or April

Patriots' Day Third Monday of April (Maine and Massachusetts only)

Memorial Day Last Monday of May

Independence Day July 4

Labor Day First Monday of September

Columbus Day Second Monday of October

Veterans Day November 11

Thanksgiving Fourth Thursday of November

Christmas Day December 25

SAFE TRAVEL

You're unlikely to come across any major problems while traveling in New England. Most of the region enjoys high standards of living; and tourists are usually well taken care of.

Outdoor Hazards

Outdoor activities, from beach-going to mountain-hiking, can be dangerous anywhere in the world. Pay attention to weather and water conditions before setting out on any sort of adventure.

➨ The White Mountains are notorious for strong winds and wild weather, but conditions can be dangerous on any of the New England mountain trails. Inquire about weather conditions with rangers before setting out.

➨ Always stay on marked trails and do not disturb wildlife while hiking.

➨ In recent years, there have been shark sightings off Cape Cod, and beaches may close for that reason. Not all public beaches are guarded, so inquire about riptides and other dangers before swimming at area beaches.

Weather

It snows a lot in New England. If you're visiting between December and March, there's a good chance you'll experience a major snow storm, possibly impeding your progress until roads are plowed.

TELEPHONE

Always dial ✆1 before toll-free (✆800, ✆888 etc) and domestic long-distance numbers. Remember that some toll-free numbers may only work within the region or from the US mainland.

All phone numbers in the US consist of a three-digit area code followed by a seven-digit local number. You now must dial ✆1 plus all 10 digits for local and long-distance calls in most areas, particularly in Eastern Massachusetts.

Pay phones aren't as readily found at shopping centers, gas stations and other public places now that cell phones are more prevalent, but keep your eyes peeled and you'll find them. Calls made within towns are local and cost 50¢.

To make direct international calls, dial ✆011 plus the country code plus the area code plus the number. (An exception is calls made to Canada, where you dial ✆1 plus the area code plus the number. International rates apply to Canada.) For international operator assistance, dial ✆0.

If you're calling New England from abroad, the international country code for the US is ✆1. All calls to New England are then followed by the area code and the seven-digit local number.

Cell Phones

The US uses a variety of cell-phone systems, and most are incompatible with the GSM 900/1800 standard used throughout

Practicalities

➡ **Discount Cards** Savings on museums, accommodations and some transport (including Amtrak trains) are available with membership in the American Automobile Association (AAA; www.aaa.com) and reciprocal clubs in the UK, Australia and elsewhere. Student discount cards include the International Student Identity Card (ISIC: www.isic.org) and Student Advantage Card (www.studentadvantage.com). US travelers aged 50 and older also qualify for discounts with membership in the American Association of Retired Persons (AARP; www.aarp.org).

➡ **Radio & TV** National Public Radio (NPR) can be found at the lower end of the FM dial. The main TV broadcasting channels are ABC, CBS, NBC, FOX and PBS (public broadcasting); the major cable channels are CNN (news), ESPN (sports), HBO (movies) and Weather Channel.

➡ **Smoking** Five out of six New England states have banned smoking in bars, restaurants and non-hospitality workplaces – so, essentially, anywhere that anyone works. Only New Hampshire is less restrictive, but smoking is nonetheless prohibited in bars and restaurants.

➡ **Media Systems** DVDs are coded for Region 1 (US and Canada only).

➡ **Weights & Measures** Weights are measured in ounces (oz), pounds (lb) and tons; liquids in fluid ounces (fl oz), pints, quarts and gallons (gal); and distance in feet (ft), yards (yd) and miles (mi).

Europe and Asia. Check with your cellular service provider before departure about using your phone in New England.

Network Coverage

Verizon has the most extensive cellular network in New England, but AT&T and Sprint also have decent coverage. Once you get up into the mountains and off the main interstates in Vermont, New Hampshire and Maine, cell-phone reception is often downright nonexistent. Forget about using it on hiking trails.

Phonecards

These private prepaid cards are available from convenience stores, supermarkets and pharmacies. Cards sold by major telecommunications companies such as AT&T may offer better deals than upstart companies.

TOURIST INFORMATION

Connecticut Office of Tourism (☑888-288-4748; www.ctvisit.com)

Greater Boston Convention & Visitors Bureau (GBCVB; ☑888-733-2678; www.bostonusa.com)

Maine Office of Tourism (☑888-624-6345; www.visitmaine.com)

Massachusetts Office of Travel & Tourism (☑617-973-8500; www.massvacation.com)

New Hampshire Division of Travel & Tourism (☑603-271-2665; www.visitnh.gov)

Rhode Island Tourism Division (☑800-556-2484; www.visitrhodeisland.com)

Vermont Division of Tourism (☑800-837-6668; www.vermontvacation.com)

Chambers of Commerce

Often associated with convention and visitors' bureaus (CVBs), these are membership organizations for local businesses including hotels, restaurants and shops. Although they often provide maps, lodging recommendations and other useful information, they focus on establishments that are members of the chamber.

A local chamber of commerce often maintains an information booth at the entrance to town or in the town center, often open only during tourist seasons.

TRAVELERS WITH DISABILITIES

Travel within New England is becoming less difficult for people with disabilities, but it's still not easy. Public buildings are now required by law to be wheelchair accessible and also to have appropriate restroom facilities. Public transportation services must be made accessible to all, and telephone companies are required to provide relay operators for the hearing impaired. Many banks provide ATM instructions in Braille, curb ramps are common, many busy intersections have audible crossing signals, and most chain hotels have suites for disabled guests.

Mobility International USA (☑541-343-1284; www.miusa.org) advises travelers with disabilities on mobility issues and runs educational international exchange programs.

Download Lonely Planet's free Accessible Travel guide from http://lptravel.to/AccessibleTravel.

VISAS

Citizens of many countries are eligible for the Visa Waiver Program, which requires prior approval via Electronic System for Travel Authorization (ESTA).

Electronic System for Travel Authorization

Since January 2009, the US has had the Electronic System for Travel Authorization (ESTA), a system that has been implemented to mitigate security risks concerning those who travel to the US by air or sea (this does not apply to those entering by land, such as via Canada). This pre-authorization system applies to citizens of all countries that fall under the Visa Waiver Program. This process requires that you register specific information online, prior to entering the US. Information required includes your name, current address and passport information, including the number and expiration date, and details about any communicable diseases you may carry (including HIV). It is recommended that you fill out the online form as early as possible, and at least 72 hours prior to departure. You will receive one of three responses:

➡ 'Authorization Approved' usually comes within minutes; most applicants can expect to receive this response.

➡ 'Authorization Pending' means you should go back online to check the status within roughly 72 hours.

➡ 'Travel not Authorized' indicates that your application is not approved and you will need to apply for a visa.

Once approved, registration is valid for two years, but note that if you renew your passport or change your name, you will need to re-register. The cost is $14. The entire process is stored electronically and linked to your passport, but it is recommended that you bring a printout of the ESTA approval just to be safe. If you don't have access to the internet, ask your travel agent, who can apply on your behalf.

Visa Applications

Documentation required for visa applications:

➡ A recent photo (50.8mm by 50.8mm).

➡ Documents of financial stability and/or guarantees from a US resident are sometimes required, particularly for those from developing countries.

➡ Visa applicants may be required to 'demonstrate binding obligations' that will ensure their return home. Because of this requirement, those planning to travel through other countries before arriving in the US are generally better off applying for their US visa while they are still in their home country rather than while on the road.

The validity period for a US visitor visa depends on your home country. The actual length of time you'll be allowed to stay in the US is determined by the Bureau of Citizenship and Immigration Services at the port of entry.

As with the Visa Waiver Program, your passport should be valid for at least six months longer than your intended stay.

Visa Waiver Program

The US has a Visa Waiver Program in which citizens of certain countries may enter the US for stays of 90 days or less without first obtaining a US visa. This list is subject to continual re-examination and bureaucratic rejigging. For an up-to-date list of countries included in the program, see the US Department of State website (http://travel.state.gov). Under the program, you must have a round-trip ticket (or onward ticket to any foreign destination) that is nonrefundable in the US and you will not be allowed to extend your stay beyond 90 days.

To participate in the Visa Waiver Program, travelers are required to have a passport that is machine readable. Also, your passport should be valid for at least six months longer than your intended stay.

BEHIND THE SCENES

SEND US YOUR FEEDBACK

We love to hear from travelers – your comments help make our books better. We read every word, and we guarantee that your feedback goes straight to the authors. Visit **lonelyplanet. com/contact** to submit your updates and suggestions.

Note: We may edit, reproduce and incorporate your comments in Lonely Planet products such as guidebooks, websites and digital products, so let us know if you don't want your comments reproduced or your name acknowledged. For a copy of our privacy policy visit lonelyplanet.com/privacy.

WRITERS' THANKS

GREGOR CLARK

Thanks to all the generous New Englanders who helped with this project, especially Katherine Quinn, Sarah Pope and Margo Whitcomb. Love and special thanks to Gaen, Meigan and Chloe, for helping me explore this beautiful region and always sharing my excitement for the road less traveled.

CAROLYN BAIN

My warmest thanks to all the chatty innkeepers, bartenders and barflies I had the good fortune to spend time with – who else would you ask for tips on the region's best beach/trail/lobster roll/craft brew etc? Sincerest thanks to the people of Nantucket for welcoming me back into your fold and embracing my nostalgia – especially to Roselyne Hatch and Tania Jones. Special mention goes to Emily Golin, Carla Tracy, Thomas Masters, and Kimberly and Barry Hunter for their kindnesses.

MARA VORHEES

Thanks to friends and neighbors who have taught me so much about New England over the years. I am grateful to my faithful travel companions, Shay and Van: it's always more fun to travel – though more difficult to write – when you're along for the ride. And thank you, Jerz, for going along with the sunrise thing, all 19 times (and counting).

BENEDICT WALKER

Massive thanks to the ever-delightful Rebecca Warren for taking me on and for your patience and guidance along the way. Huge hugs to my twin in the Big Apple, Lyndal Hunt, for your love and hospitality, to my buddy Peter Falso in Newport for fun and laughs, to my always-awesome pals Heather, Pete and Wendy and to the master architect Tom Zook for your friendship, knowledge and support. Finally, thanks Mum: I love you to the moon and back.

ACKNOWLEDGMENTS

Climate map data adapted from Peel MC, Finlayson BL & McMahon TA (2007) 'Updated World Map of the Köppen-Geiger Climate Classification', *Hydrology and Earth System Sciences*, 11, 1633 44.

Front cover photographs (clockwise from top): Farmhouse, New Hampshire, Danita Delimont Stock/AWL©; Lobster shack, Maine, Walter Bibikow/AWL©; Vintage car, Weston, Vermont, Hoffmann Photography/Alamy©

Back cover photograph: Sleepy Hollow Farm, Woodstock, Vermont, Tim Mannakee/4Corners©

THIS BOOK

This 3rd edition of Lonely Planet's *New England's Best Trips* guidebook was curated by Gregor Clark, and researched and written by Gregor Clark, Carolyn Bain, Mara Vorhees and Benedict Walker. The previous edition was written by Mara Vorhees, Amy C Balfour, Paula Hardy and Caroline Sieg. This guidebook was produced by the following:

Destination Editor Rebecca Warren

Product Editor Grace Dobell

Senior Cartographer Alison Lyall

Book Designer Wendy Wright

Assisting Editors Sarah Bailey, Bruce Evans, Helen Koehne, Ali Lemer, Rosie Nicholson, Kristin Odijk, Saralinda Turner

Cover Researcher Brendan Dempsey-Spencer

Thanks to Cathelijne Augustijn, David Callow, Katherine Davis-Young, Amy Irvine, Christina Jacobi, Doreen Nicol, Sheela O Regan, Kirsten Rawlings, Victoria Smith, Luna Soo, Dora Whitaker, Tony Wheeler, Tracy Whitmey

INDEX

MARA VORHEES

Born and raised in St Clair Shores, Michigan, Mara traveled the world (if not the universe) before settling in the Hub. The pen-wielding traveler covers destinations as diverse as Belize and Russia, as well as her home of New England. She lives in a pink house in Somerville, Massachusetts with her husband, two kiddies and two kitties.

Read more about Mara at: https://auth.lonelyplanet.com/profiles/mvorhees

BENEDICT WALKER

Born in Newcastle, Australia, Ben holds notions of the beach core to his idea of self, though he's traveled hundreds of thousands of kilometres from the sandy shores of home. Ben was given his first Lonely Planet guide *(Japan)* when he was 12. Two decades later, he'd write chapters for the same publication: a dream come true. A communications graduate and travel agent by trade, Ben whittled away his twenties gallivanting around the globe. He thinks the best thing about travel isn't as much about where you go as who you meet: living vicariously through the stories of kind strangers enriches one's own experience. Ben has also written and directed a play, toured Australia managing the travel logistics for top-billing music festivals and is experimenting with a return to his original craft of photography and film-making.

Read more about Ben at: https://auth.lonelyplanet.com/profiles/BenedictWalker

OUR WRITERS

OUR STORY

A beat-up old car, a few dollars in the pocket and a sense of adventure. In 1972 that's all Tony and Maureen Wheeler needed for the trip of a lifetime – across Europe and Asia overland to Australia. It took several months, and at the end – broke but inspired – they sat at their kitchen table writing and stapling together their first travel guide, *Across Asia on the Cheap*. Within a week they'd sold 1500 copies. Lonely Planet was born.

Today, Lonely Planet has offices in Franklin, London, Melbourne, Oakland, Dublin, Beijing and Delhi, with more than 600 staff and writers. We share Tony's belief that 'a great guidebook should do three things: inform, educate and amuse'.

GREGOR CLARK

Gregor Clark has been exploring New England's back roads since childhood, when he rode bikes through Cape Cod's dunes, skated on frozen ponds in northwestern Connecticut and saw his first shooting star in Vermont's Green Mountains. A lifelong polyglot with an insatiable curiosity for what lies around the next bend, Gregor has contributed to over three dozen Lonely Planet guides, with an emphasis on North America, Latin America and Europe. He lives with his wife and daughters in Middlebury, VT.

Read more about Gregor at: https://auth. lonelyplanet.com/profiles/gregorclark

CAROLYN BAIN

Australian-born Carolyn worked a glorious season on Nantucket a decade or so back – and like countless visitors before her, she fell in love with Cape Cod at first sight. Sand dunes and salt spray, history and wholesomeness, cozy inns and seafood feasts: this was (and still is) the USA at its most charming. On this trip, Maine made an awesome adjunct, and she relished the chance to go beyond lighthouses and lobsters to uncover craft brews, moose trails and road-tripping nirvana.

Read more about Carolyn at: https://auth. lonelyplanet.com/profiles/carolynbain

 MORE WRITERS

31901062980364

Published by Lonely Planet Global Limited
CRN 554153
3rd edition – Feb 2017
ISBN 978 1 7865 723 18
© Lonely Planet 2017
Photographs © as indicated 2017
10 9 8 7 6 5 4 3 2 1
Printed in China

MIX
Paper from responsible sources
FSC™ C021741

Paper in this book is certified against the Forest Stewardship Council™ standards. FSC™ promotes environmentally responsible, socially beneficial and economically viable management of the world's forests.